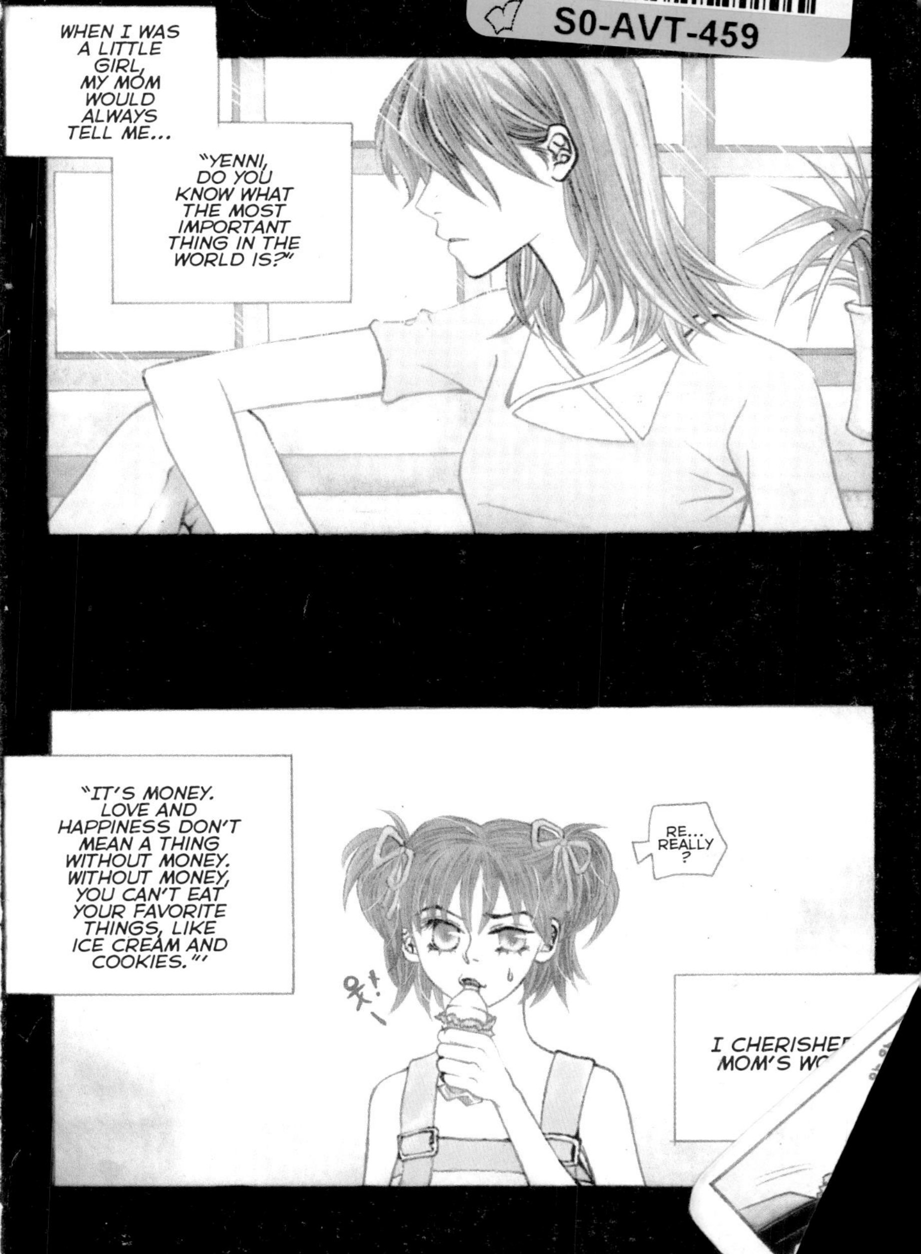
WHEN I WAS A LITTLE GIRL, MY MOM WOULD ALWAYS TELL ME...
"YENNI, DO YOU KNOW WHAT THE MOST IMPORTANT THING IN THE WORLD IS?"
"IT'S MONEY. LOVE AND HAPPINESS DON'T MEAN A THING WITHOUT MONEY. WITHOUT MONEY, YOU CAN'T EAT YOUR FAVORITE THINGS, LIKE ICE CREAM AND COOKIES."
RE... REALLY?
I CHERISHE
MOM'S WO

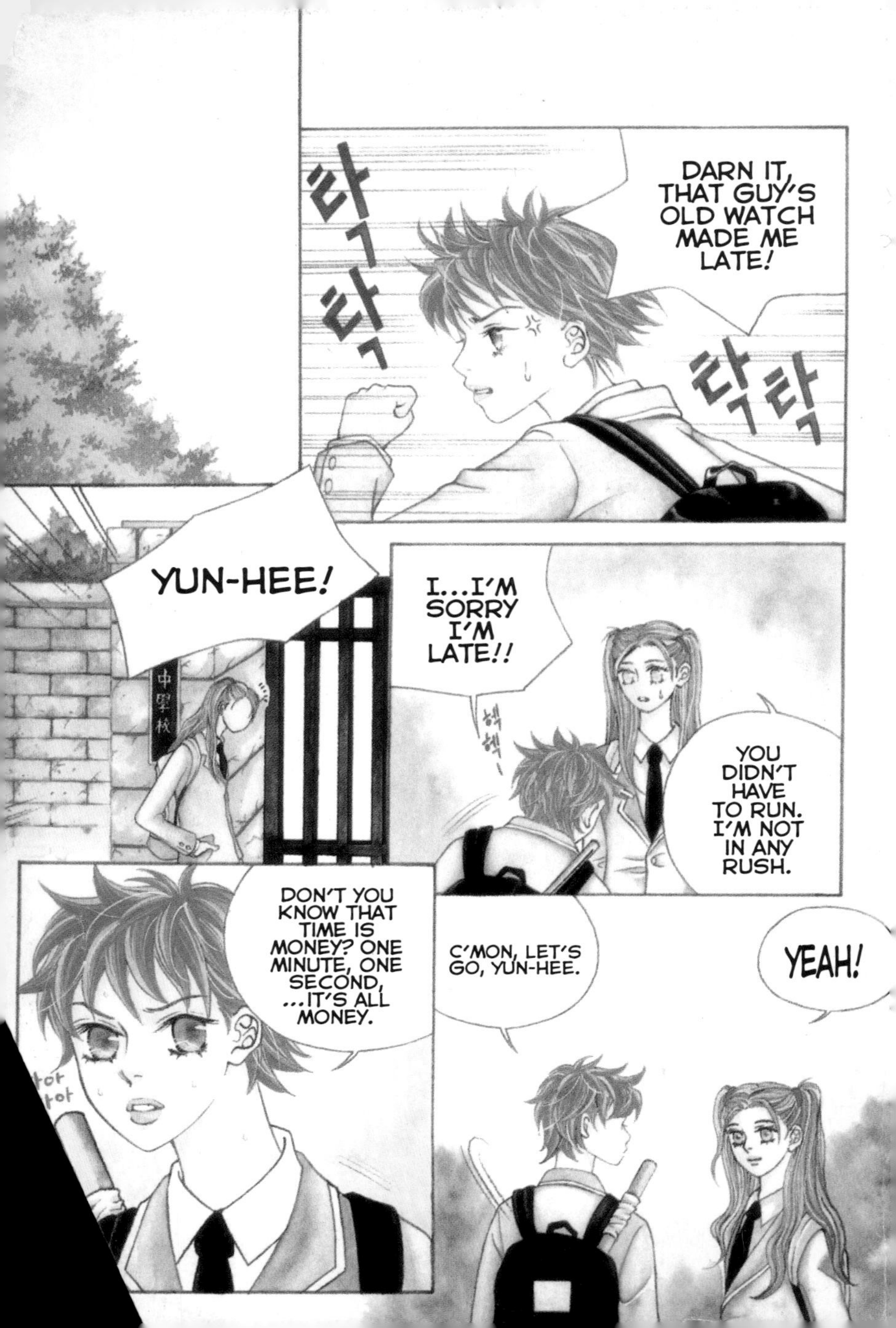

탁탁
DARN IT, THAT GUY'S OLD WATCH MADE ME LATE!
탁탁
YUN-HEE!
中學校
I...I'M SORRY I'M LATE!!
헉헉
YOU DIDN'T HAVE TO RUN. I'M NOT IN ANY RUSH.
DON'T YOU KNOW THAT TIME IS MONEY? ONE MINUTE, ONE SECOND, ...IT'S ALL MONEY.
C'MON, LET'S GO, YUN-HEE.
YEAH!

LOVE OR MONEY

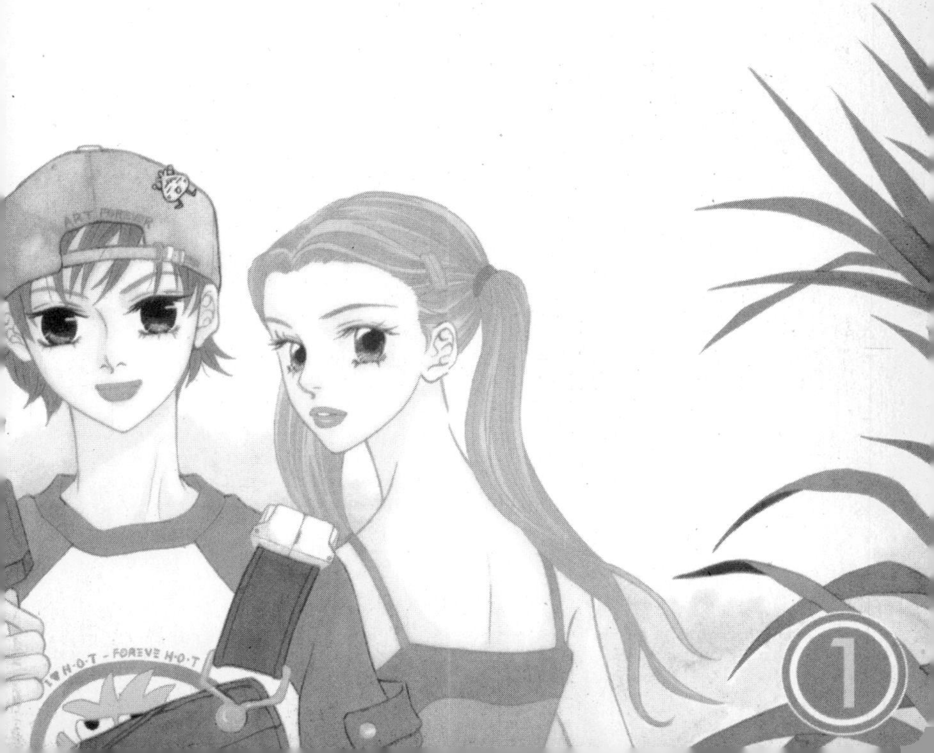
1

Love or Money, Volume 1
created by Sang-Eun Lee

Translation - Grace Min
English Adaptation - Avra Douglas
Copy Editor - Aaron Sparrow
Retouch and Lettering - Jose Macasocol, Jr.
Production Artist - Jacqueline Del Monte
Cover Design - Anna Kernbaum

Editor - Julie Taylor
Digital Imaging Manager - Chris Buford
Pre-Press Manager - Antonio DePietro
Production Managers - Jennifer Miller and Mutsumi Miyazaki
Art Director - Matt Alford
Managing Editor - Jill Freshney
VP of Production - Ron Klamert
Editor-in-Chief - Mike Kiley
President and C.O.O. - John Parker
Publisher and C.E.O. - Stuart Levy

A  Manga

TOKYOPOP Inc.
5900 Wilshire Blvd. Suite 2000
Los Angeles, CA 90036

E-mail: info@TOKYOPOP.com
Come visit us online at www.TOKYOPOP.com

ISBN: 1-59532-248-5
First TOKYOPOP printing: December 2004
10 9 8 7 6 5 4 3 2 1
Printed in the USA

LOVE OR MONEY

Volume 1

by
Sang-Eun Lee

HAMBURG // LONDON // LOS ANGELES // TOKYO

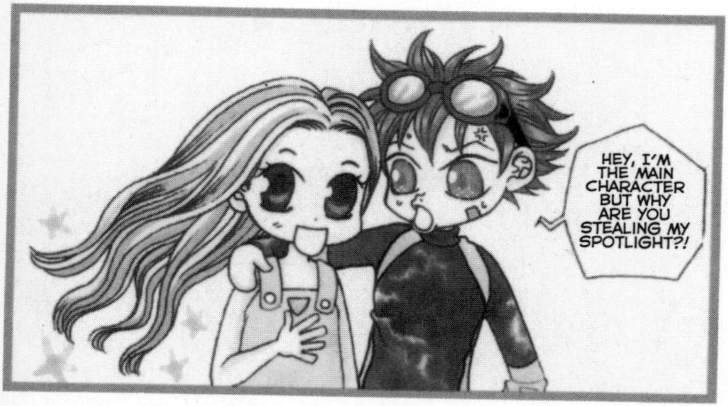
HEY, I'M THE MAIN CHARACTER BUT WHY ARE YOU STEALING MY SPOTLIGHT?!

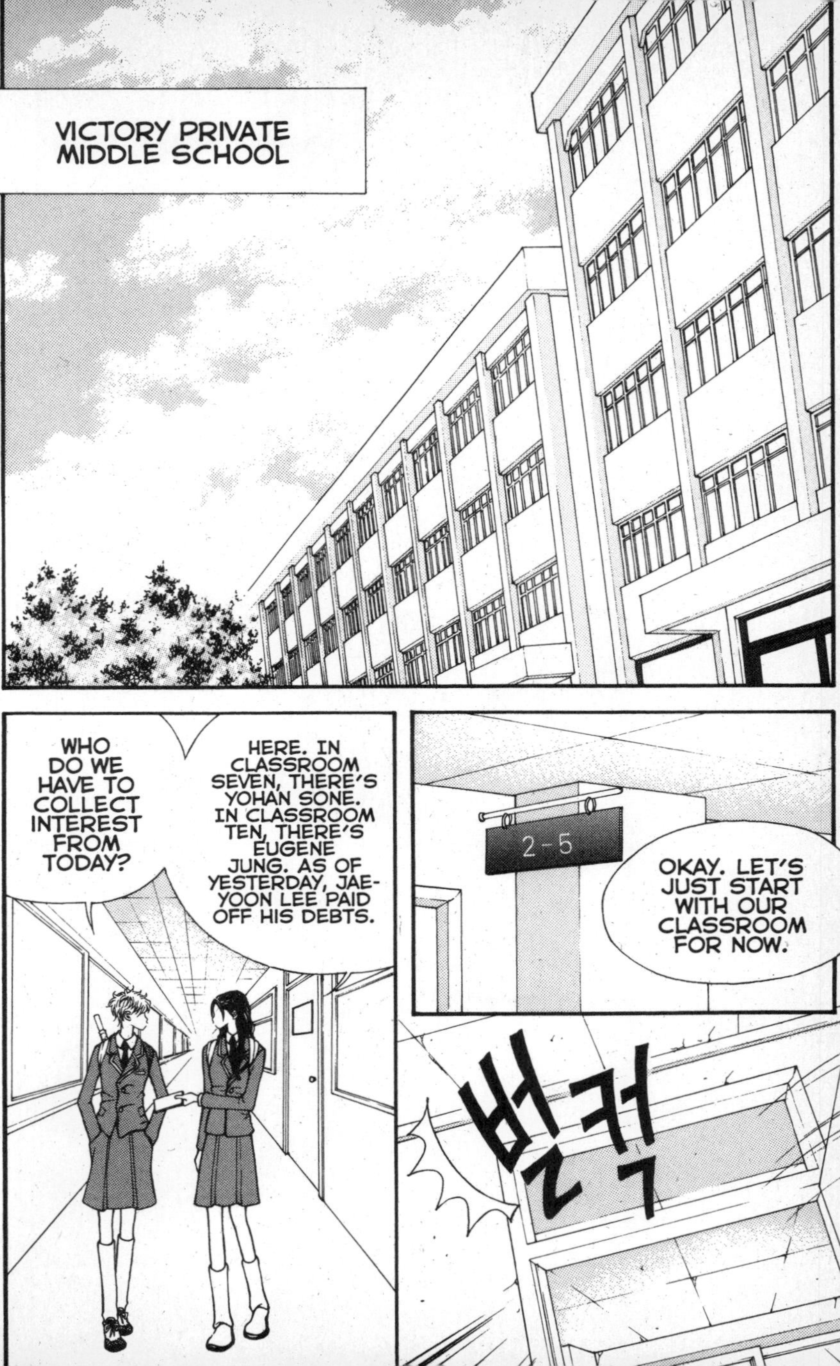
VICTORY PRIVATE MIDDLE SCHOOL
WHO DO WE HAVE TO COLLECT INTEREST FROM TODAY?
HERE. IN CLASSROOM SEVEN, THERE'S YOHAN SONE. IN CLASSROOM TEN, THERE'S EUGENE JUNG. AS OF YESTERDAY, JAE-YOON LEE PAID OFF HIS DEBTS.
2-5
OKAY. LET'S JUST START WITH OUR CLASSROOM FOR NOW.
벌컥

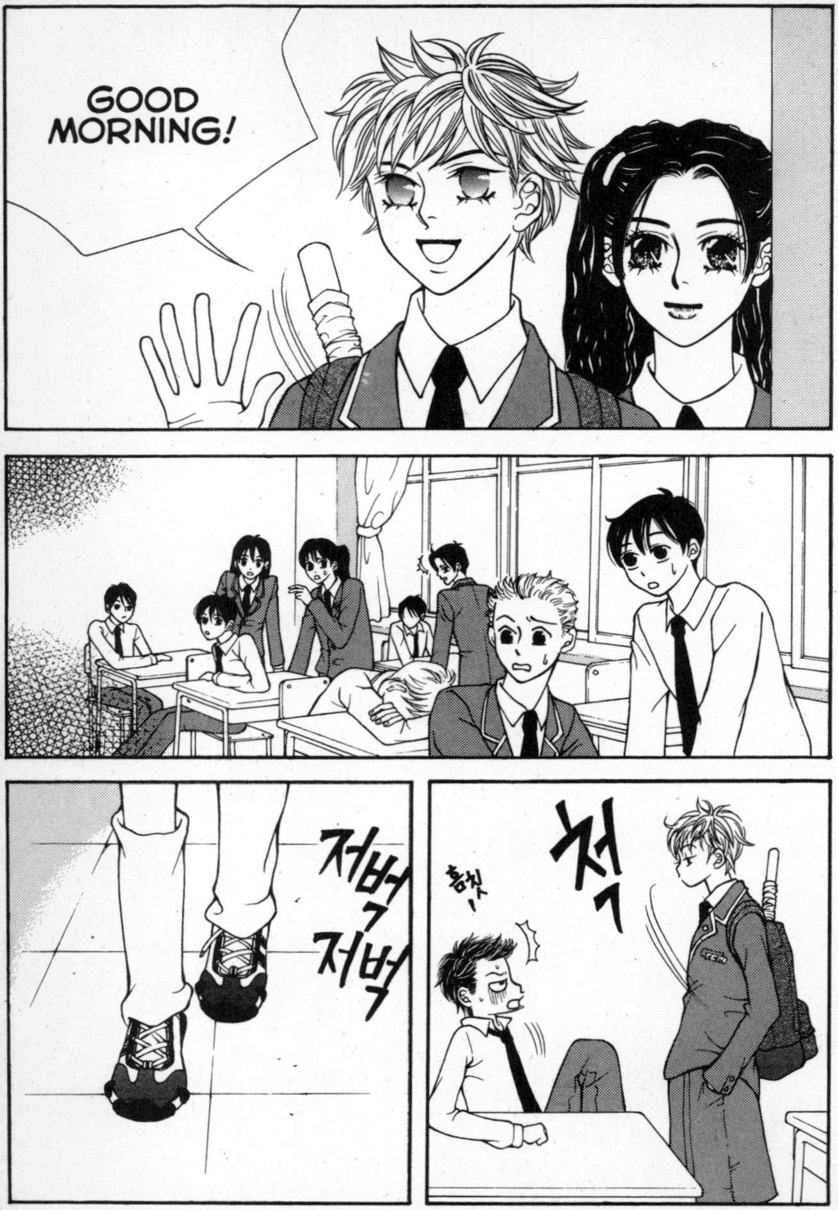
GOOD MORNING!
저벅 저벅
척
흠칫

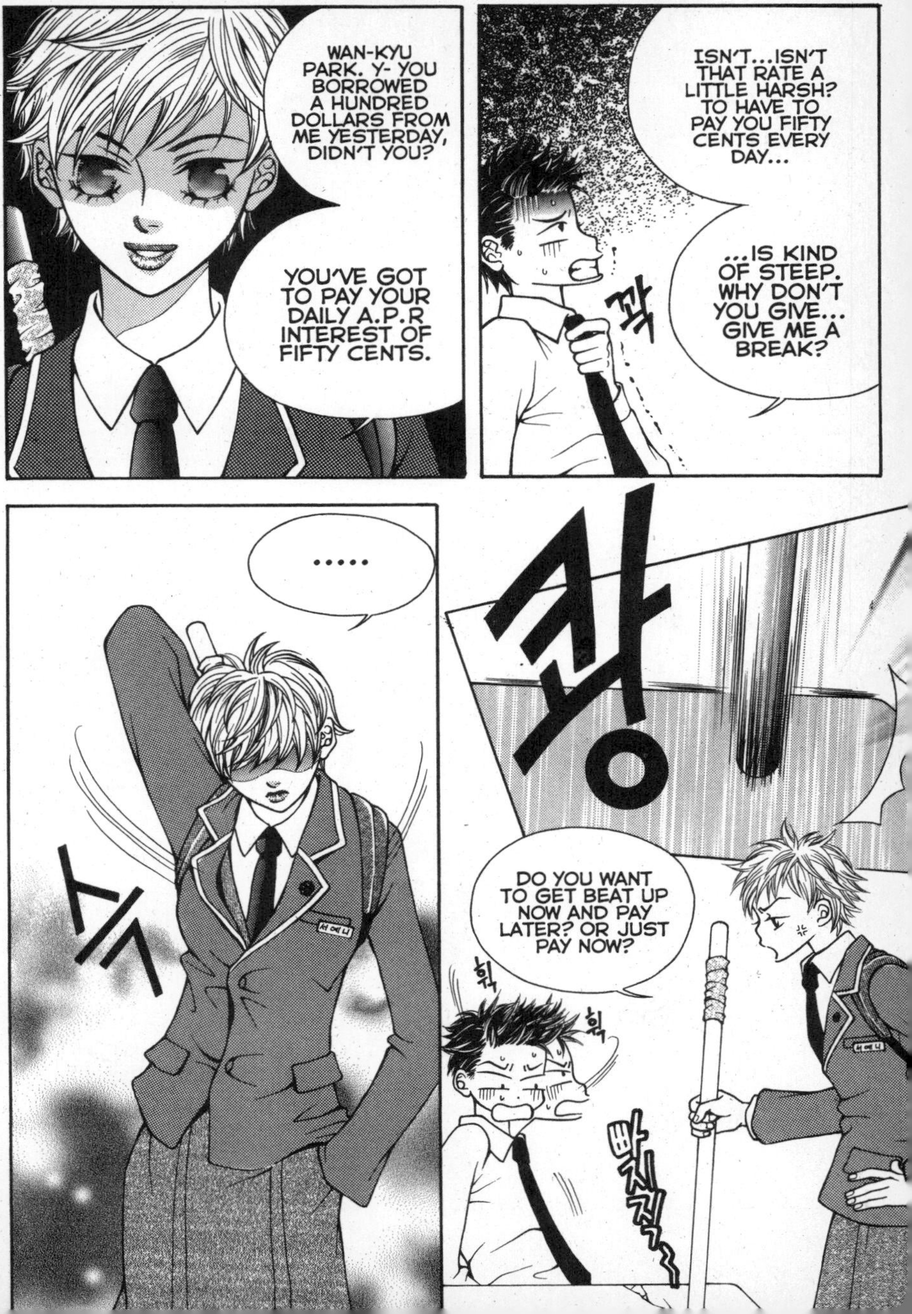
WAN-KYU PARK. Y- YOU BORROWED A HUNDRED DOLLARS FROM ME YESTERDAY, DIDN'T YOU?
YOU'VE GOT TO PAY YOUR DAILY A.P.R INTEREST OF FIFTY CENTS.
ISN'T...ISN'T THAT RATE A LITTLE HARSH? TO HAVE TO PAY YOU FIFTY CENTS EVERY DAY...
...IS KIND OF STEEP. WHY DON'T YOU GIVE... GIVE ME A BREAK?
꽉
.....
쾅
DO YOU WANT TO GET BEAT UP NOW AND PAY LATER? OR JUST PAY NOW?
휙
휙

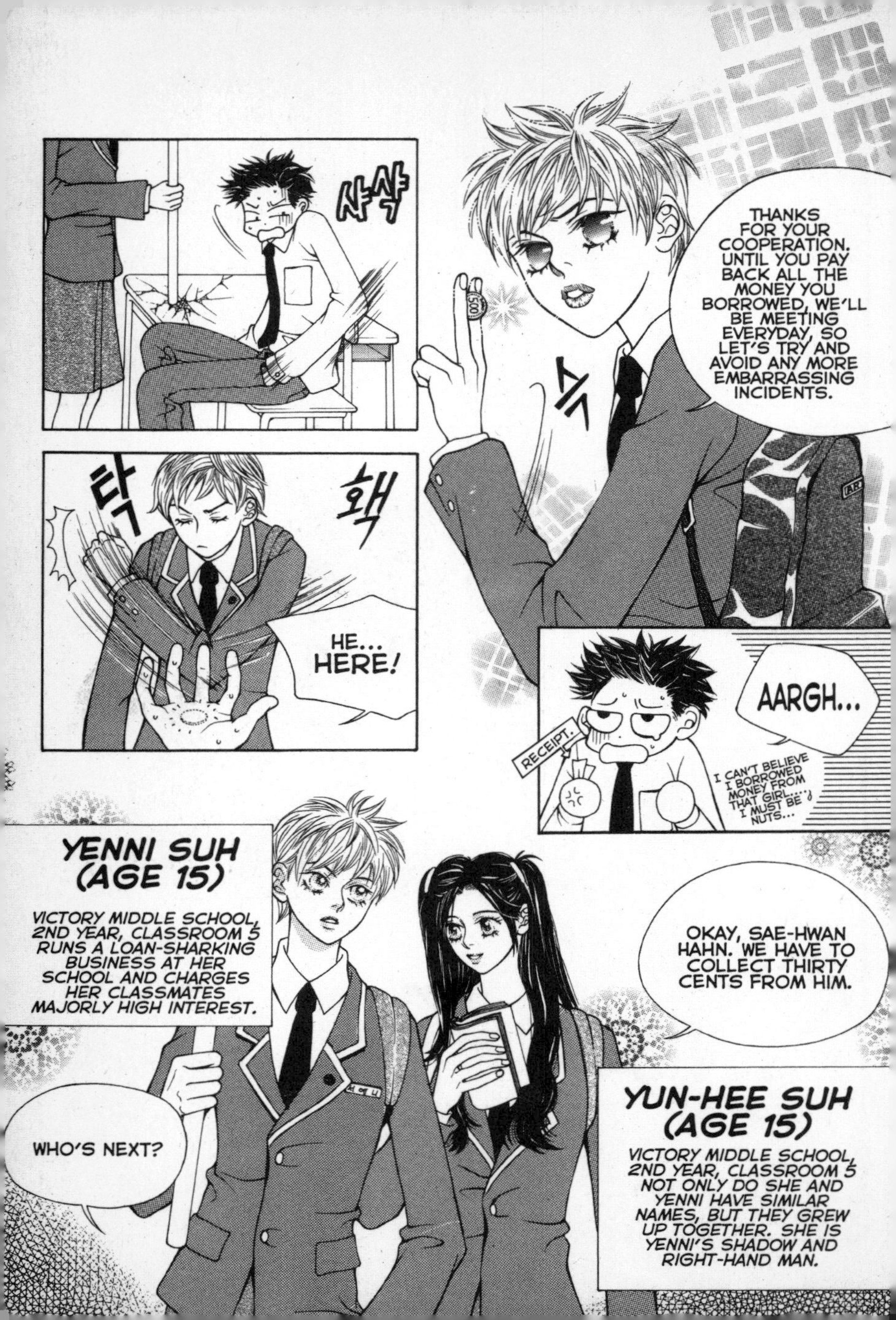
샤샥
탁
홱
HE... HERE!
슥
THANKS FOR YOUR COOPERATION. UNTIL YOU PAY BACK ALL THE MONEY YOU BORROWED, WE'LL BE MEETING EVERYDAY, SO LET'S TRY AND AVOID ANY MORE EMBARRASSING INCIDENTS.
RECEIPT.
AARGH...
I CAN'T BELIEVE I BORROWED MONEY FROM THAT GIRL.... I MUST BE NUTS...
YENNI SUH (AGE 15)
VICTORY MIDDLE SCHOOL, 2ND YEAR, CLASSROOM 5 RUNS A LOAN-SHARKING BUSINESS AT HER SCHOOL AND CHARGES HER CLASSMATES MAJORLY HIGH INTEREST.
OKAY, SAE-HWAN HAHN. WE HAVE TO COLLECT THIRTY CENTS FROM HIM.
WHO'S NEXT?
YUN-HEE SUH (AGE 15)
VICTORY MIDDLE SCHOOL, 2ND YEAR, CLASSROOM 5 NOT ONLY DO SHE AND YENNI HAVE SIMILAR NAMES, BUT THEY GREW UP TOGETHER. SHE IS YENNI'S SHADOW AND RIGHT-HAND MAN.

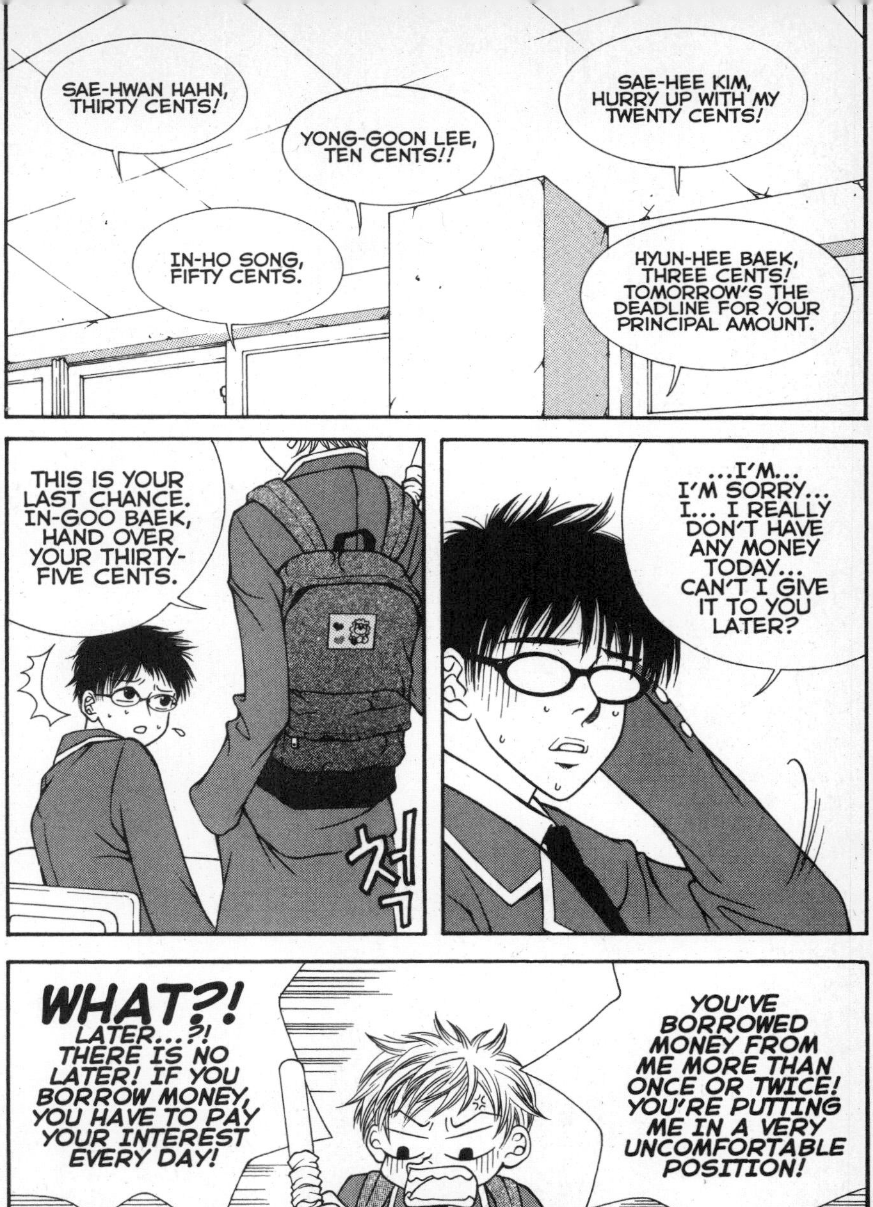
SAE-HWAN HAHN, THIRTY CENTS!
YONG-GOON LEE, TEN CENTS!!
SAE-HEE KIM, HURRY UP WITH MY TWENTY CENTS!
IN-HO SONG, FIFTY CENTS.
HYUN-HEE BAEK, THREE CENTS! TOMORROW'S THE DEADLINE FOR YOUR PRINCIPAL AMOUNT.
THIS IS YOUR LAST CHANCE. IN-GOO BAEK, HAND OVER YOUR THIRTY-FIVE CENTS.
척
...I'M... I'M SORRY... I... I REALLY DON'T HAVE ANY MONEY TODAY... CAN'T I GIVE IT TO YOU LATER?
WHAT?! LATER...?! THERE IS NO LATER! IF YOU BORROW MONEY, YOU HAVE TO PAY YOUR INTEREST EVERY DAY!
YOU'VE BORROWED MONEY FROM ME MORE THAN ONCE OR TWICE! YOU'RE PUTTING ME IN A VERY UNCOMFORTABLE POSITION!

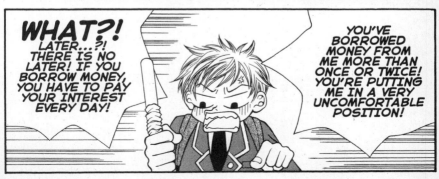

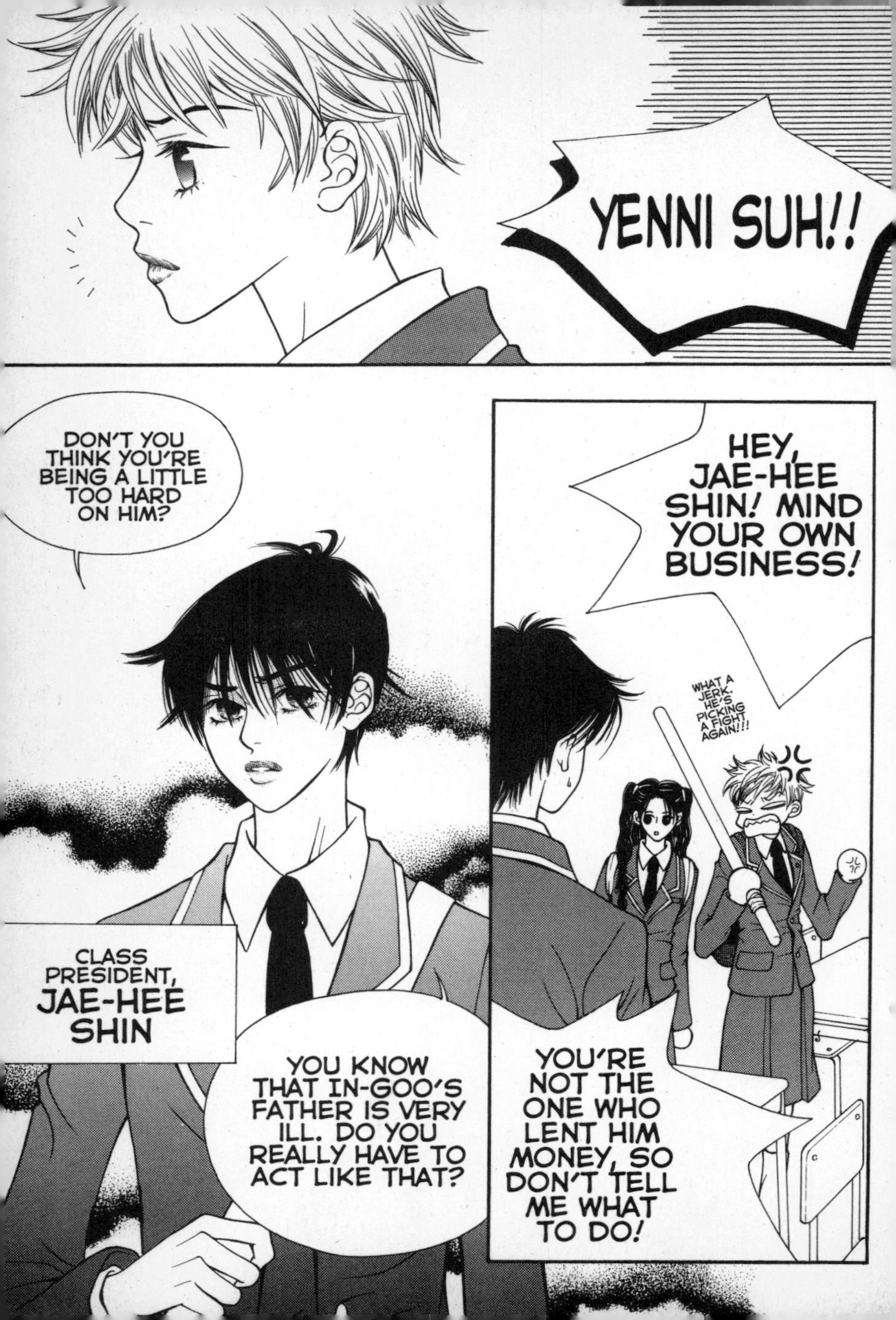
YENNI SUH!!
DON'T YOU THINK YOU'RE BEING A LITTLE TOO HARD ON HIM?
CLASS PRESIDENT, JAE-HEE SHIN
YOU KNOW THAT IN-GOO'S FATHER IS VERY ILL. DO YOU REALLY HAVE TO ACT LIKE THAT?
HEY, JAE-HEE SHIN! MIND YOUR OWN BUSINESS!
WHAT A JERK. HE'S PICKING A FIGHT AGAIN!!!
YOU'RE NOT THE ONE WHO LENT HIM MONEY, SO DON'T TELL ME WHAT TO DO!

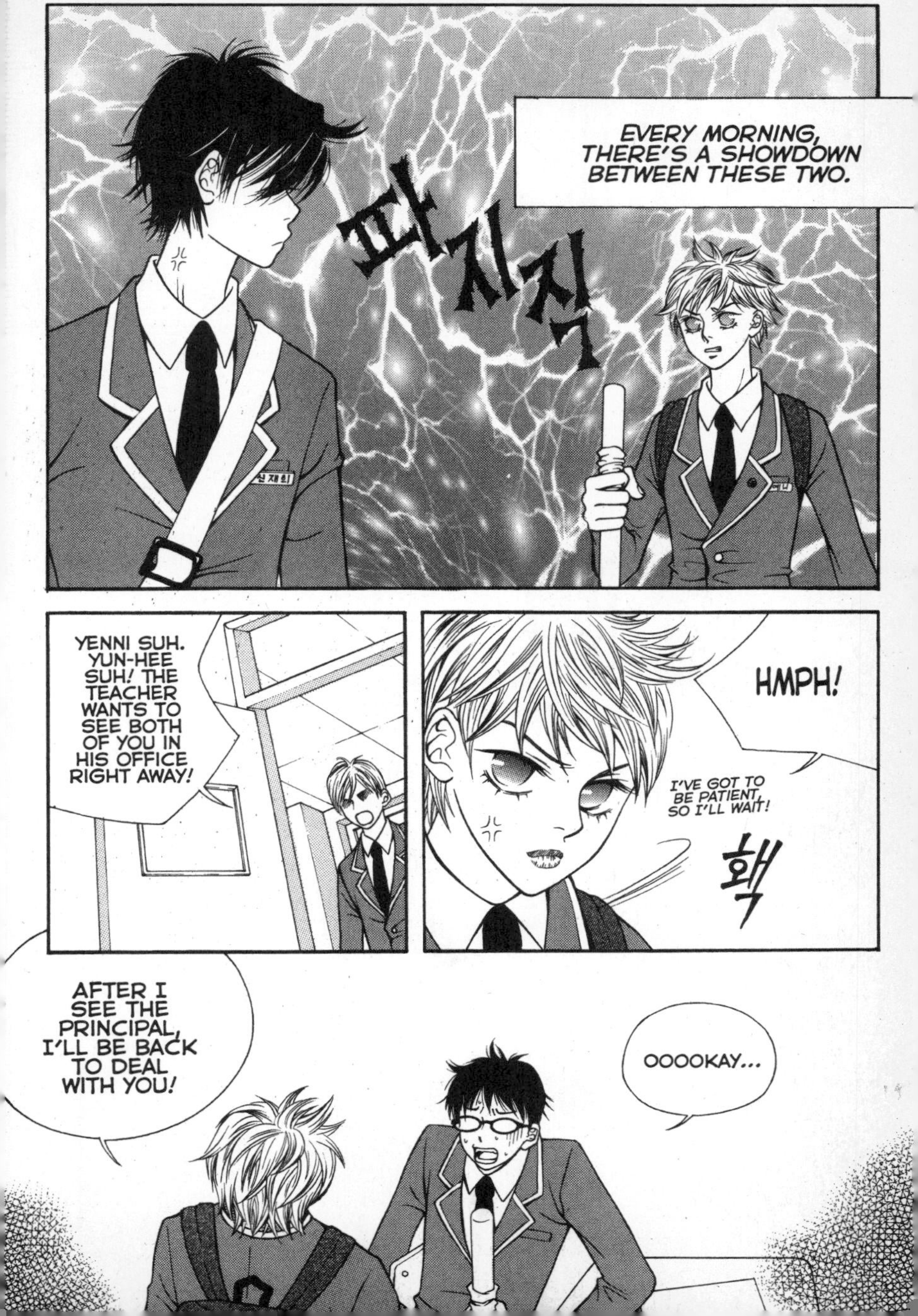
EVERY MORNING, THERE'S A SHOWDOWN BETWEEN THESE TWO.
파지직
YENNI SUH. YUN-HEE SUH! THE TEACHER WANTS TO SEE BOTH OF YOU IN HIS OFFICE RIGHT AWAY!
HMPH!
I'VE GOT TO BE PATIENT, SO I'LL WAIT!
홱
AFTER I SEE THE PRINCIPAL, I'LL BE BACK TO DEAL WITH YOU!
OOOOKAY...

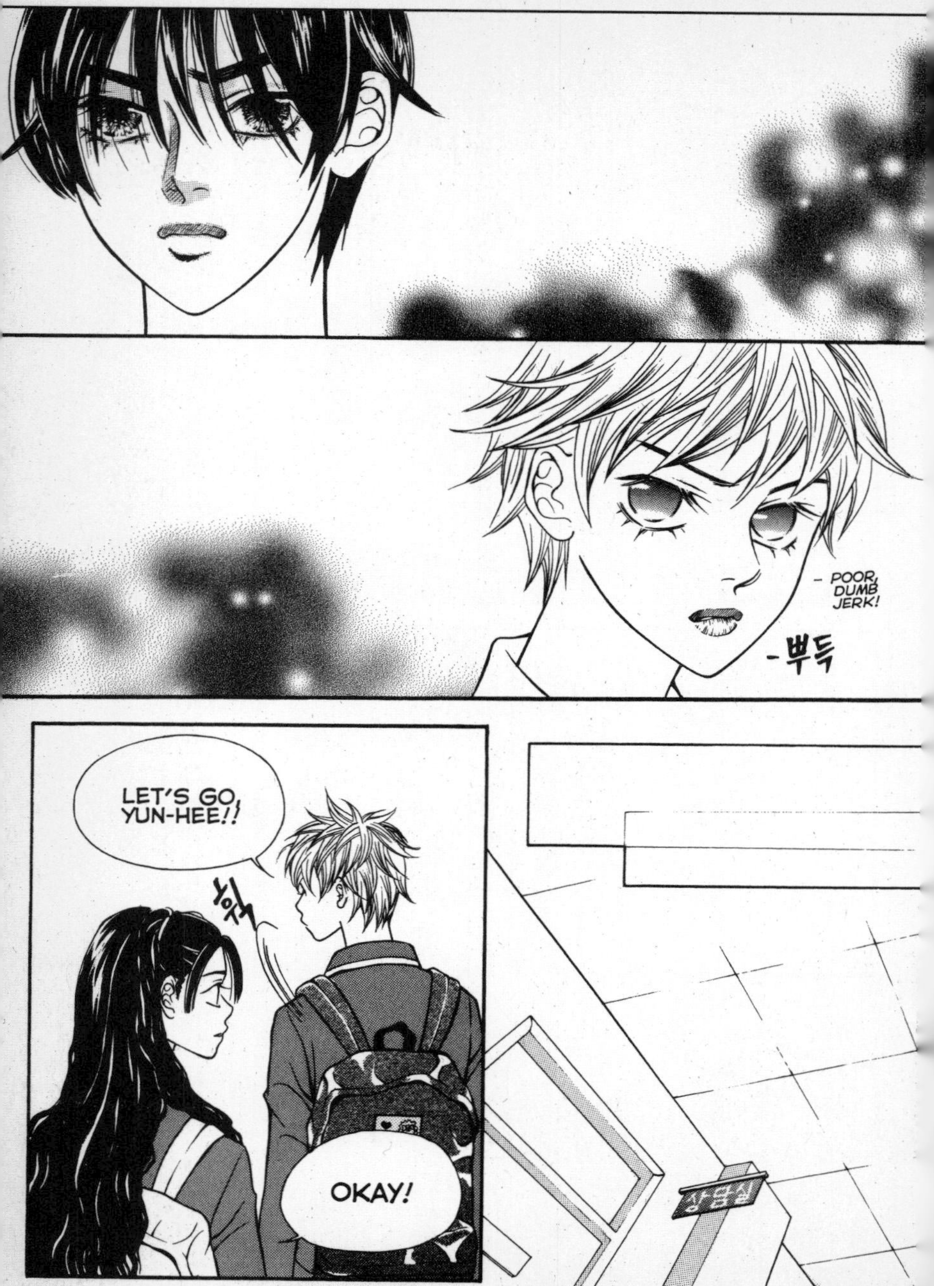
- POOR, DUMB JERK!
-뿌득
LET'S GO, YUN-HEE!!
OKAY!
상담실

*SIGN: COUNSELOR'S OFFICE.

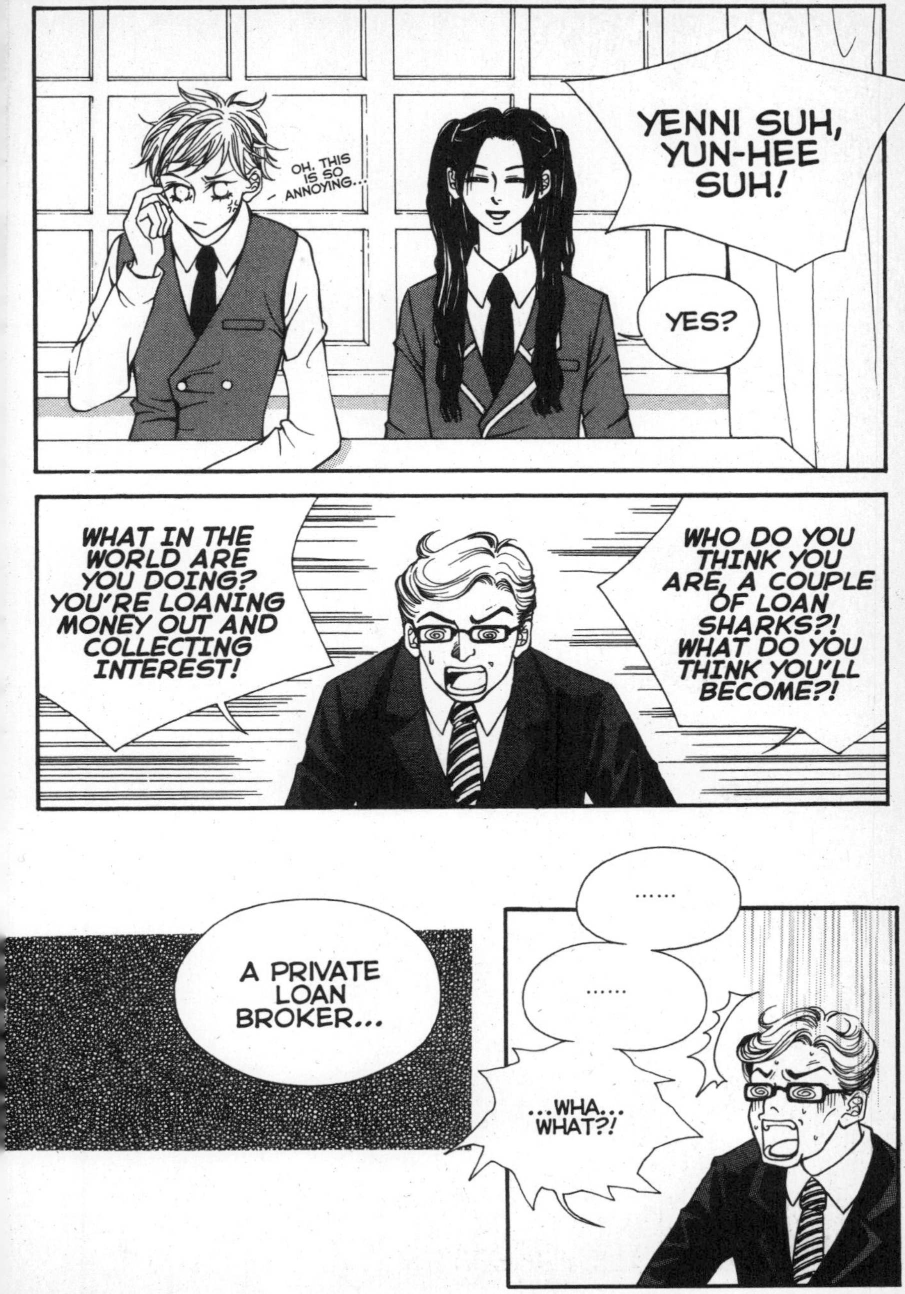
OH, THIS IS SO ANNOYING...
YENNI SUH, YUN-HEE SUH!
YES?
WHAT IN THE WORLD ARE YOU DOING? YOU'RE LOANING MONEY OUT AND COLLECTING INTEREST!
WHO DO YOU THINK YOU ARE, A COUPLE OF LOAN SHARKS?! WHAT DO YOU THINK YOU'LL BECOME?!
A PRIVATE LOAN BROKER...
......
......
...WHA... WHAT?!

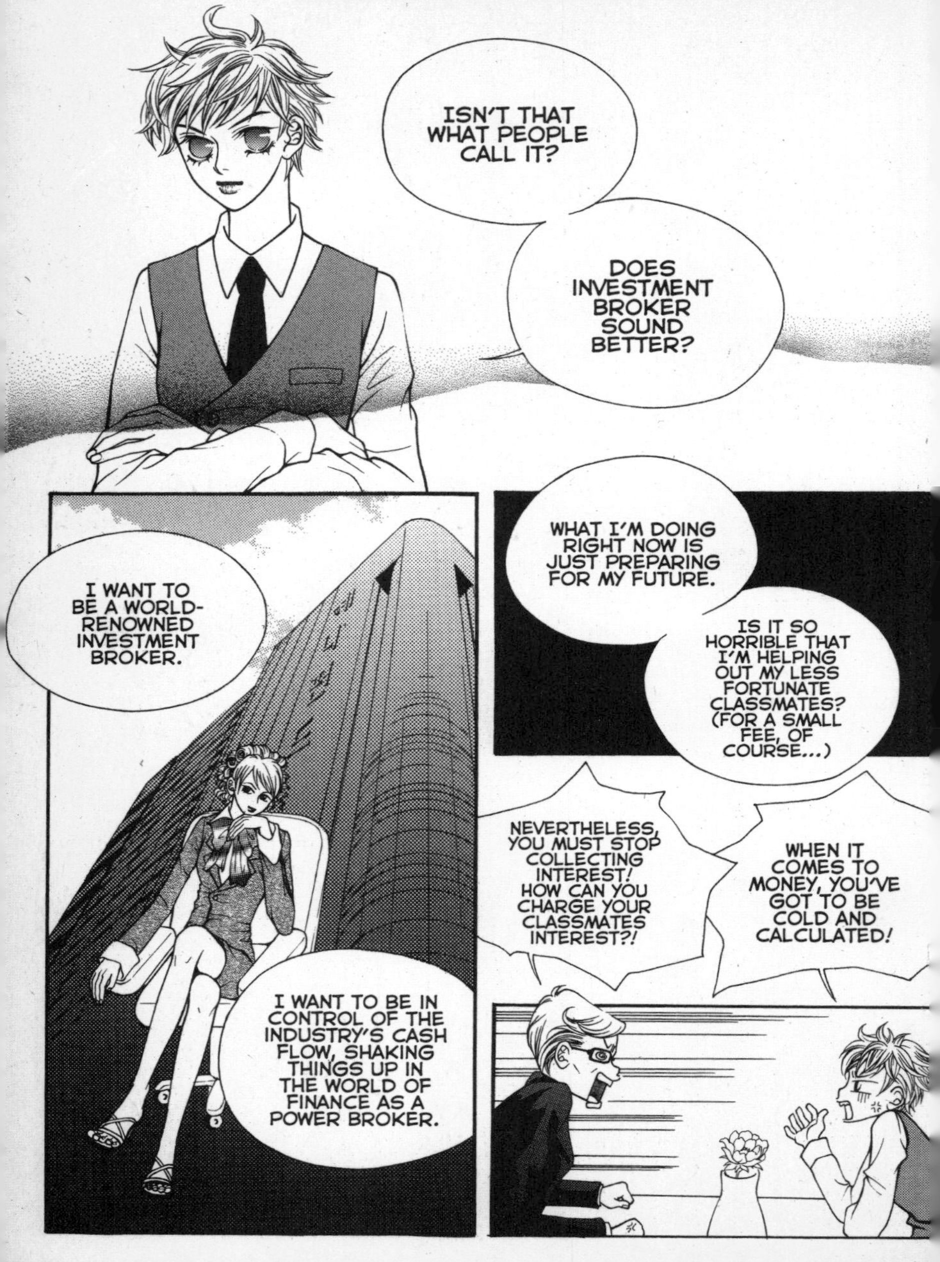
ISN'T THAT WHAT PEOPLE CALL IT?
DOES INVESTMENT BROKER SOUND BETTER?
I WANT TO BE A WORLD-RENOWNED INVESTMENT BROKER.
I WANT TO BE IN CONTROL OF THE INDUSTRY'S CASH FLOW, SHAKING THINGS UP IN THE WORLD OF FINANCE AS A POWER BROKER.
WHAT I'M DOING RIGHT NOW IS JUST PREPARING FOR MY FUTURE.
IS IT SO HORRIBLE THAT I'M HELPING OUT MY LESS FORTUNATE CLASSMATES? (FOR A SMALL FEE, OF COURSE...)
NEVERTHELESS, YOU MUST STOP COLLECTING INTEREST! HOW CAN YOU CHARGE YOUR CLASSMATES INTEREST?!
WHEN IT COMES TO MONEY, YOU'VE GOT TO BE COLD AND CALCULATED!

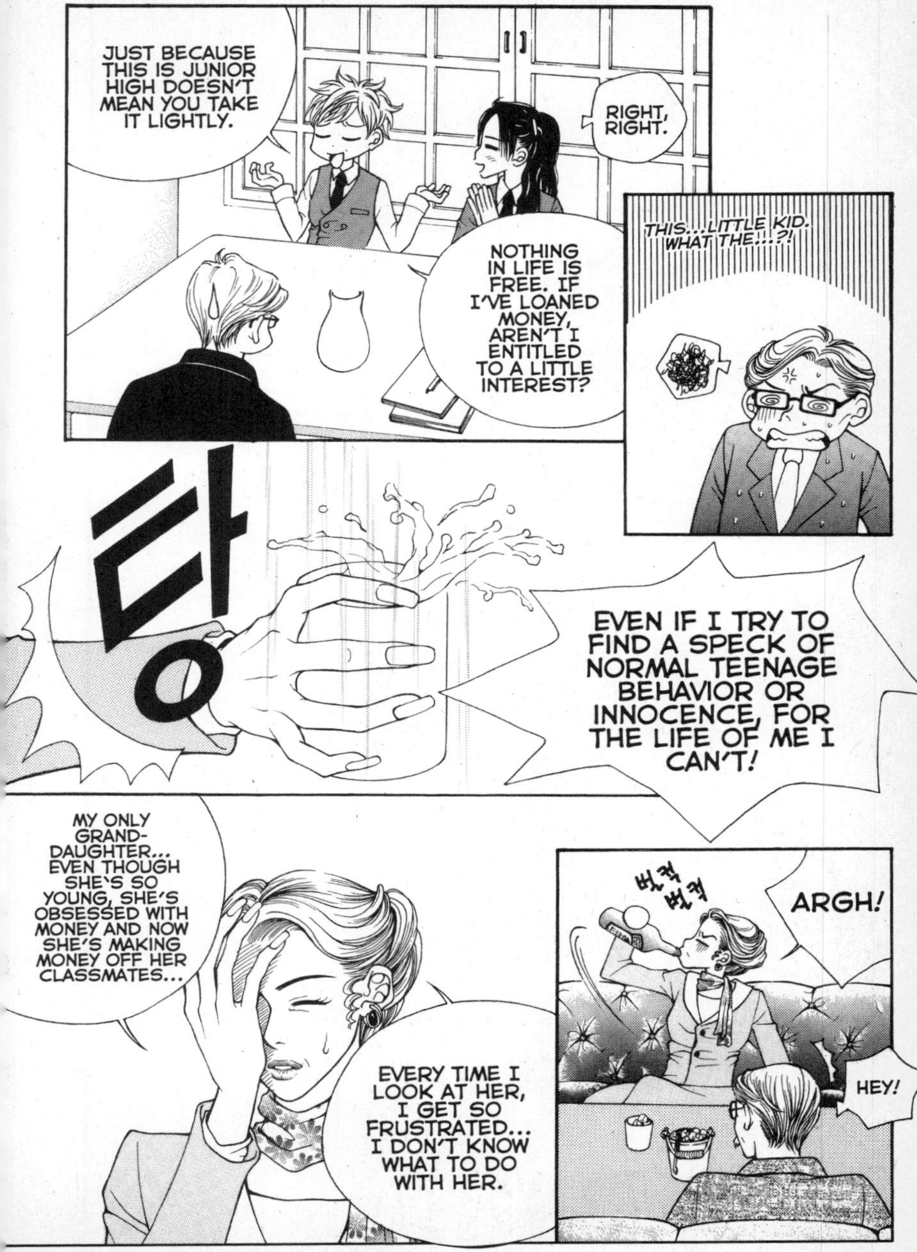
JUST BECAUSE THIS IS JUNIOR HIGH DOESN'T MEAN YOU TAKE IT LIGHTLY.
RIGHT, RIGHT.
NOTHING IN LIFE IS FREE. IF I'VE LOANED MONEY, AREN'T I ENTITLED TO A LITTLE INTEREST?
THIS...LITTLE KID. WHAT THE...?!
탕
EVEN IF I TRY TO FIND A SPECK OF NORMAL TEENAGE BEHAVIOR OR INNOCENCE, FOR THE LIFE OF ME I CAN'T!
MY ONLY GRAND-DAUGHTER... EVEN THOUGH SHE'S SO YOUNG, SHE'S OBSESSED WITH MONEY AND NOW SHE'S MAKING MONEY OFF HER CLASSMATES...
EVERY TIME I LOOK AT HER, I GET SO FRUSTRATED... I DON'T KNOW WHAT TO DO WITH HER.
벌컥 벌컥
ARGH!
HEY!

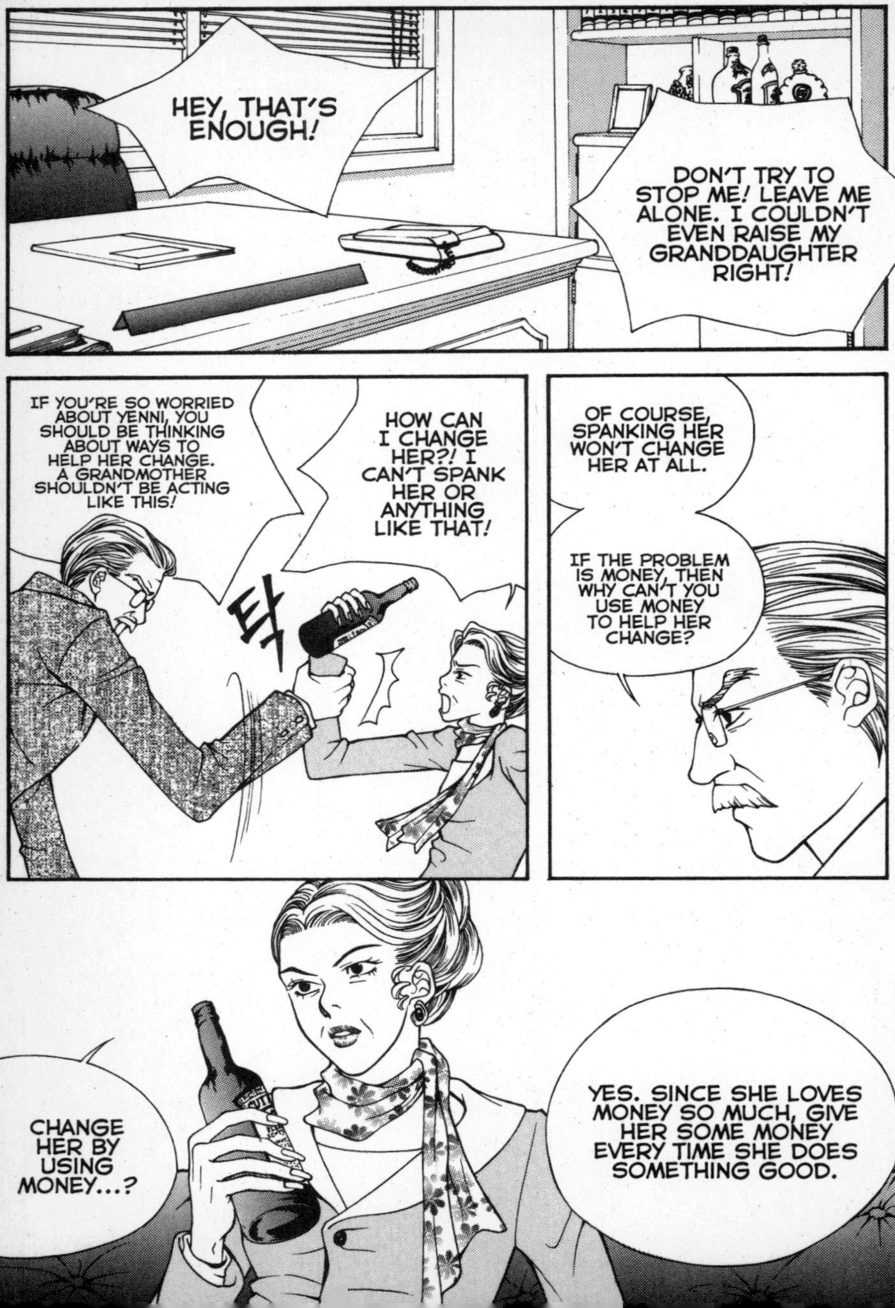
HEY, THAT'S ENOUGH!
DON'T TRY TO STOP ME! LEAVE ME ALONE. I COULDN'T EVEN RAISE MY GRANDDAUGHTER RIGHT!
IF YOU'RE SO WORRIED ABOUT YENNI, YOU SHOULD BE THINKING ABOUT WAYS TO HELP HER CHANGE. A GRANDMOTHER SHOULDN'T BE ACTING LIKE THIS!
HOW CAN I CHANGE HER?! I CAN'T SPANK HER OR ANYTHING LIKE THAT!
탁
OF COURSE, SPANKING HER WON'T CHANGE HER AT ALL.
IF THE PROBLEM IS MONEY, THEN WHY CAN'T YOU USE MONEY TO HELP HER CHANGE?
CHANGE HER BY USING MONEY...?
YES. SINCE SHE LOVES MONEY SO MUCH, GIVE HER SOME MONEY EVERY TIME SHE DOES SOMETHING GOOD.

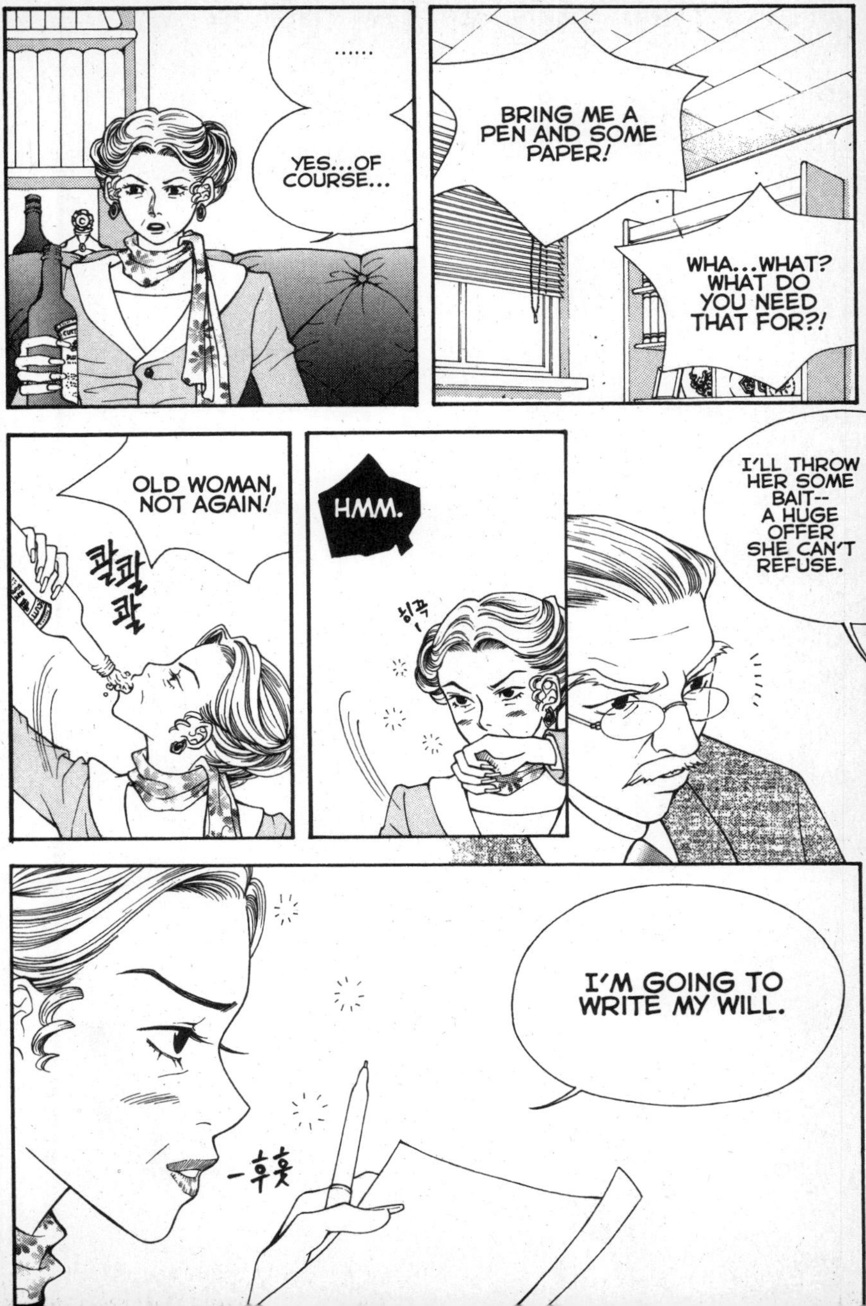
......
YES...OF COURSE...
BRING ME A PEN AND SOME PAPER!
WHA...WHAT? WHAT DO YOU NEED THAT FOR?!
OLD WOMAN, NOT AGAIN!
콸콸콸
HMM.
힝끅
I'LL THROW HER SOME BAIT-- A HUGE OFFER SHE CAN'T REFUSE.
I'M GOING TO WRITE MY WILL.
ㅡ후훗

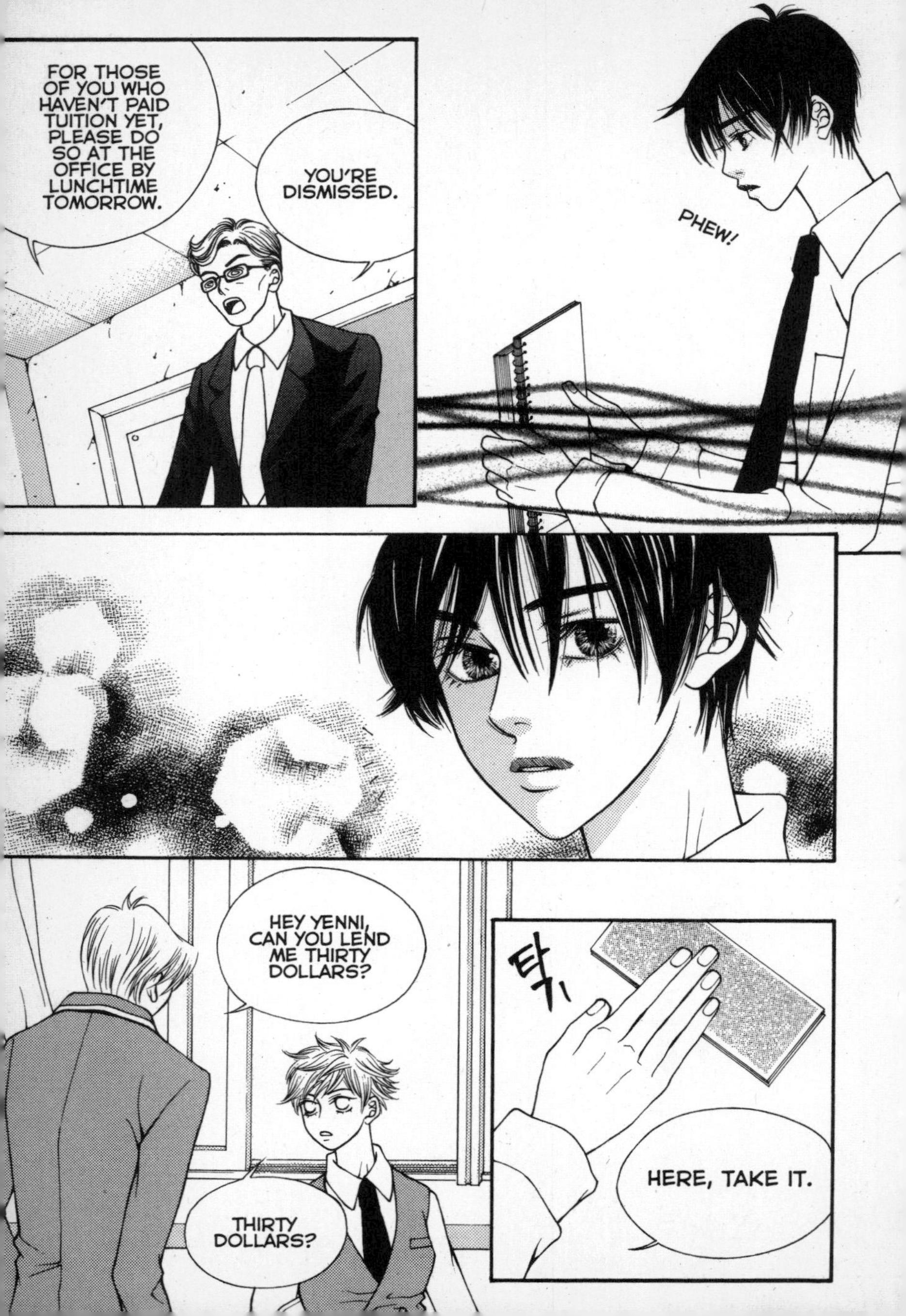
FOR THOSE OF YOU WHO HAVEN'T PAID TUITION YET, PLEASE DO SO AT THE OFFICE BY LUNCHTIME TOMORROW.
YOU'RE DISMISSED.
PHEW!
HEY YENNI, CAN YOU LEND ME THIRTY DOLLARS?
THIRTY DOLLARS?
탁
HERE, TAKE IT.

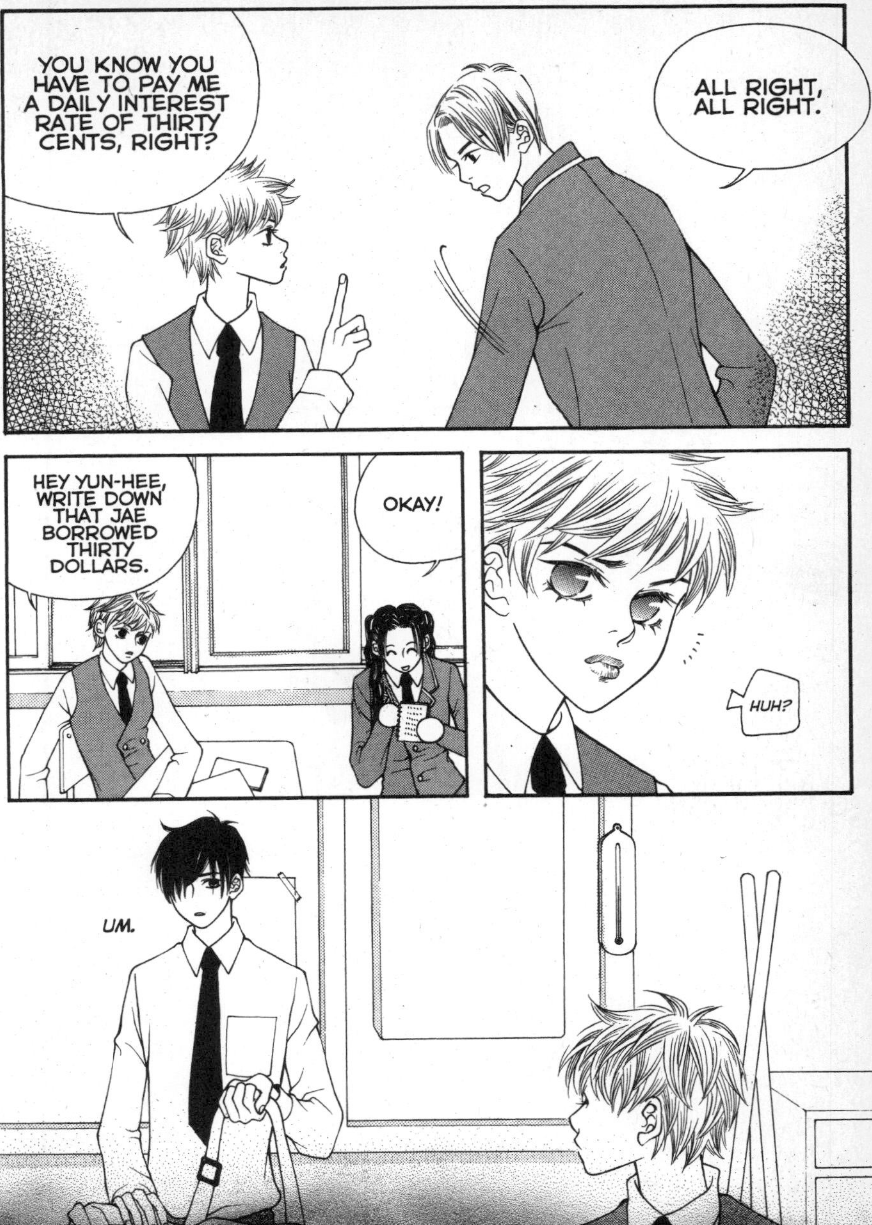
YOU KNOW YOU HAVE TO PAY ME A DAILY INTEREST RATE OF THIRTY CENTS, RIGHT?
ALL RIGHT, ALL RIGHT.
HEY YUN-HEE, WRITE DOWN THAT JAE BORROWED THIRTY DOLLARS.
OKAY!
HUH?
UM.

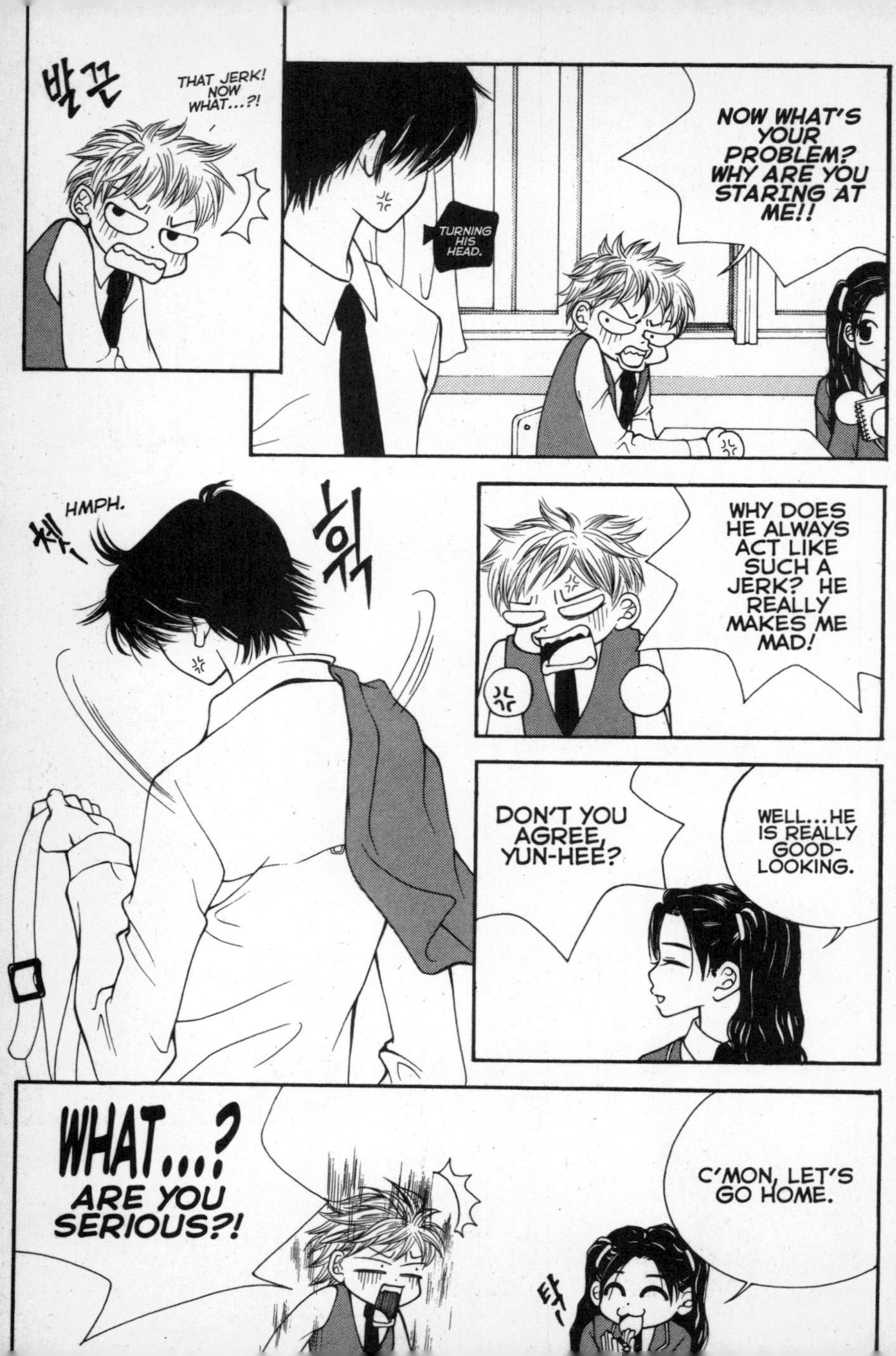
발끈
THAT JERK! NOW WHAT...?!
TURNING HIS HEAD.
NOW WHAT'S YOUR PROBLEM? WHY ARE YOU STARING AT ME!!
쳇
HMPH.
휙
WHY DOES HE ALWAYS ACT LIKE SUCH A JERK? HE REALLY MAKES ME MAD!
DON'T YOU AGREE, YUN-HEE?
WELL...HE IS REALLY GOOD-LOOKING.
WHAT...? ARE YOU SERIOUS?!
탁
C'MON, LET'S GO HOME.

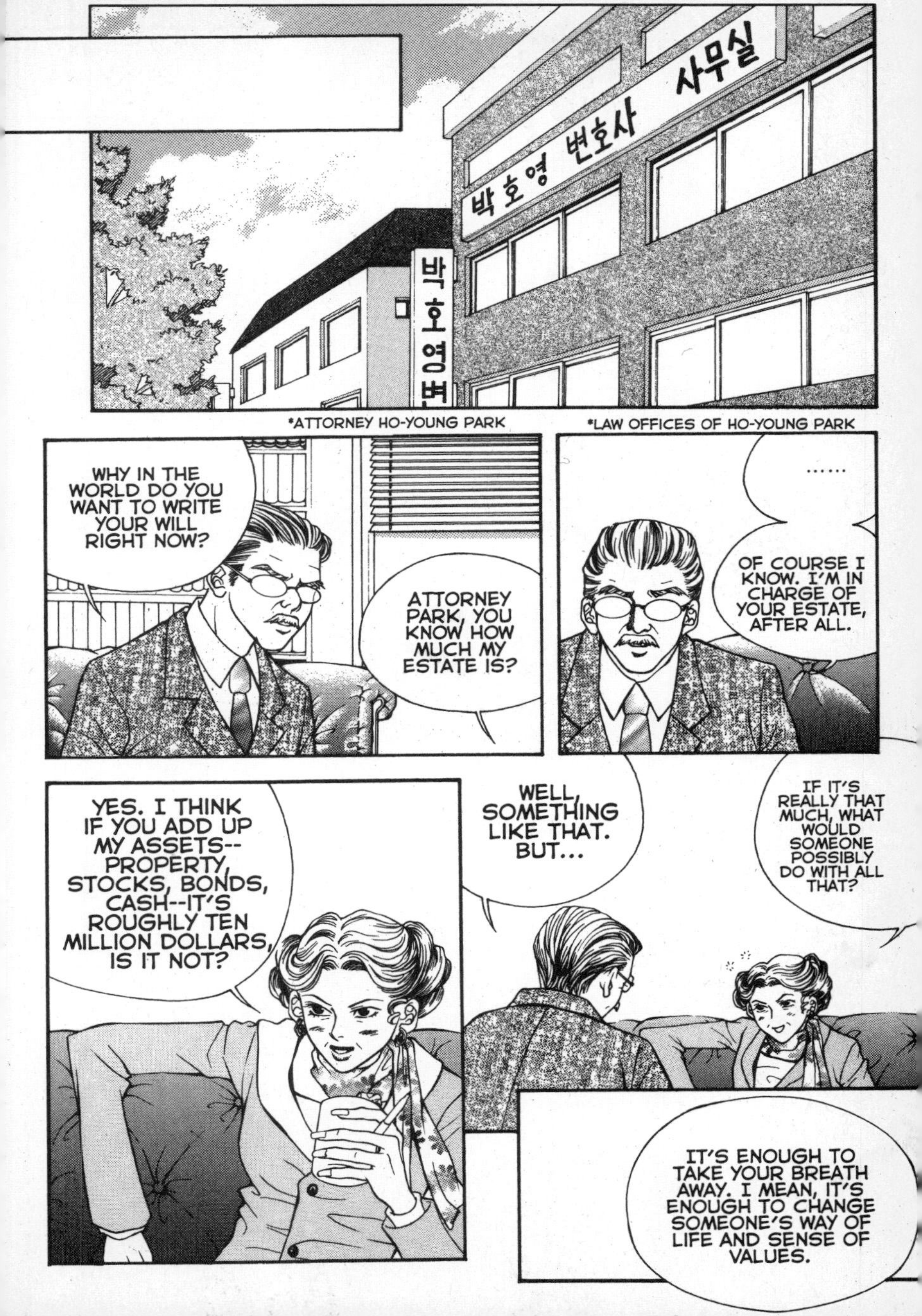

박호영
*ATTORNEY HO-YOUNG PARK
박호영 변호사 사무실
*LAW OFFICES OF HO-YOUNG PARK
WHY IN THE WORLD DO YOU WANT TO WRITE YOUR WILL RIGHT NOW?
ATTORNEY PARK, YOU KNOW HOW MUCH MY ESTATE IS?
......
OF COURSE I KNOW. I'M IN CHARGE OF YOUR ESTATE, AFTER ALL.
YES. I THINK IF YOU ADD UP MY ASSETS--PROPERTY, STOCKS, BONDS, CASH--IT'S ROUGHLY TEN MILLION DOLLARS, IS IT NOT?
WELL, SOMETHING LIKE THAT. BUT...
IF IT'S REALLY THAT MUCH, WHAT WOULD SOMEONE POSSIBLY DO WITH ALL THAT?
IT'S ENOUGH TO TAKE YOUR BREATH AWAY. I MEAN, IT'S ENOUGH TO CHANGE SOMEONE'S WAY OF LIFE AND SENSE OF VALUES.

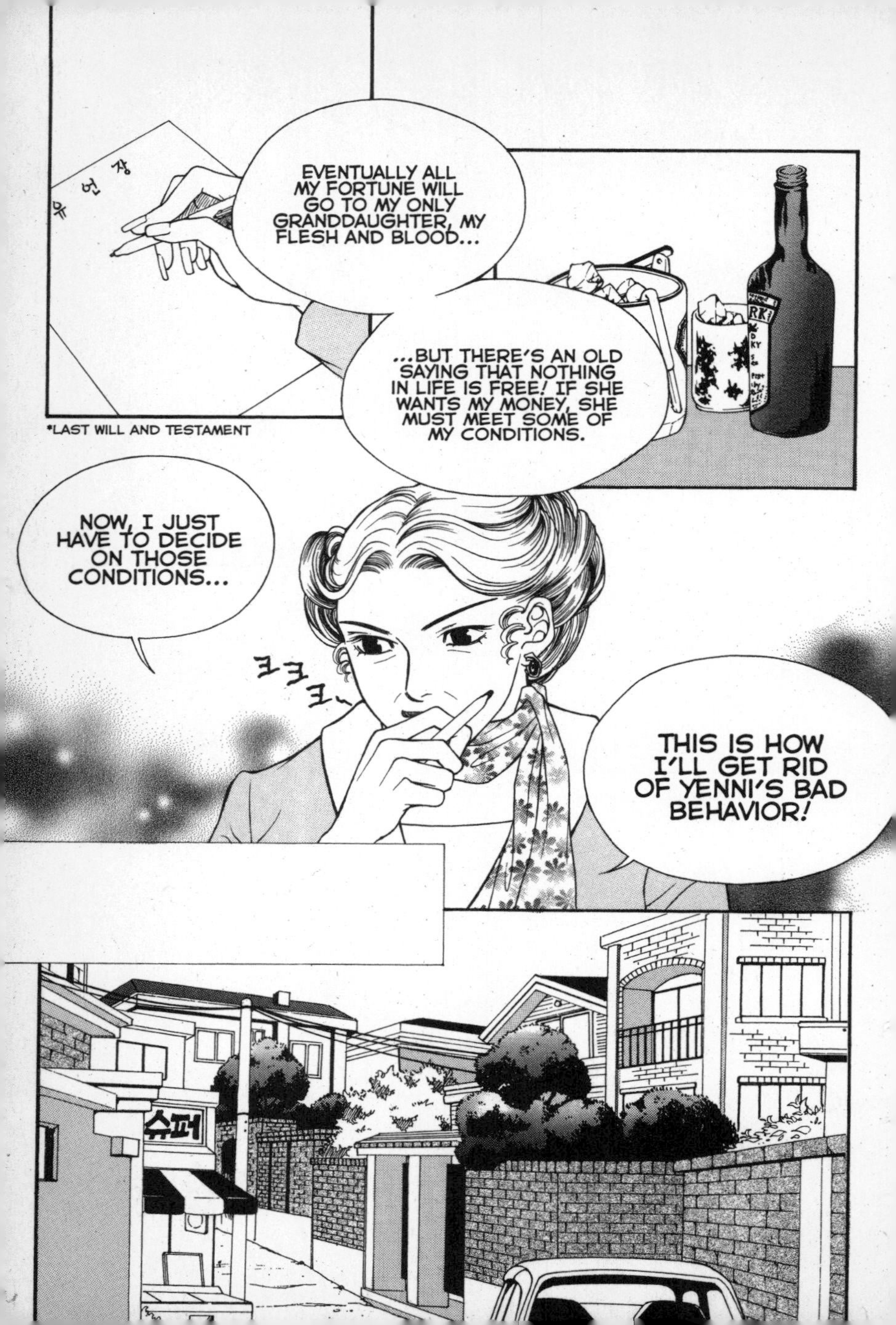
유언장
*LAST WILL AND TESTAMENT
EVENTUALLY ALL MY FORTUNE WILL GO TO MY ONLY GRANDDAUGHTER, MY FLESH AND BLOOD...
...BUT THERE'S AN OLD SAYING THAT NOTHING IN LIFE IS FREE! IF SHE WANTS MY MONEY, SHE MUST MEET SOME OF MY CONDITIONS.
NOW, I JUST HAVE TO DECIDE ON THOSE CONDITIONS...
ㅋㅋㅋ~
THIS IS HOW I'LL GET RID OF YENNI'S BAD BEHAVIOR!
슈퍼

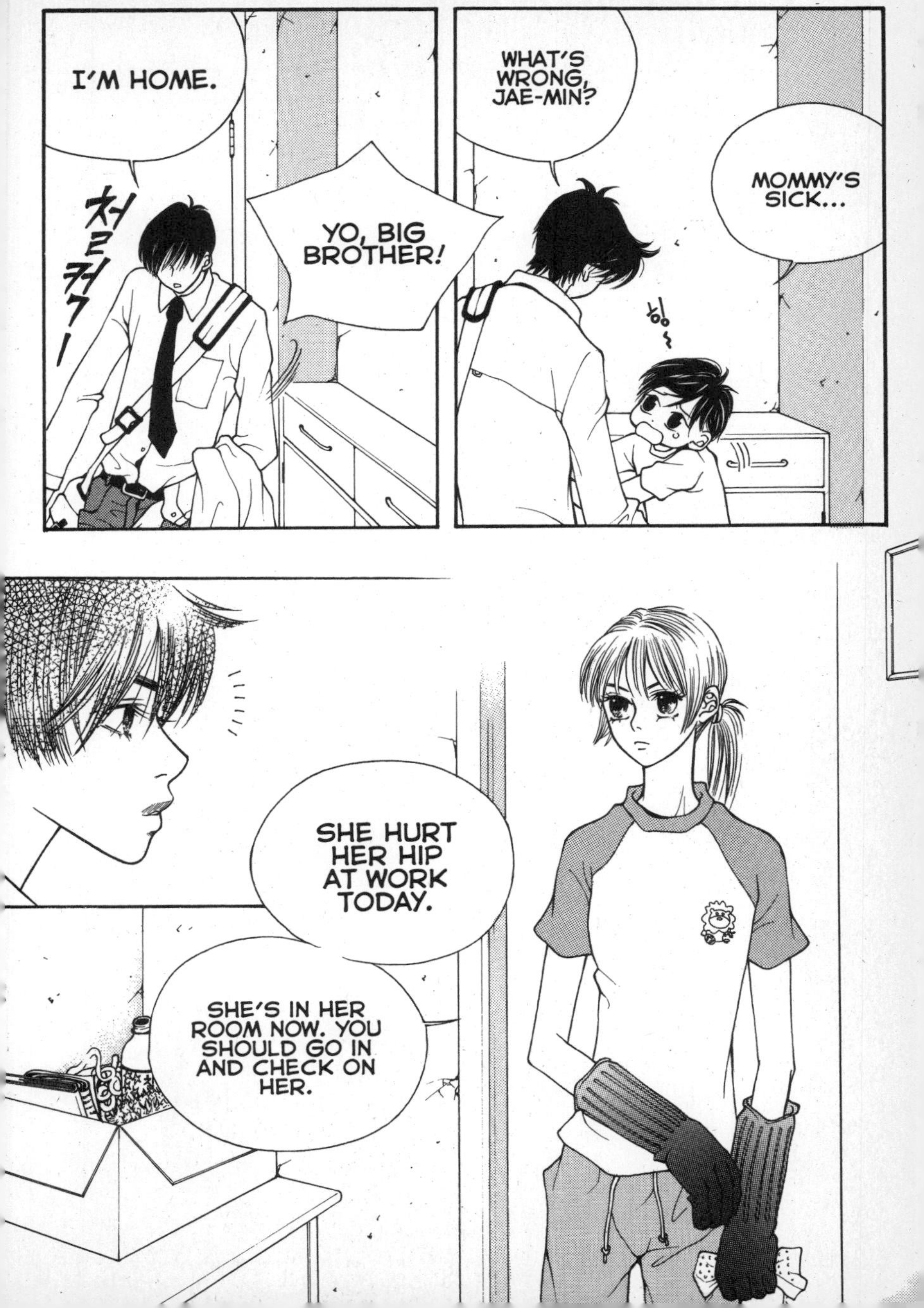
I'M HOME.
YO, BIG BROTHER!
WHAT'S WRONG, JAE-MIN?
MOMMY'S SICK...
힝
SHE HURT HER HIP AT WORK TODAY.
SHE'S IN HER ROOM NOW. YOU SHOULD GO IN AND CHECK ON HER.

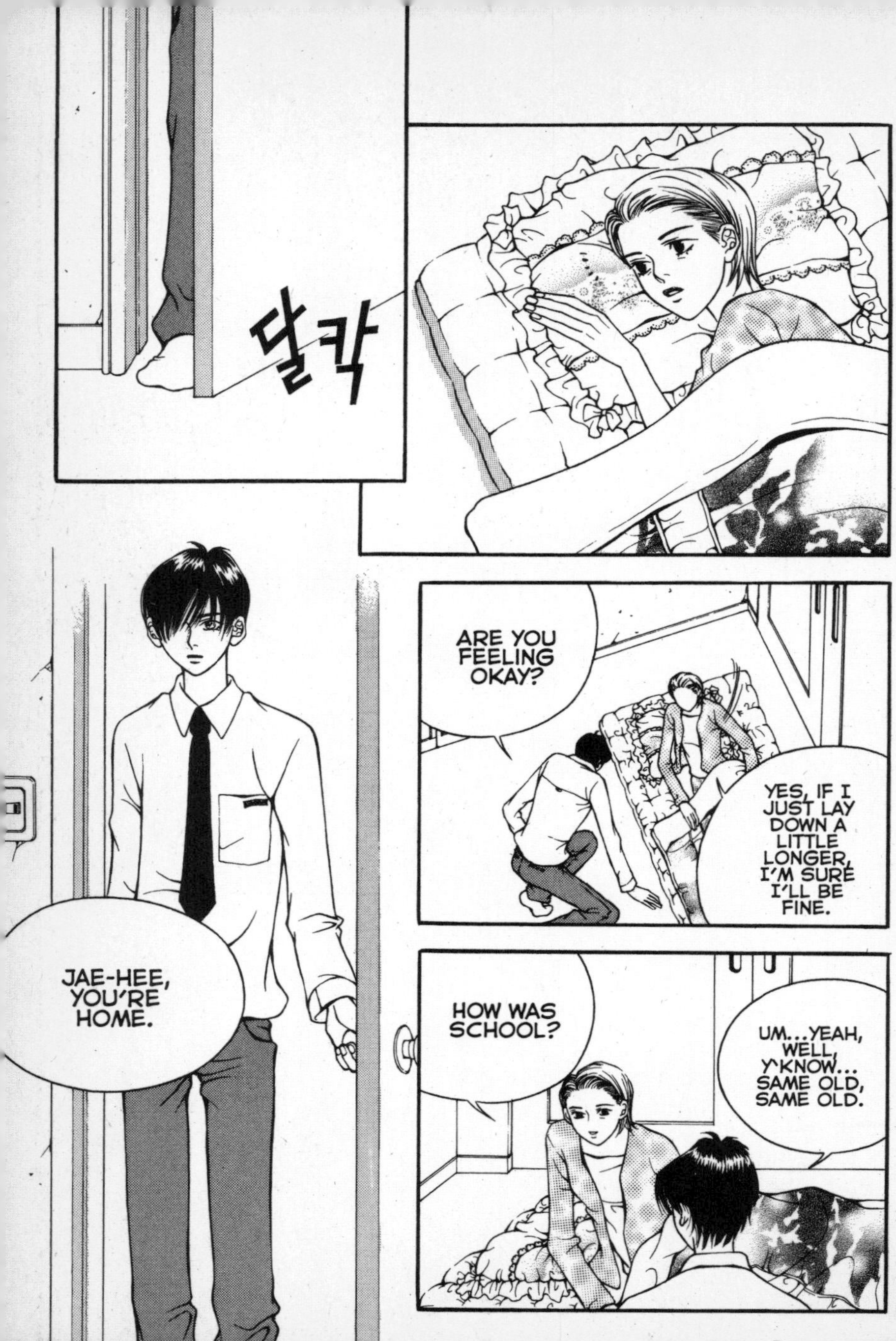
달칵
JAE-HEE, YOU'RE HOME.
ARE YOU FEELING OKAY?
YES, IF I JUST LAY DOWN A LITTLE LONGER, I'M SURE I'LL BE FINE.
HOW WAS SCHOOL?
UM...YEAH, WELL, Y'KNOW... SAME OLD, SAME OLD.

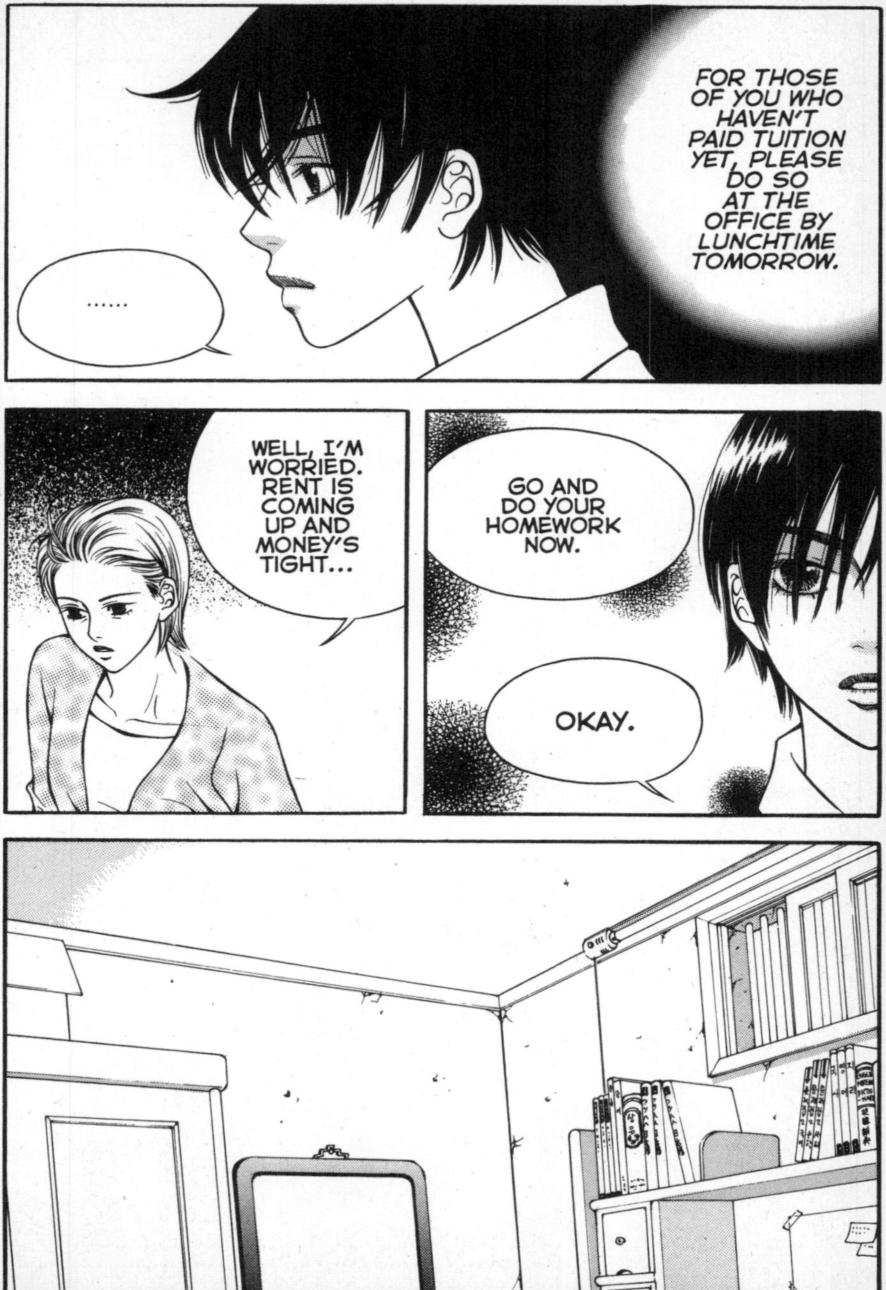
FOR THOSE OF YOU WHO HAVEN'T PAID TUITION YET, PLEASE DO SO AT THE OFFICE BY LUNCHTIME TOMORROW.
......
WELL, I'M WORRIED. RENT IS COMING UP AND MONEY'S TIGHT...
GO AND DO YOUR HOMEWORK NOW.
OKAY.

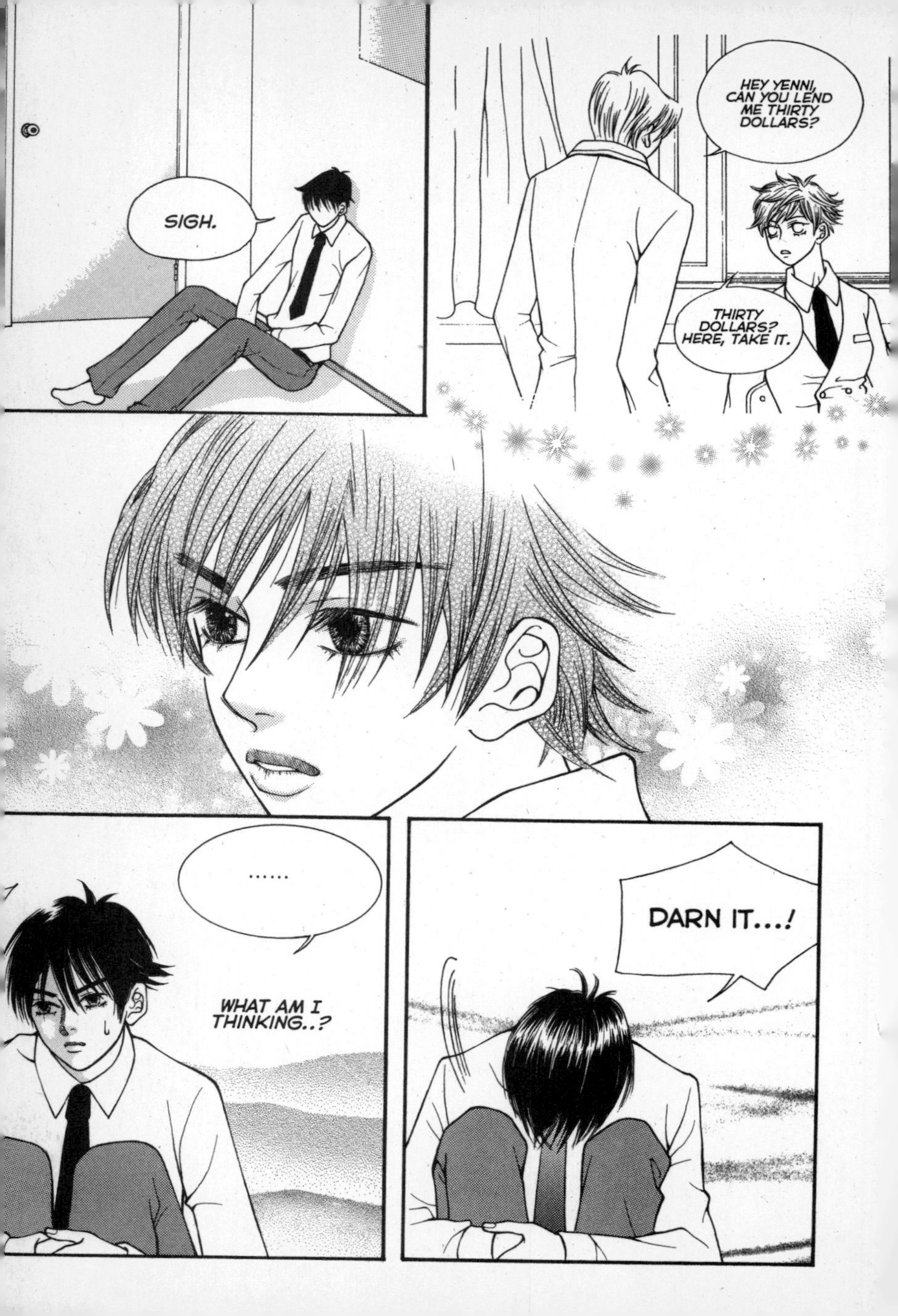
SIGH.
HEY YENNI, CAN YOU LEND ME THIRTY DOLLARS?
THIRTY DOLLARS? HERE, TAKE IT.
......
WHAT AM I THINKING..?
DARN IT...!

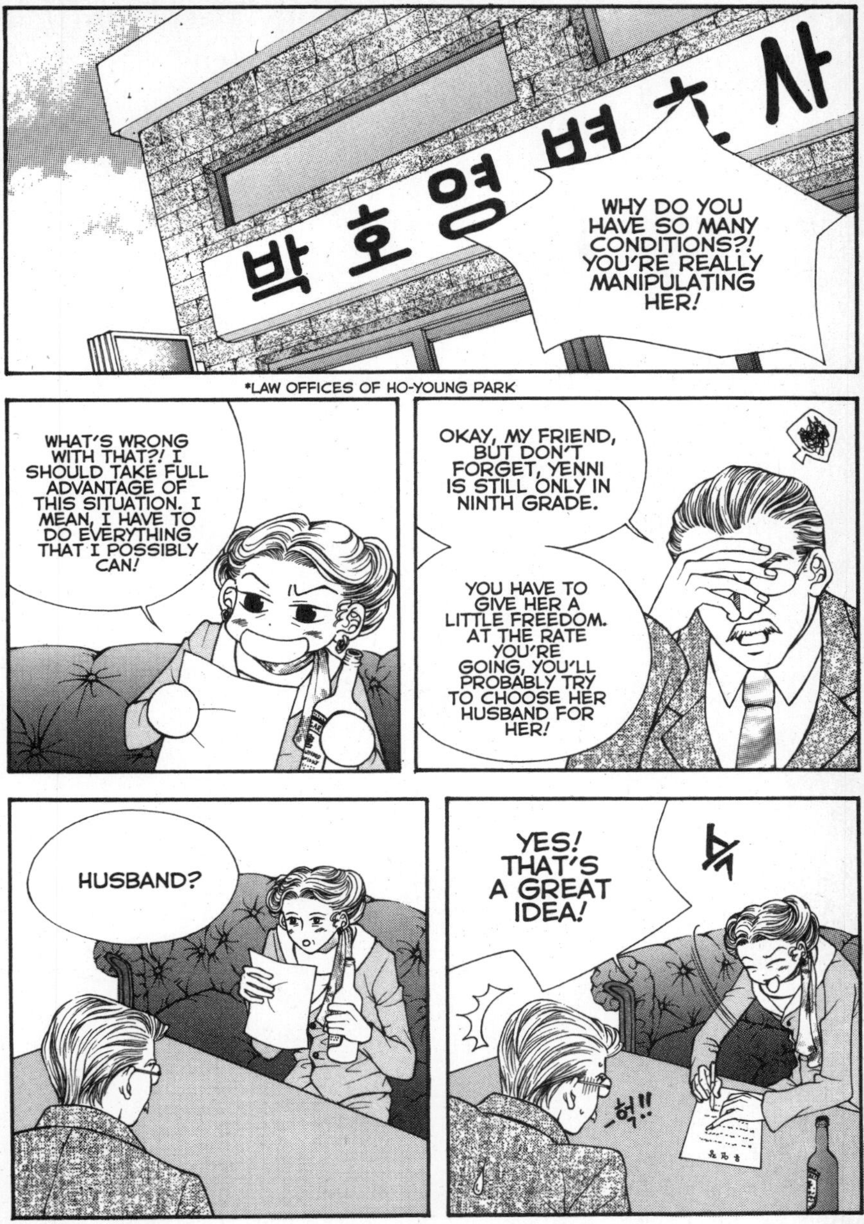
WHY DO YOU HAVE SO MANY CONDITIONS?! YOU'RE REALLY MANIPULATING HER!
*LAW OFFICES OF HO-YOUNG PARK
WHAT'S WRONG WITH THAT?! I SHOULD TAKE FULL ADVANTAGE OF THIS SITUATION. I MEAN, I HAVE TO DO EVERYTHING THAT I POSSIBLY CAN!
OKAY, MY FRIEND, BUT DON'T FORGET, YENNI IS STILL ONLY IN NINTH GRADE.
YOU HAVE TO GIVE HER A LITTLE FREEDOM. AT THE RATE YOU'RE GOING, YOU'LL PROBABLY TRY TO CHOOSE HER HUSBAND FOR HER!
HUSBAND?
YES! THAT'S A GREAT IDEA!
헉!!

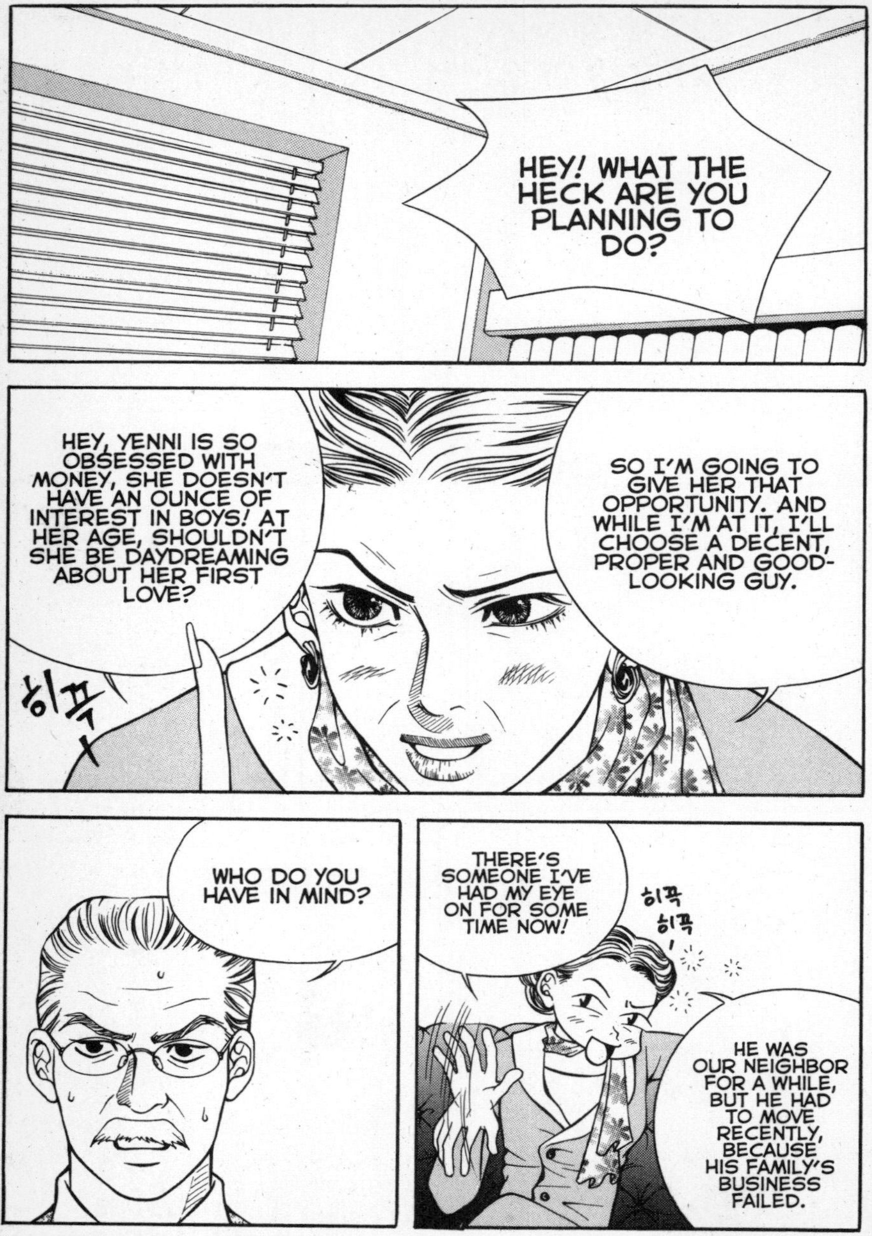
HEY! WHAT THE HECK ARE YOU PLANNING TO DO?
HEY, YENNI IS SO OBSESSED WITH MONEY, SHE DOESN'T HAVE AN OUNCE OF INTEREST IN BOYS! AT HER AGE, SHOULDN'T SHE BE DAYDREAMING ABOUT HER FIRST LOVE?
히끅
SO I'M GOING TO GIVE HER THAT OPPORTUNITY. AND WHILE I'M AT IT, I'LL CHOOSE A DECENT, PROPER AND GOOD-LOOKING GUY.
WHO DO YOU HAVE IN MIND?
THERE'S SOMEONE I'VE HAD MY EYE ON FOR SOME TIME NOW!
히끅
히끅
HE WAS OUR NEIGHBOR FOR A WHILE, BUT HE HAD TO MOVE RECENTLY, BECAUSE HIS FAMILY'S BUSINESS FAILED.

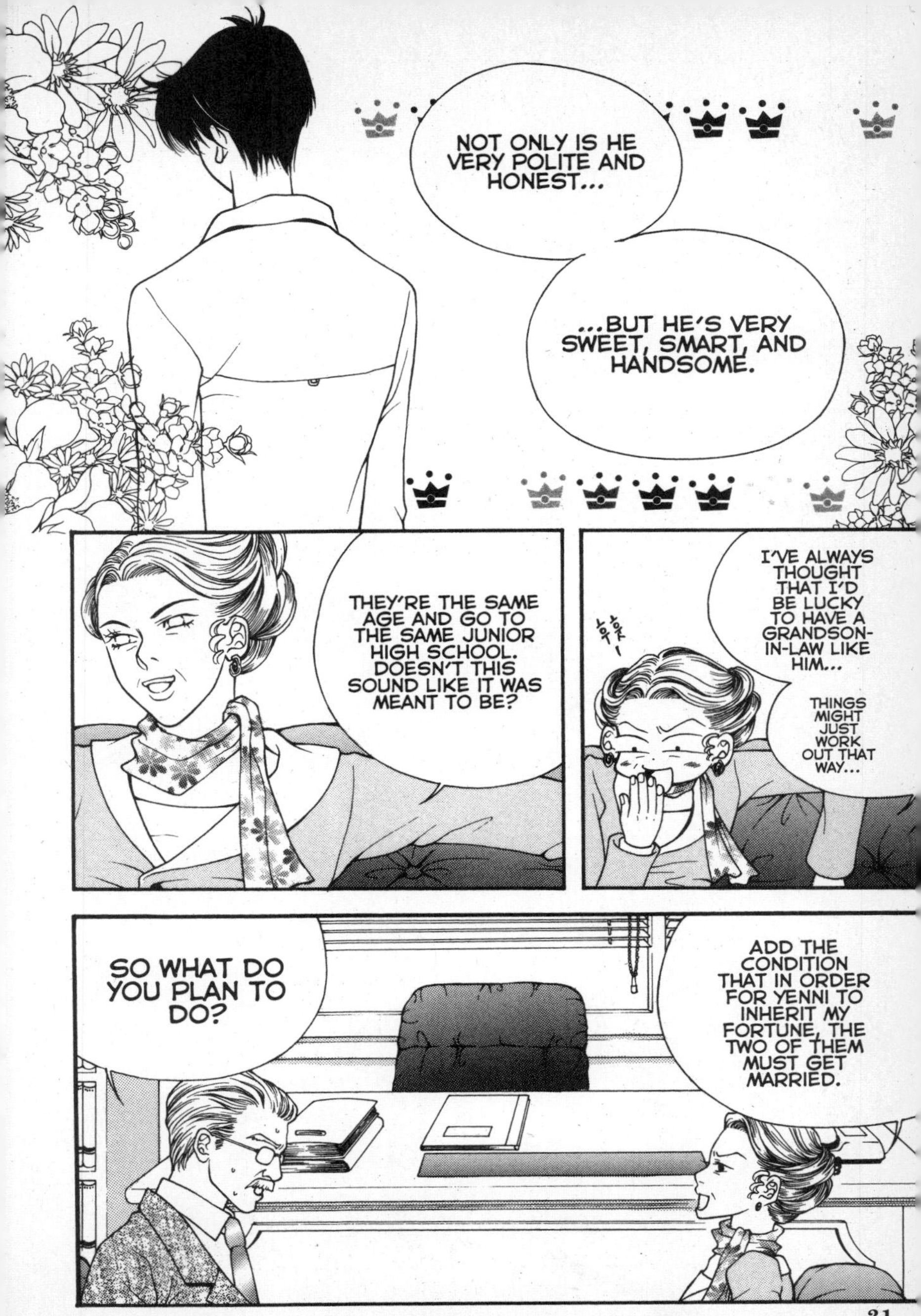
NOT ONLY IS HE VERY POLITE AND HONEST...
...BUT HE'S VERY SWEET, SMART, AND HANDSOME.
THEY'RE THE SAME AGE AND GO TO THE SAME JUNIOR HIGH SCHOOL. DOESN'T THIS SOUND LIKE IT WAS MEANT TO BE?
후훗!
I'VE ALWAYS THOUGHT THAT I'D BE LUCKY TO HAVE A GRANDSON-IN-LAW LIKE HIM...
THINGS MIGHT JUST WORK OUT THAT WAY...
SO WHAT DO YOU PLAN TO DO?
ADD THE CONDITION THAT IN ORDER FOR YENNI TO INHERIT MY FORTUNE, THE TWO OF THEM MUST GET MARRIED.

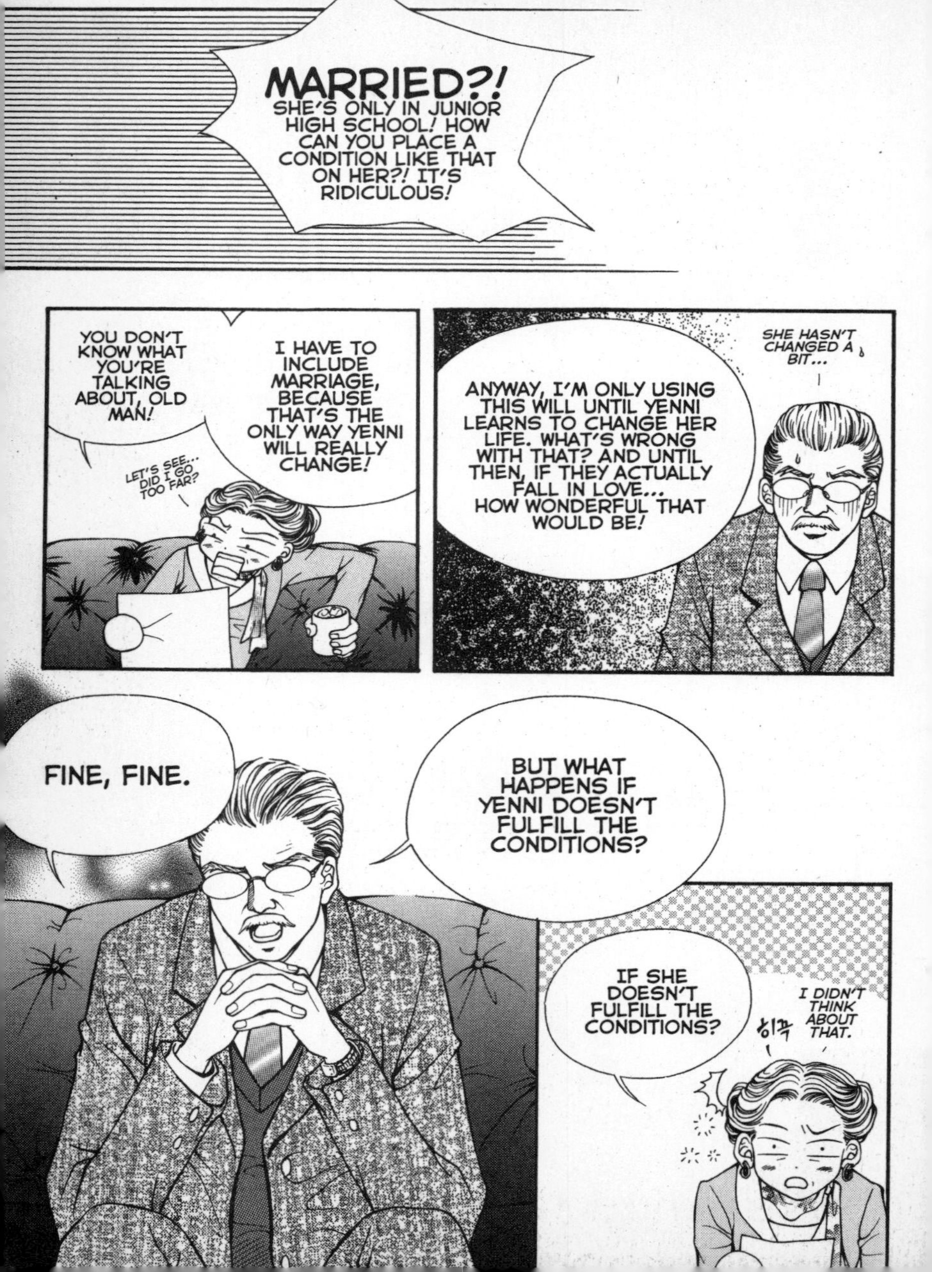
MARRIED?! SHE'S ONLY IN JUNIOR HIGH SCHOOL! HOW CAN YOU PLACE A CONDITION LIKE THAT ON HER?! IT'S RIDICULOUS!
YOU DON'T KNOW WHAT YOU'RE TALKING ABOUT, OLD MAN!
I HAVE TO INCLUDE MARRIAGE, BECAUSE THAT'S THE ONLY WAY YENNI WILL REALLY CHANGE!
LET'S SEE... DID I GO TOO FAR?
ANYWAY, I'M ONLY USING THIS WILL UNTIL YENNI LEARNS TO CHANGE HER LIFE. WHAT'S WRONG WITH THAT? AND UNTIL THEN, IF THEY ACTUALLY FALL IN LOVE... HOW WONDERFUL THAT WOULD BE!
SHE HASN'T CHANGED A BIT...
FINE, FINE.
BUT WHAT HAPPENS IF YENNI DOESN'T FULFILL THE CONDITIONS?
IF SHE DOESN'T FULFILL THE CONDITIONS?
히끅
I DIDN'T THINK ABOUT THAT.

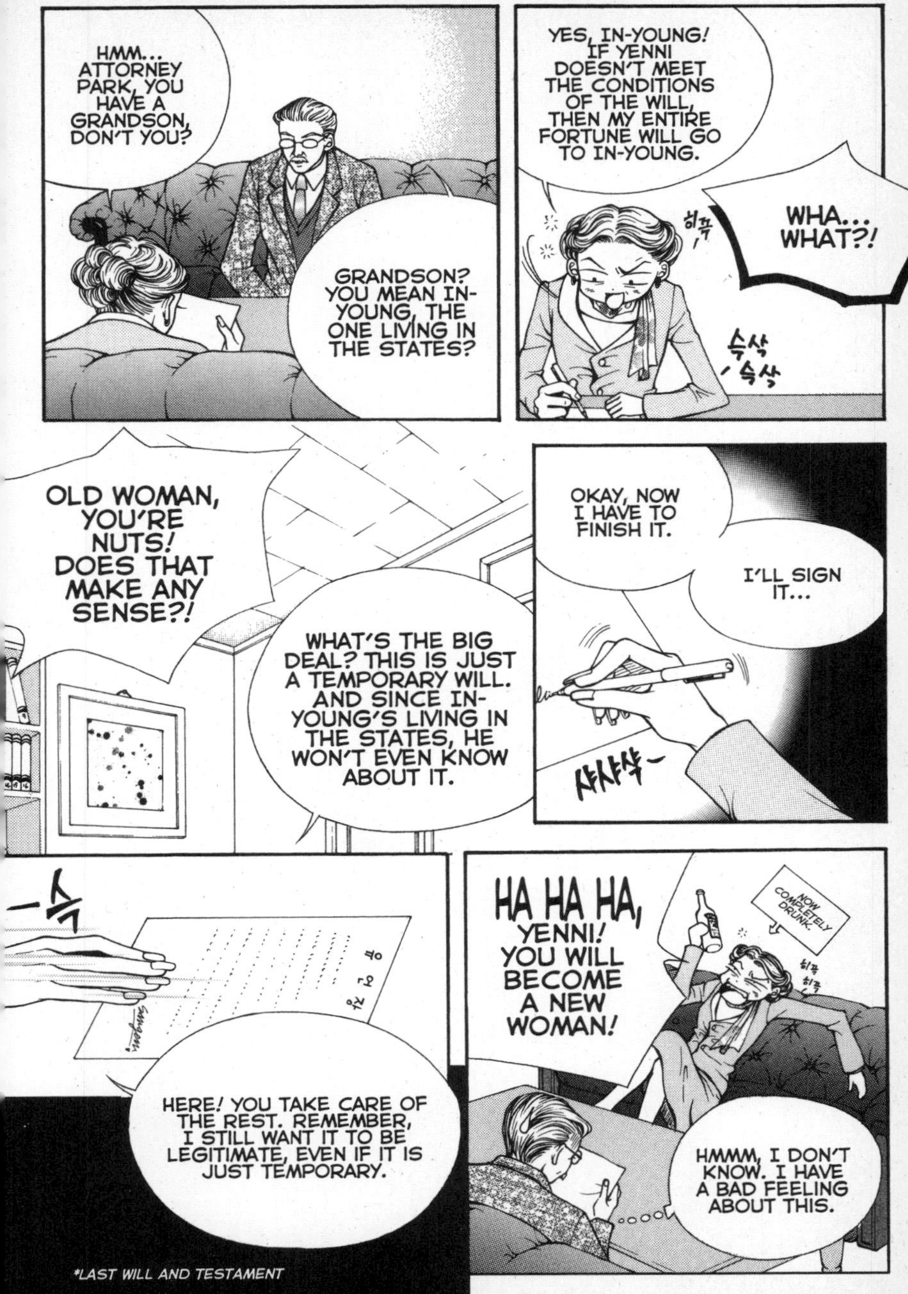
HMM... ATTORNEY PARK, YOU HAVE A GRANDSON, DON'T YOU?
GRANDSON? YOU MEAN IN-YOUNG, THE ONE LIVING IN THE STATES?
YES, IN-YOUNG! IF YENNI DOESN'T MEET THE CONDITIONS OF THE WILL, THEN MY ENTIRE FORTUNE WILL GO TO IN-YOUNG.
슥삭 슥삭
WHA... WHAT?!
OLD WOMAN, YOU'RE NUTS! DOES THAT MAKE ANY SENSE?!
WHAT'S THE BIG DEAL? THIS IS JUST A TEMPORARY WILL. AND SINCE IN-YOUNG'S LIVING IN THE STATES, HE WON'T EVEN KNOW ABOUT IT.
OKAY, NOW I HAVE TO FINISH IT.
I'LL SIGN IT...
HERE! YOU TAKE CARE OF THE REST. REMEMBER, I STILL WANT IT TO BE LEGITIMATE, EVEN IF IT IS JUST TEMPORARY.
HA HA HA, YENNI! YOU WILL BECOME A NEW WOMAN!
NOW COMPLETELY DRUNK.
HMMM, I DON'T KNOW. I HAVE A BAD FEELING ABOUT THIS.
*LAST WILL AND TESTAMENT

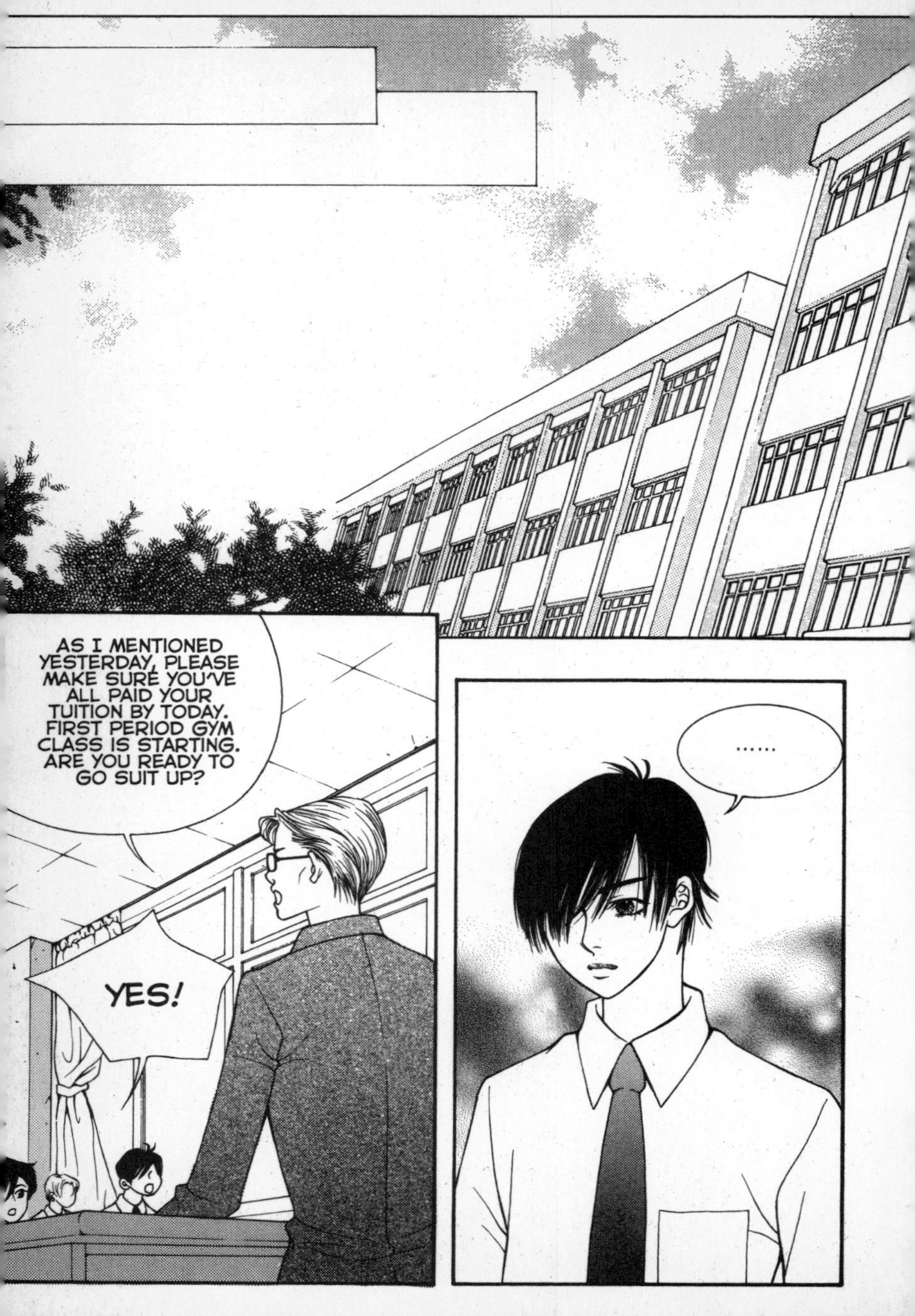
AS I MENTIONED YESTERDAY, PLEASE MAKE SURE YOU'VE ALL PAID YOUR TUITION BY TODAY. FIRST PERIOD GYM CLASS IS STARTING. ARE YOU READY TO GO SUIT UP?
YES!
......

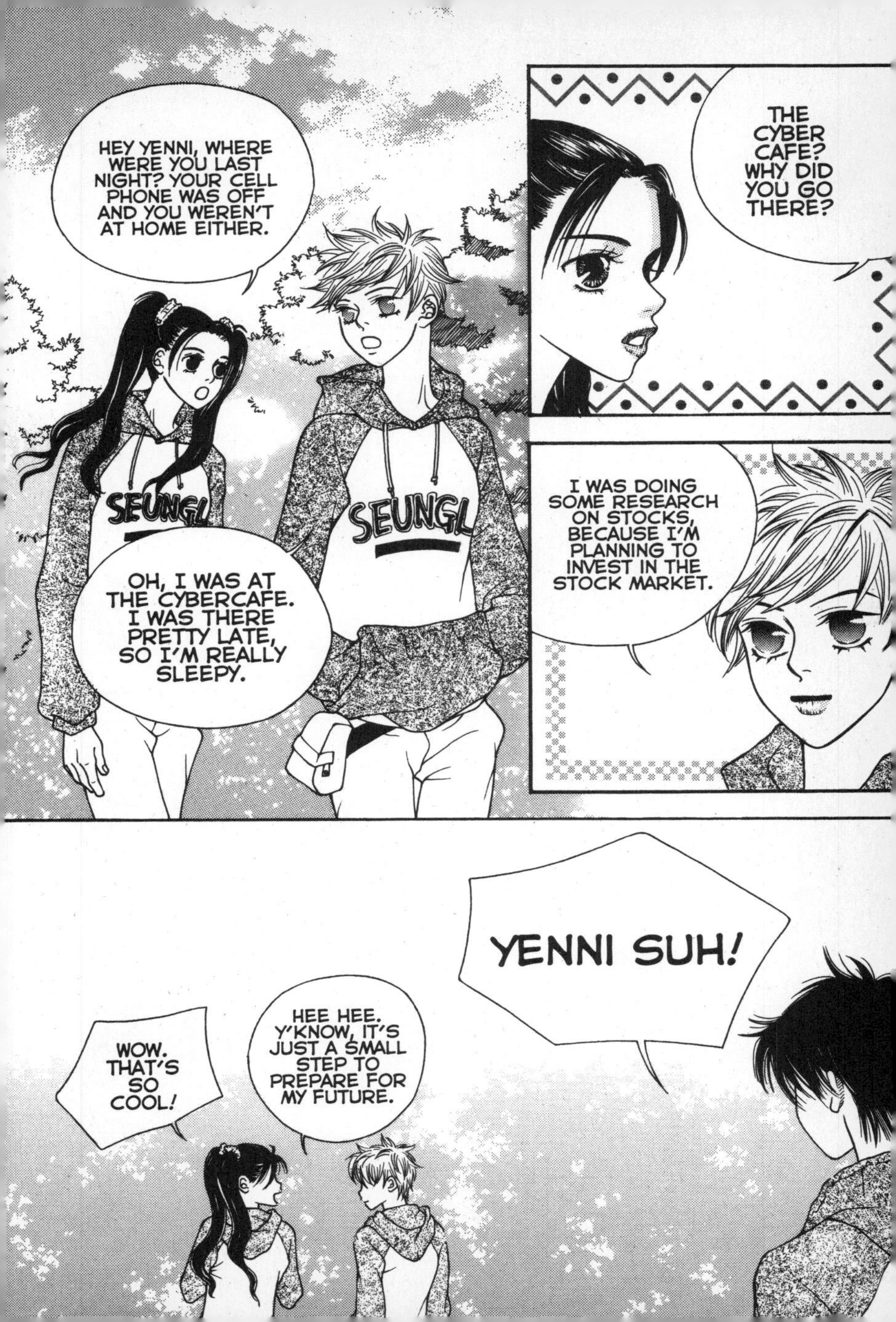
HEY YENNI, WHERE WERE YOU LAST NIGHT? YOUR CELL PHONE WAS OFF AND YOU WEREN'T AT HOME EITHER.
OH, I WAS AT THE CYBERCAFE. I WAS THERE PRETTY LATE, SO I'M REALLY SLEEPY.
THE CYBER CAFE? WHY DID YOU GO THERE?
I WAS DOING SOME RESEARCH ON STOCKS, BECAUSE I'M PLANNING TO INVEST IN THE STOCK MARKET.
WOW. THAT'S SO COOL!
HEE HEE. Y'KNOW, IT'S JUST A SMALL STEP TO PREPARE FOR MY FUTURE.
YENNI SUH!

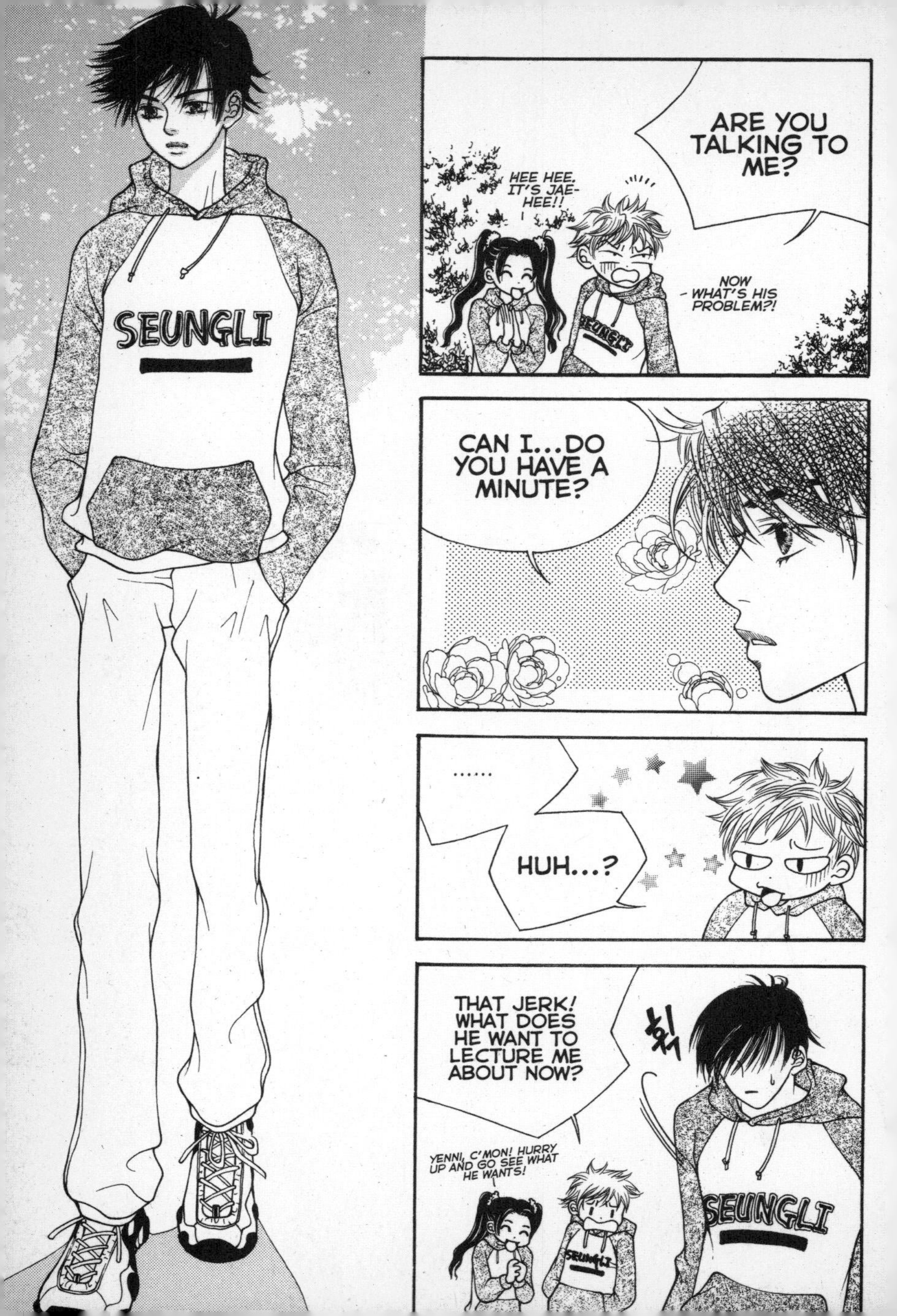
SEUNGLI
HEE HEE. IT'S JAE-HEE!!
ARE YOU TALKING TO ME?
NOW - WHAT'S HIS PROBLEM?!
CAN I...DO YOU HAVE A MINUTE?
......
HUH...?
THAT JERK! WHAT DOES HE WANT TO LECTURE ME ABOUT NOW?
YENNI, C'MON! HURRY UP AND GO SEE WHAT HE WANTS!
SEUNGLI

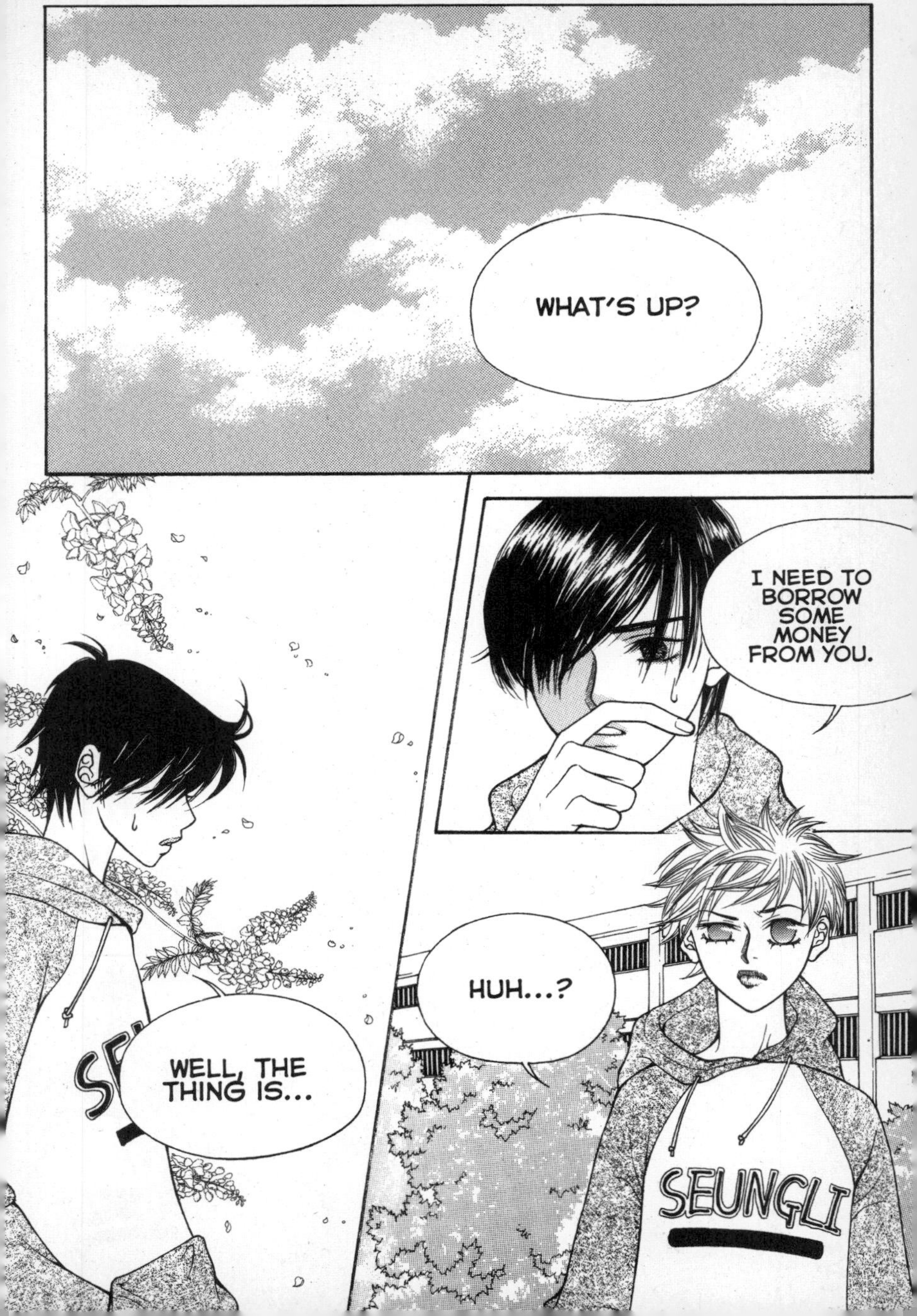
WHAT'S UP?
WELL, THE THING IS...
I NEED TO BORROW SOME MONEY FROM YOU.
HUH...?

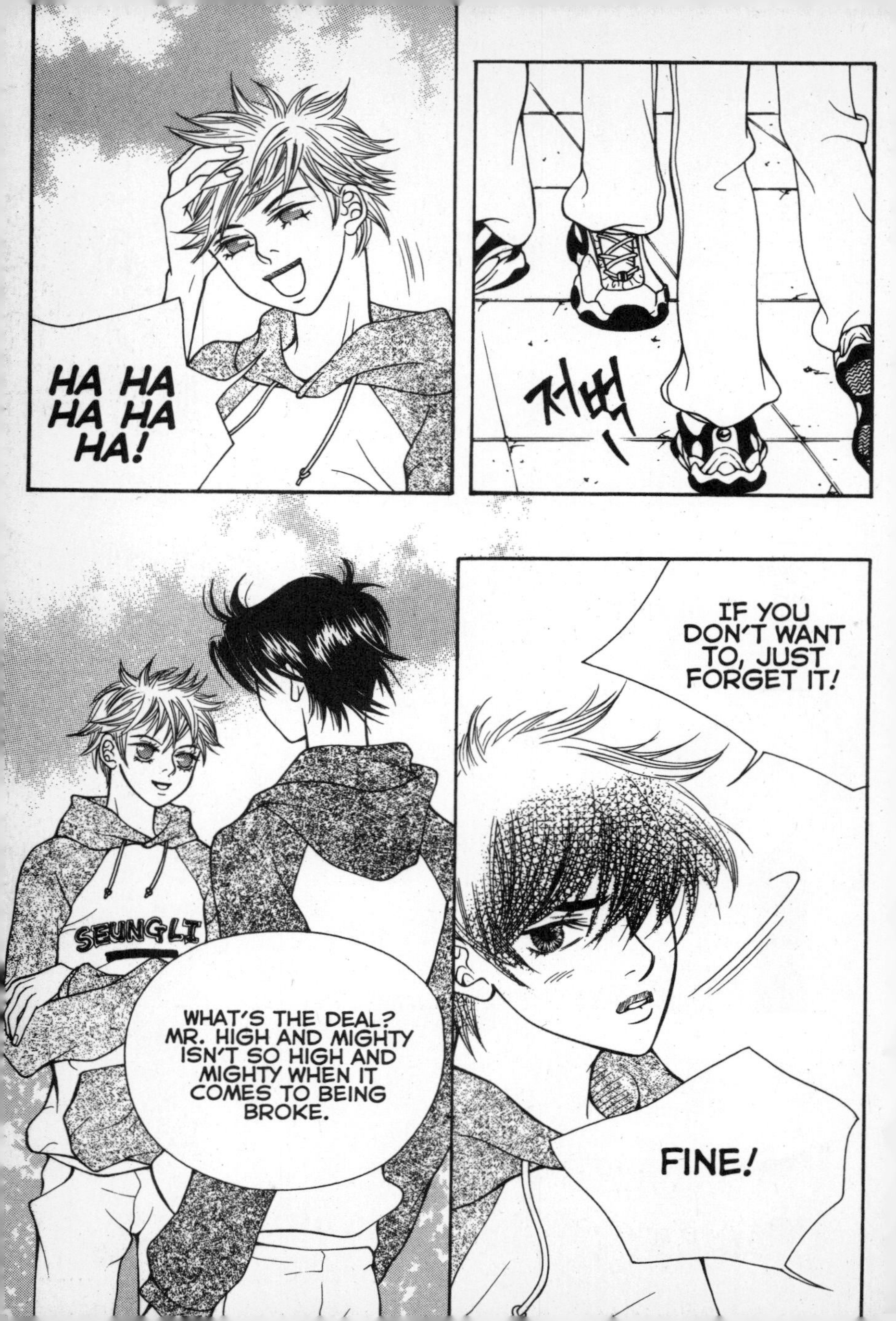
HA HA HA HA HA!
저벅
WHAT'S THE DEAL? MR. HIGH AND MIGHTY ISN'T SO HIGH AND MIGHTY WHEN IT COMES TO BEING BROKE.
SEUNGLI
IF YOU DON'T WANT TO, JUST FORGET IT!
FINE!

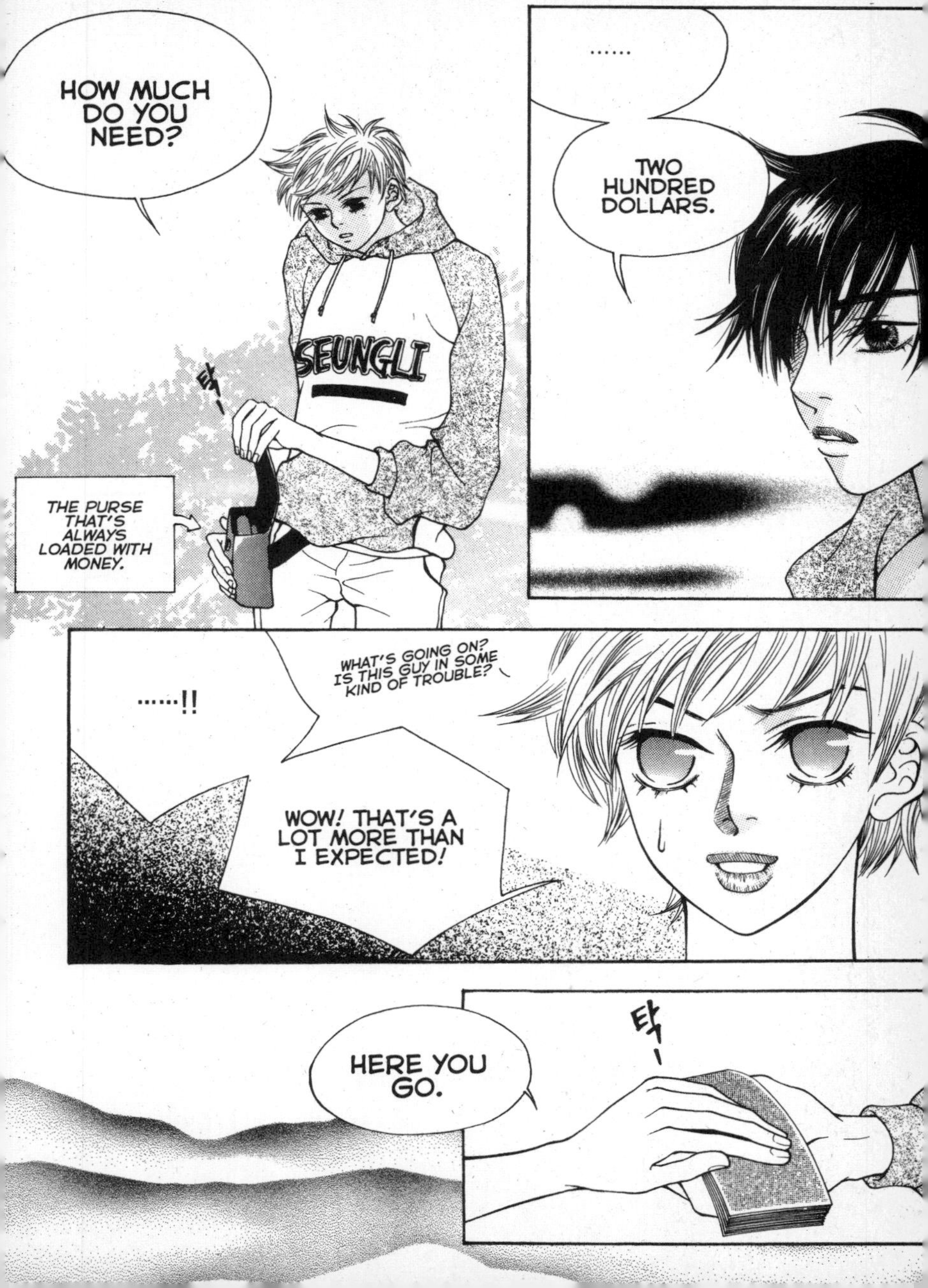
HOW MUCH DO YOU NEED?
탁
THE PURSE THAT'S ALWAYS LOADED WITH MONEY.
......
TWO HUNDRED DOLLARS.
......!!
WHAT'S GOING ON? IS THIS GUY IN SOME KIND OF TROUBLE?
WOW! THAT'S A LOT MORE THAN I EXPECTED!
HERE YOU GO.
탁

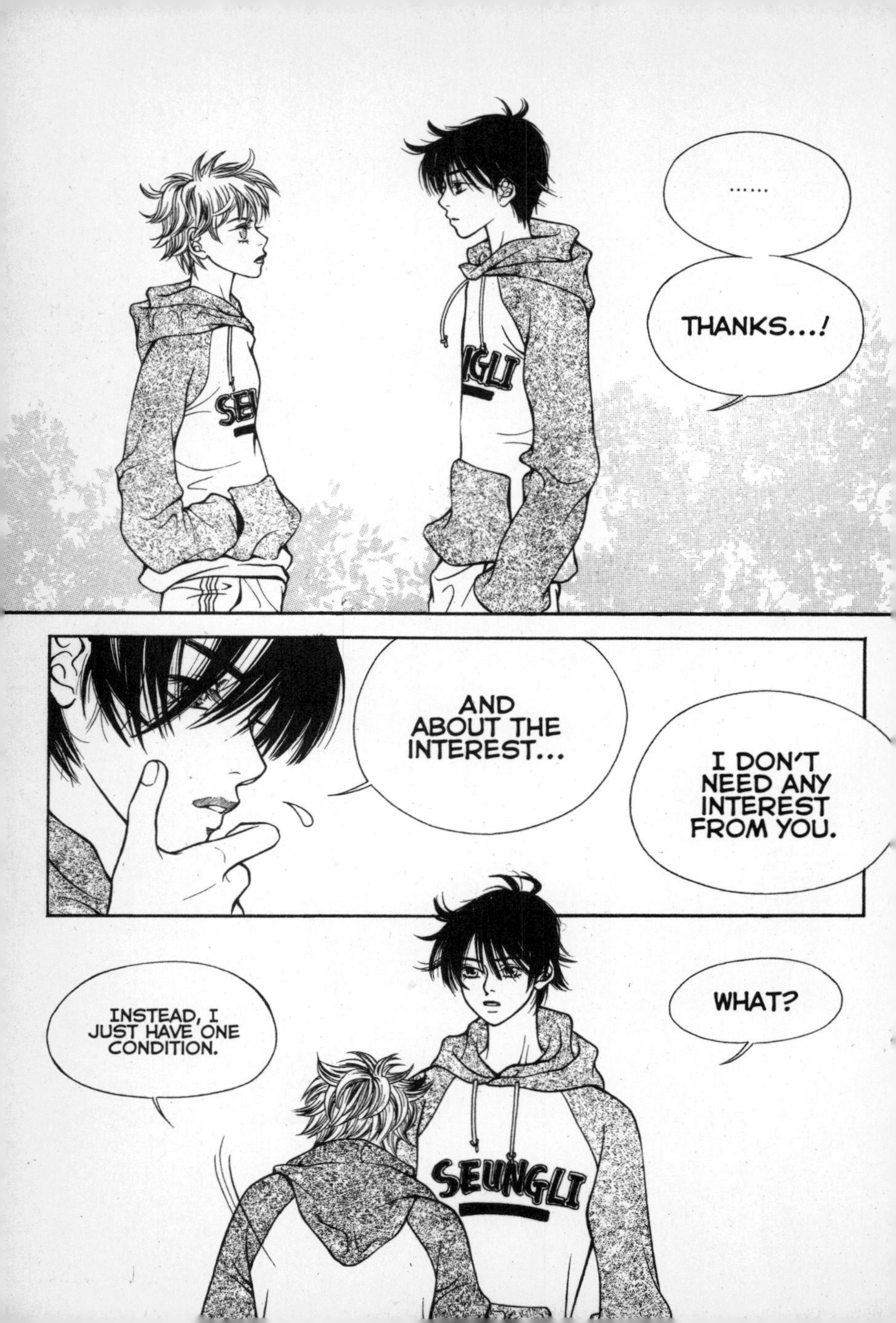
......
THANKS...!
AND ABOUT THE INTEREST...
I DON'T NEED ANY INTEREST FROM YOU.
INSTEAD, I JUST HAVE ONE CONDITION.
WHAT?

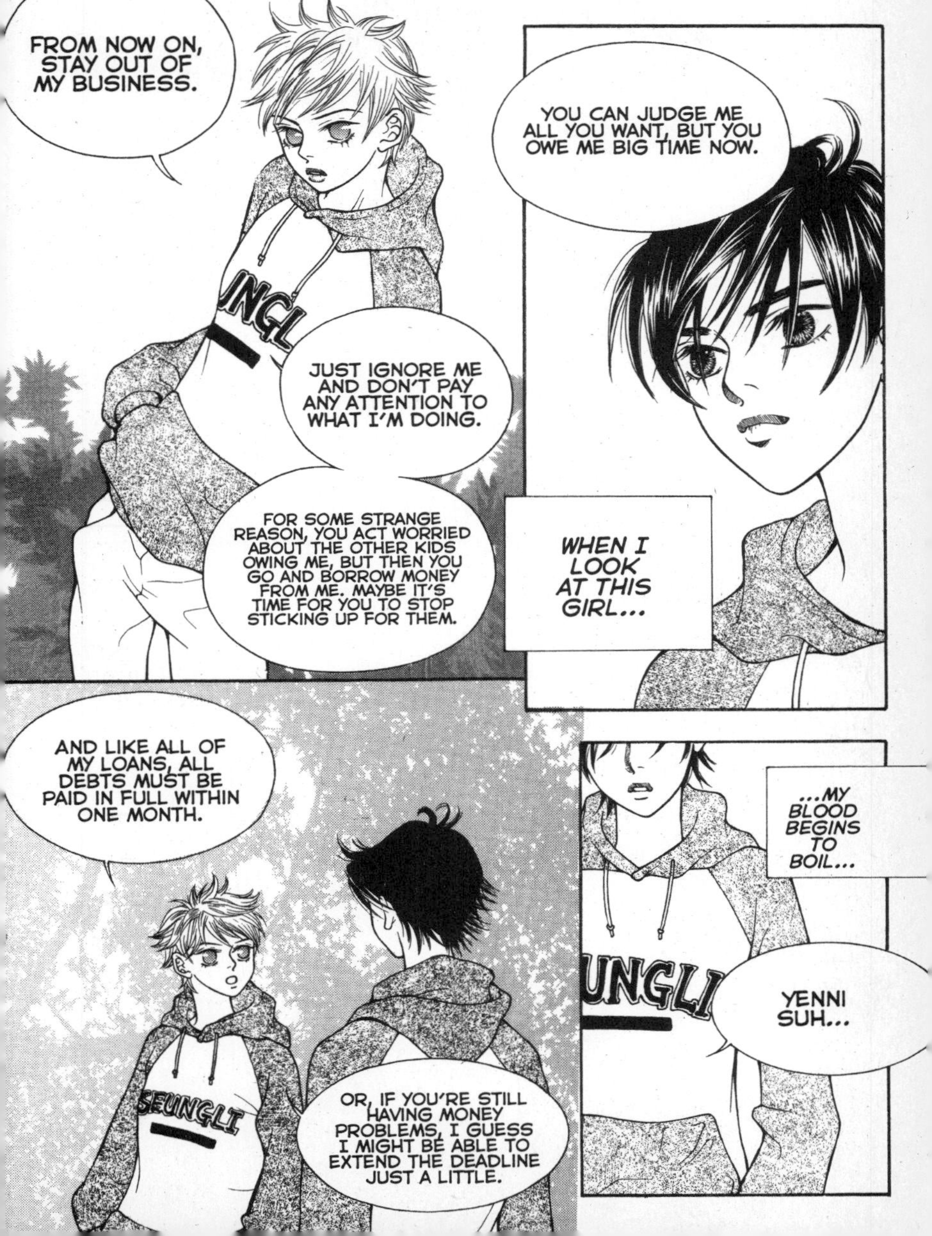
FROM NOW ON, STAY OUT OF MY BUSINESS.
JUST IGNORE ME AND DON'T PAY ANY ATTENTION TO WHAT I'M DOING.
FOR SOME STRANGE REASON, YOU ACT WORRIED ABOUT THE OTHER KIDS OWING ME, BUT THEN YOU GO AND BORROW MONEY FROM ME. MAYBE IT'S TIME FOR YOU TO STOP STICKING UP FOR THEM.
YOU CAN JUDGE ME ALL YOU WANT, BUT YOU OWE ME BIG TIME NOW.
WHEN I LOOK AT THIS GIRL...
AND LIKE ALL OF MY LOANS, ALL DEBTS MUST BE PAID IN FULL WITHIN ONE MONTH.
SEUNGLI
OR, IF YOU'RE STILL HAVING MONEY PROBLEMS, I GUESS I MIGHT BE ABLE TO EXTEND THE DEADLINE JUST A LITTLE.
...MY BLOOD BEGINS TO BOIL...
YENNI SUH...

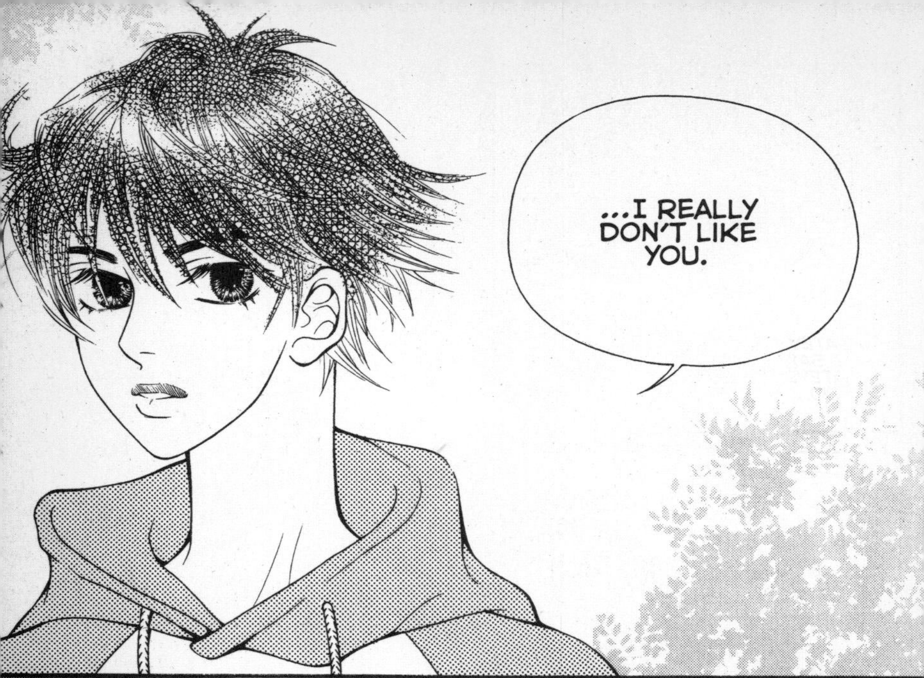
...I REALLY DON'T LIKE YOU.
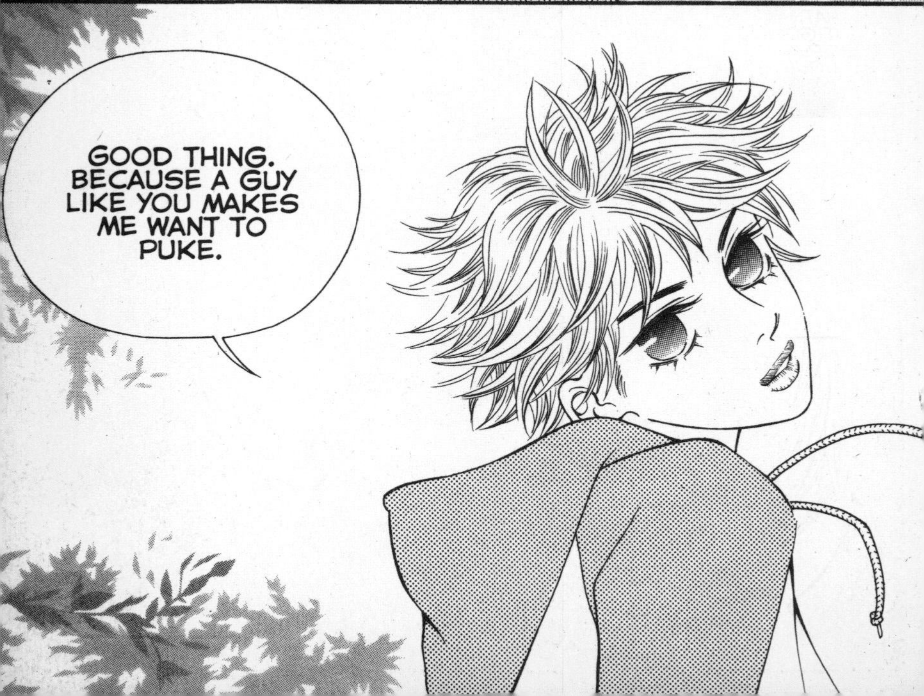
GOOD THING. BECAUSE A GUY LIKE YOU MAKES ME WANT TO PUKE.

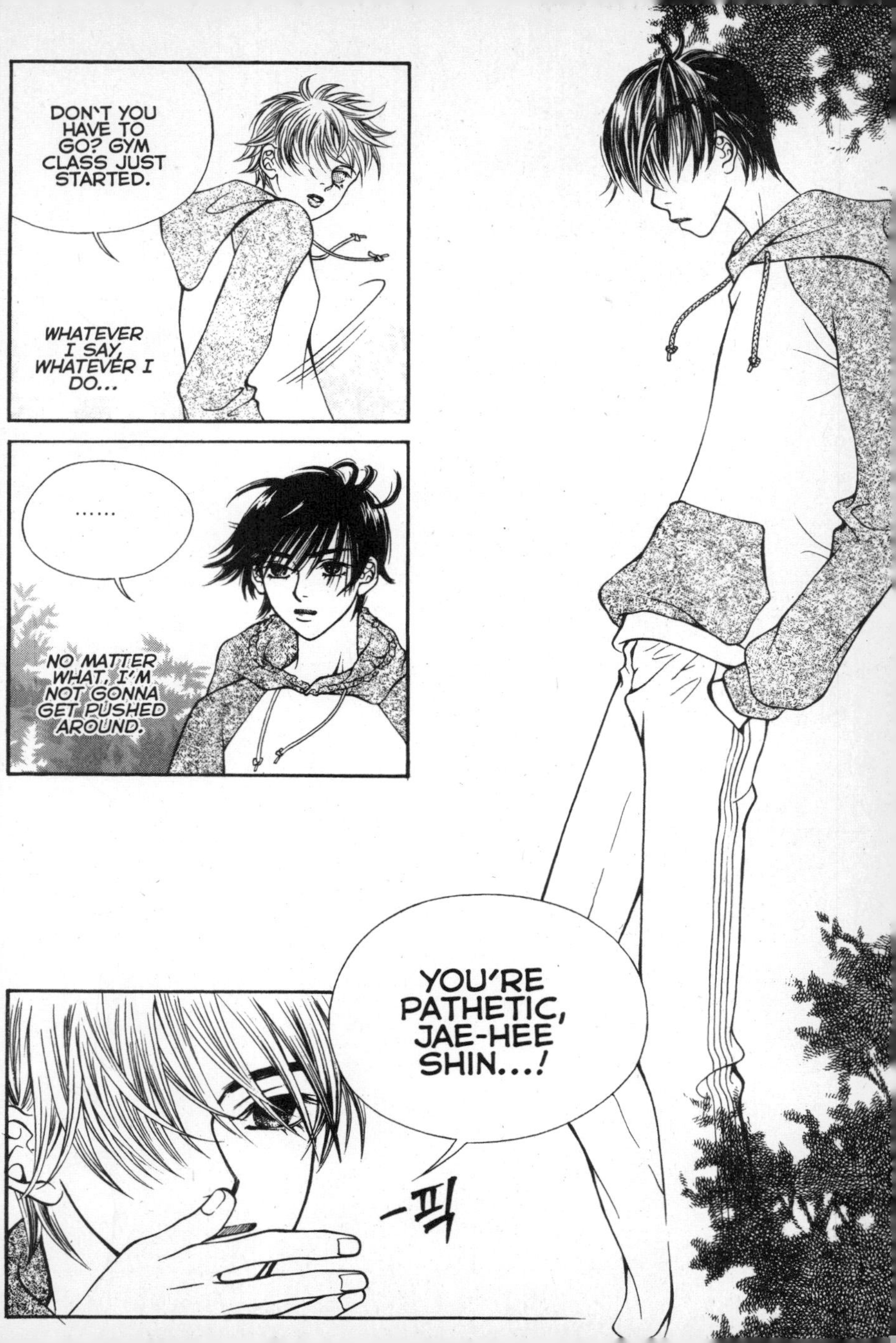
DON'T YOU HAVE TO GO? GYM CLASS JUST STARTED.
WHATEVER I SAY, WHATEVER I DO...
......
NO MATTER WHAT, I'M NOT GONNA GET PUSHED AROUND.
YOU'RE PATHETIC, JAE-HEE SHIN...!
픽

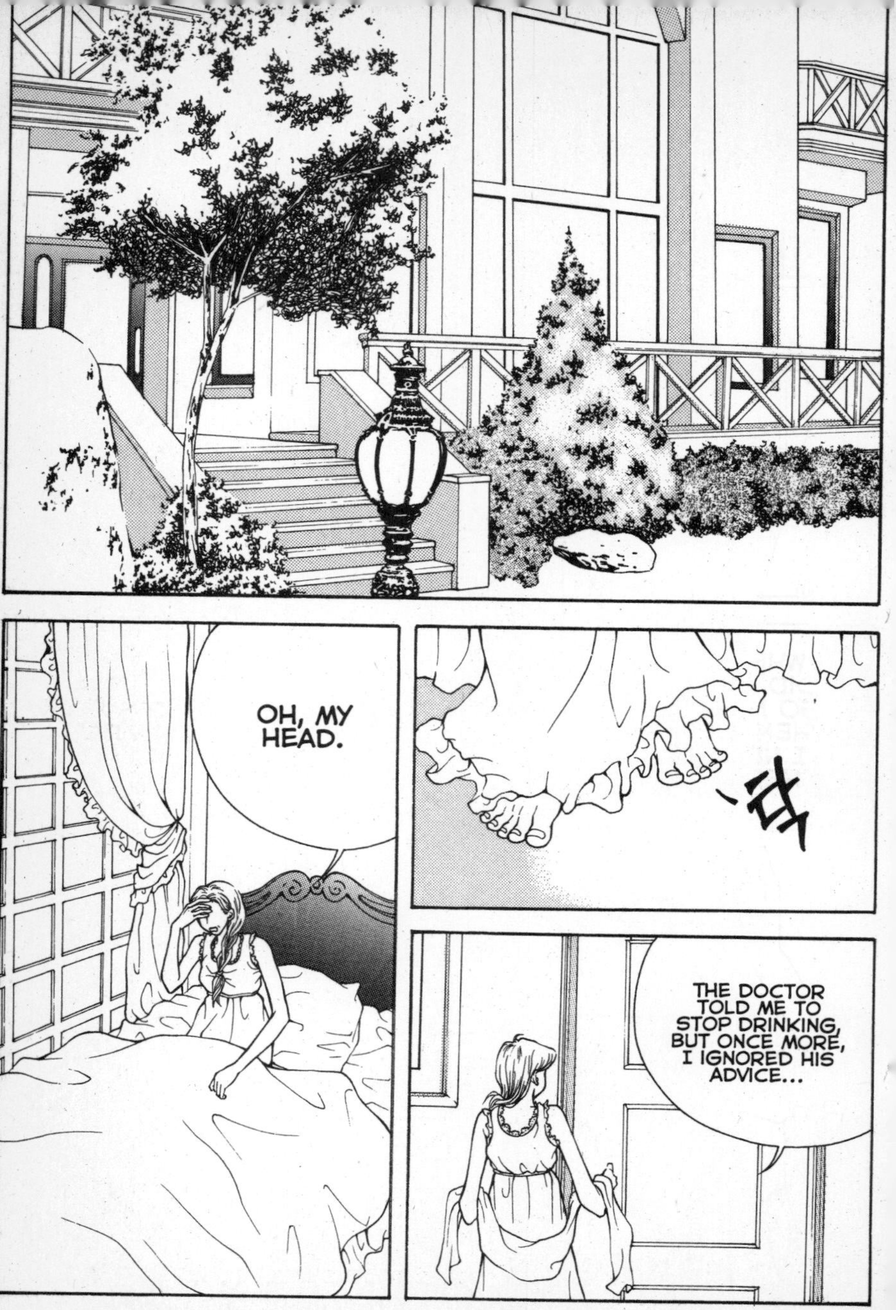
OH, MY HEAD.
THE DOCTOR TOLD ME TO STOP DRINKING, BUT ONCE MORE, I IGNORED HIS ADVICE...

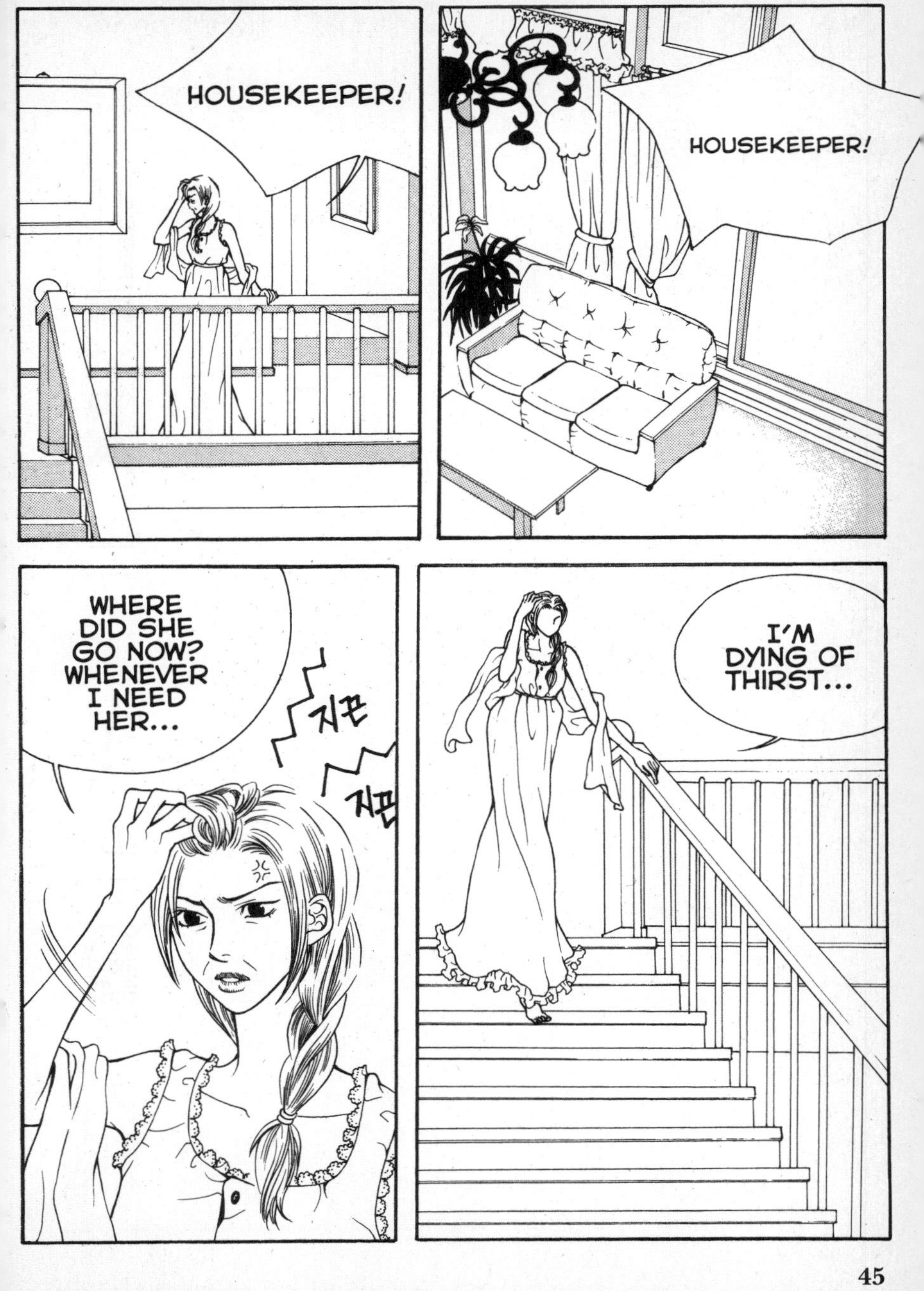
HOUSEKEEPER!
HOUSEKEEPER!
WHERE DID SHE GO NOW? WHENEVER I NEED HER...
지끈
지끈
I'M DYING OF THIRST...

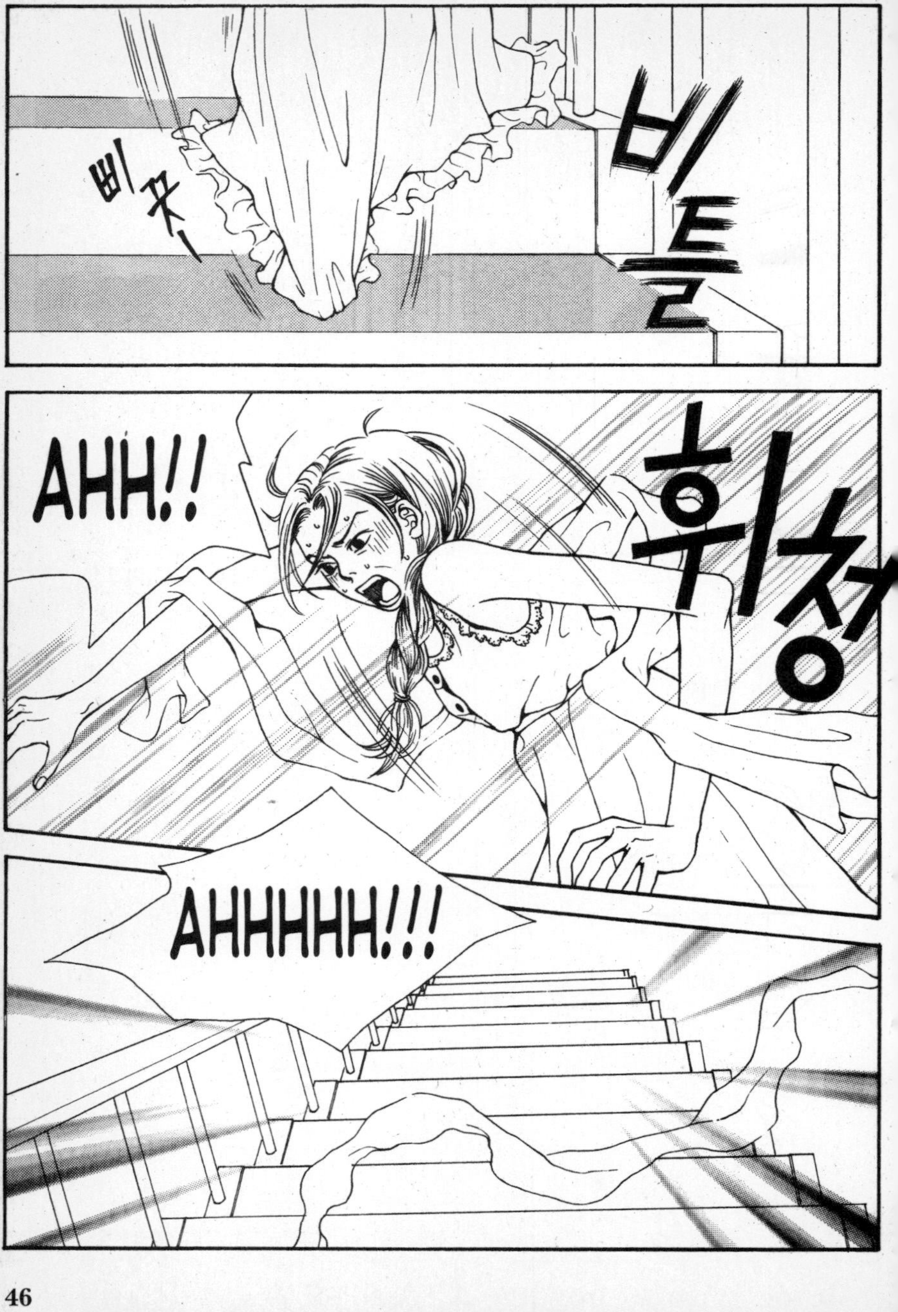
삐끗!
비틀
AHH!!
휘청
AHHHHH!!!

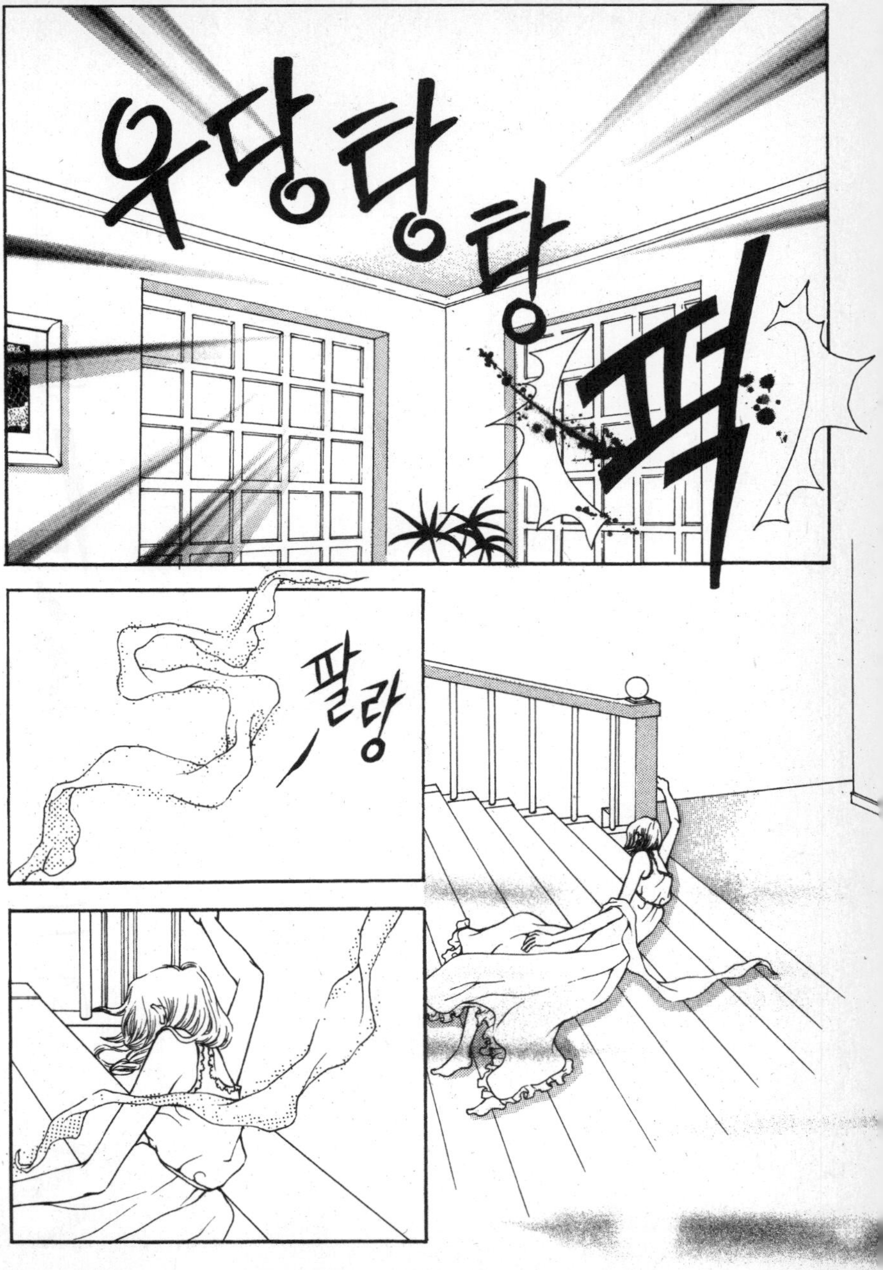
우당당탕
퍽
팔랑

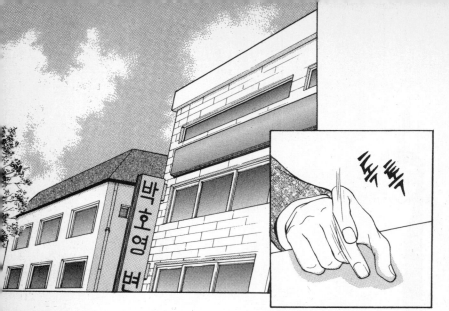

I WONDER IF THE OL' BAG IS OKAY...

SHE HAS A BAD HEART AND SHE DRANK SO MUCH LAST NIGHT...

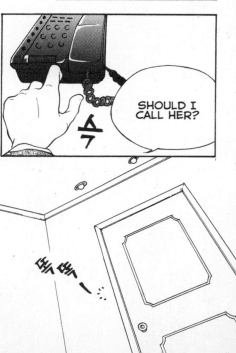

SHOULD I CALL HER?

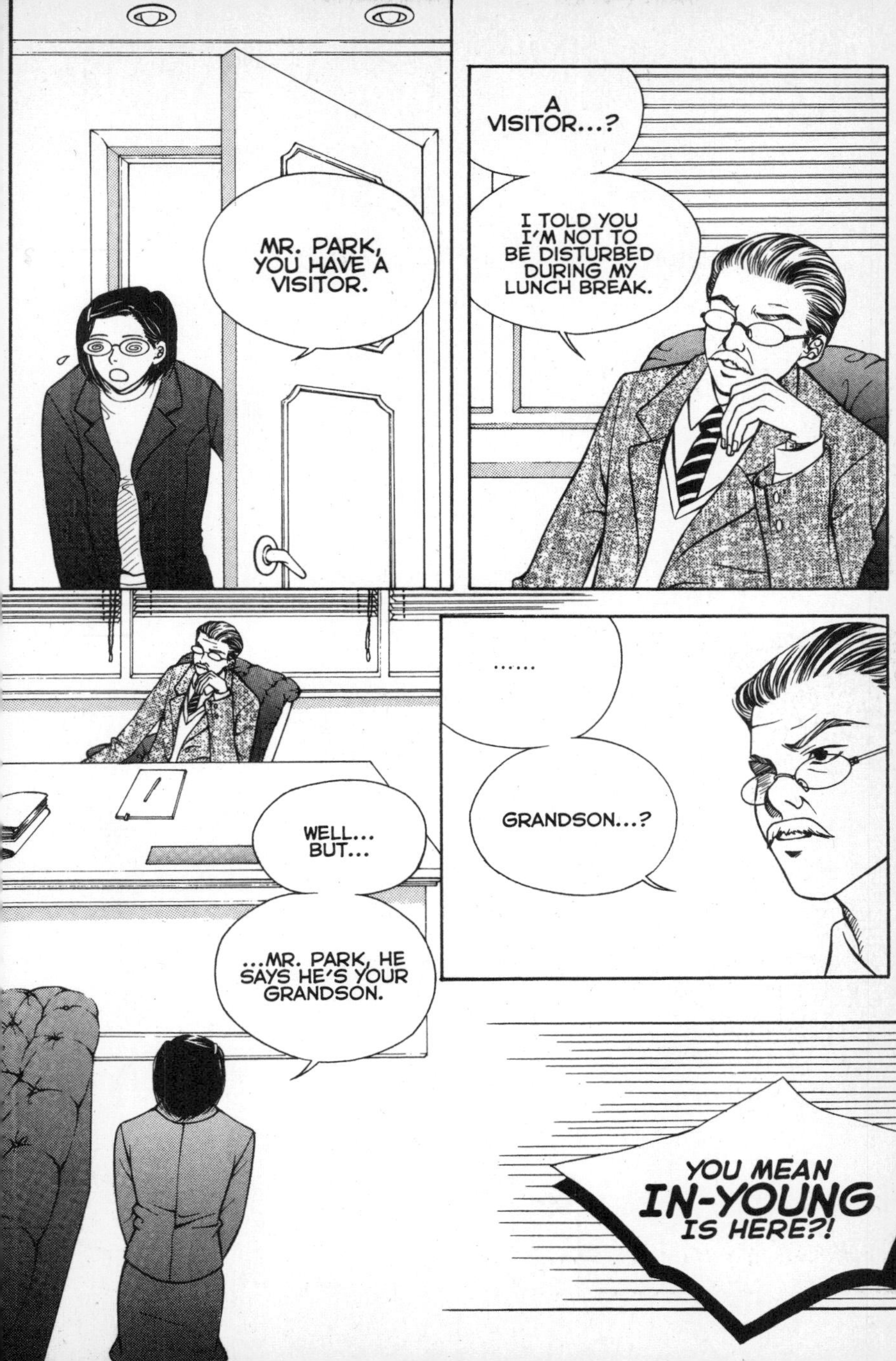
MR. PARK, YOU HAVE A VISITOR.
A VISITOR...?
I TOLD YOU I'M NOT TO BE DISTURBED DURING MY LUNCH BREAK.
WELL... BUT...
...MR. PARK, HE SAYS HE'S YOUR GRANDSON.
......
GRANDSON...?
YOU MEAN IN-YOUNG IS HERE?!

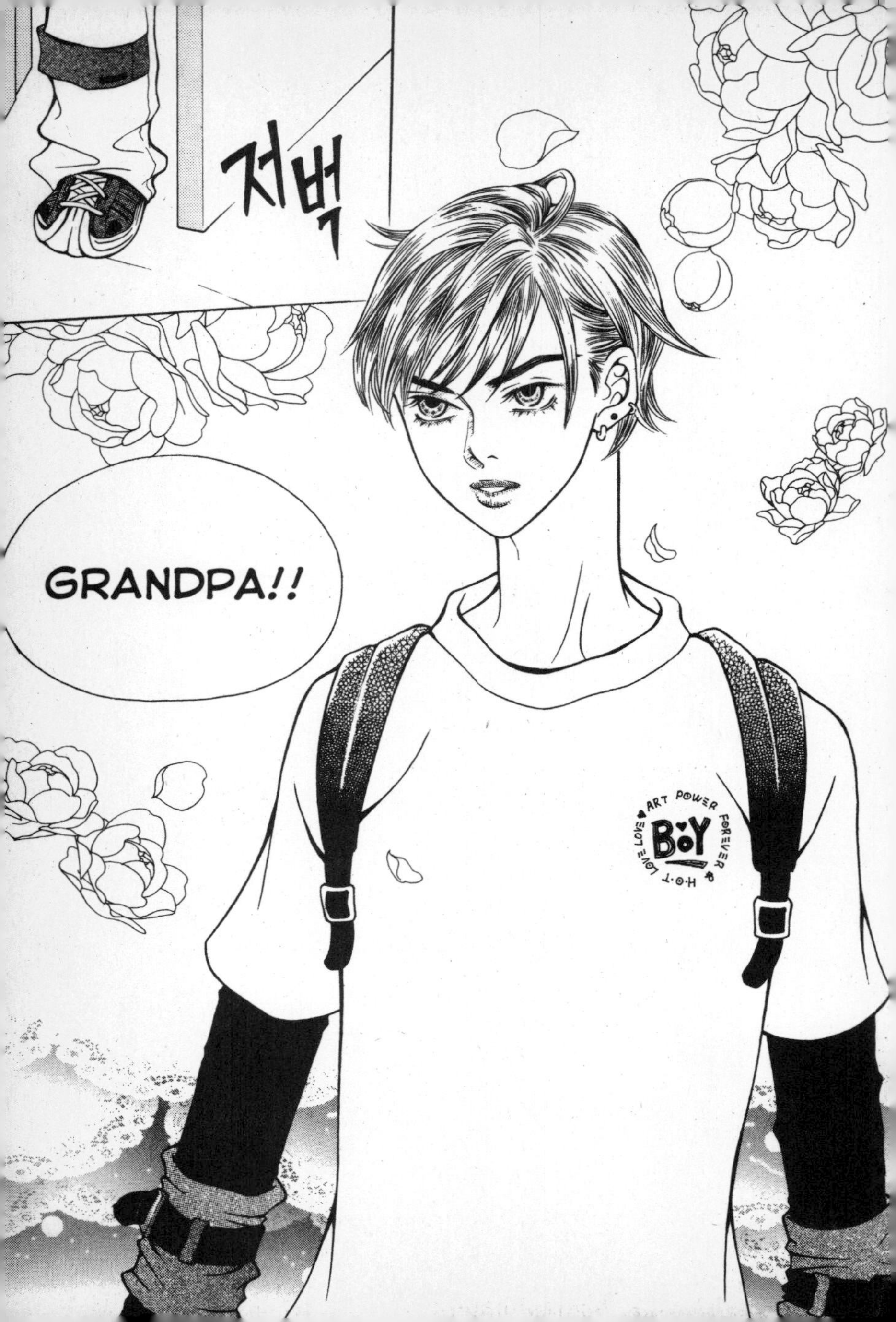
저벅
GRANDPA!!
LOVE LOVE ART POWER FOREVER
BoY
H·O·T

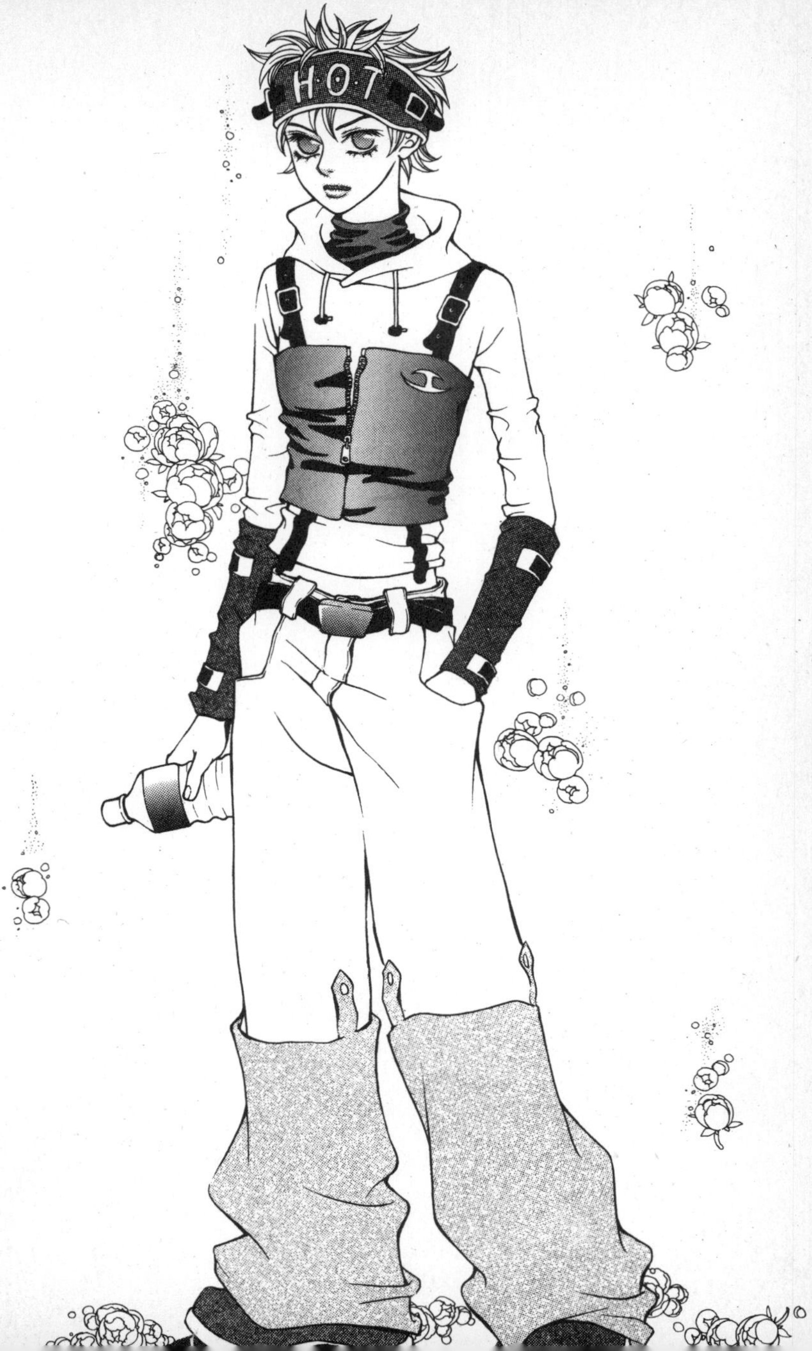
H·O·T

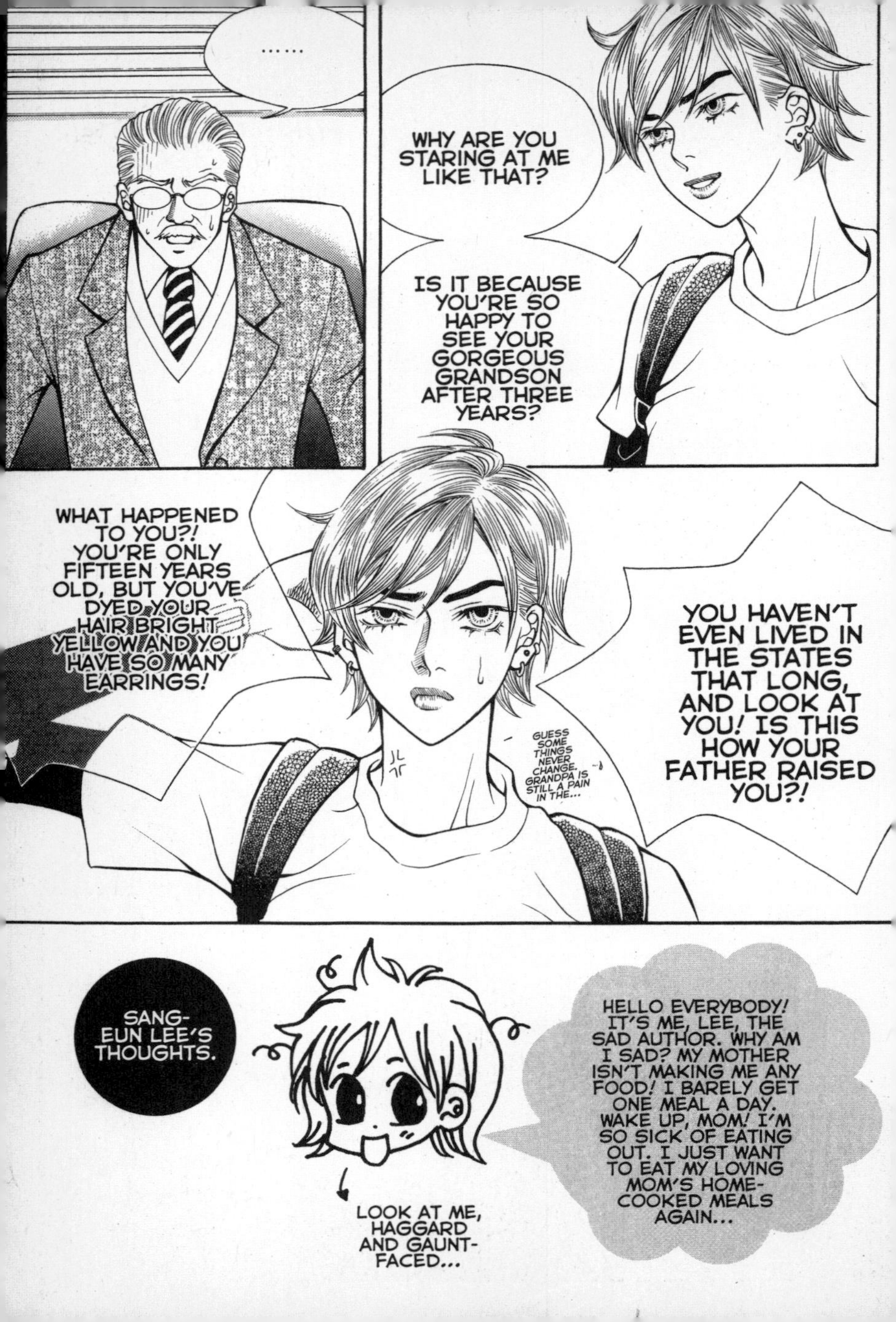
......
WHY ARE YOU STARING AT ME LIKE THAT?
IS IT BECAUSE YOU'RE SO HAPPY TO SEE YOUR GORGEOUS GRANDSON AFTER THREE YEARS?
WHAT HAPPENED TO YOU?! YOU'RE ONLY FIFTEEN YEARS OLD, BUT YOU'VE DYED YOUR HAIR BRIGHT YELLOW AND YOU HAVE SO MANY EARRINGS!
YOU HAVEN'T EVEN LIVED IN THE STATES THAT LONG, AND LOOK AT YOU! IS THIS HOW YOUR FATHER RAISED YOU?!
GUESS SOME THINGS NEVER CHANGE. GRANDPA IS STILL A PAIN IN THE...
SANG-EUN LEE'S THOUGHTS.
HELLO EVERYBODY! IT'S ME, LEE, THE SAD AUTHOR. WHY AM I SAD? MY MOTHER ISN'T MAKING ME ANY FOOD! I BARELY GET ONE MEAL A DAY. WAKE UP, MOM! I'M SO SICK OF EATING OUT. I JUST WANT TO EAT MY LOVING MOM'S HOME-COOKED MEALS AGAIN...
LOOK AT ME, HAGGARD AND GAUNT-FACED...

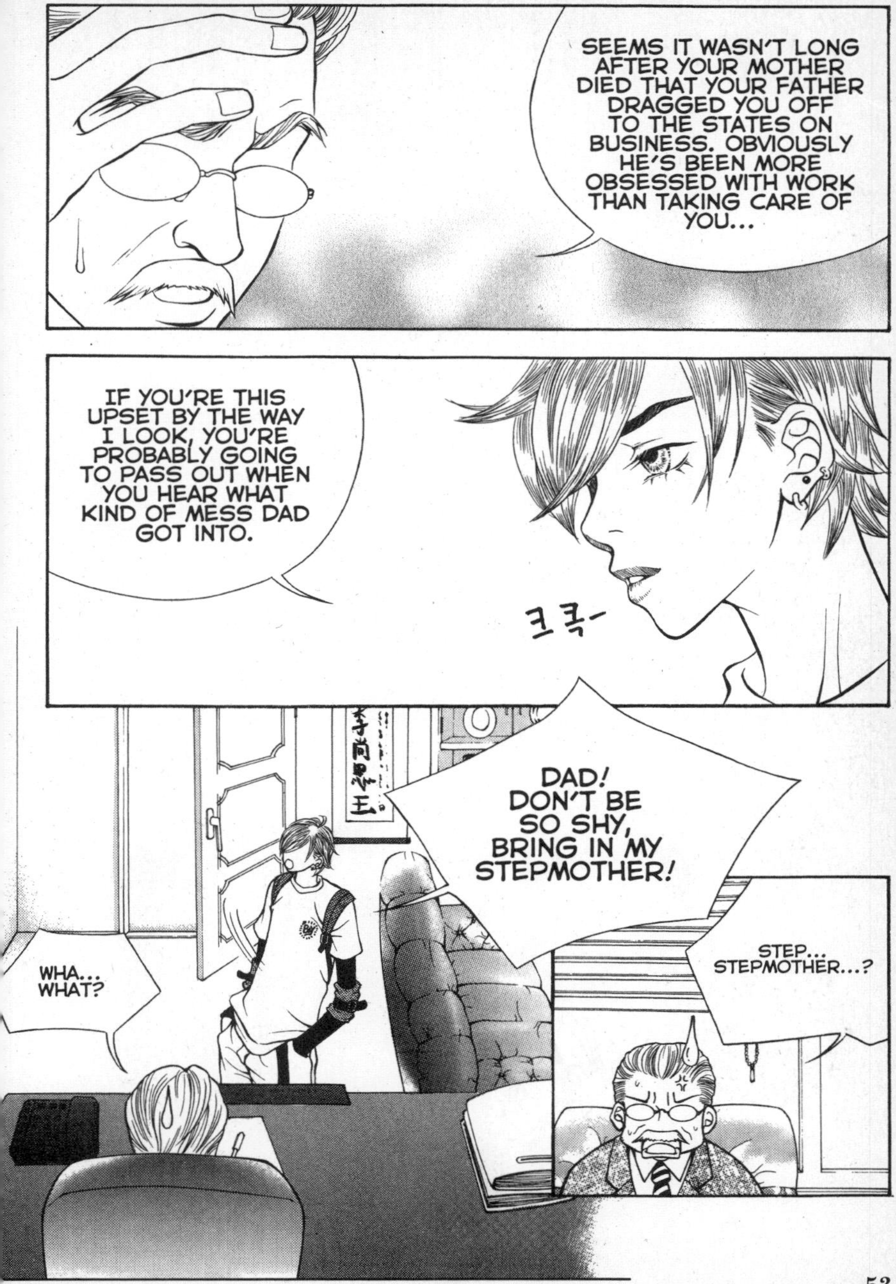
SEEMS IT WASN'T LONG AFTER YOUR MOTHER DIED THAT YOUR FATHER DRAGGED YOU OFF TO THE STATES ON BUSINESS. OBVIOUSLY HE'S BEEN MORE OBSESSED WITH WORK THAN TAKING CARE OF YOU...
IF YOU'RE THIS UPSET BY THE WAY I LOOK, YOU'RE PROBABLY GOING TO PASS OUT WHEN YOU HEAR WHAT KIND OF MESS DAD GOT INTO.
크큭-
DAD! DON'T BE SO SHY, BRING IN MY STEPMOTHER!
WHA... WHAT?
STEP... STEPMOTHER...?

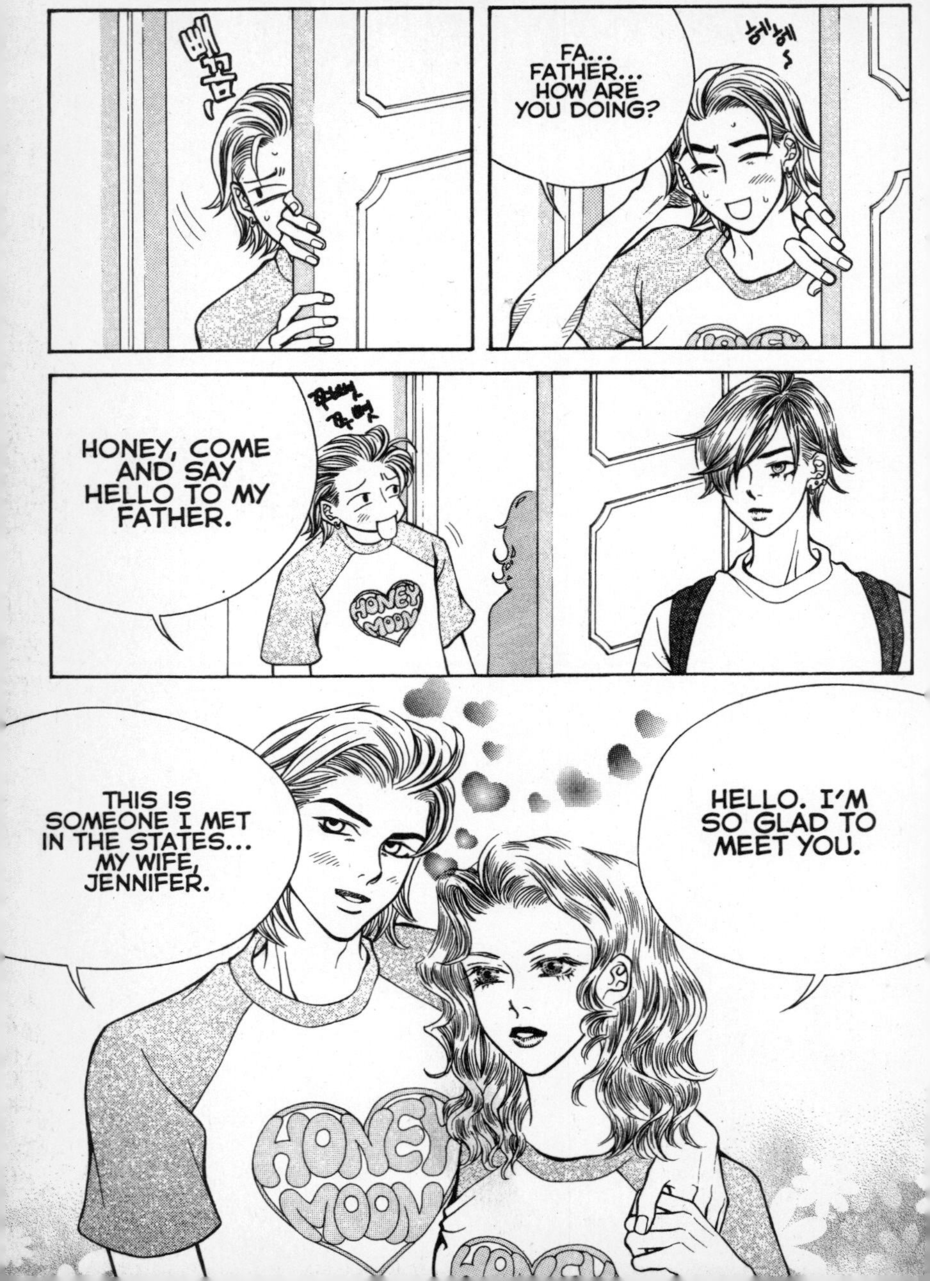
빼꼼
FA... FATHER... HOW ARE YOU DOING?
헤헤~
HONEY, COME AND SAY HELLO TO MY FATHER.
THIS IS SOMEONE I MET IN THE STATES... MY WIFE, JENNIFER.
HELLO. I'M SO GLAD TO MEET YOU.
HONEY MOON

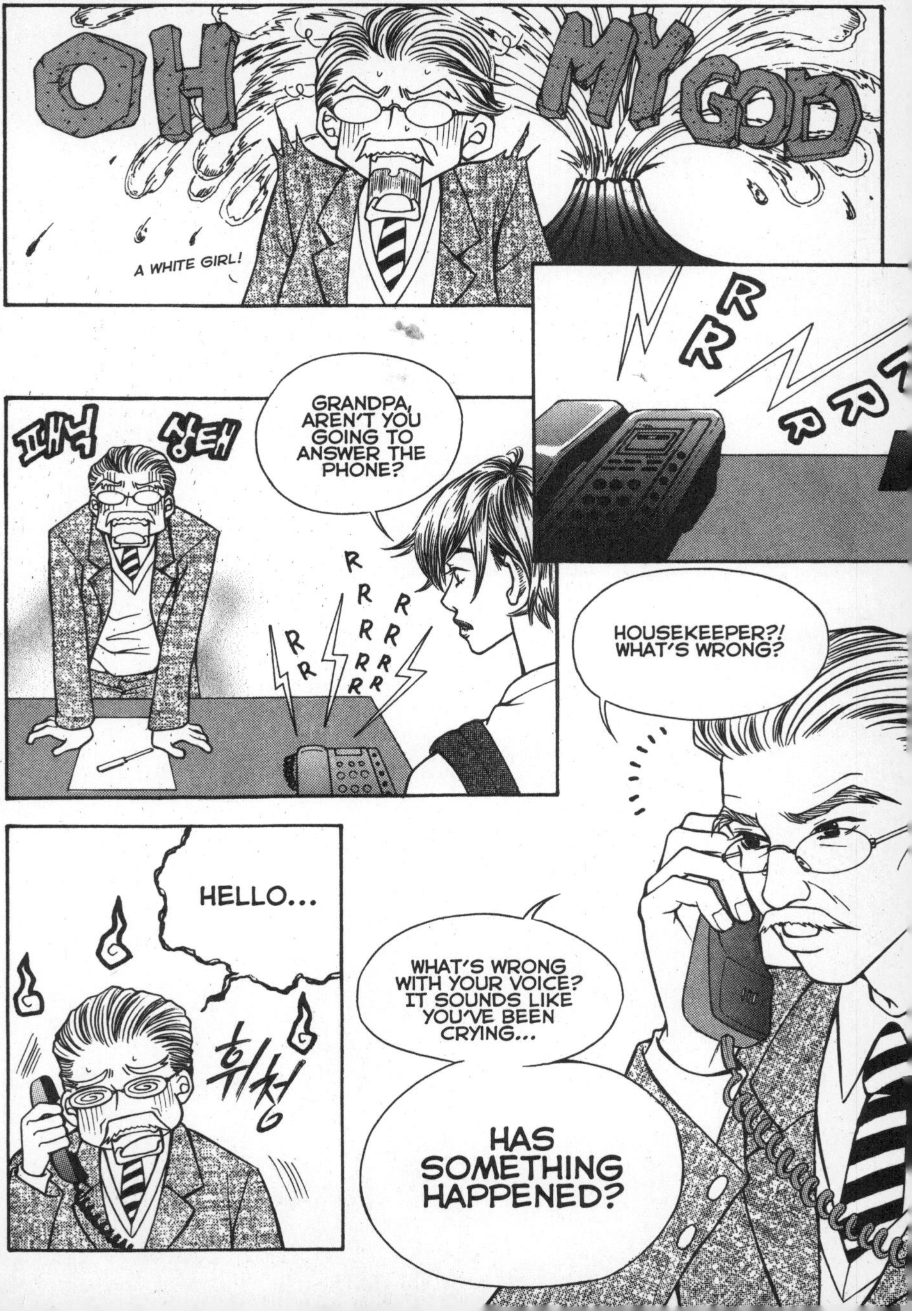
OH MY GOD
A WHITE GIRL!
패닉 상태
GRANDPA, AREN'T YOU GOING TO ANSWER THE PHONE?
R R R R R R R R R R R R
R R R R R
HELLO...
휘청
HOUSEKEEPER?! WHAT'S WRONG?
WHAT'S WRONG WITH YOUR VOICE? IT SOUNDS LIKE YOU'VE BEEN CRYING...
HAS SOMETHING HAPPENED?

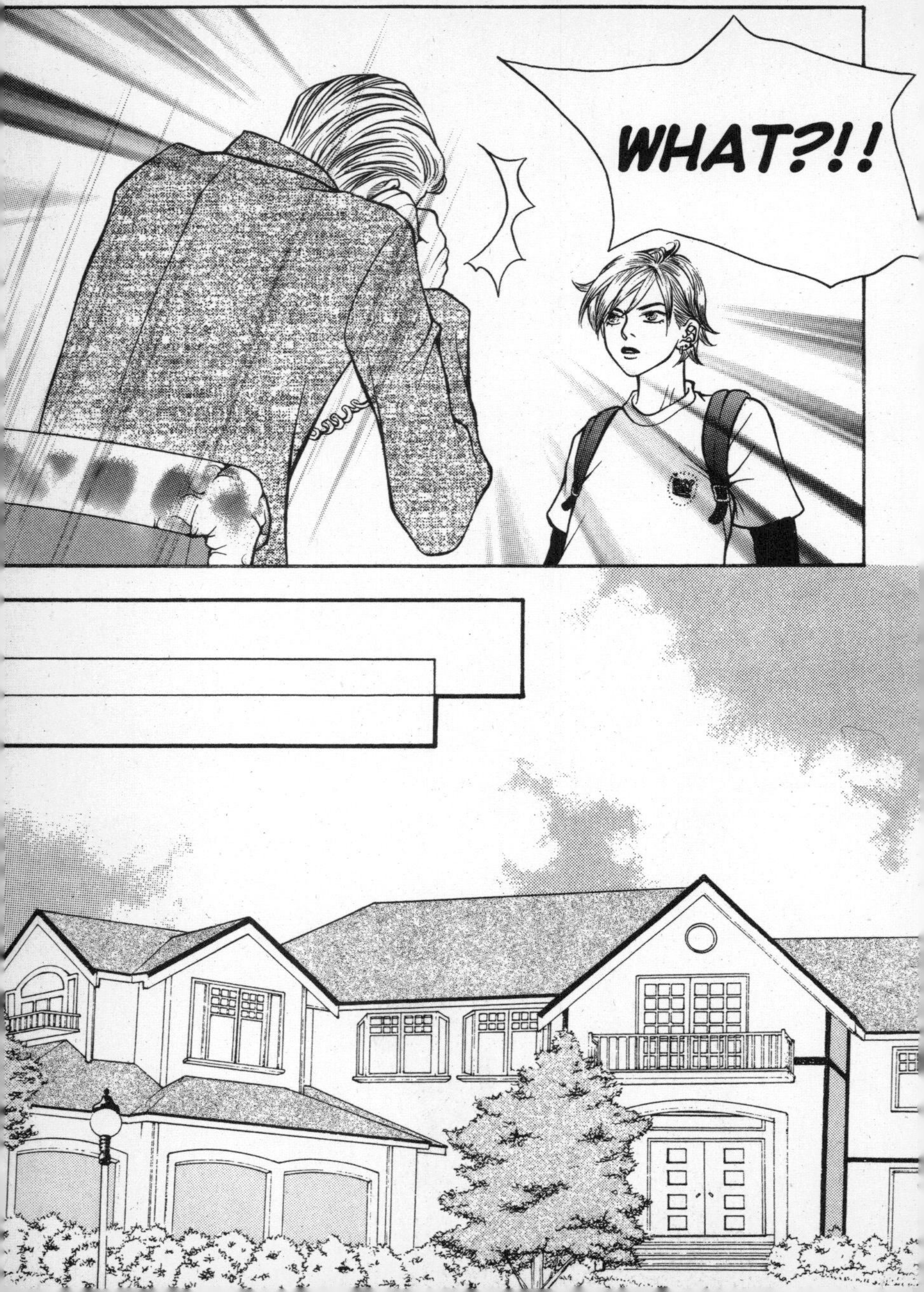
WHAT?!!

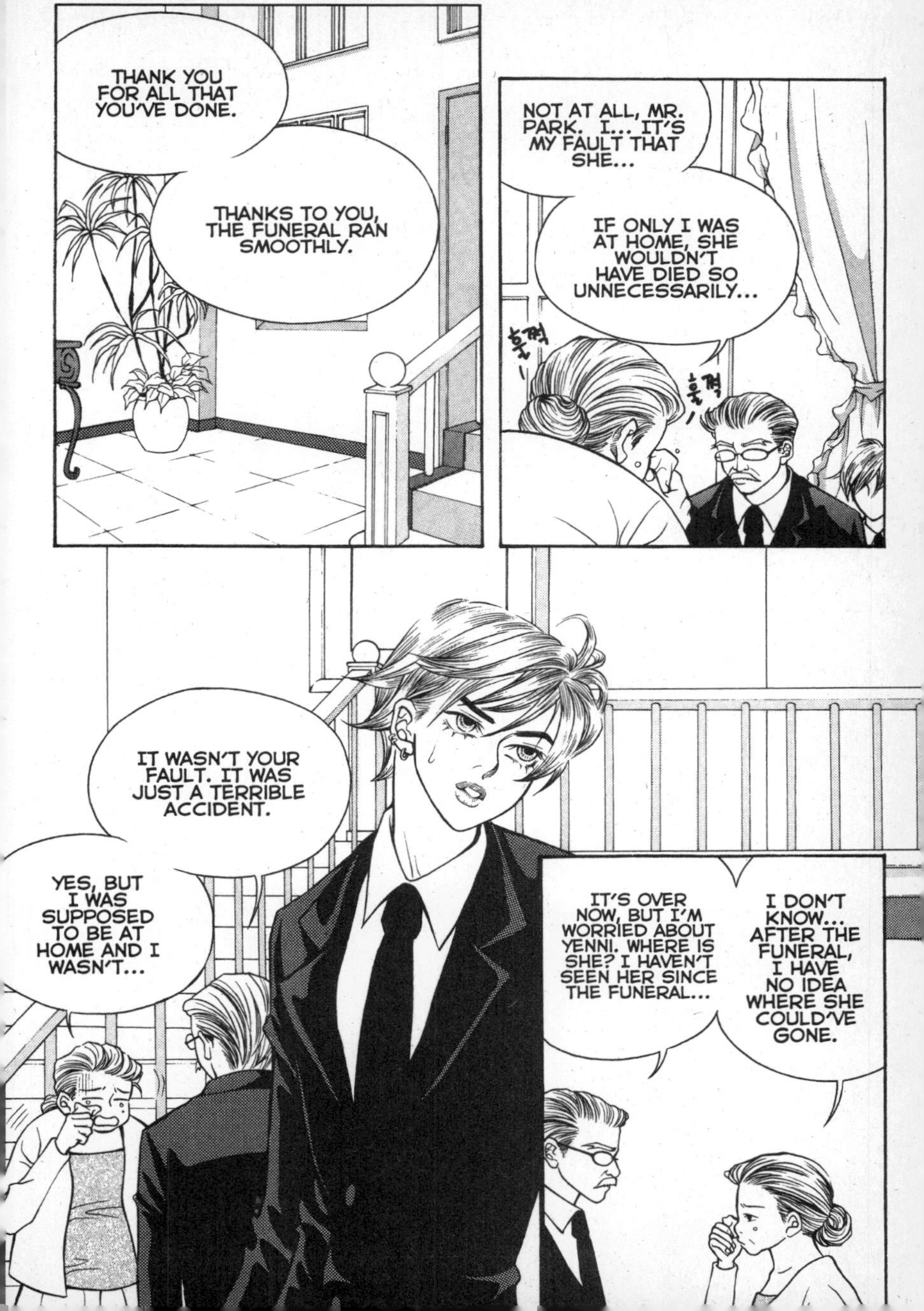
THANK YOU FOR ALL THAT YOU'VE DONE.
THANKS TO YOU, THE FUNERAL RAN SMOOTHLY.
NOT AT ALL, MR. PARK. I... IT'S MY FAULT THAT SHE...
IF ONLY I WAS AT HOME, SHE WOULDN'T HAVE DIED SO UNNECESSARILY...
훌쩍
훌쩍
IT WASN'T YOUR FAULT. IT WAS JUST A TERRIBLE ACCIDENT.
YES, BUT I WAS SUPPOSED TO BE AT HOME AND I WASN'T...
IT'S OVER NOW, BUT I'M WORRIED ABOUT YENNI. WHERE IS SHE? I HAVEN'T SEEN HER SINCE THE FUNERAL...
I DON'T KNOW... AFTER THE FUNERAL, I HAVE NO IDEA WHERE SHE COULD'VE GONE.

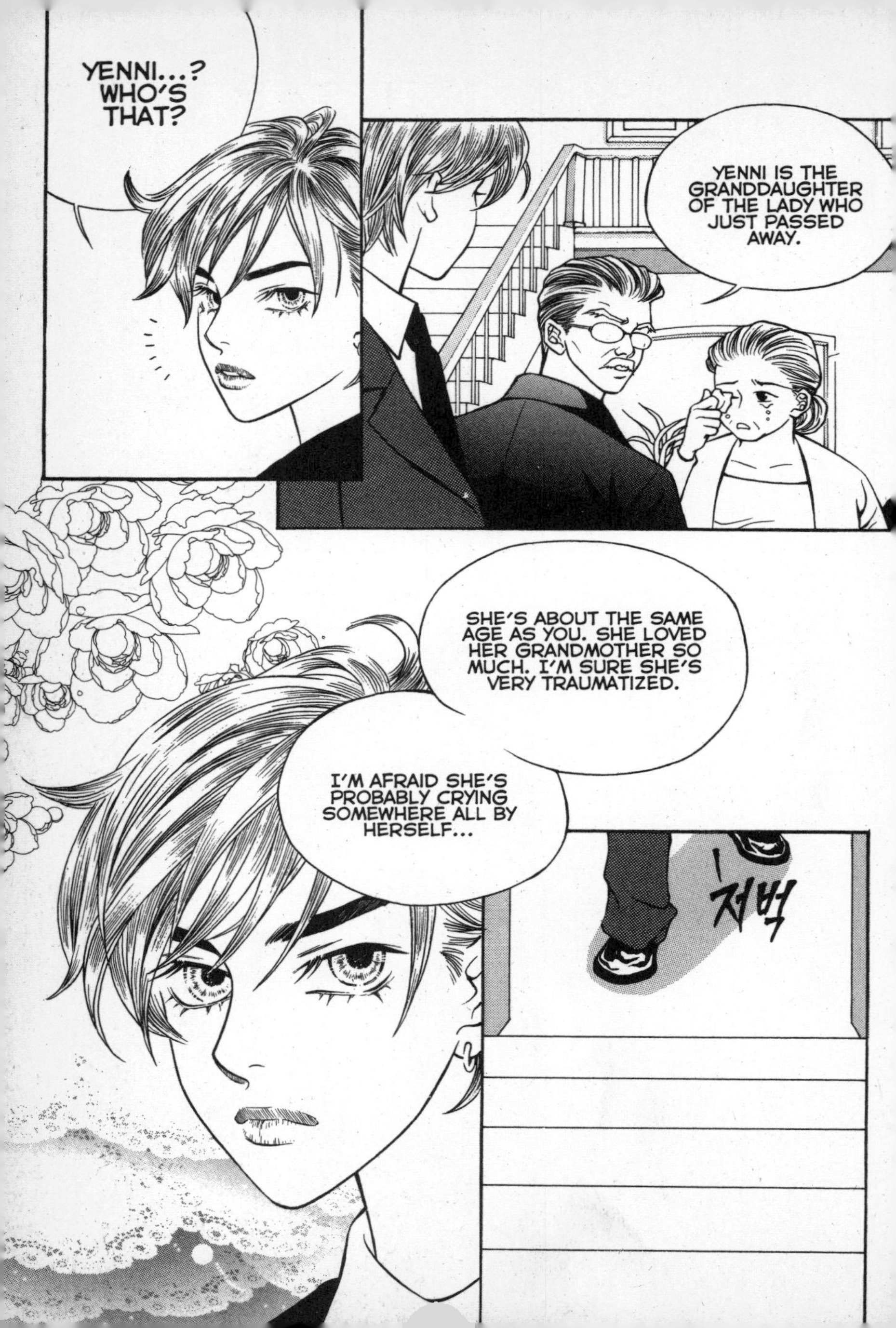
YENNI...? WHO'S THAT?
YENNI IS THE GRANDDAUGHTER OF THE LADY WHO JUST PASSED AWAY.
SHE'S ABOUT THE SAME AGE AS YOU. SHE LOVED HER GRANDMOTHER SO MUCH. I'M SURE SHE'S VERY TRAUMATIZED.
I'M AFRAID SHE'S PROBABLY CRYING SOMEWHERE ALL BY HERSELF...
저벅

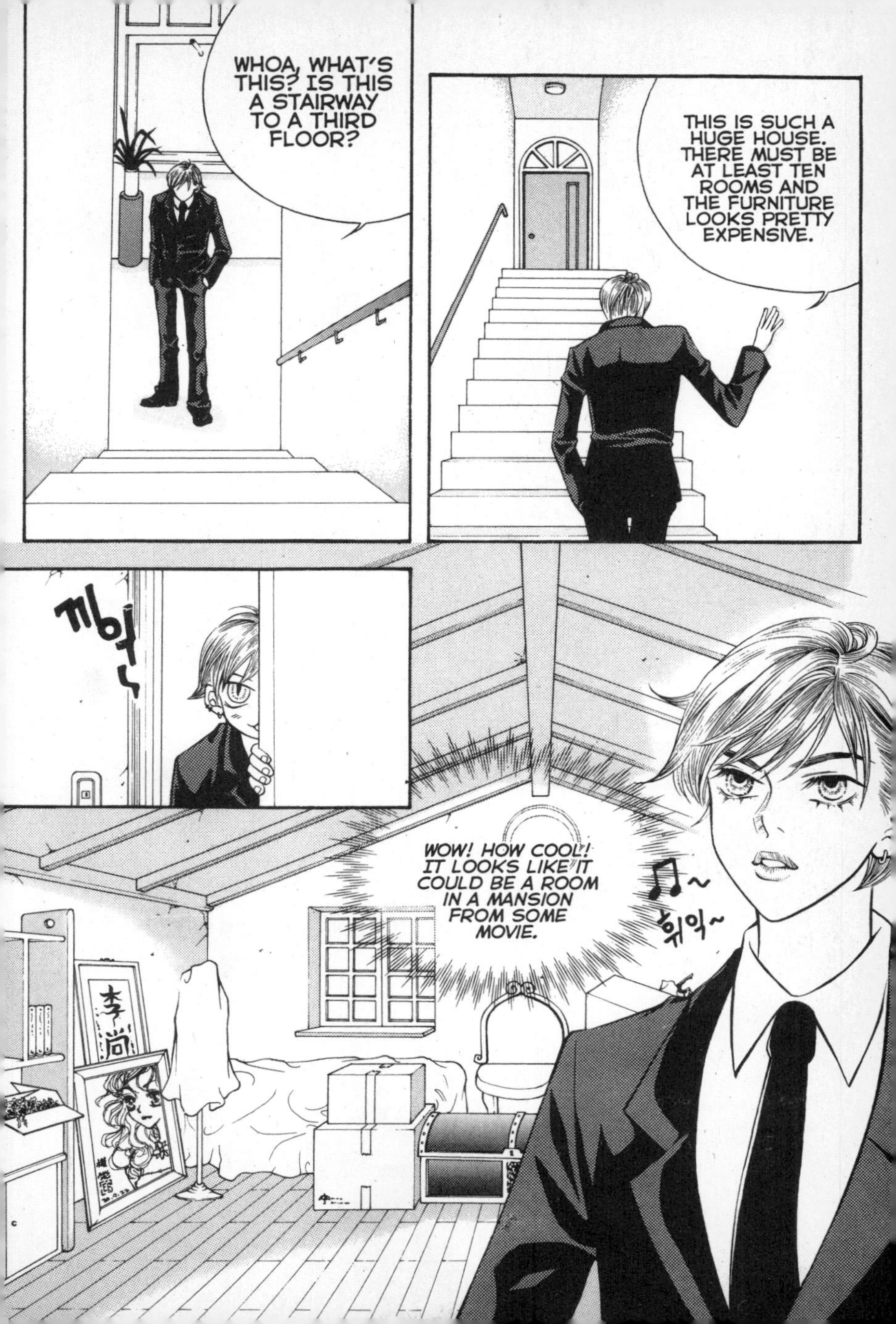
WHOA, WHAT'S THIS? IS THIS A STAIRWAY TO A THIRD FLOOR?
THIS IS SUCH A HUGE HOUSE. THERE MUST BE AT LEAST TEN ROOMS AND THE FURNITURE LOOKS PRETTY EXPENSIVE.
끼익~
WOW! HOW COOL! IT LOOKS LIKE IT COULD BE A ROOM IN A MANSION FROM SOME MOVIE.
♪~
휘익~

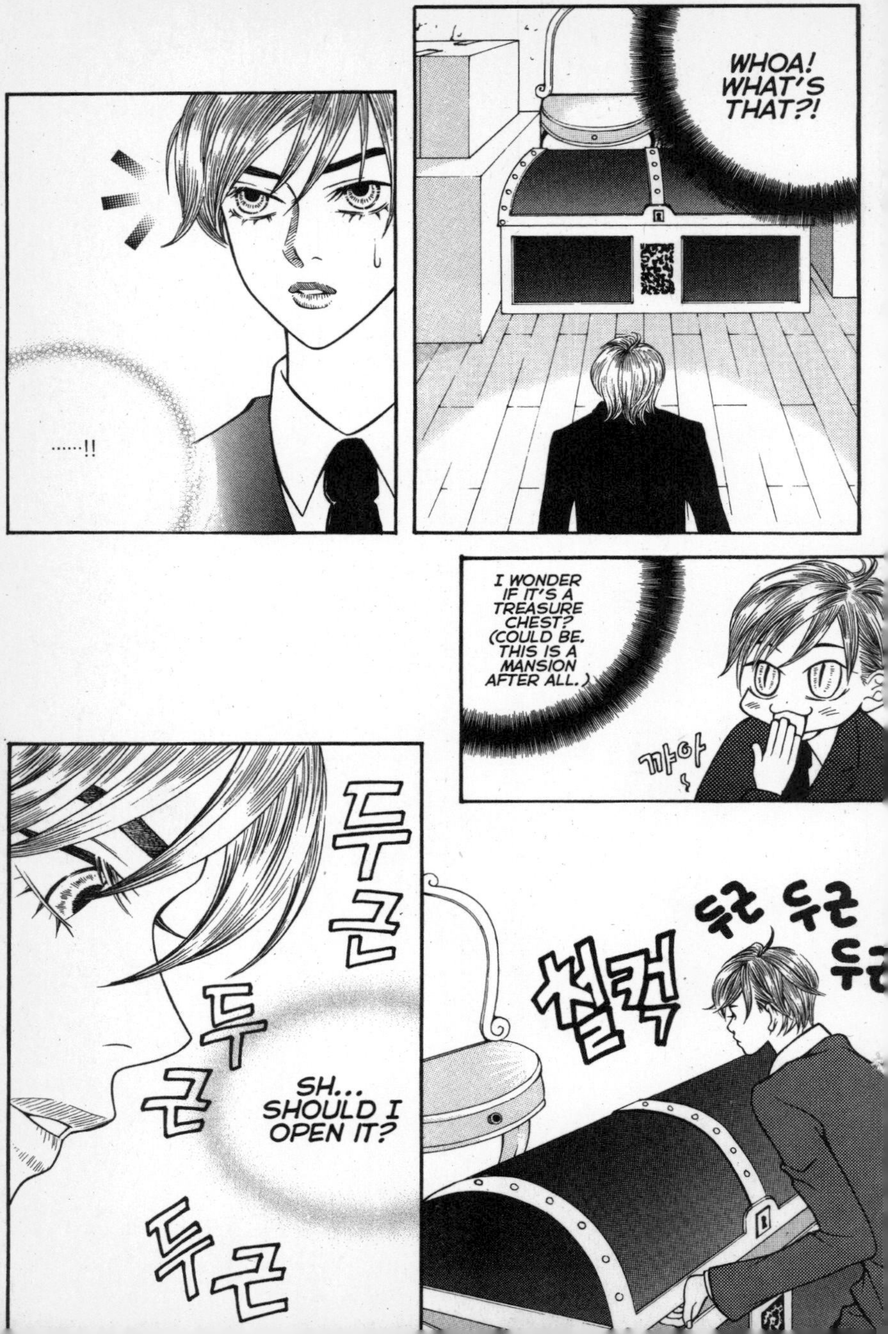
......!!
WHOA! WHAT'S THAT?!
I WONDER IF IT'S A TREASURE CHEST? (COULD BE. THIS IS A MANSION AFTER ALL.)
꺄아
두근
두근
두근
SH... SHOULD I OPEN IT?
철컥
두근 두근

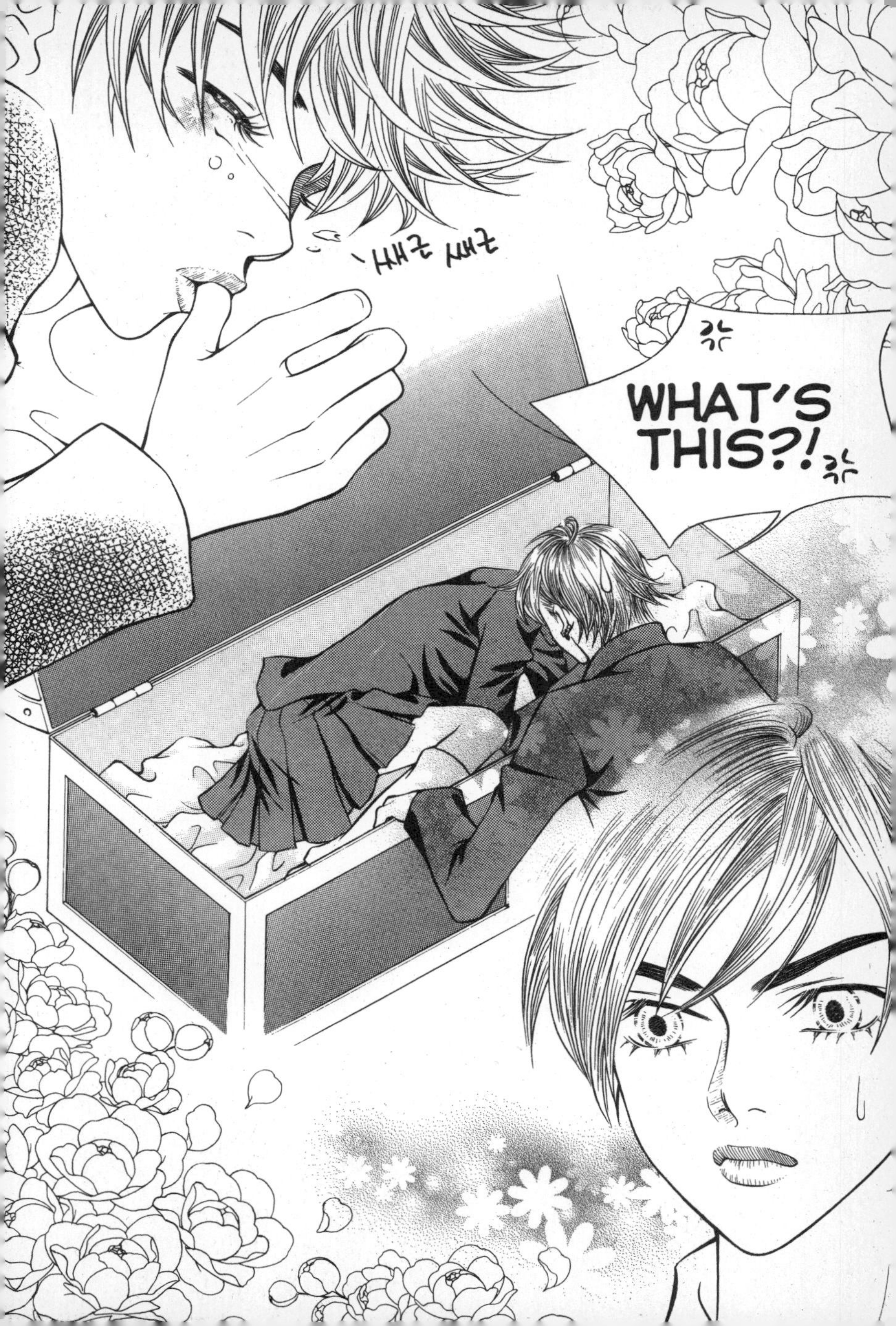
WHAT'S THIS?!

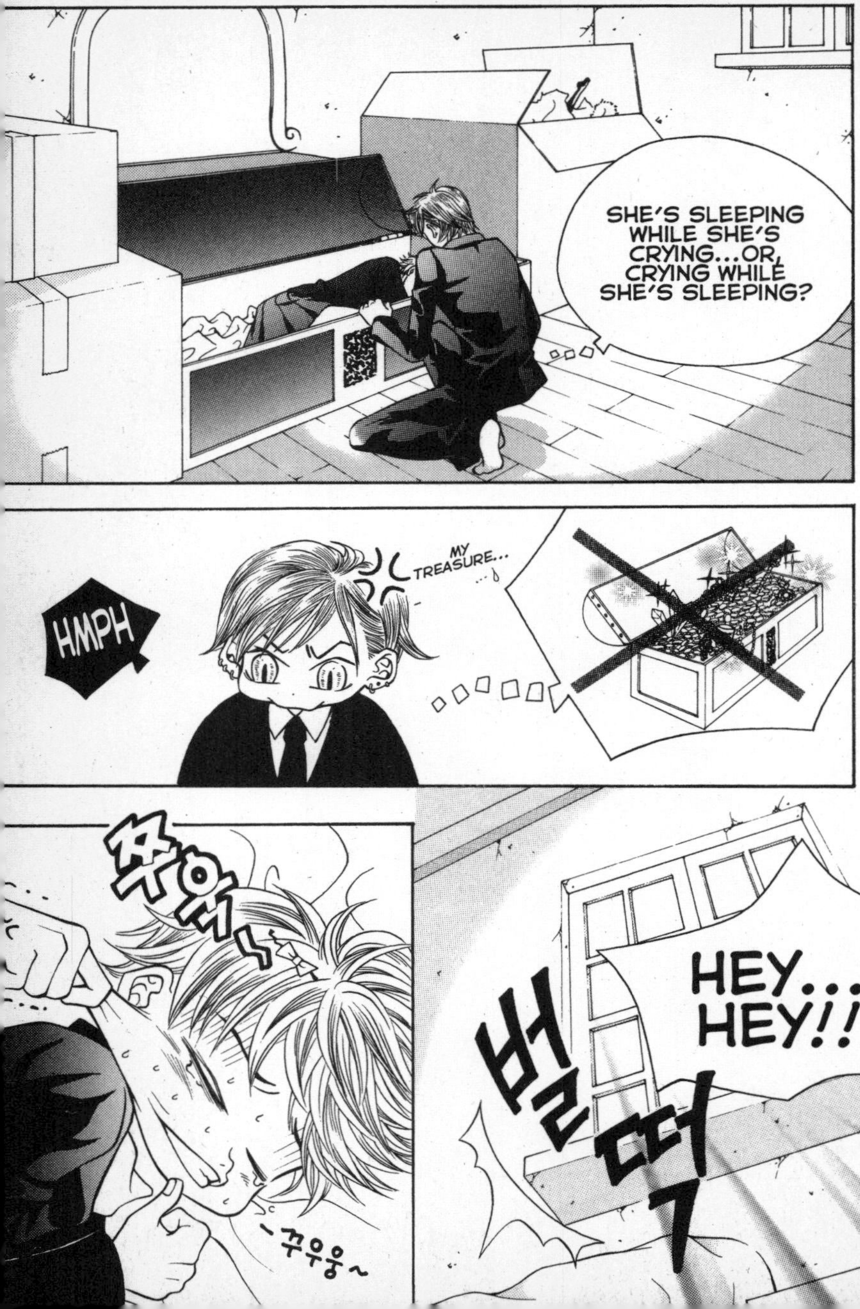
SHE'S SLEEPING WHILE SHE'S CRYING...OR, CRYING WHILE SHE'S SLEEPING?
HMPH
MY TREASURE...
쭈욱~
~꾸우웅~
HEY... HEY!!
벌떡

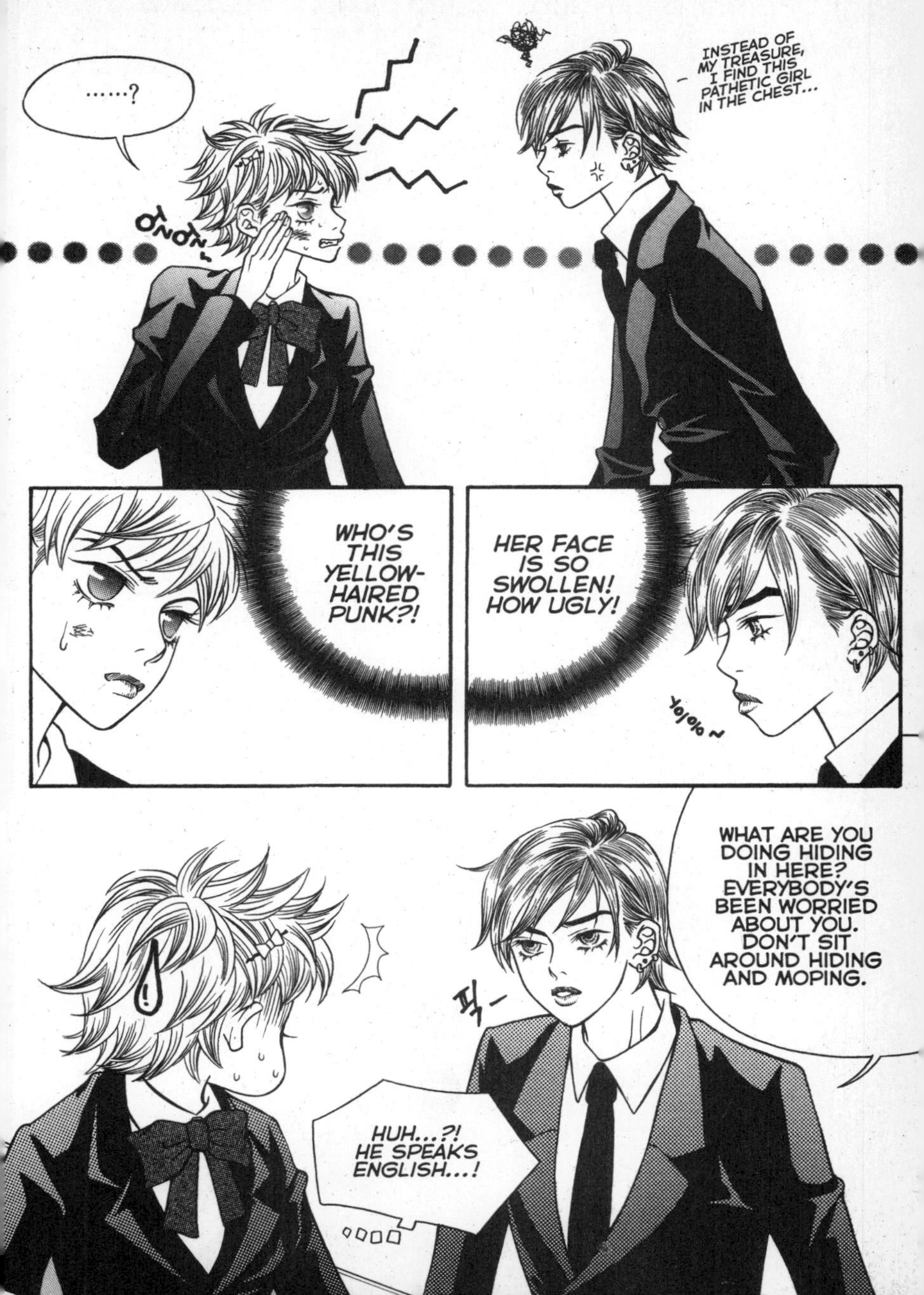
......?
INSTEAD OF MY TREASURE, I FIND THIS PATHETIC GIRL IN THE CHEST...
WHO'S THIS YELLOW-HAIRED PUNK?!
HER FACE IS SO SWOLLEN! HOW UGLY!
WHAT ARE YOU DOING HIDING IN HERE? EVERYBODY'S BEEN WORRIED ABOUT YOU. DON'T SIT AROUND HIDING AND MOPING.
HUH...?! HE SPEAKS ENGLISH...!

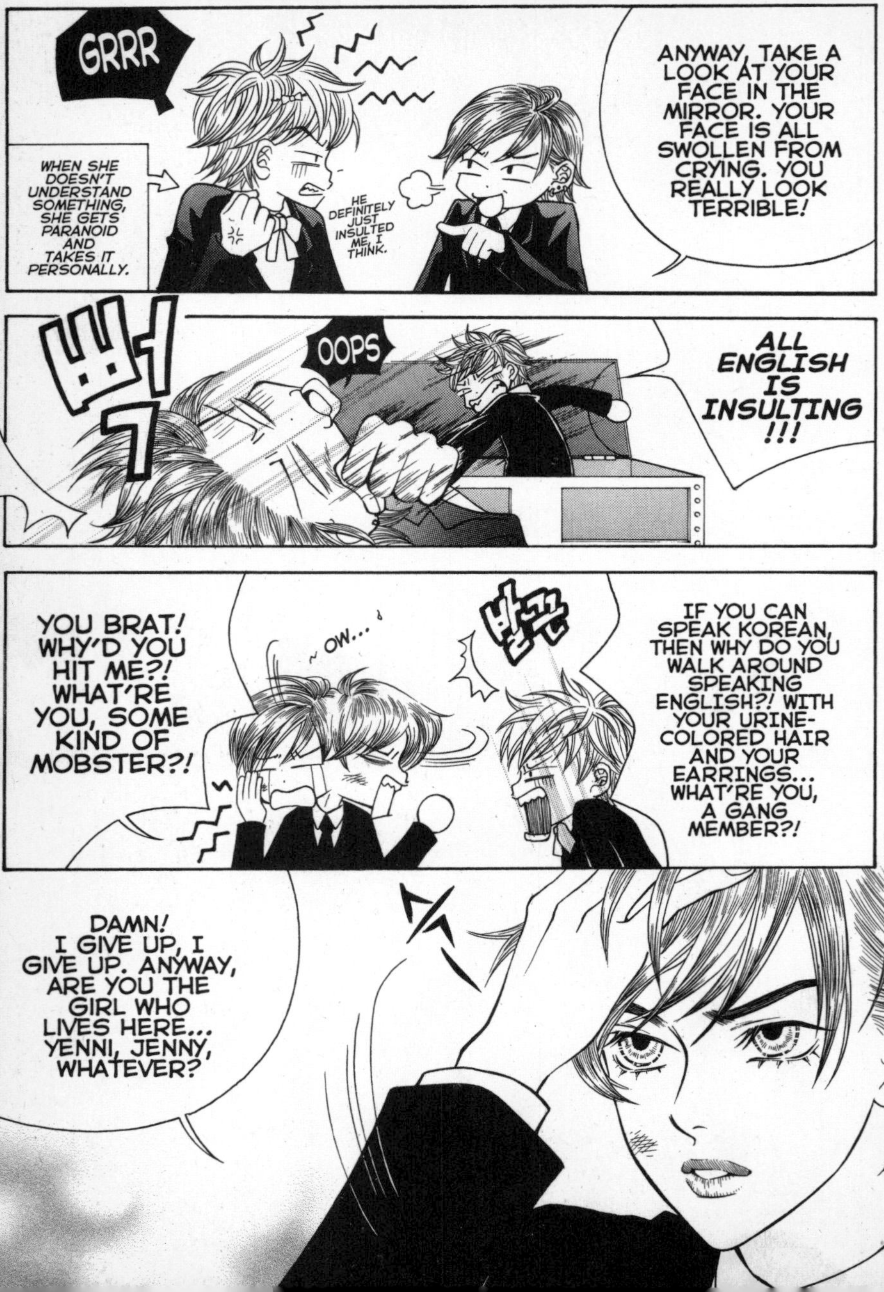
GRRR
WHEN SHE DOESN'T UNDERSTAND SOMETHING, SHE GETS PARANOID AND TAKES IT PERSONALLY.
HE DEFINITELY JUST INSULTED ME, I THINK.
ANYWAY, TAKE A LOOK AT YOUR FACE IN THE MIRROR. YOUR FACE IS ALL SWOLLEN FROM CRYING. YOU REALLY LOOK TERRIBLE!
빡
OOPS
ALL ENGLISH IS INSULTING !!!
YOU BRAT! WHY'D YOU HIT ME?! WHAT'RE YOU, SOME KIND OF MOBSTER?!
~OW...
발끈
IF YOU CAN SPEAK KOREAN, THEN WHY DO YOU WALK AROUND SPEAKING ENGLISH?! WITH YOUR URINE-COLORED HAIR AND YOUR EARRINGS... WHAT'RE YOU, A GANG MEMBER?!
DAMN! I GIVE UP, I GIVE UP. ANYWAY, ARE YOU THE GIRL WHO LIVES HERE... YENNI, JENNY, WHATEVER?

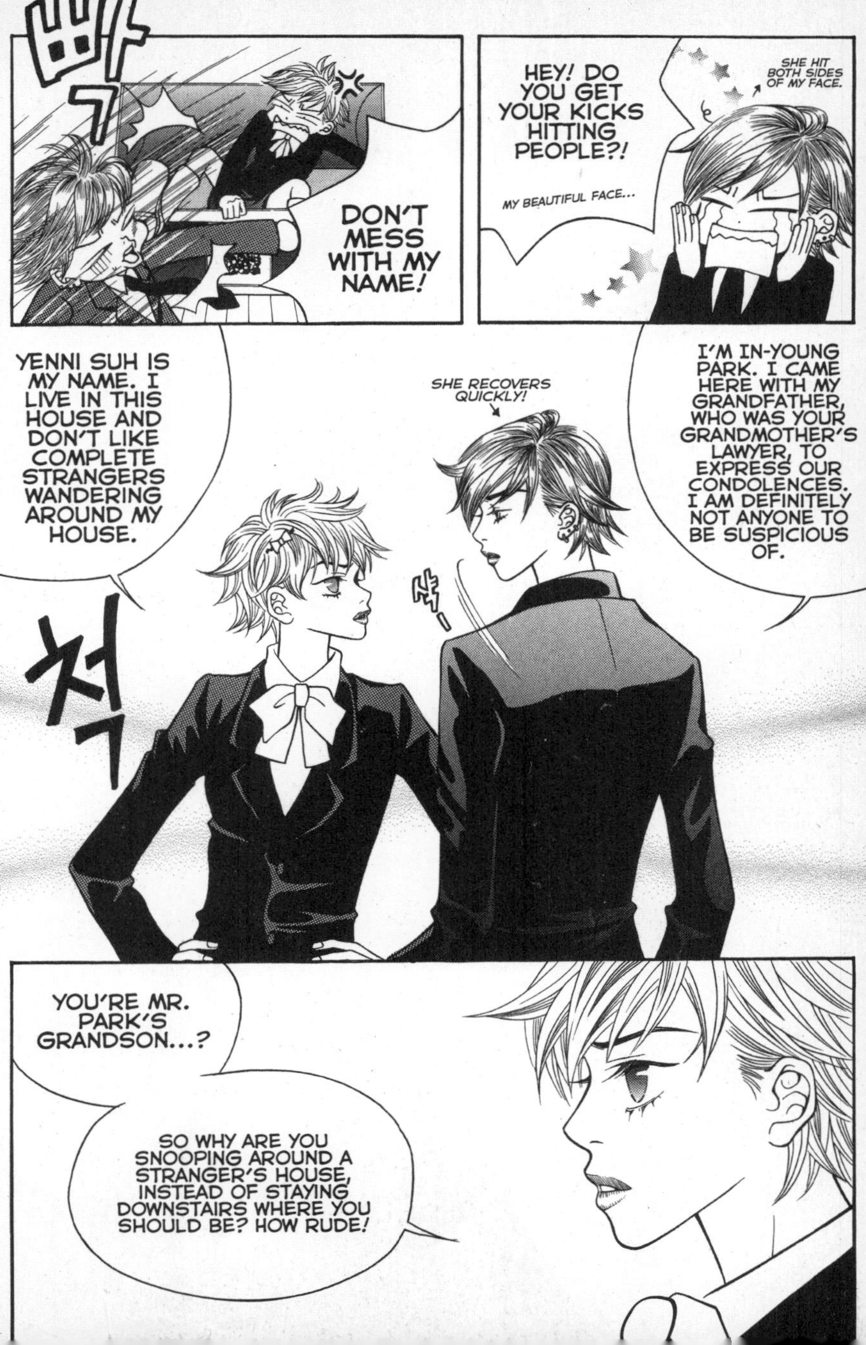
빡
DON'T MESS WITH MY NAME!
HEY! DO YOU GET YOUR KICKS HITTING PEOPLE?!
SHE HIT BOTH SIDES OF MY FACE.
MY BEAUTIFUL FACE...
YENNI SUH IS MY NAME. I LIVE IN THIS HOUSE AND DON'T LIKE COMPLETE STRANGERS WANDERING AROUND MY HOUSE.
척
SHE RECOVERS QUICKLY!
I'M IN-YOUNG PARK. I CAME HERE WITH MY GRANDFATHER, WHO WAS YOUR GRANDMOTHER'S LAWYER, TO EXPRESS OUR CONDOLENCES. I AM DEFINITELY NOT ANYONE TO BE SUSPICIOUS OF.
YOU'RE MR. PARK'S GRANDSON...?
SO WHY ARE YOU SNOOPING AROUND A STRANGER'S HOUSE, INSTEAD OF STAYING DOWNSTAIRS WHERE YOU SHOULD BE? HOW RUDE!

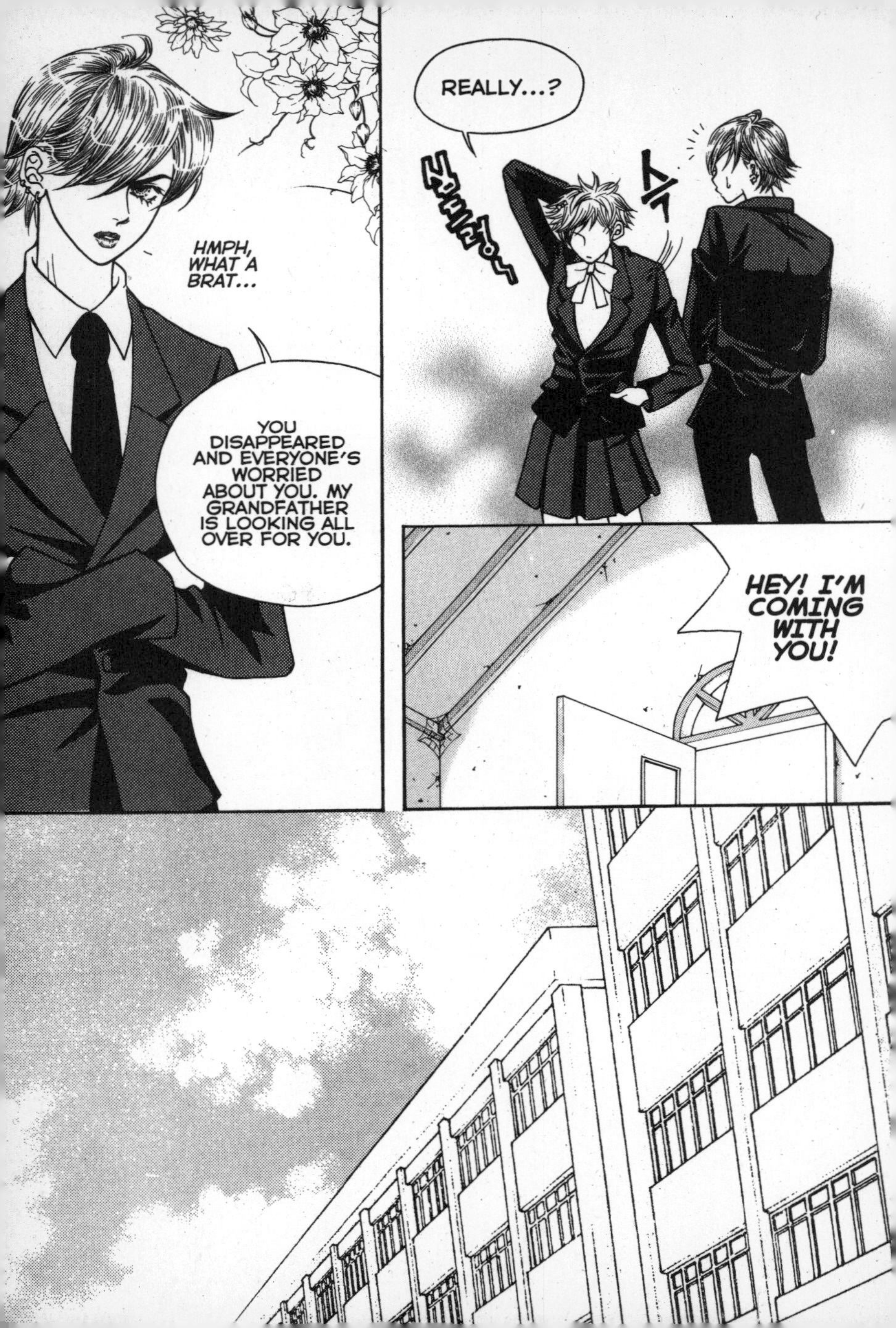
HMPH, WHAT A BRAT...
YOU DISAPPEARED AND EVERYONE'S WORRIED ABOUT YOU. MY GRANDFATHER IS LOOKING ALL OVER FOR YOU.
REALLY...?
HEY! I'M COMING WITH YOU!

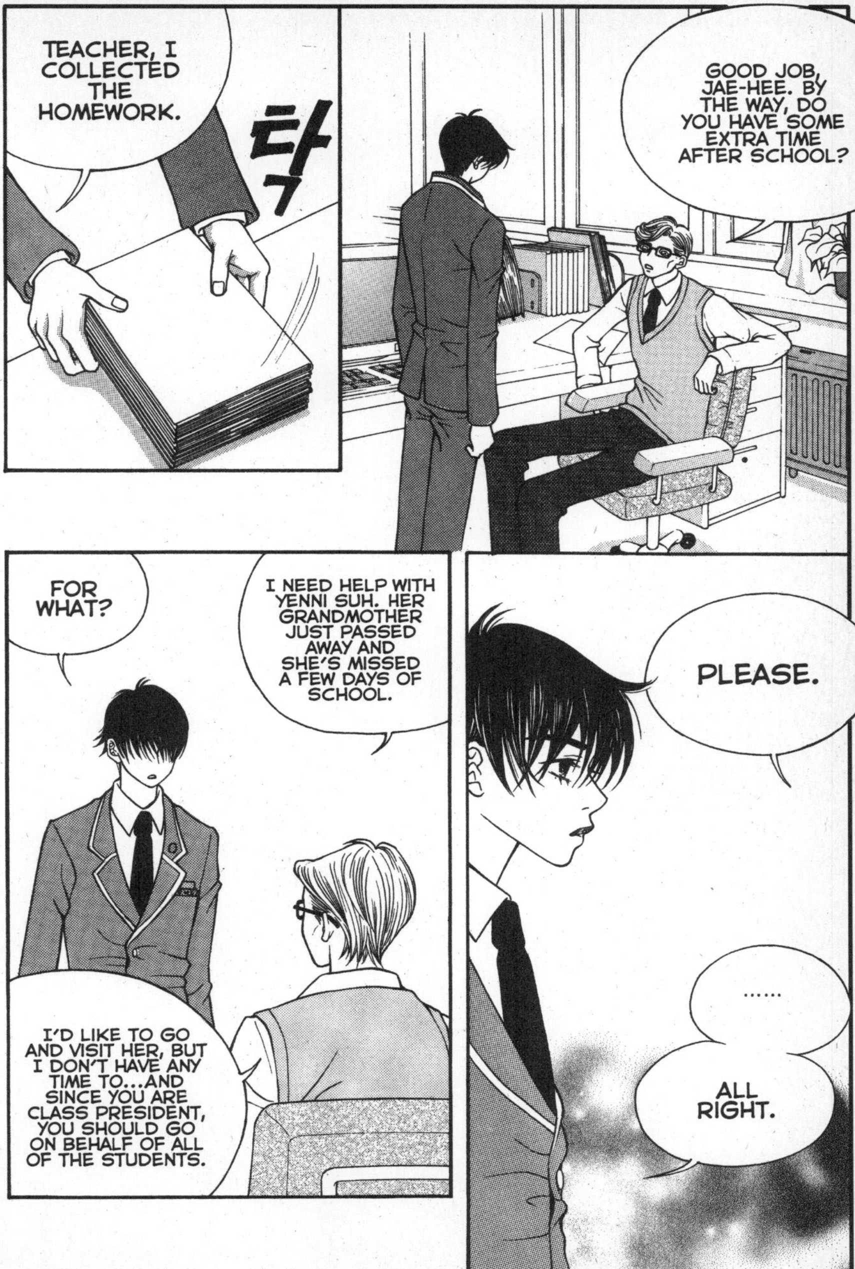
TEACHER, I COLLECTED THE HOMEWORK.
탁
GOOD JOB, JAE-HEE. BY THE WAY, DO YOU HAVE SOME EXTRA TIME AFTER SCHOOL?
FOR WHAT?
I NEED HELP WITH YENNI SUH. HER GRANDMOTHER JUST PASSED AWAY AND SHE'S MISSED A FEW DAYS OF SCHOOL.
I'D LIKE TO GO AND VISIT HER, BUT I DON'T HAVE ANY TIME TO...AND SINCE YOU ARE CLASS PRESIDENT, YOU SHOULD GO ON BEHALF OF ALL OF THE STUDENTS.
PLEASE.
......
ALL RIGHT.

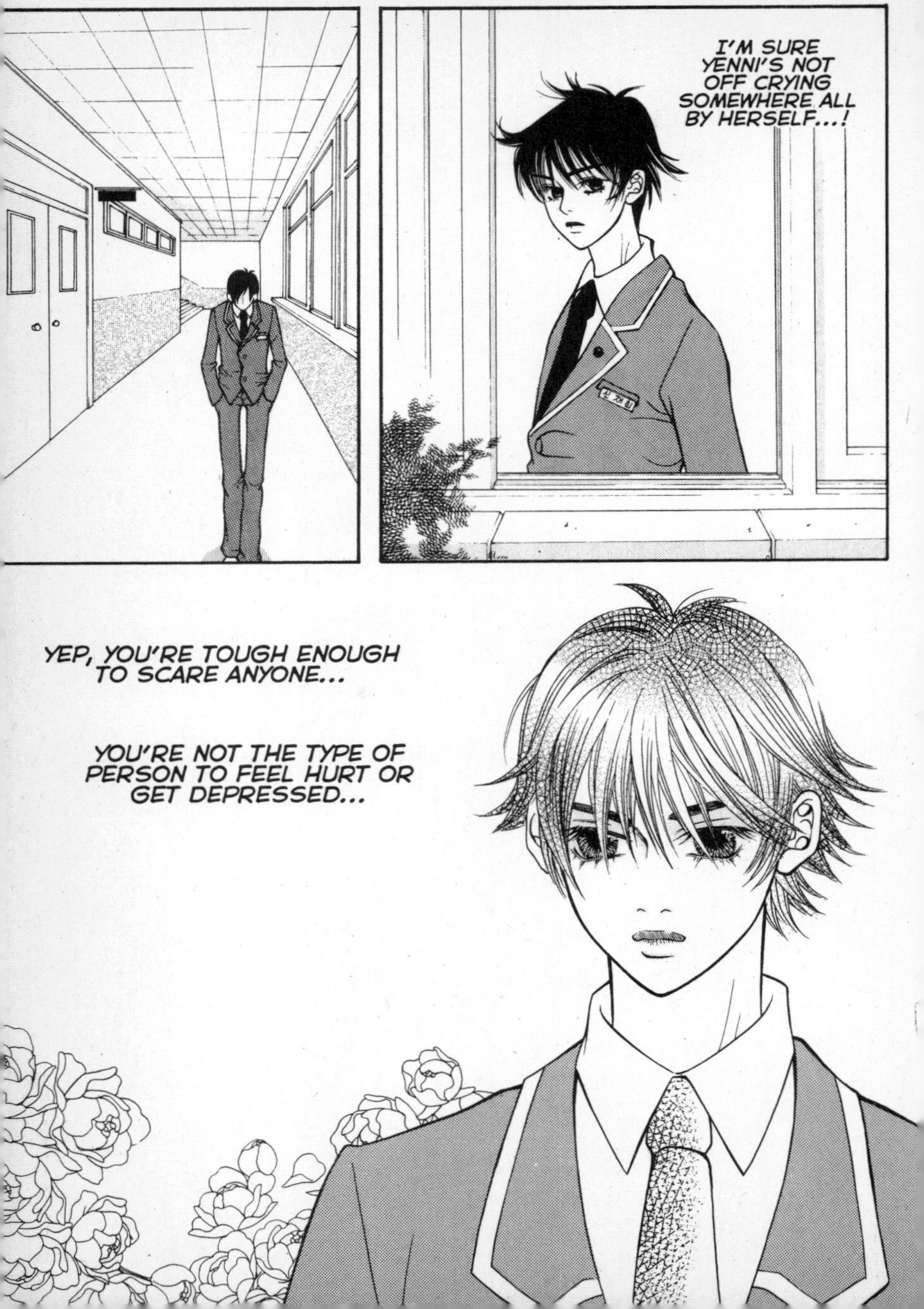
I'M SURE YENNI'S NOT OFF CRYING SOMEWHERE ALL BY HERSELF...!
YEP, YOU'RE TOUGH ENOUGH TO SCARE ANYONE...
YOU'RE NOT THE TYPE OF PERSON TO FEEL HURT OR GET DEPRESSED...

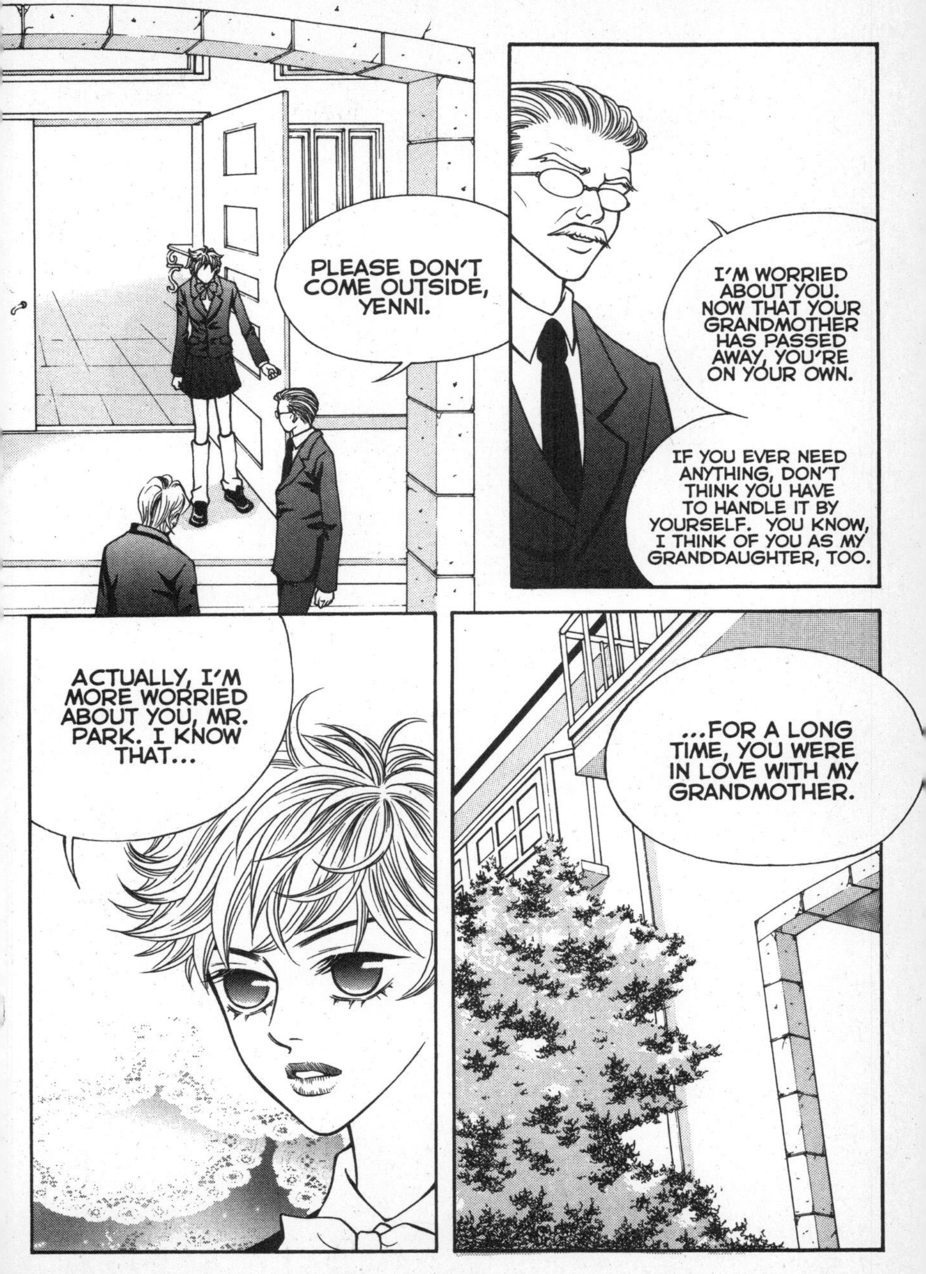
PLEASE DON'T COME OUTSIDE, YENNI.
I'M WORRIED ABOUT YOU. NOW THAT YOUR GRANDMOTHER HAS PASSED AWAY, YOU'RE ON YOUR OWN.
IF YOU EVER NEED ANYTHING, DON'T THINK YOU HAVE TO HANDLE IT BY YOURSELF. YOU KNOW, I THINK OF YOU AS MY GRANDDAUGHTER, TOO.
ACTUALLY, I'M MORE WORRIED ABOUT YOU, MR. PARK. I KNOW THAT...
...FOR A LONG TIME, YOU WERE IN LOVE WITH MY GRANDMOTHER.

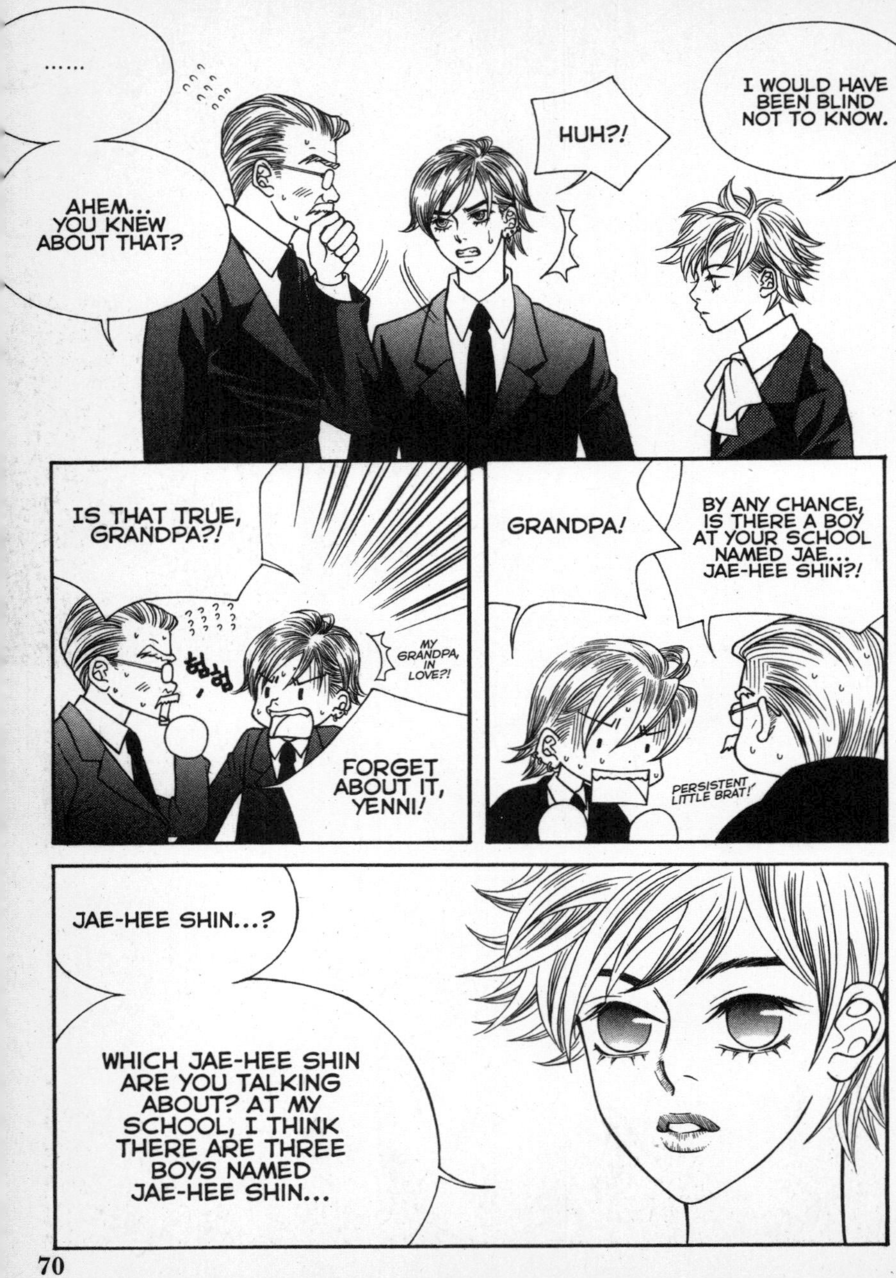
......
AHEM... YOU KNEW ABOUT THAT?
HUH?!
I WOULD HAVE BEEN BLIND NOT TO KNOW.
IS THAT TRUE, GRANDPA?!
험험
MY GRANDPA, IN LOVE?!
FORGET ABOUT IT, YENNI!
GRANDPA!
BY ANY CHANCE, IS THERE A BOY AT YOUR SCHOOL NAMED JAE... JAE-HEE SHIN?!
PERSISTENT LITTLE BRAT!
JAE-HEE SHIN...?
WHICH JAE-HEE SHIN ARE YOU TALKING ABOUT? AT MY SCHOOL, I THINK THERE ARE THREE BOYS NAMED JAE-HEE SHIN...

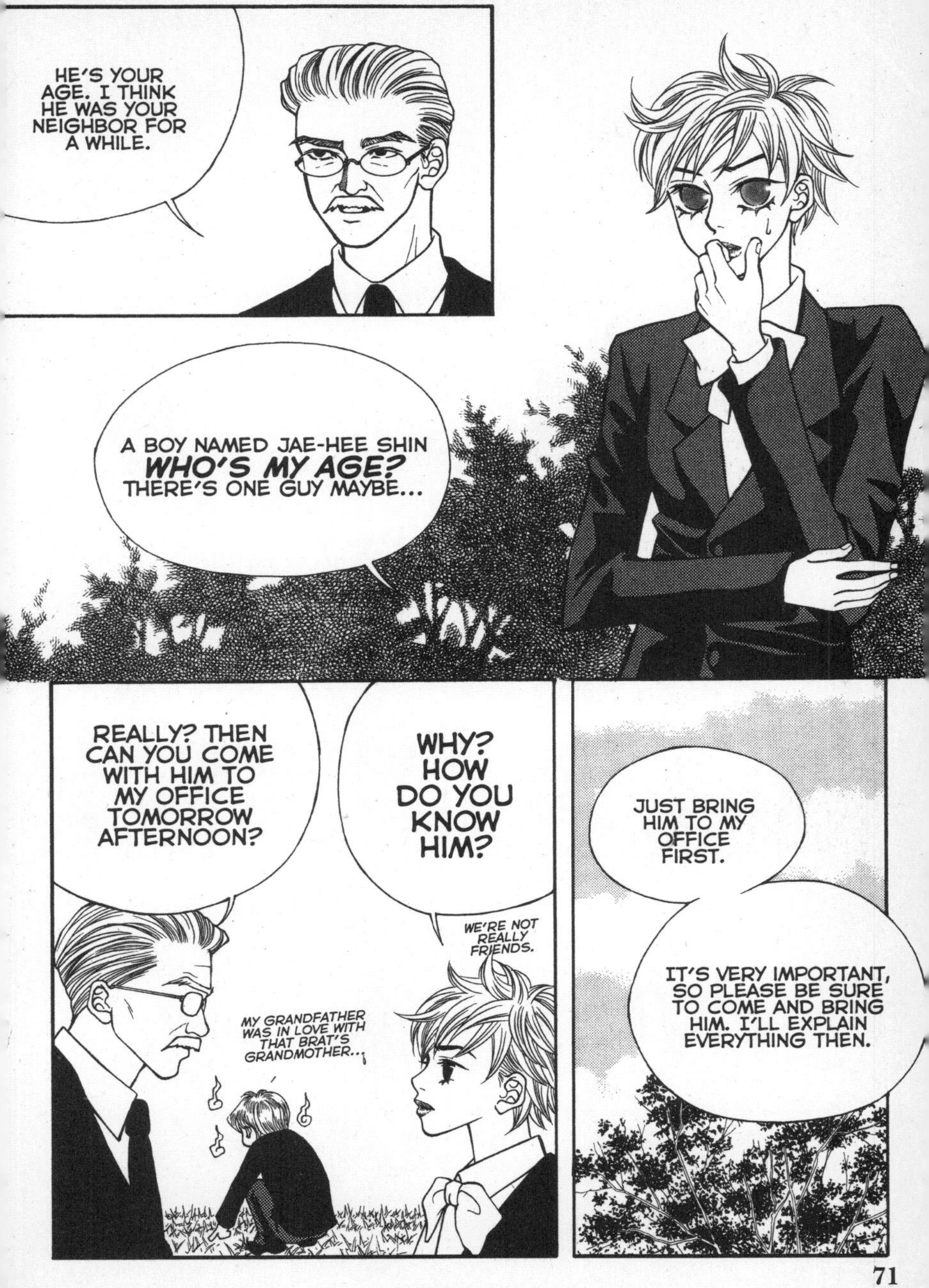
HE'S YOUR AGE. I THINK HE WAS YOUR NEIGHBOR FOR A WHILE.
A BOY NAMED JAE-HEE SHIN *WHO'S MY AGE?* THERE'S ONE GUY MAYBE...
REALLY? THEN CAN YOU COME WITH HIM TO MY OFFICE TOMORROW AFTERNOON?
WHY? HOW DO YOU KNOW HIM?
WE'RE NOT REALLY FRIENDS.
MY GRANDFATHER WAS IN LOVE WITH THAT BRAT'S GRANDMOTHER...
JUST BRING HIM TO MY OFFICE FIRST.
IT'S VERY IMPORTANT, SO PLEASE BE SURE TO COME AND BRING HIM. I'LL EXPLAIN EVERYTHING THEN.

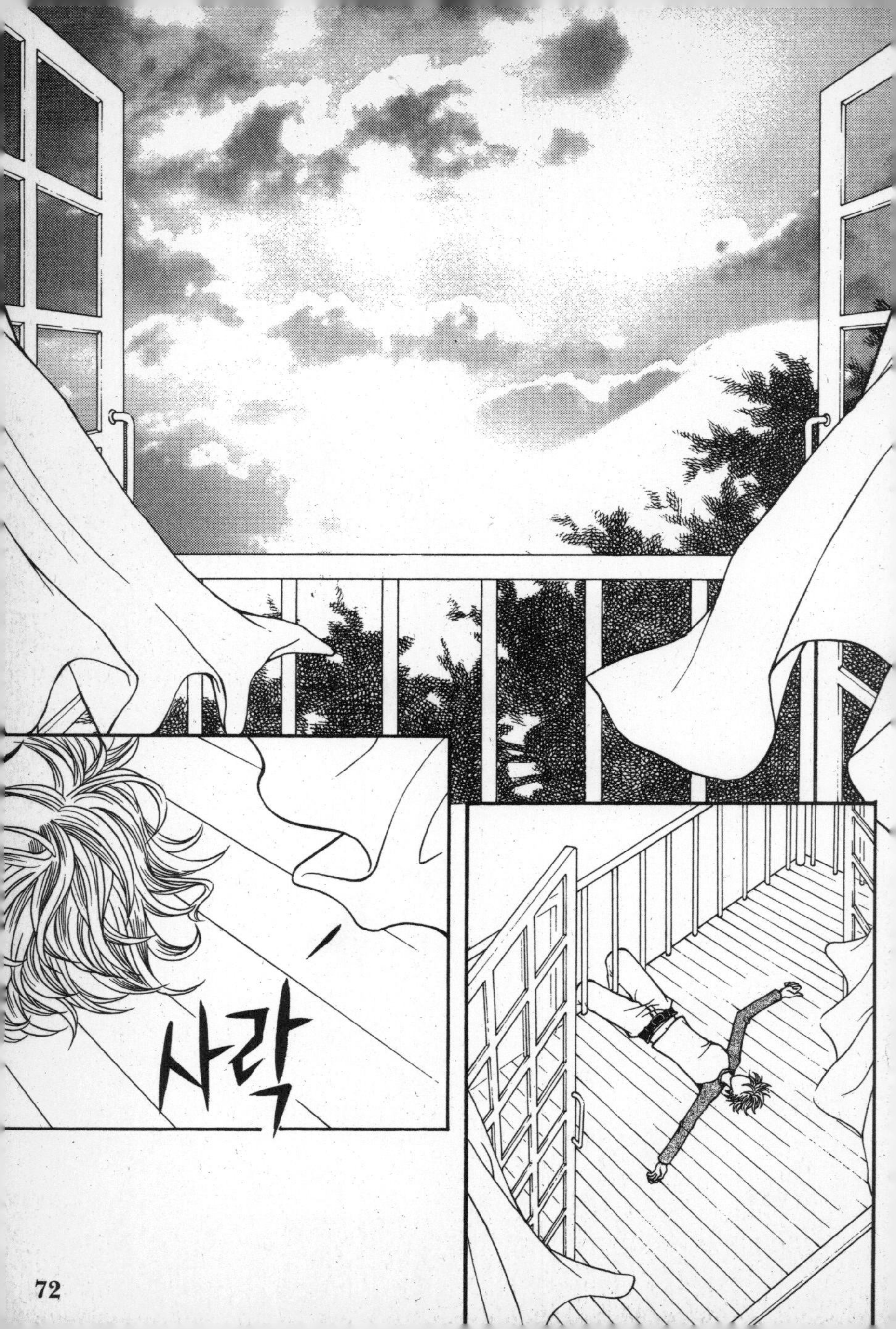
사락

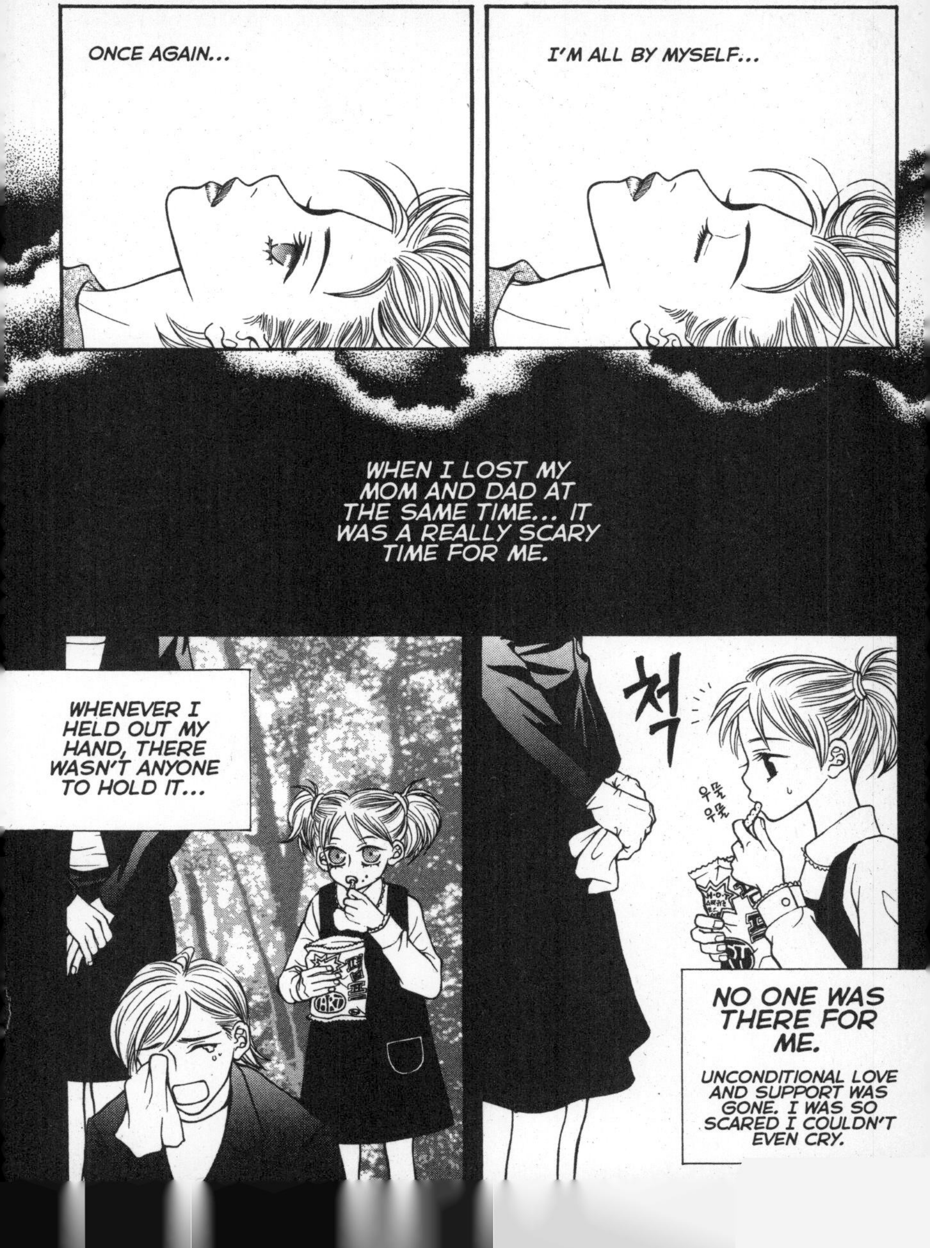
ONCE AGAIN...
I'M ALL BY MYSELF...
WHEN I LOST MY MOM AND DAD AT THE SAME TIME... IT WAS A REALLY SCARY TIME FOR ME.
WHENEVER I HELD OUT MY HAND, THERE WASN'T ANYONE TO HOLD IT...
척
우물 우물
NO ONE WAS THERE FOR ME.
UNCONDITIONAL LOVE AND SUPPORT WAS GONE. I WAS SO SCARED I COULDN'T EVEN CRY.

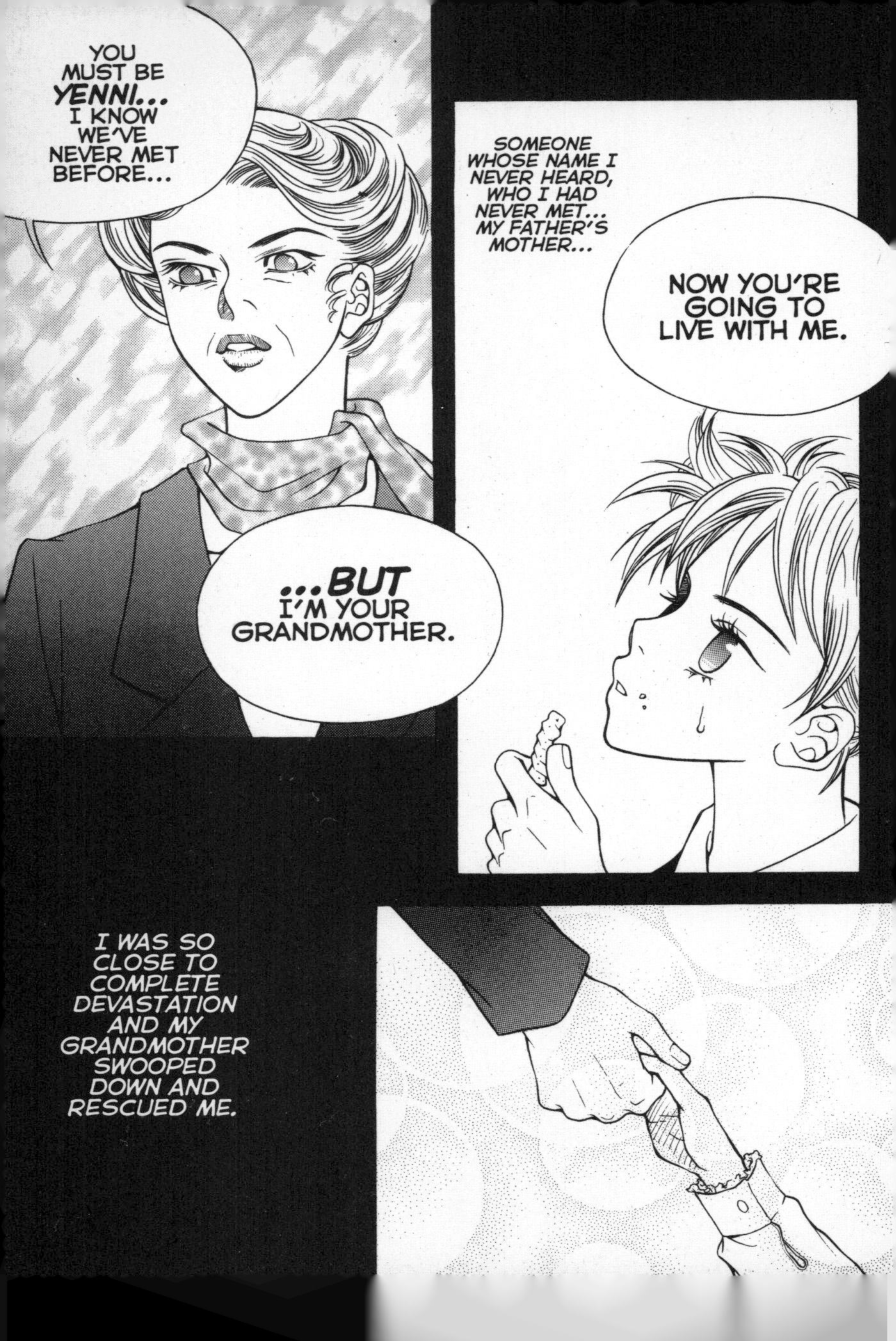
YOU MUST BE YENNI... I KNOW WE'VE NEVER MET BEFORE...
...BUT I'M YOUR GRANDMOTHER.
SOMEONE WHOSE NAME I NEVER HEARD, WHO I HAD NEVER MET... MY FATHER'S MOTHER...
NOW YOU'RE GOING TO LIVE WITH ME.
I WAS SO CLOSE TO COMPLETE DEVASTATION AND MY GRANDMOTHER SWOOPED DOWN AND RESCUED ME.

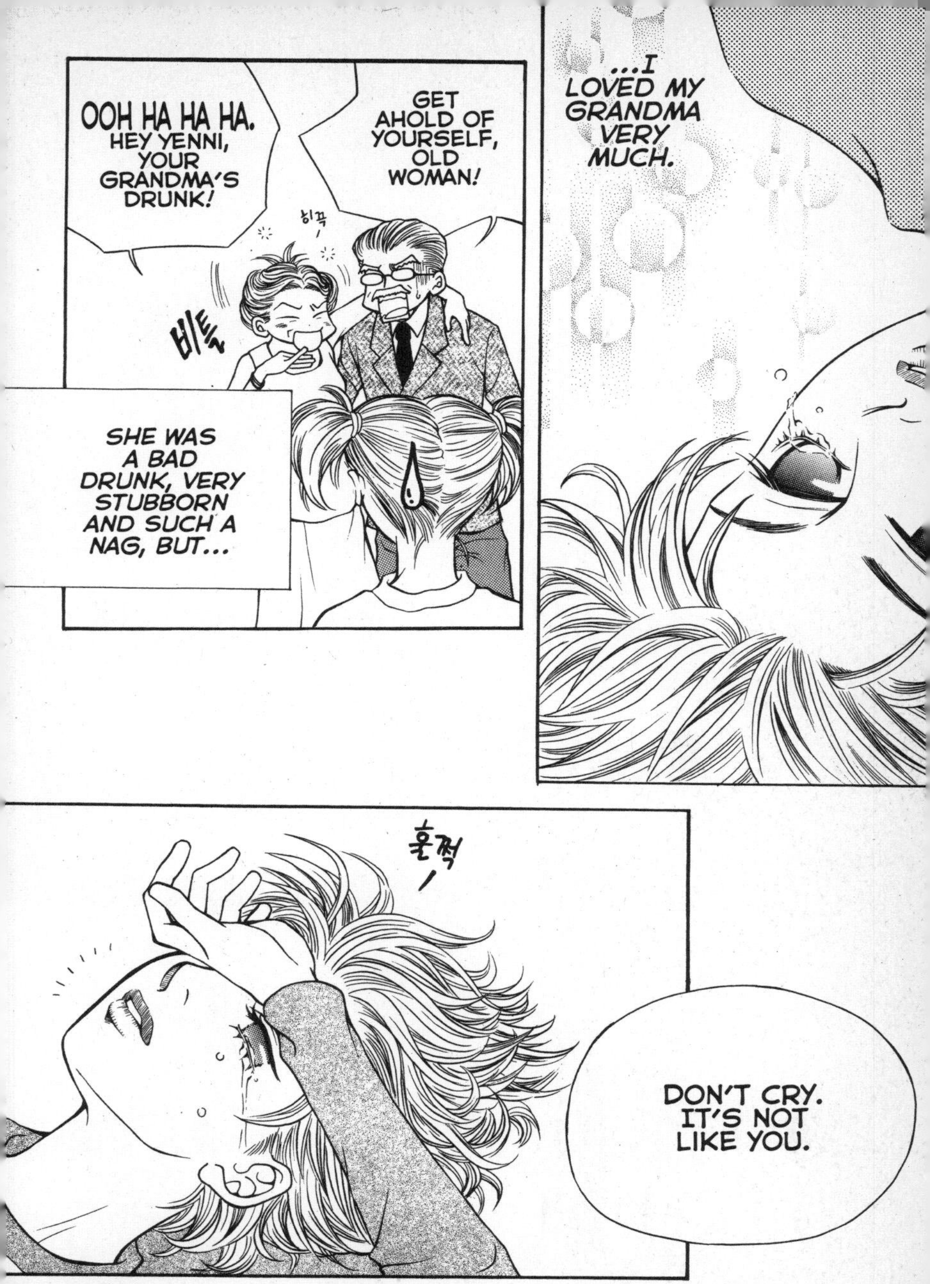
OOH HA HA HA. HEY YENNI, YOUR GRANDMA'S DRUNK!
GET AHOLD OF YOURSELF, OLD WOMAN!
히끅
비틀
SHE WAS A BAD DRUNK, VERY STUBBORN AND SUCH A NAG, BUT...
...I LOVED MY GRANDMA VERY MUCH.
훌쩍
DON'T CRY. IT'S NOT LIKE YOU.

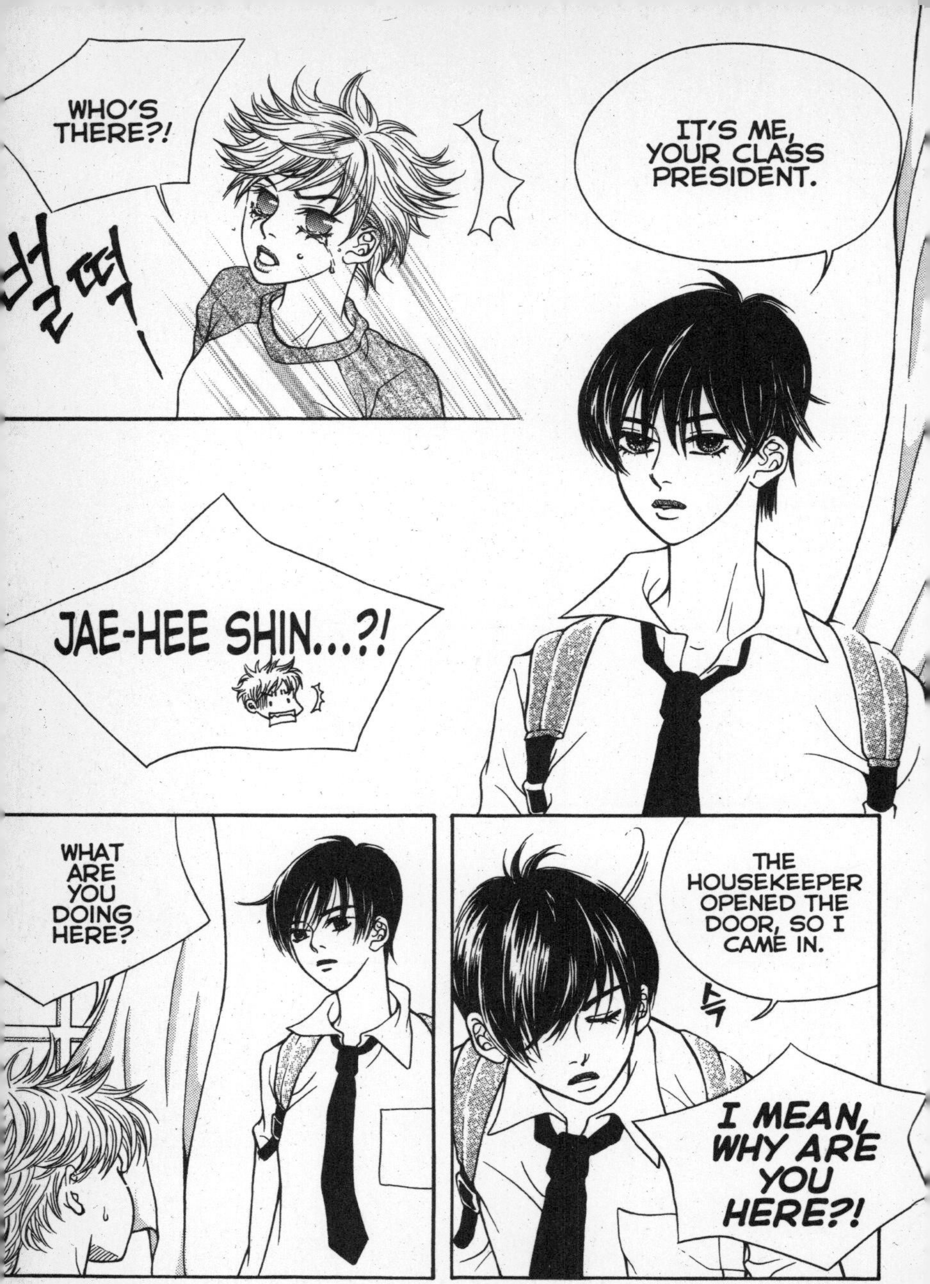
WHO'S THERE?!
벌떡
IT'S ME, YOUR CLASS PRESIDENT.
JAE-HEE SHIN...?!
WHAT ARE YOU DOING HERE?
THE HOUSEKEEPER OPENED THE DOOR, SO I CAME IN.
슥
I MEAN, WHY ARE YOU HERE?!

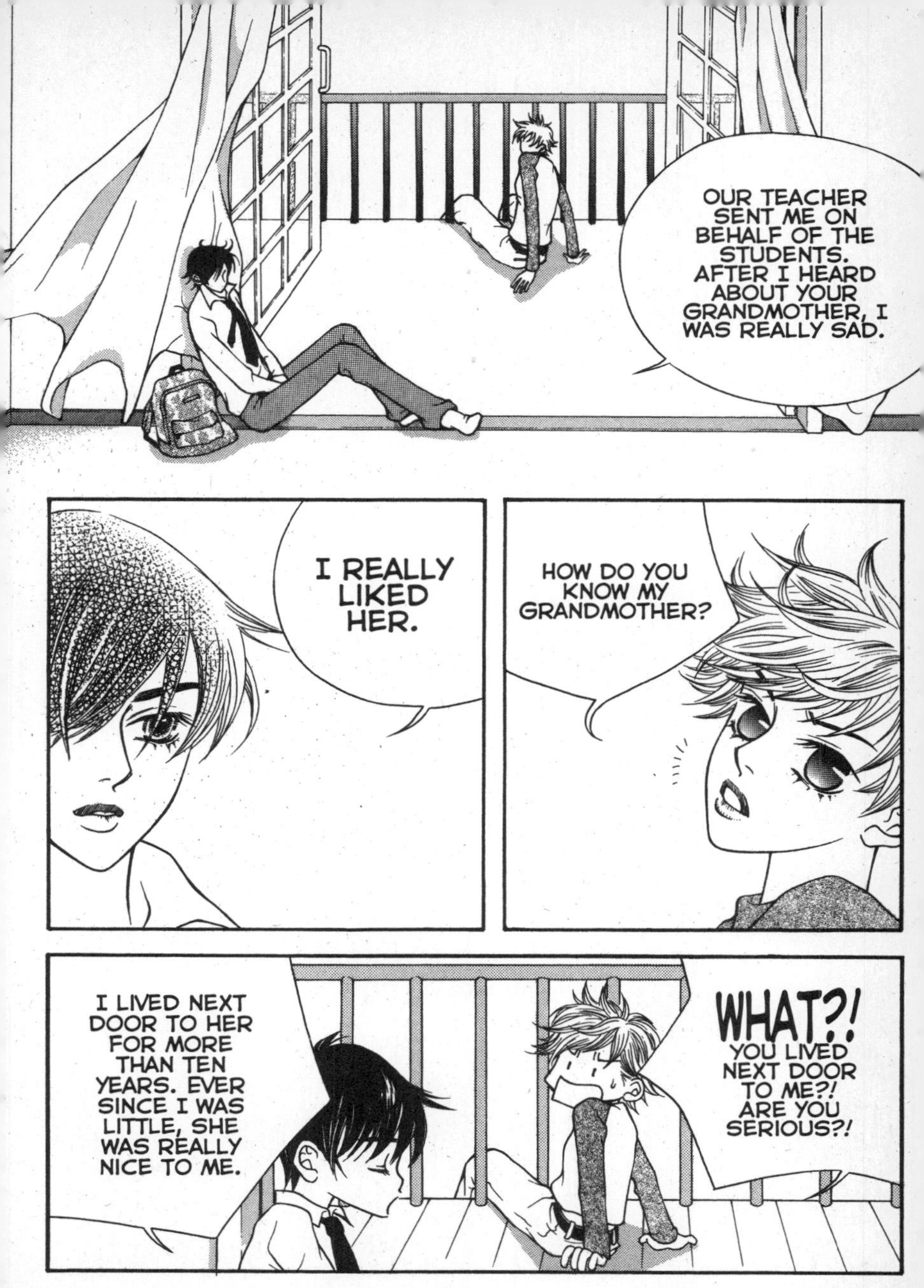
OUR TEACHER SENT ME ON BEHALF OF THE STUDENTS. AFTER I HEARD ABOUT YOUR GRANDMOTHER, I WAS REALLY SAD.
I REALLY LIKED HER.
HOW DO YOU KNOW MY GRANDMOTHER?
I LIVED NEXT DOOR TO HER FOR MORE THAN TEN YEARS. EVER SINCE I WAS LITTLE, SHE WAS REALLY NICE TO ME.
WHAT?! YOU LIVED NEXT DOOR TO ME?! ARE YOU SERIOUS?!

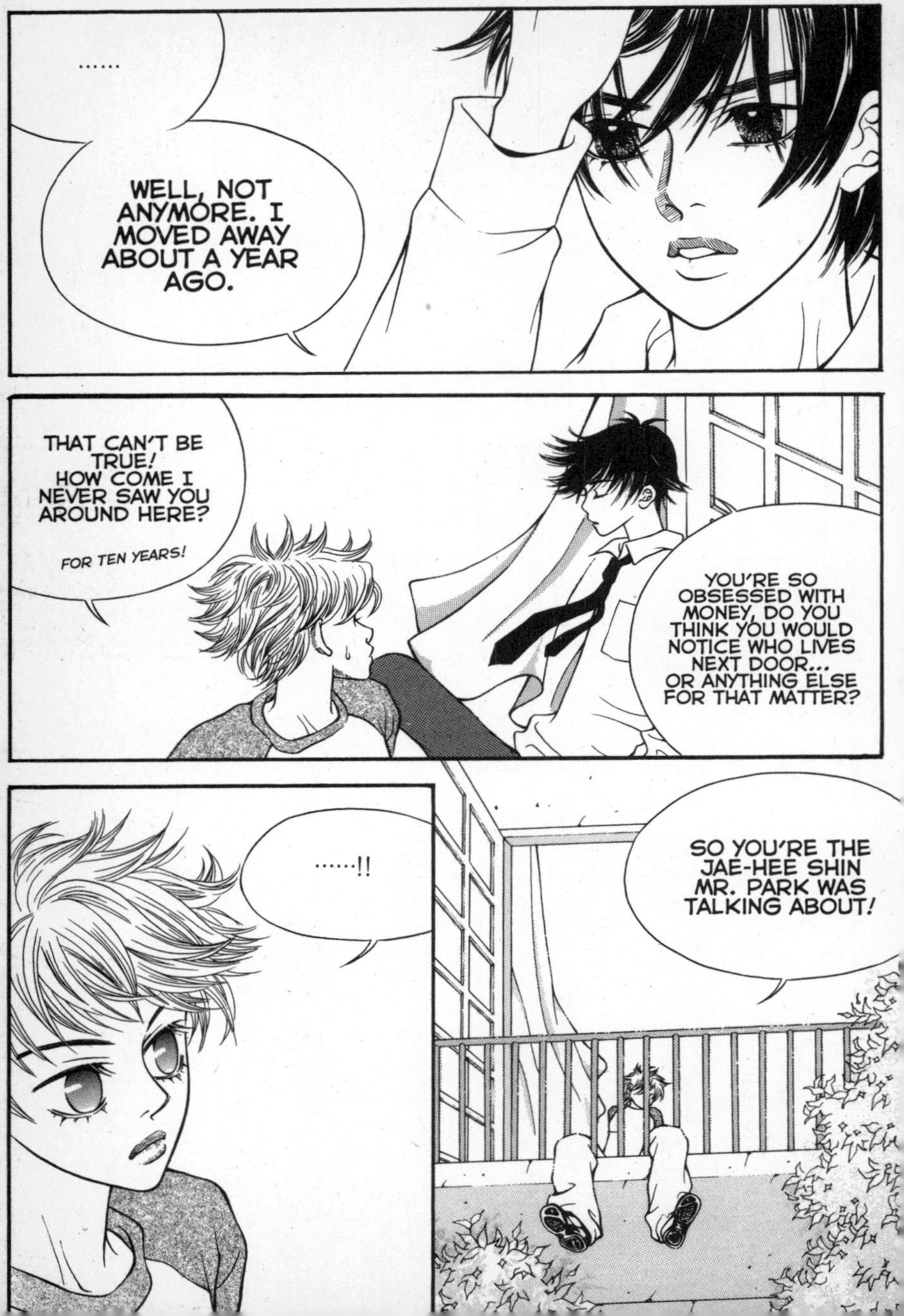
......
WELL, NOT ANYMORE. I MOVED AWAY ABOUT A YEAR AGO.
THAT CAN'T BE TRUE! HOW COME I NEVER SAW YOU AROUND HERE?
FOR TEN YEARS!
YOU'RE SO OBSESSED WITH MONEY, DO YOU THINK YOU WOULD NOTICE WHO LIVES NEXT DOOR... OR ANYTHING ELSE FOR THAT MATTER?
......!!
SO YOU'RE THE JAE-HEE SHIN MR. PARK WAS TALKING ABOUT!

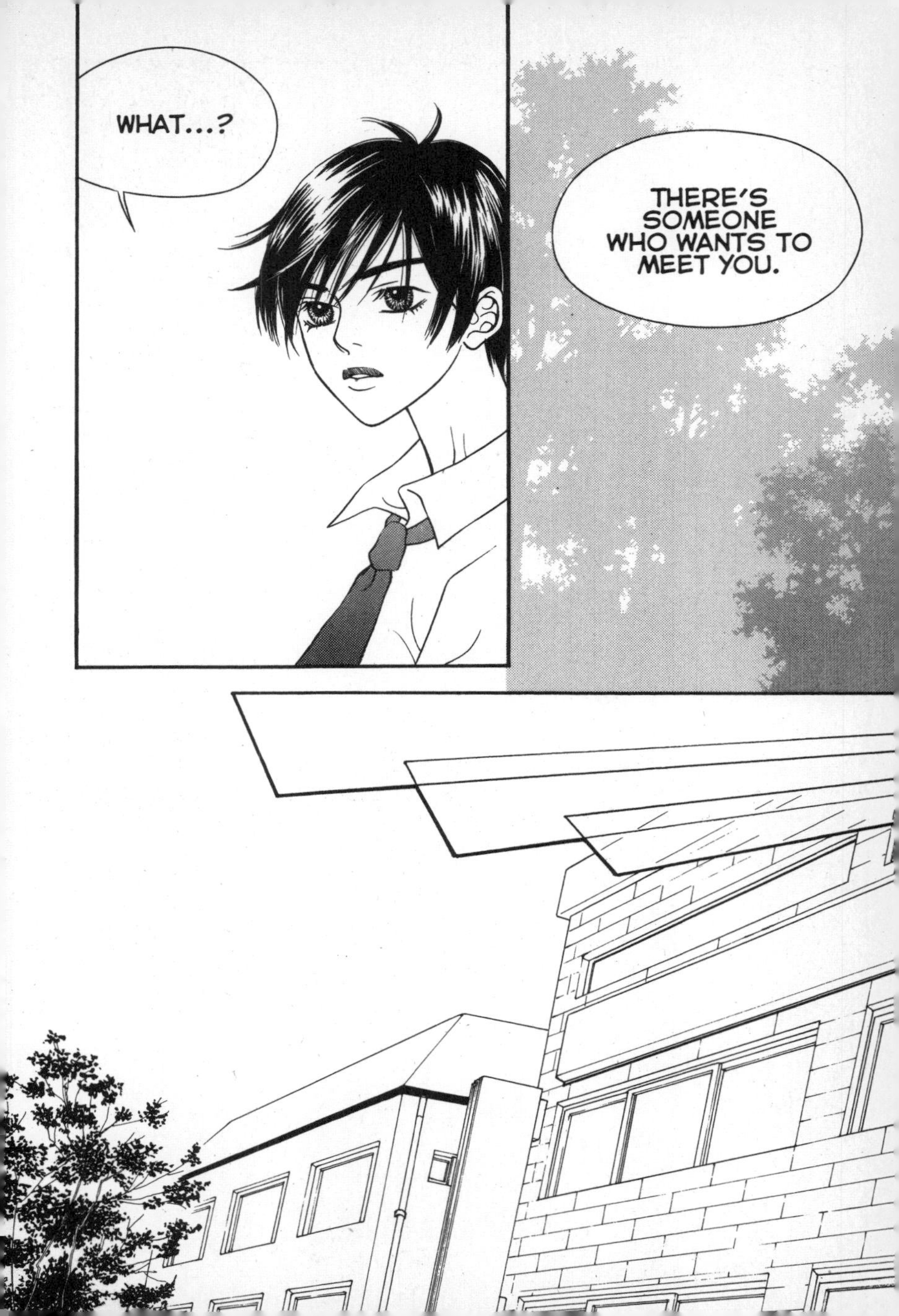
WHAT...?
THERE'S SOMEONE WHO WANTS TO MEET YOU.

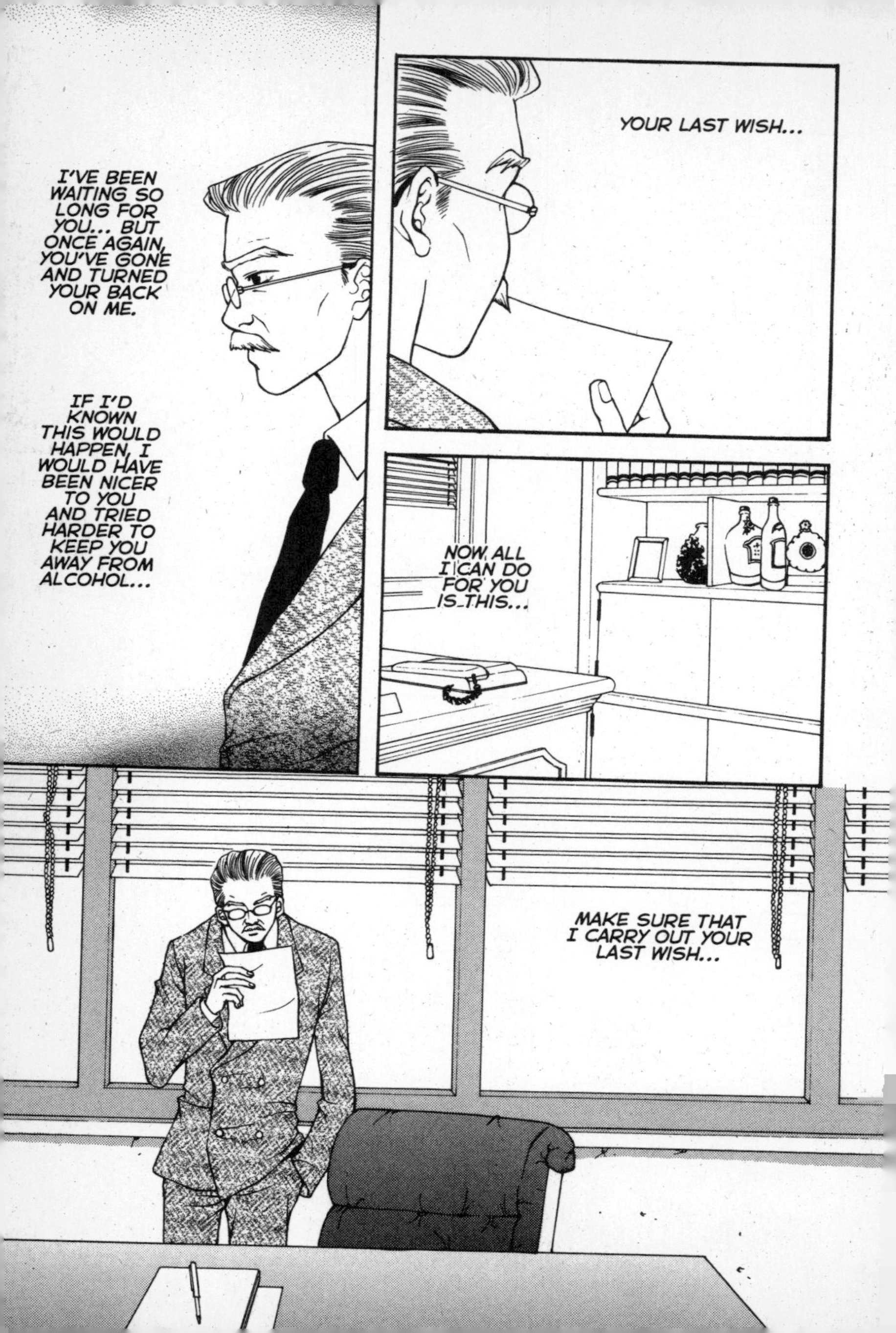
I'VE BEEN WAITING SO LONG FOR YOU... BUT ONCE AGAIN, YOU'VE GONE AND TURNED YOUR BACK ON ME.
IF I'D KNOWN THIS WOULD HAPPEN, I WOULD HAVE BEEN NICER TO YOU AND TRIED HARDER TO KEEP YOU AWAY FROM ALCOHOL...
YOUR LAST WISH...
NOW ALL I CAN DO FOR YOU IS THIS...
MAKE SURE THAT I CARRY OUT YOUR LAST WISH...

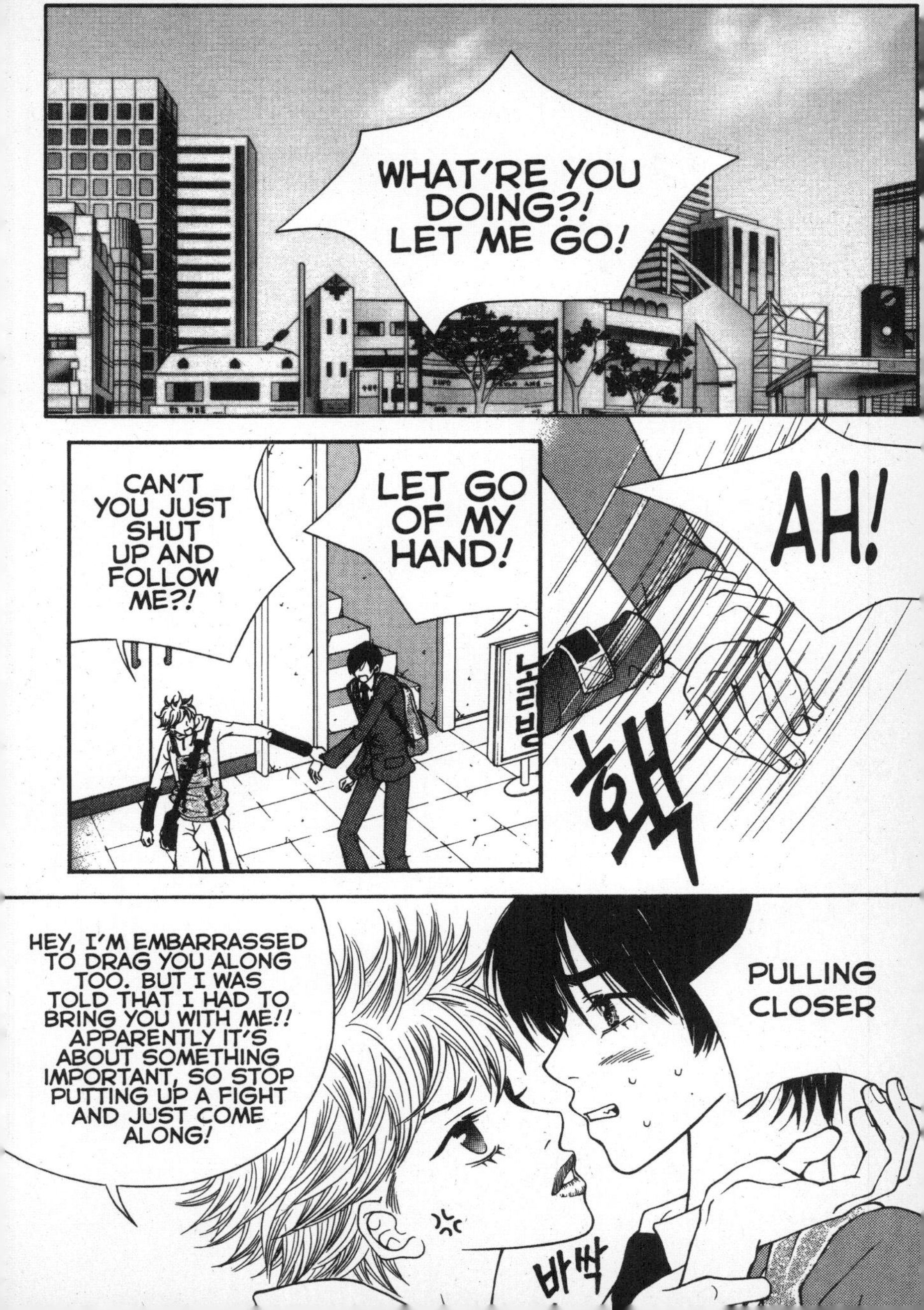
WHAT'RE YOU DOING?! LET ME GO!
CAN'T YOU JUST SHUT UP AND FOLLOW ME?!
LET GO OF MY HAND!
AH!
홱
HEY, I'M EMBARRASSED TO DRAG YOU ALONG TOO. BUT I WAS TOLD THAT I HAD TO BRING YOU WITH ME!! APPARENTLY IT'S ABOUT SOMETHING IMPORTANT, SO STOP PUTTING UP A FIGHT AND JUST COME ALONG!
PULLING CLOSER
바싹

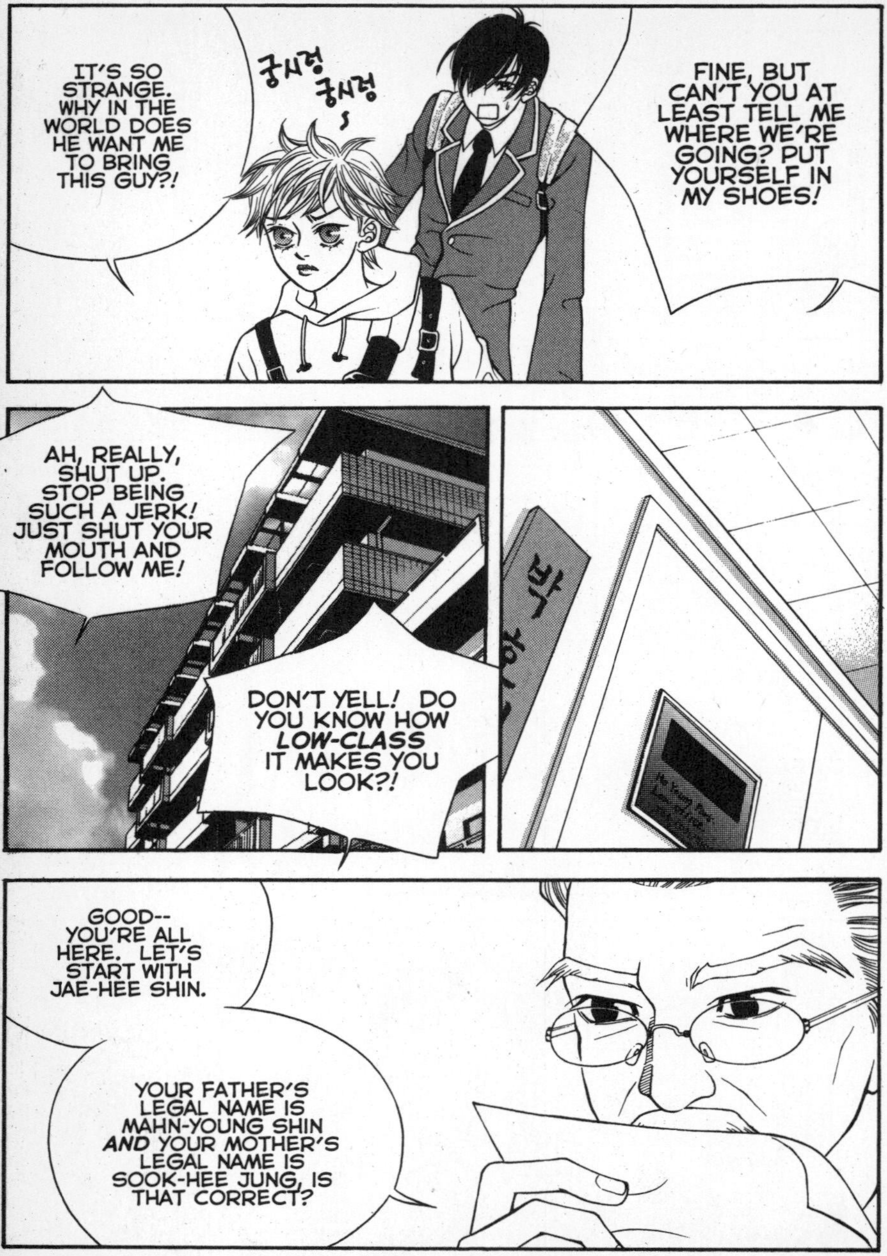
IT'S SO STRANGE. WHY IN THE WORLD DOES HE WANT ME TO BRING THIS GUY?!
궁시렁 궁시렁
FINE, BUT CAN'T YOU AT LEAST TELL ME WHERE WE'RE GOING? PUT YOURSELF IN MY SHOES!
AH, REALLY, SHUT UP. STOP BEING SUCH A JERK! JUST SHUT YOUR MOUTH AND FOLLOW ME!
DON'T YELL! DO YOU KNOW HOW *LOW-CLASS* IT MAKES YOU LOOK?!
박
GOOD-- YOU'RE ALL HERE. LET'S START WITH JAE-HEE SHIN.
YOUR FATHER'S LEGAL NAME IS MAHN-YOUNG SHIN *AND* YOUR MOTHER'S LEGAL NAME IS SOOK-HEE JUNG, IS THAT CORRECT?

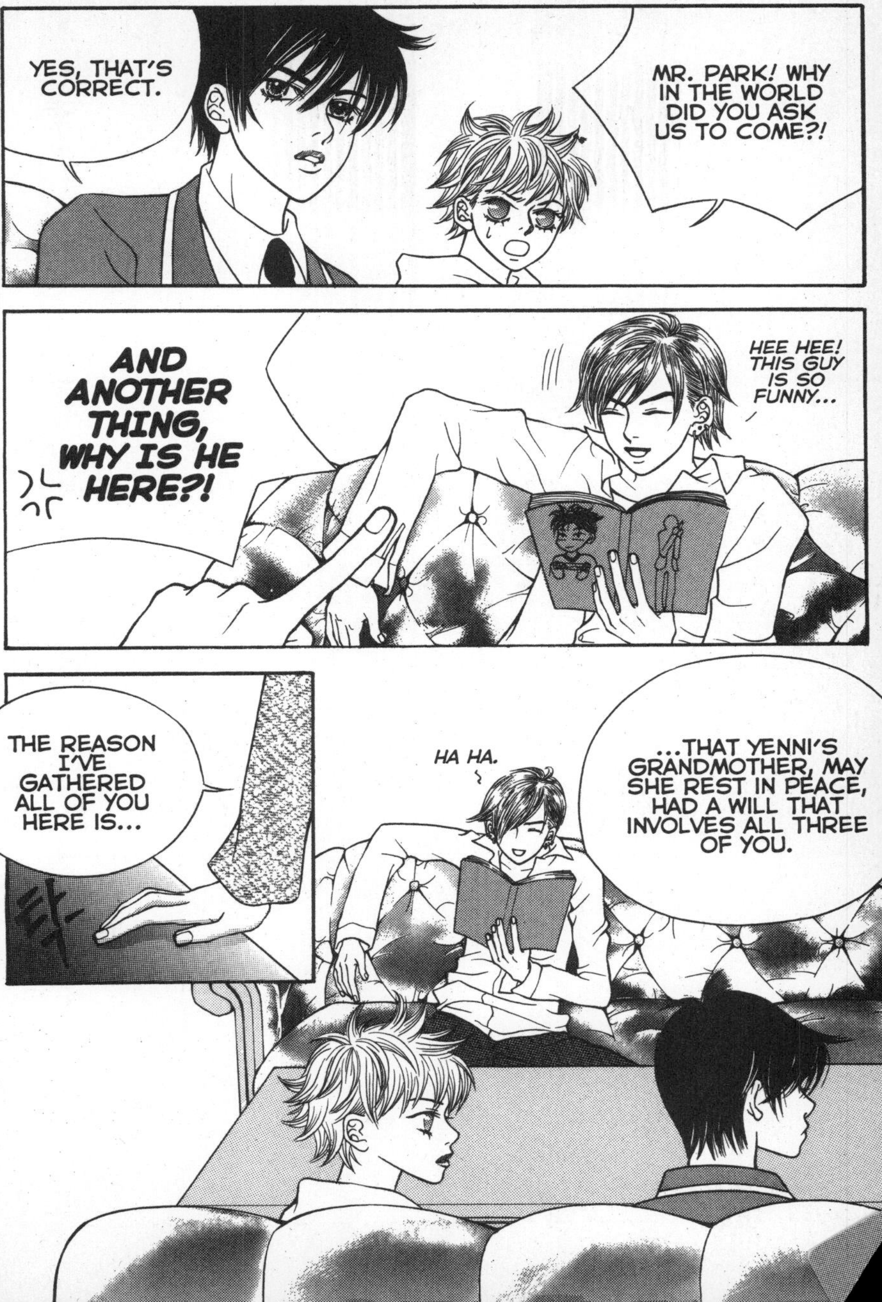
YES, THAT'S CORRECT.
MR. PARK! WHY IN THE WORLD DID YOU ASK US TO COME?!
AND ANOTHER THING, WHY IS HE HERE?!
HEE HEE! THIS GUY IS SO FUNNY...
THE REASON I'VE GATHERED ALL OF YOU HERE IS...
HA HA.
...THAT YENNI'S GRANDMOTHER, MAY SHE REST IN PEACE, HAD A WILL THAT INVOLVES ALL THREE OF YOU.

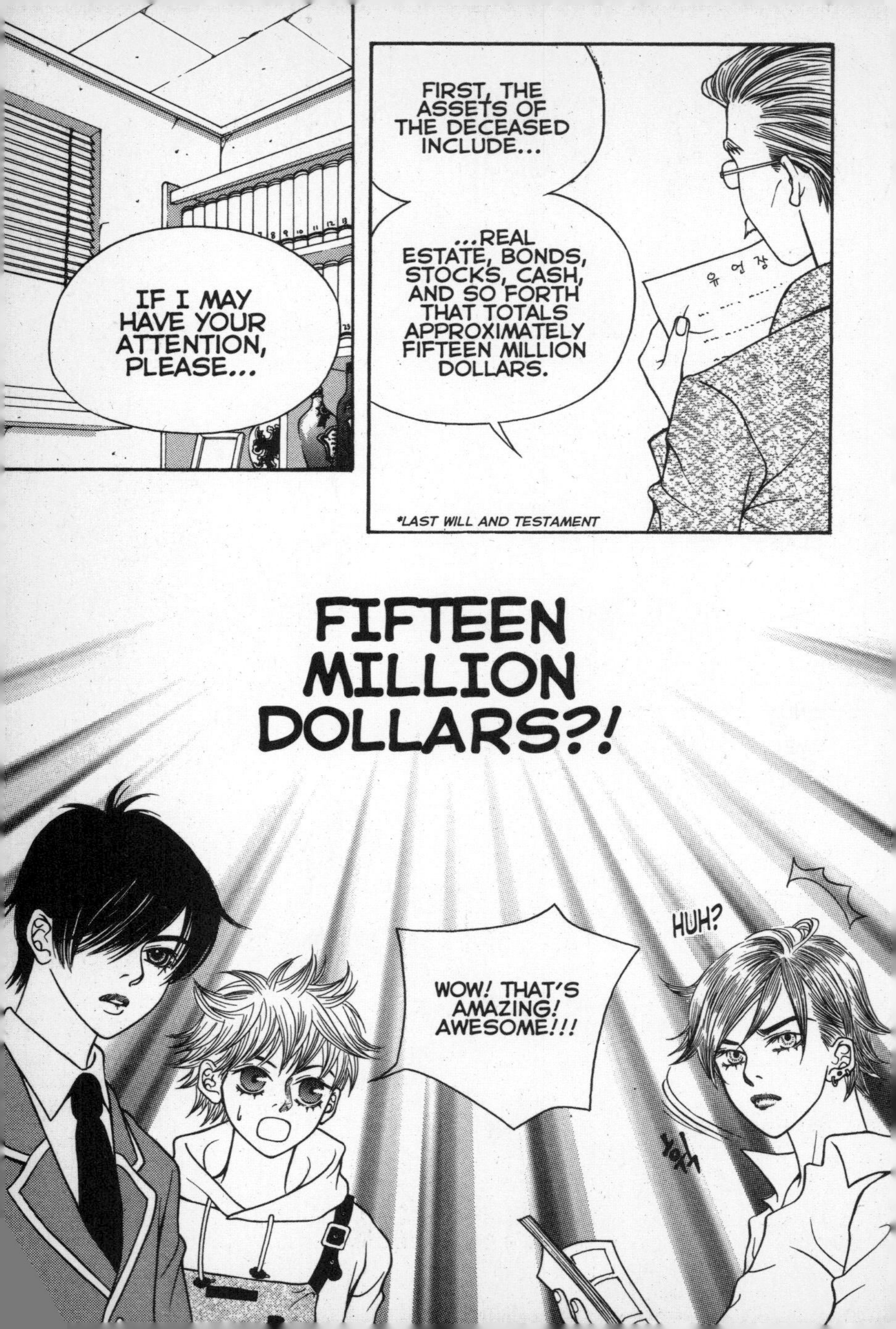
IF I MAY HAVE YOUR ATTENTION, PLEASE...
FIRST, THE ASSETS OF THE DECEASED INCLUDE...
...REAL ESTATE, BONDS, STOCKS, CASH, AND SO FORTH THAT TOTALS APPROXIMATELY FIFTEEN MILLION DOLLARS.
유언장
*LAST WILL AND TESTAMENT
FIFTEEN MILLION DOLLARS?!
WOW! THAT'S AMAZING! AWESOME!!!
HUH?

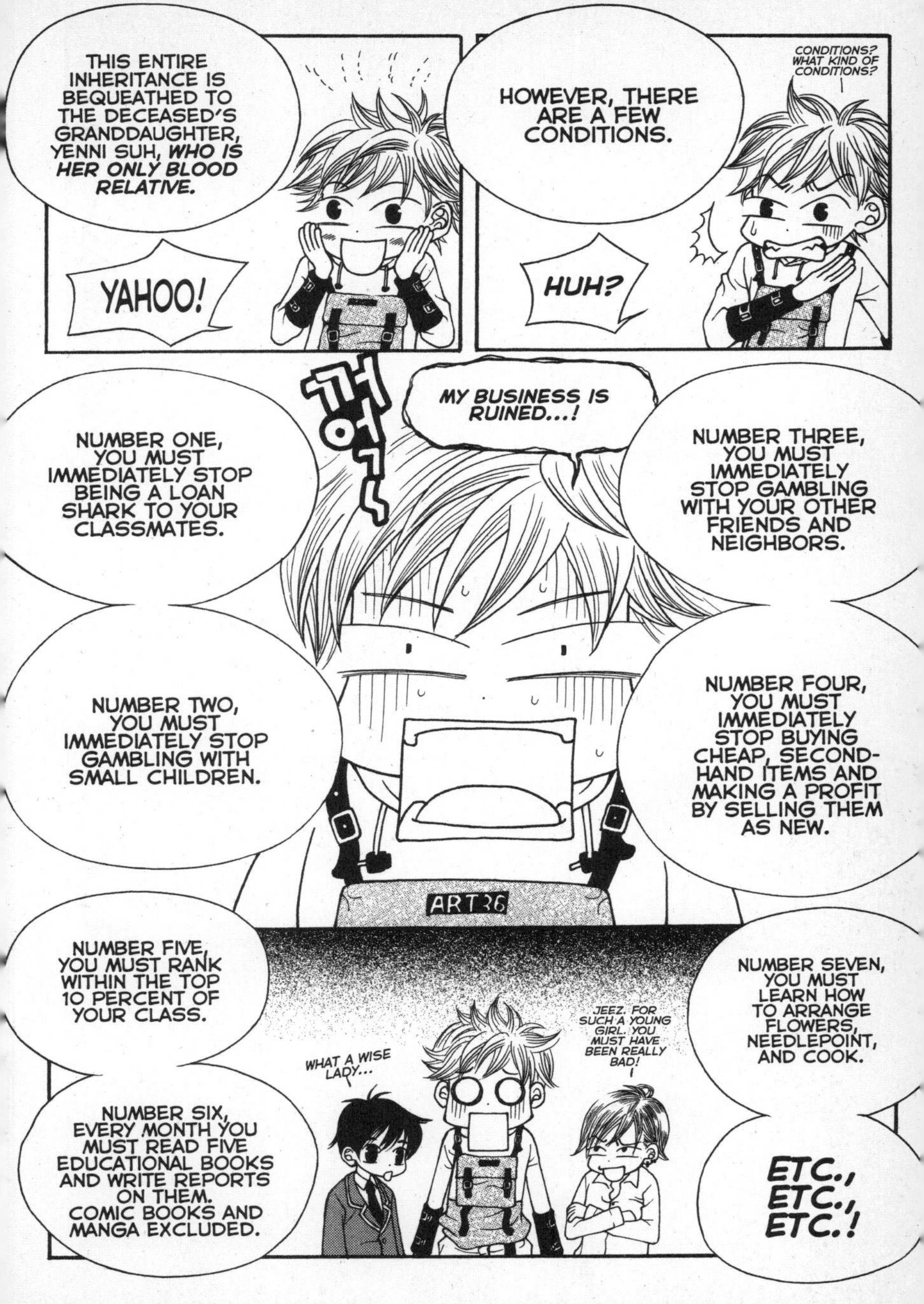
THIS ENTIRE INHERITANCE IS BEQUEATHED TO THE DECEASED'S GRANDDAUGHTER, YENNI SUH, *WHO IS HER ONLY BLOOD RELATIVE.*
YAHOO!
HOWEVER, THERE ARE A FEW CONDITIONS.
CONDITIONS? WHAT KIND OF CONDITIONS?
HUH?
NUMBER ONE, YOU MUST IMMEDIATELY STOP BEING A LOAN SHARK TO YOUR CLASSMATES.
NUMBER TWO, YOU MUST IMMEDIATELY STOP GAMBLING WITH SMALL CHILDREN.
NUMBER THREE, YOU MUST IMMEDIATELY STOP GAMBLING WITH YOUR OTHER FRIENDS AND NEIGHBORS.
NUMBER FOUR, YOU MUST IMMEDIATELY STOP BUYING CHEAP, SECOND-HAND ITEMS AND MAKING A PROFIT BY SELLING THEM AS NEW.
MY BUSINESS IS RUINED...!
ART36
NUMBER FIVE, YOU MUST RANK WITHIN THE TOP 10 PERCENT OF YOUR CLASS.
NUMBER SIX, EVERY MONTH YOU MUST READ FIVE EDUCATIONAL BOOKS AND WRITE REPORTS ON THEM. COMIC BOOKS AND MANGA EXCLUDED.
WHAT A WISE LADY...
JEEZ. FOR SUCH A YOUNG GIRL, YOU MUST HAVE BEEN REALLY BAD!
NUMBER SEVEN, YOU MUST LEARN HOW TO ARRANGE FLOWERS, NEEDLEPOINT, AND COOK.
ETC., ETC., ETC.!

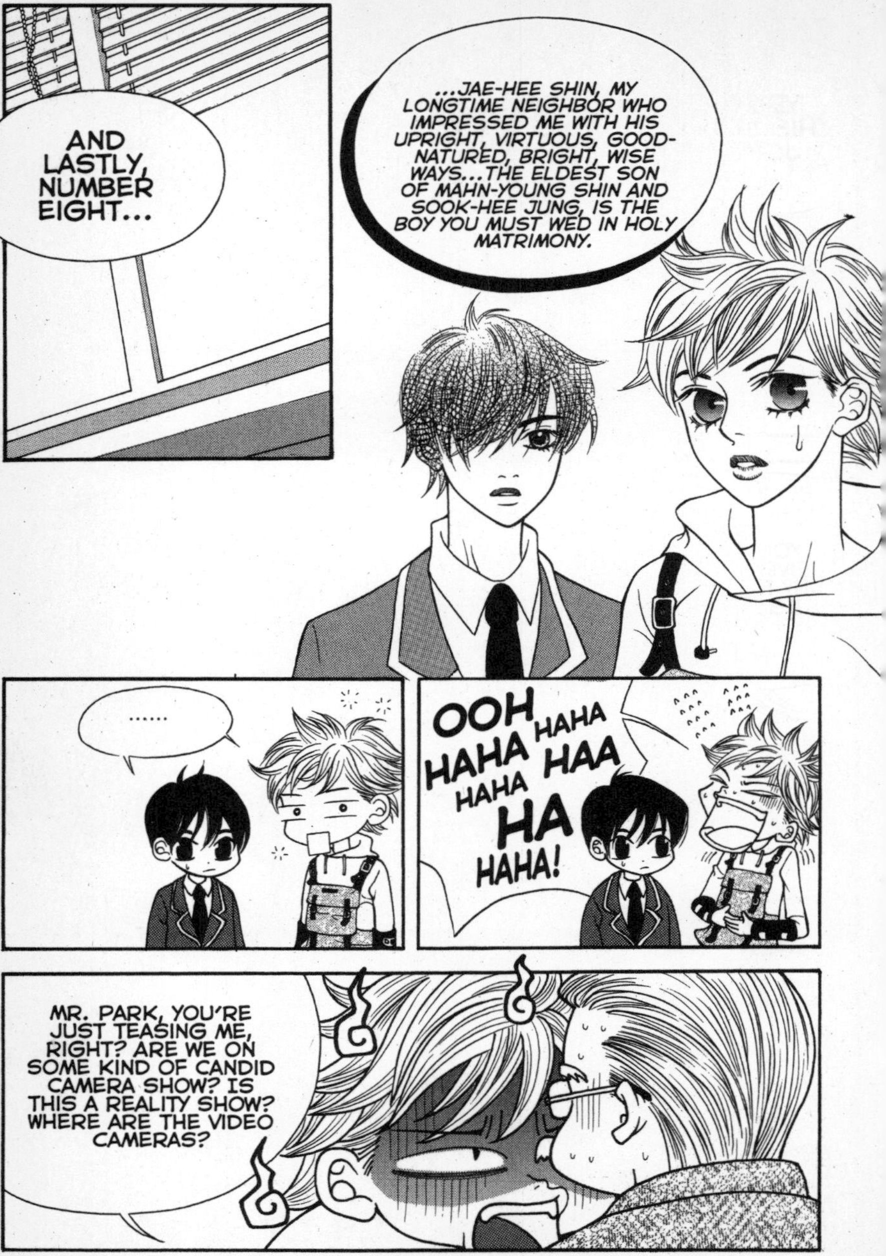
AND LASTLY, NUMBER EIGHT...
...JAE-HEE SHIN, MY LONGTIME NEIGHBOR WHO IMPRESSED ME WITH HIS UPRIGHT, VIRTUOUS, GOOD-NATURED, BRIGHT, WISE WAYS...THE ELDEST SON OF MAHN-YOUNG SHIN AND SOOK-HEE JUNG, IS THE BOY YOU MUST WED IN HOLY MATRIMONY.
......
OOH HAHA HAHA HAHA HAA HA HAHA!
MR. PARK, YOU'RE JUST TEASING ME, RIGHT? ARE WE ON SOME KIND OF CANDID CAMERA SHOW? IS THIS A REALITY SHOW? WHERE ARE THE VIDEO CAMERAS?

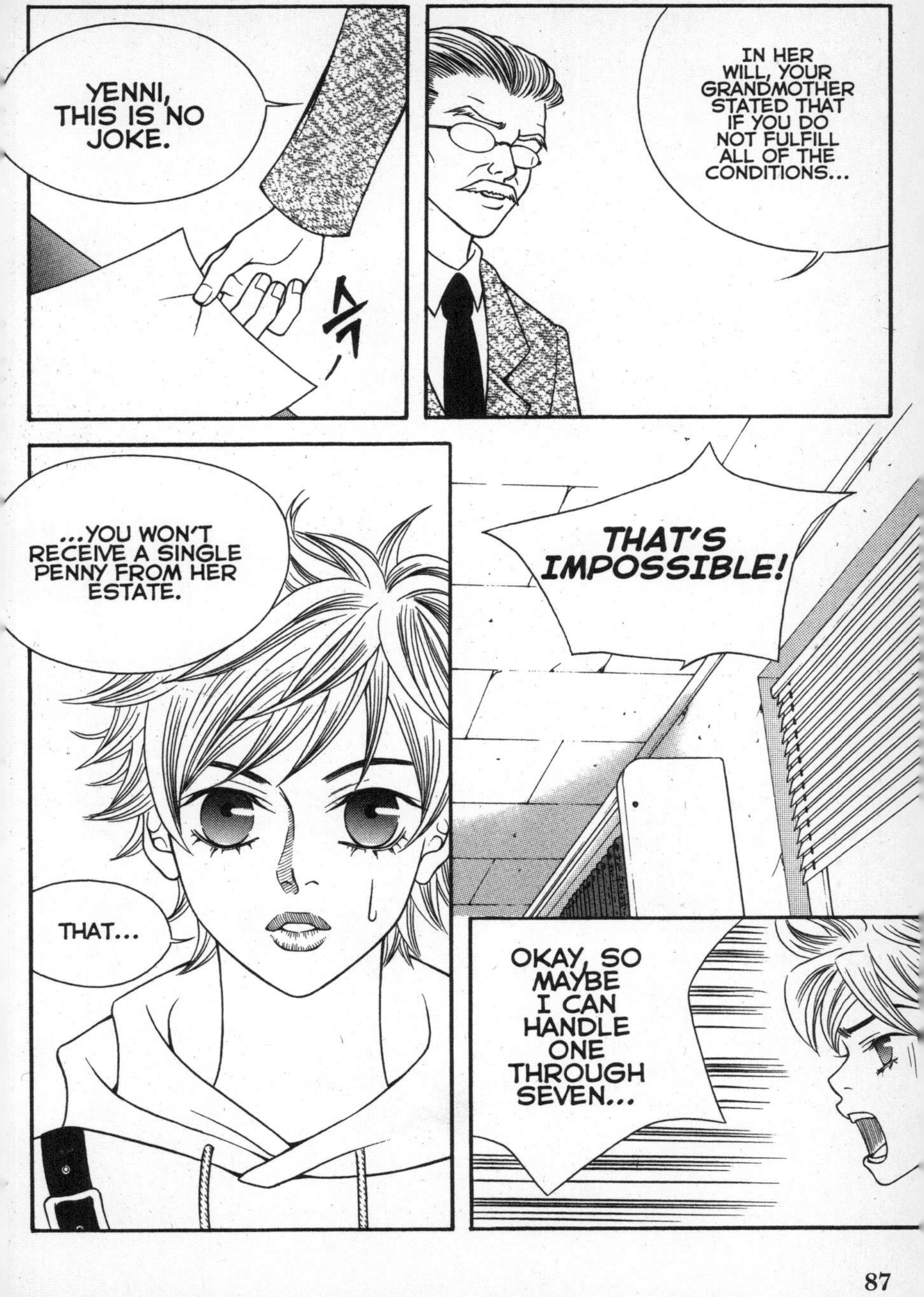
YENNI, THIS IS NO JOKE.
IN HER WILL, YOUR GRANDMOTHER STATED THAT IF YOU DO NOT FULFILL ALL OF THE CONDITIONS...
...YOU WON'T RECEIVE A SINGLE PENNY FROM HER ESTATE.
THAT...
THAT'S IMPOSSIBLE!
OKAY, SO MAYBE I CAN HANDLE ONE THROUGH SEVEN...

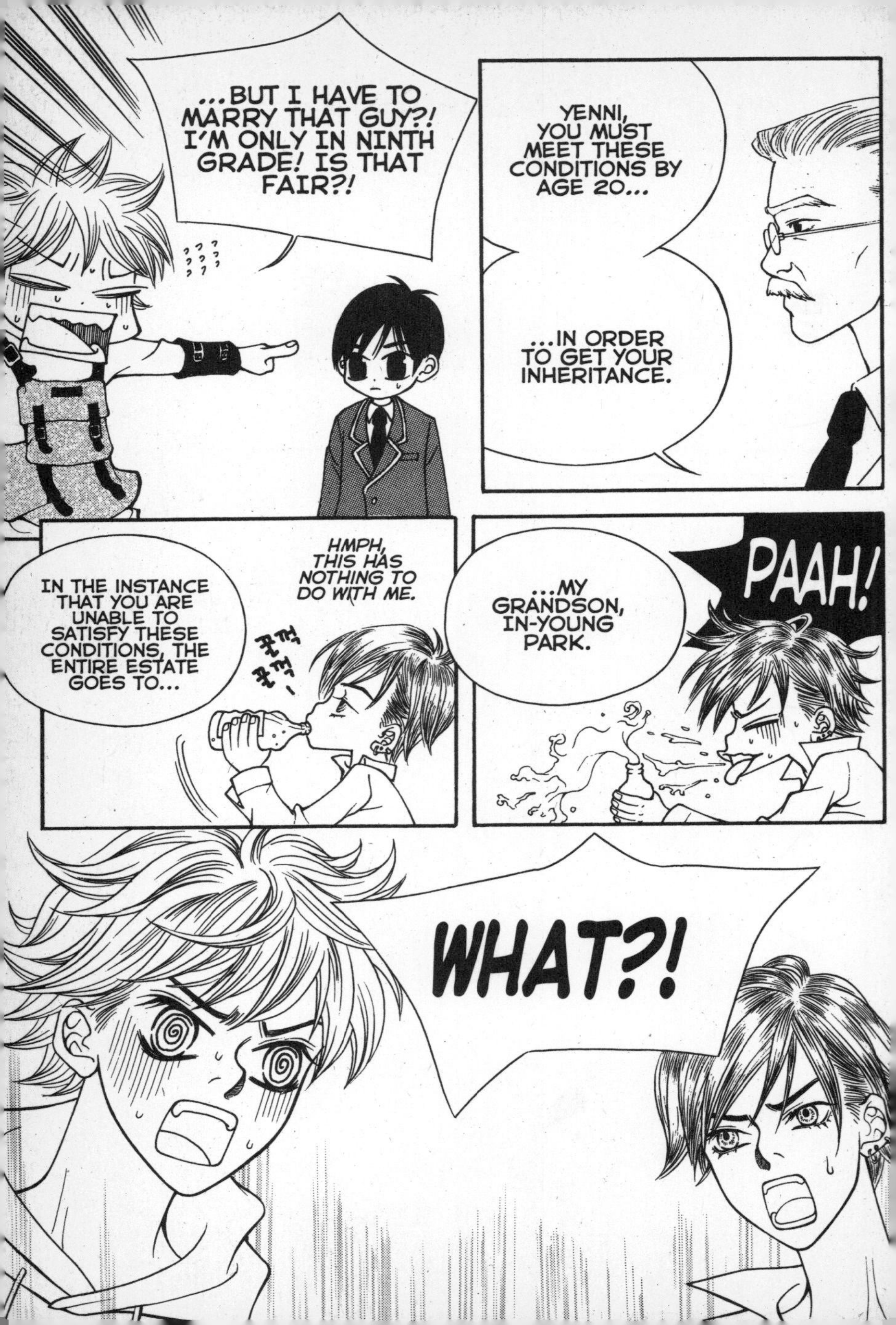
...BUT I HAVE TO MARRY THAT GUY?! I'M ONLY IN NINTH GRADE! IS THAT FAIR?!
YENNI, YOU MUST MEET THESE CONDITIONS BY AGE 20...
...IN ORDER TO GET YOUR INHERITANCE.
IN THE INSTANCE THAT YOU ARE UNABLE TO SATISFY THESE CONDITIONS, THE ENTIRE ESTATE GOES TO...
HMPH, THIS HAS NOTHING TO DO WITH ME.
꿀꺽 꿀꺽
...MY GRANDSON, IN-YOUNG PARK.
PAAH!
WHAT?!

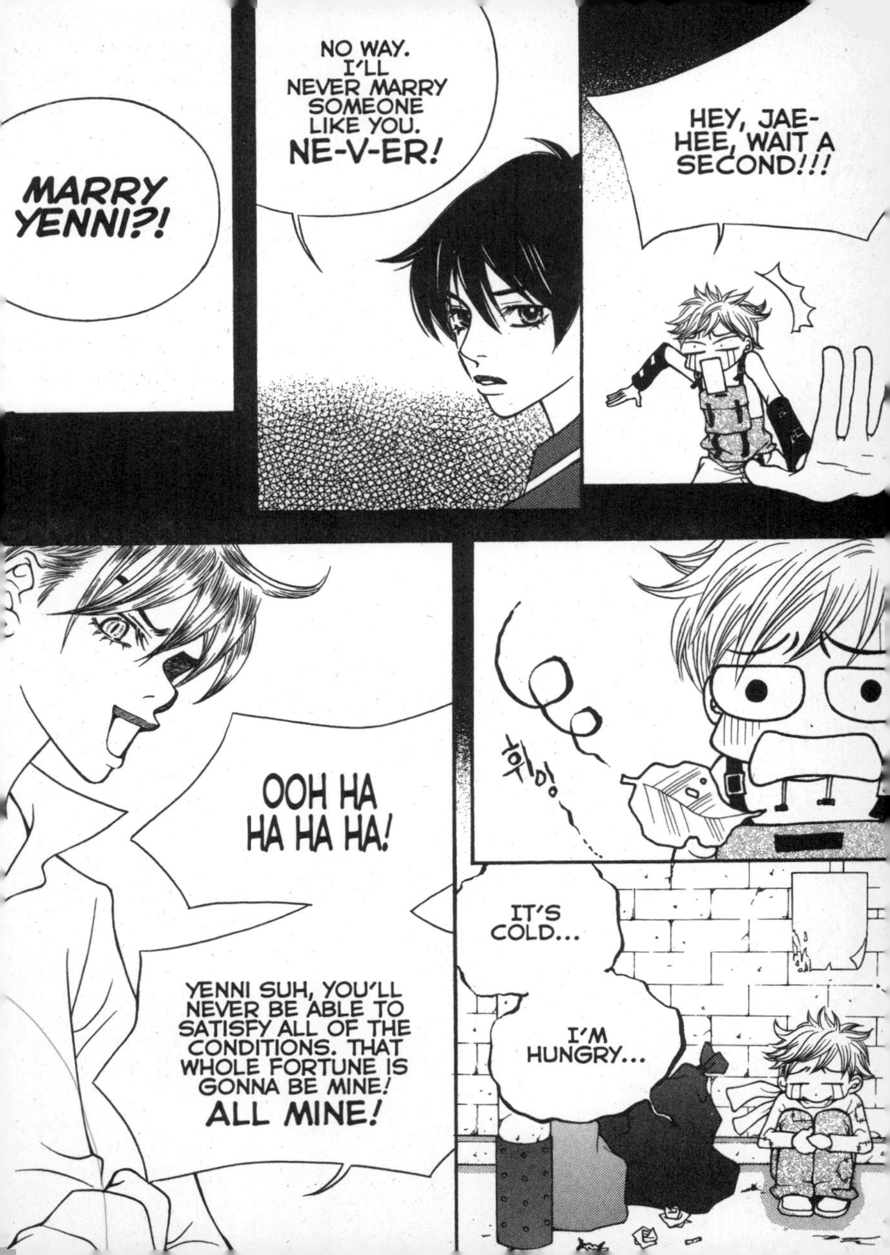
MARRY YENNI?!
NO WAY. I'LL NEVER MARRY SOMEONE LIKE YOU. NE-V-ER!
HEY, JAE-HEE, WAIT A SECOND!!!
OOH HA HA HA HA!
YENNI SUH, YOU'LL NEVER BE ABLE TO SATISFY ALL OF THE CONDITIONS. THAT WHOLE FORTUNE IS GONNA BE MINE! ALL MINE!
휘잉
IT'S COLD...
I'M HUNGRY...

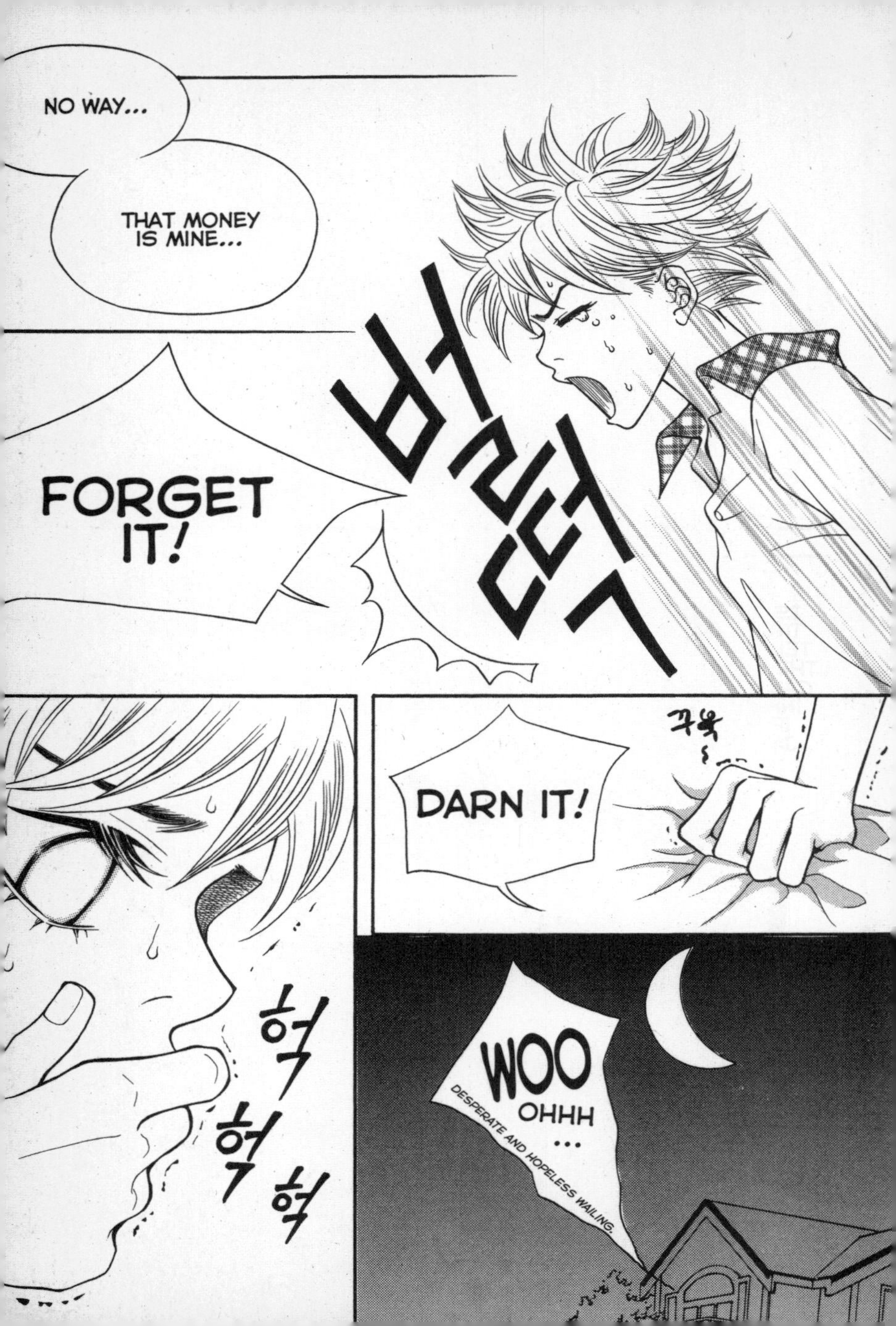
NO WAY...
THAT MONEY IS MINE...
FORGET IT!
벌떡
헉
헉
헉
DARN IT!
WOO OHHH ...
DESPERATE AND HOPELESS WAILING.

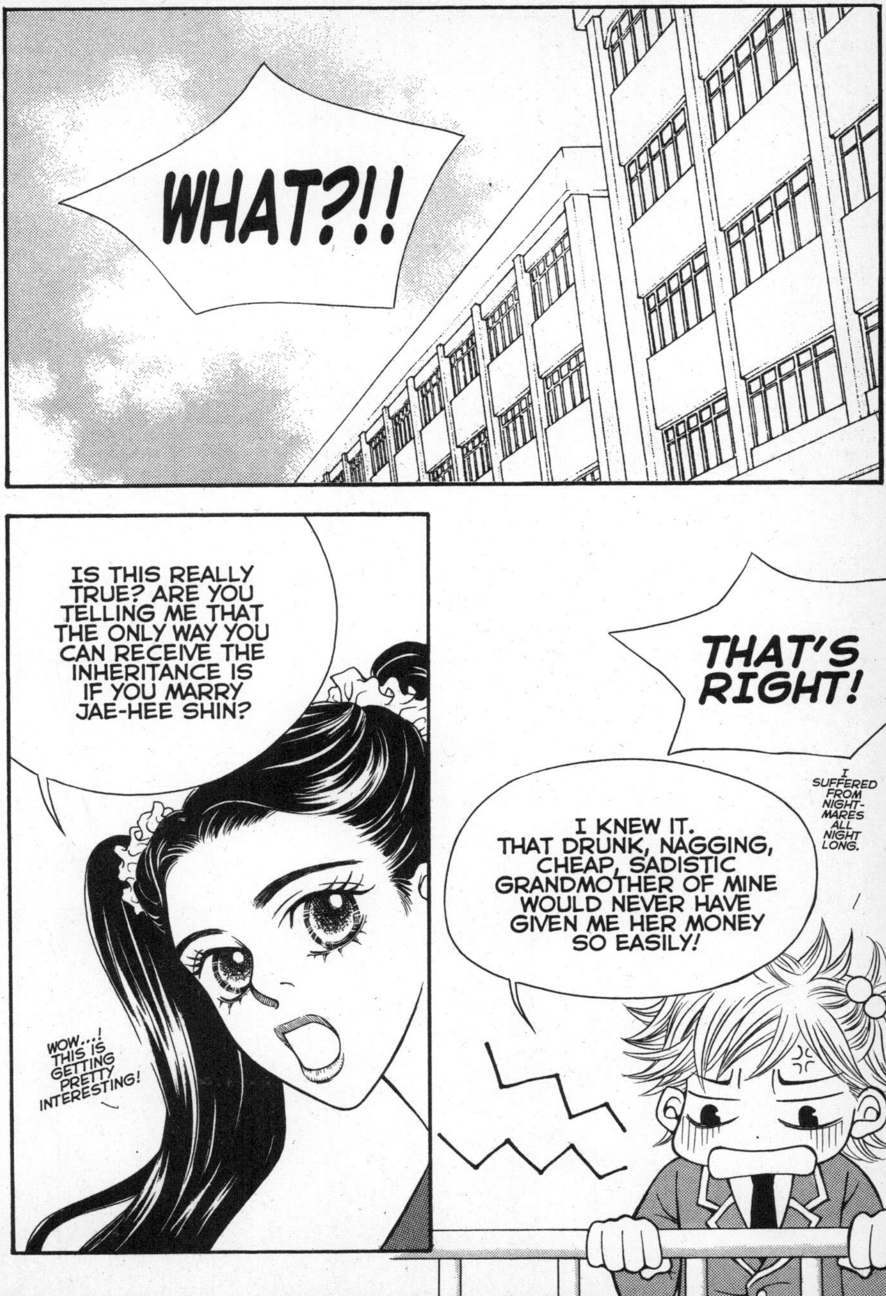
WHAT?!!
IS THIS REALLY TRUE? ARE YOU TELLING ME THAT THE ONLY WAY YOU CAN RECEIVE THE INHERITANCE IS IF YOU MARRY JAE-HEE SHIN?
WOW...! THIS IS GETTING PRETTY INTERESTING!
THAT'S RIGHT!
I KNEW IT. THAT DRUNK, NAGGING, CHEAP, SADISTIC GRANDMOTHER OF MINE WOULD NEVER HAVE GIVEN ME HER MONEY SO EASILY!
I SUFFERED FROM NIGHT-MARES ALL NIGHT LONG.

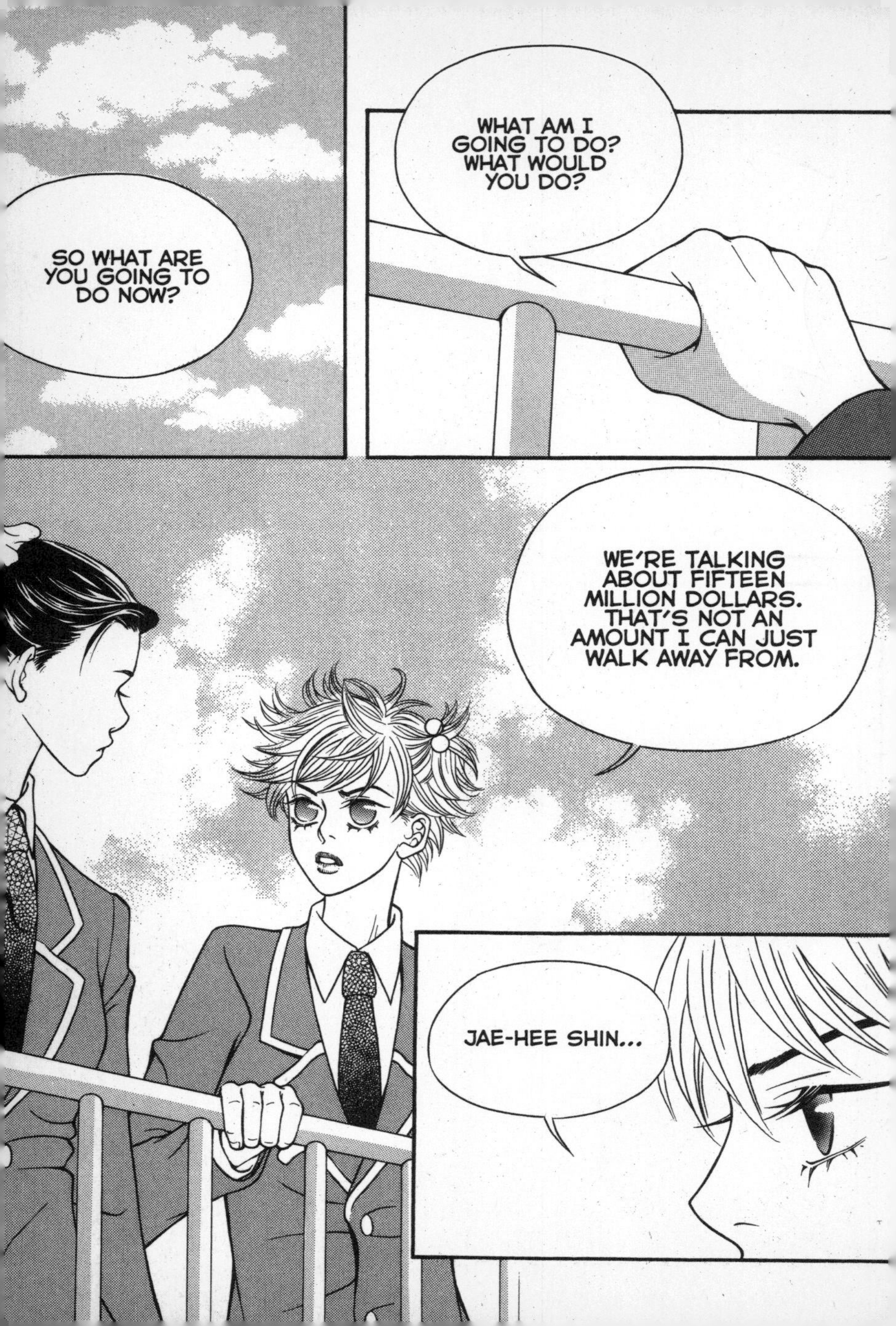
SO WHAT ARE YOU GOING TO DO NOW?
WHAT AM I GOING TO DO? WHAT WOULD YOU DO?
WE'RE TALKING ABOUT FIFTEEN MILLION DOLLARS. THAT'S NOT AN AMOUNT I CAN JUST WALK AWAY FROM.
JAE-HEE SHIN...

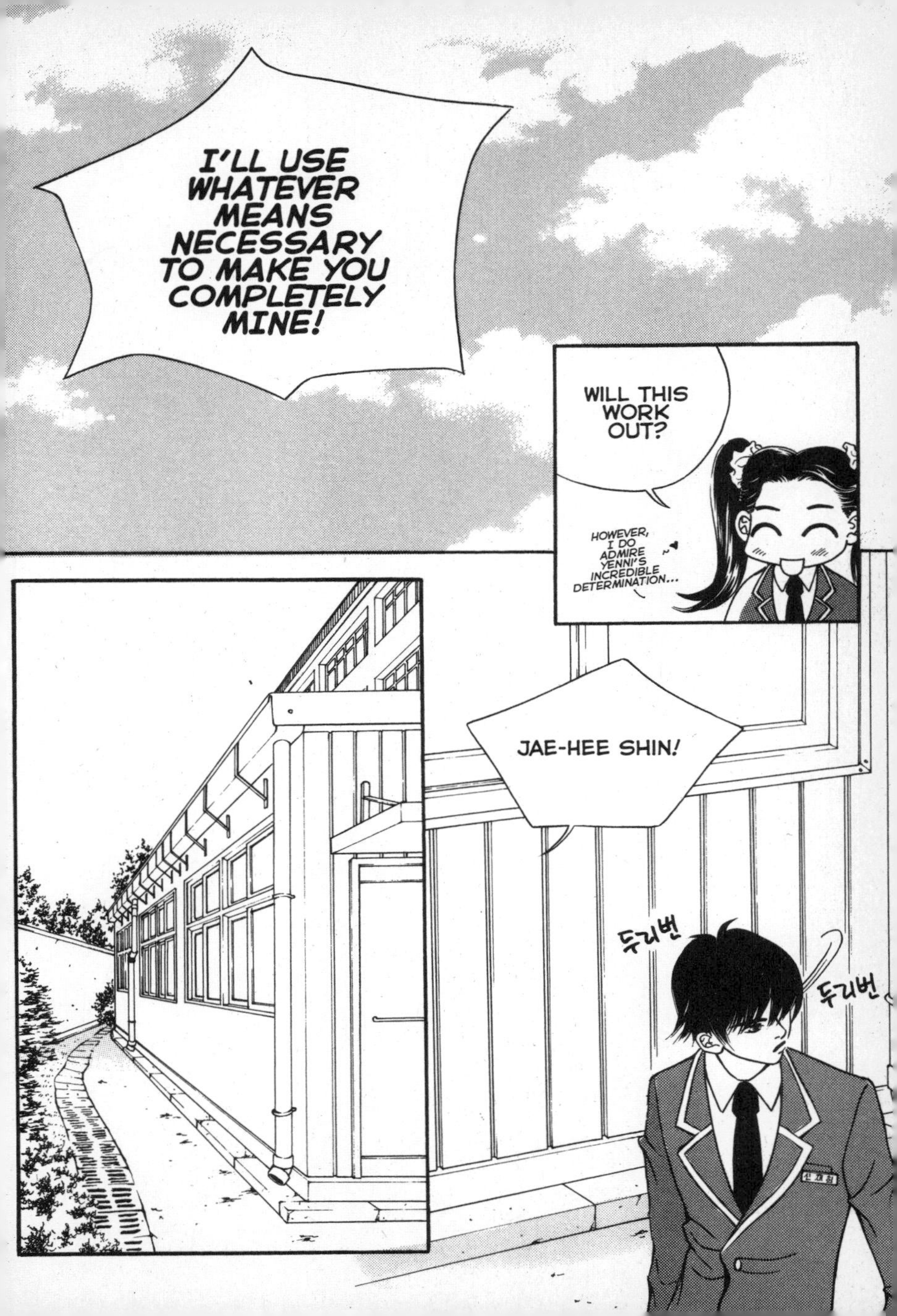
I'LL USE WHATEVER MEANS NECESSARY TO MAKE YOU COMPLETELY MINE!
WILL THIS WORK OUT?
HOWEVER, I DO ADMIRE YENNI'S INCREDIBLE DETERMINATION...
JAE-HEE SHIN!
두리번
두리번

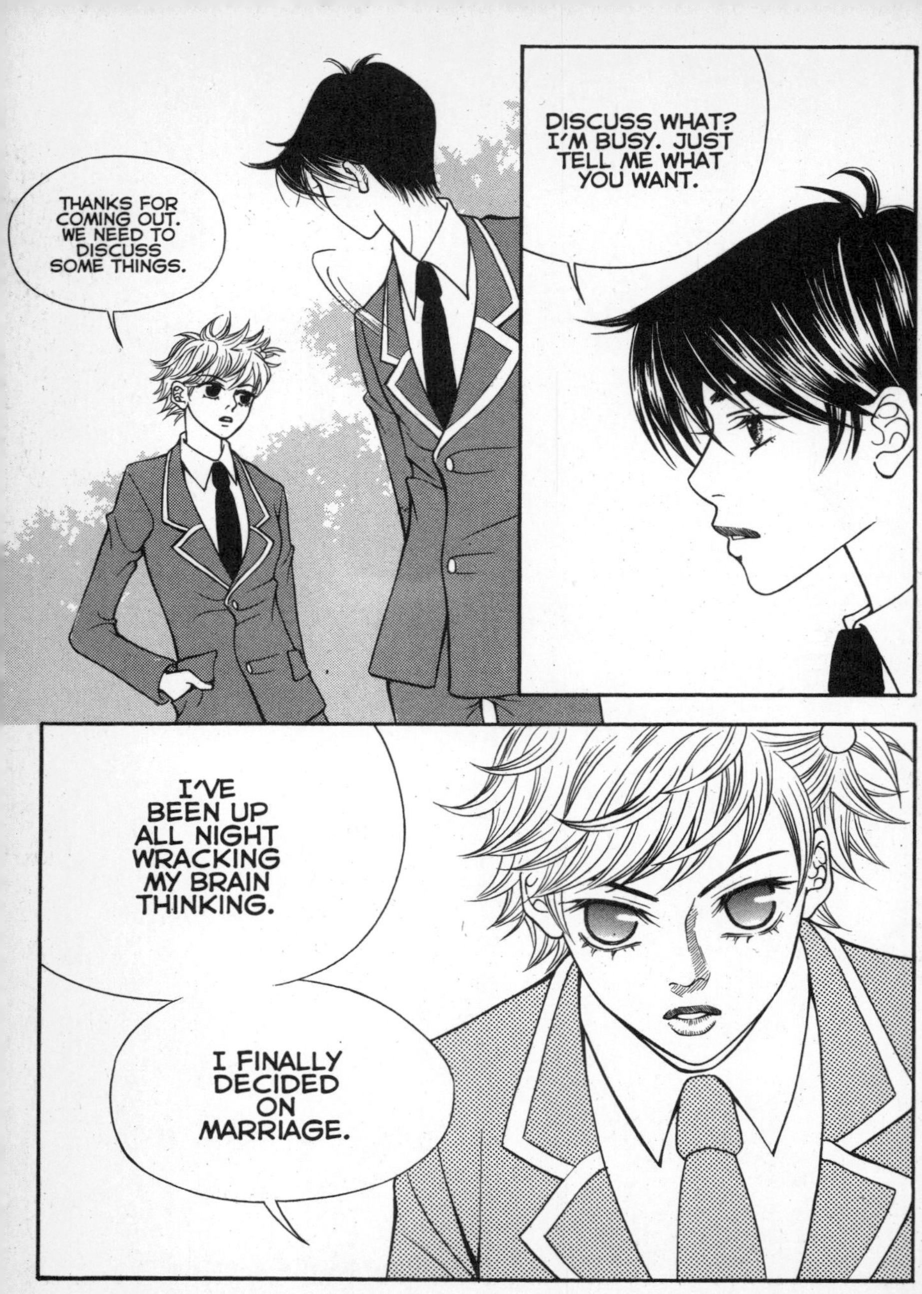
THANKS FOR COMING OUT. WE NEED TO DISCUSS SOME THINGS.
DISCUSS WHAT? I'M BUSY. JUST TELL ME WHAT YOU WANT.
I'VE BEEN UP ALL NIGHT WRACKING MY BRAIN THINKING.
I FINALLY DECIDED ON MARRIAGE.

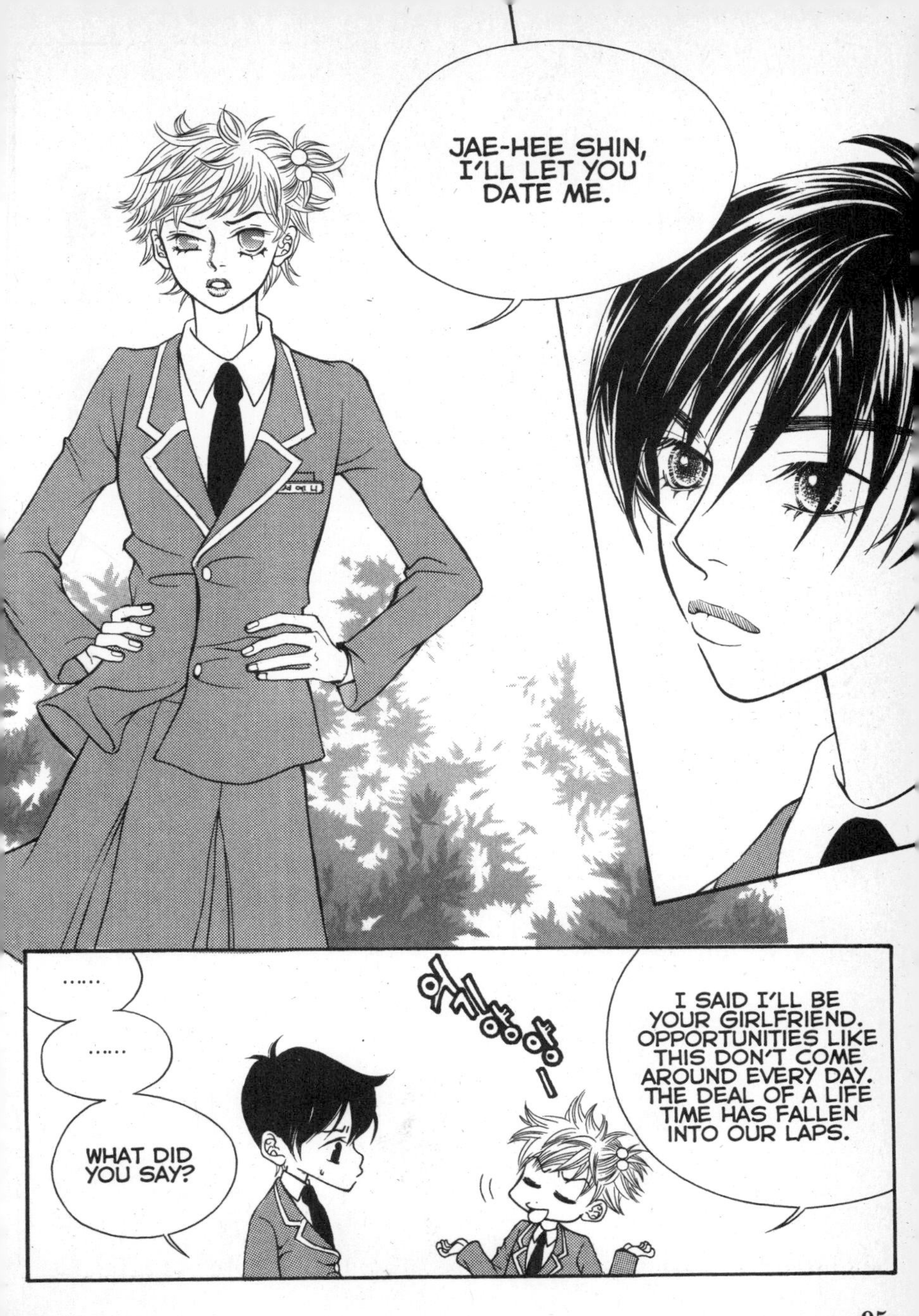
JAE-HEE SHIN, I'LL LET YOU DATE ME.
……
……
WHAT DID YOU SAY?
I SAID I'LL BE YOUR GIRLFRIEND. OPPORTUNITIES LIKE THIS DON'T COME AROUND EVERY DAY. THE DEAL OF A LIFE TIME HAS FALLEN INTO OUR LAPS.

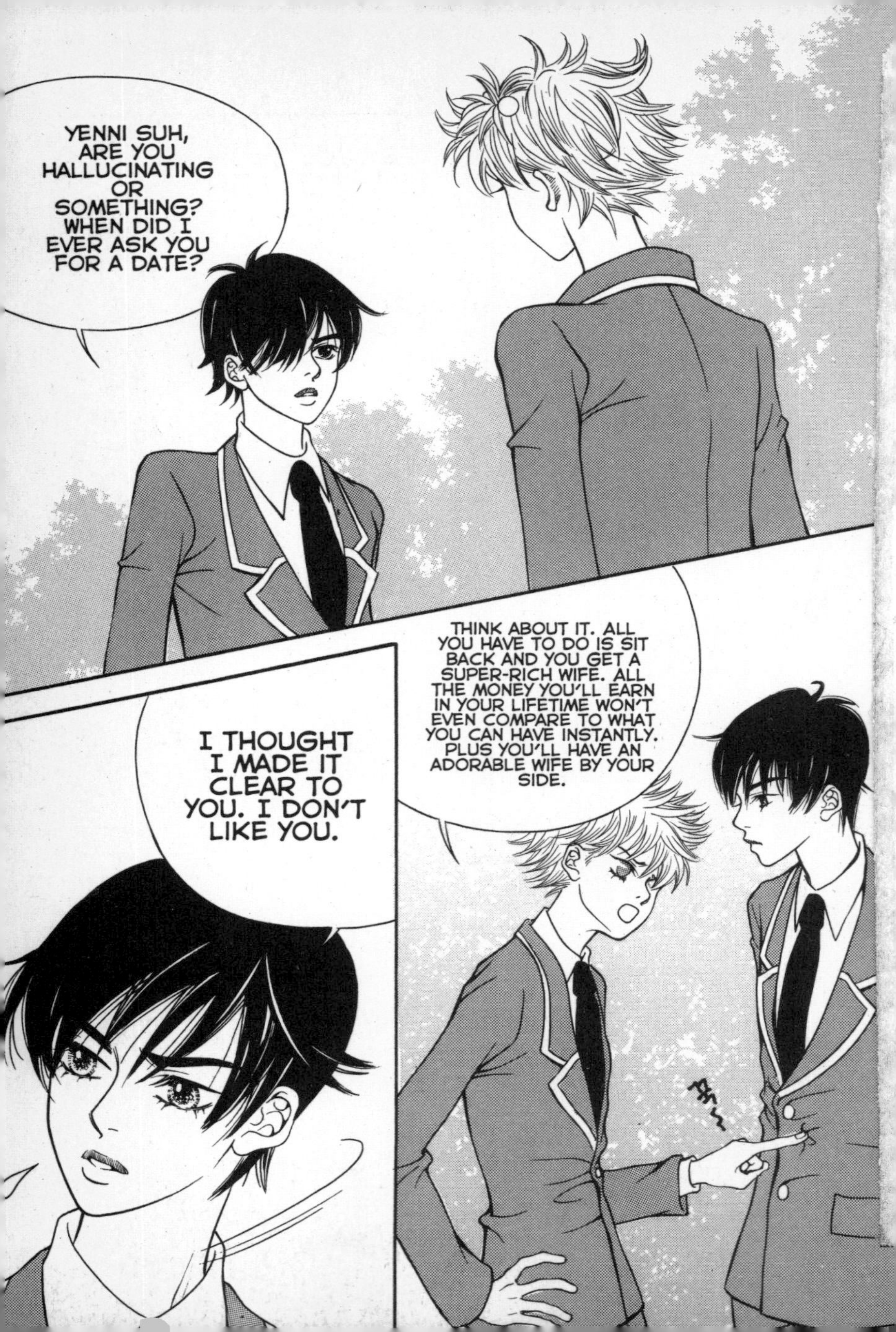
YENNI SUH, ARE YOU HALLUCINATING OR SOMETHING? WHEN DID I EVER ASK YOU FOR A DATE?
I THOUGHT I MADE IT CLEAR TO YOU. I DON'T LIKE YOU.
THINK ABOUT IT. ALL YOU HAVE TO DO IS SIT BACK AND YOU GET A SUPER-RICH WIFE. ALL THE MONEY YOU'LL EARN IN YOUR LIFETIME WON'T EVEN COMPARE TO WHAT YOU CAN HAVE INSTANTLY. PLUS YOU'LL HAVE AN ADORABLE WIFE BY YOUR SIDE.

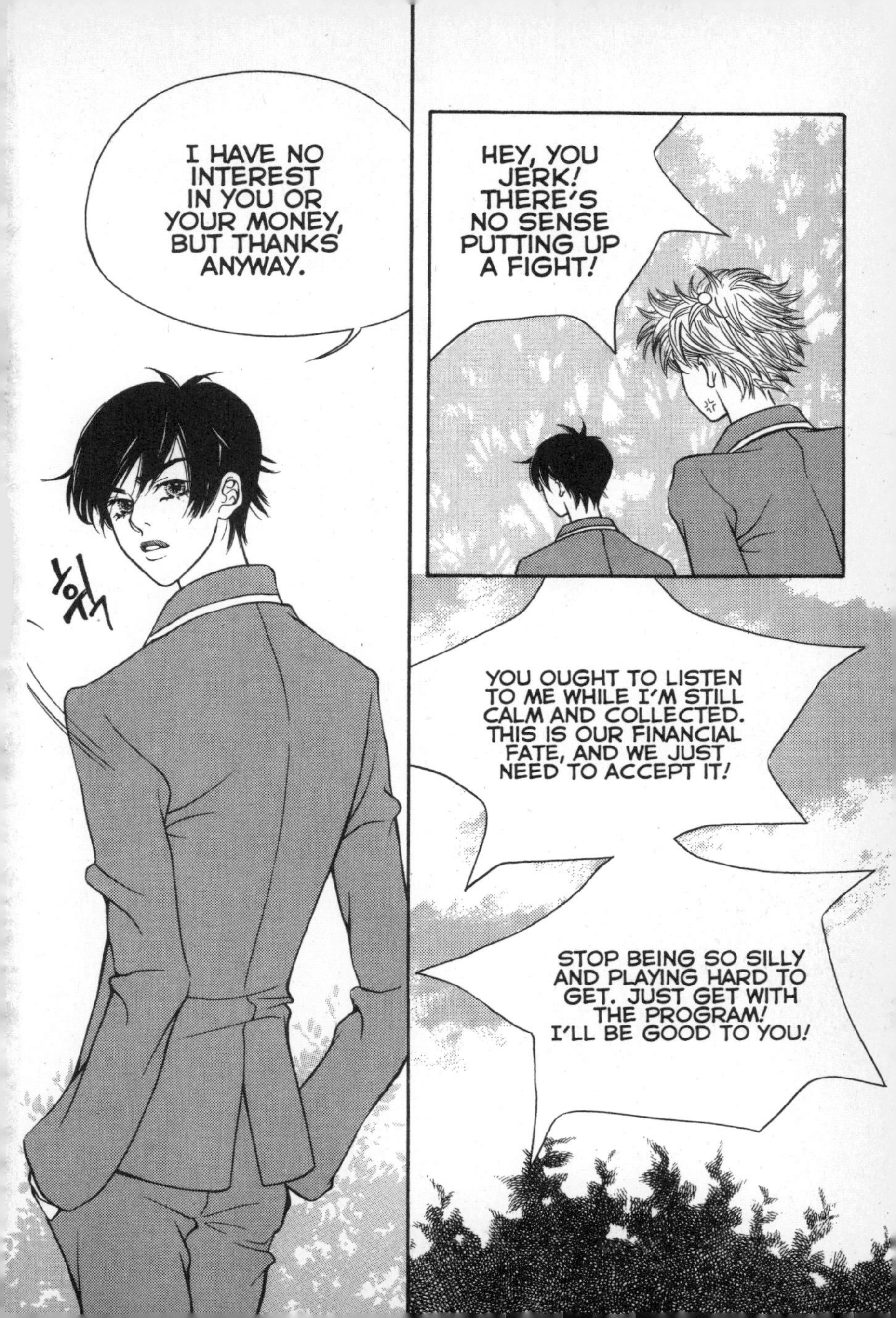
I HAVE NO INTEREST IN YOU OR YOUR MONEY, BUT THANKS ANYWAY.
HEY, YOU JERK! THERE'S NO SENSE PUTTING UP A FIGHT!
YOU OUGHT TO LISTEN TO ME WHILE I'M STILL CALM AND COLLECTED. THIS IS OUR FINANCIAL FATE, AND WE JUST NEED TO ACCEPT IT!
STOP BEING SO SILLY AND PLAYING HARD TO GET. JUST GET WITH THE PROGRAM! I'LL BE GOOD TO YOU!

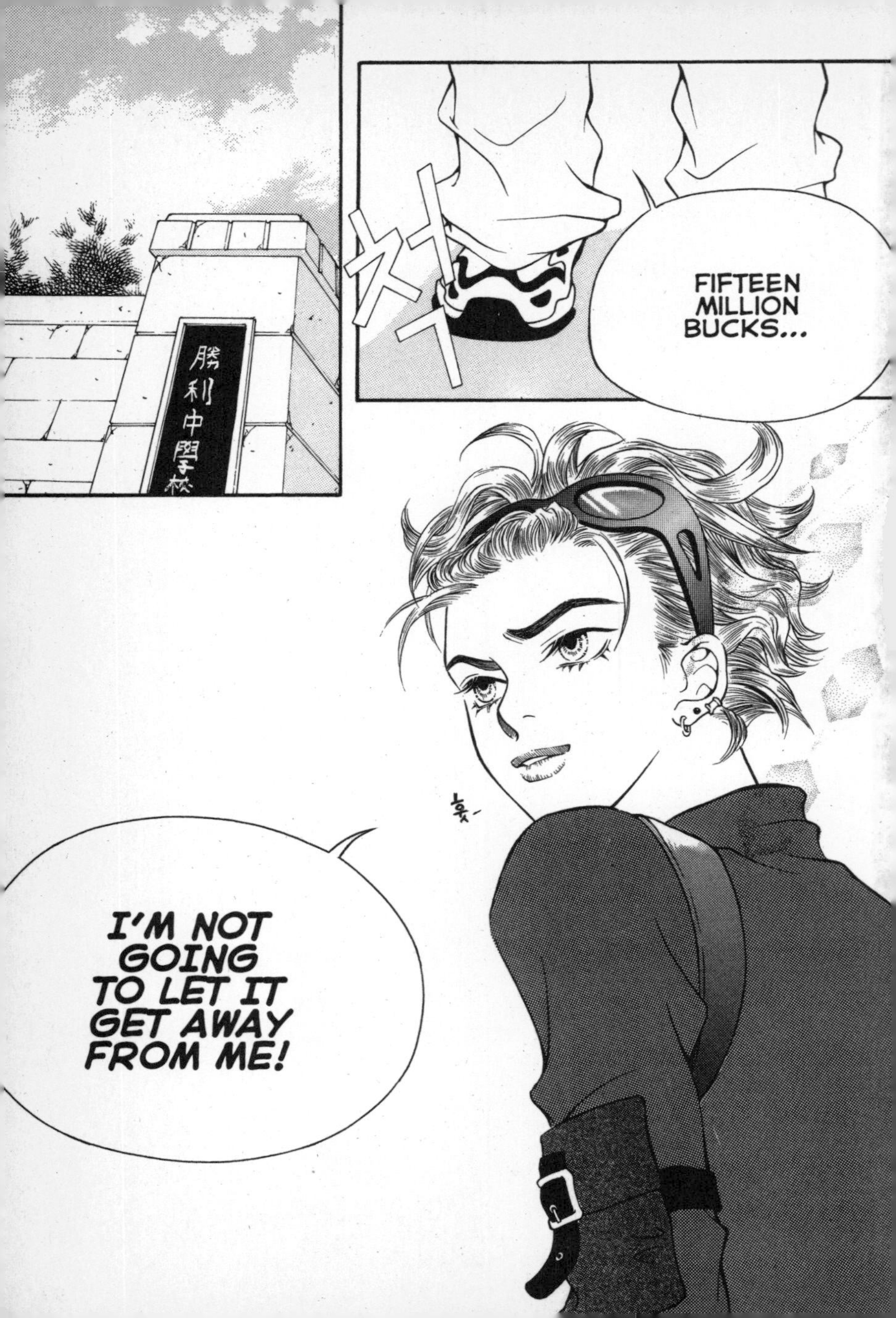
勝利中學校
FIFTEEN MILLION BUCKS...
I'M NOT GOING TO LET IT GET AWAY FROM ME!

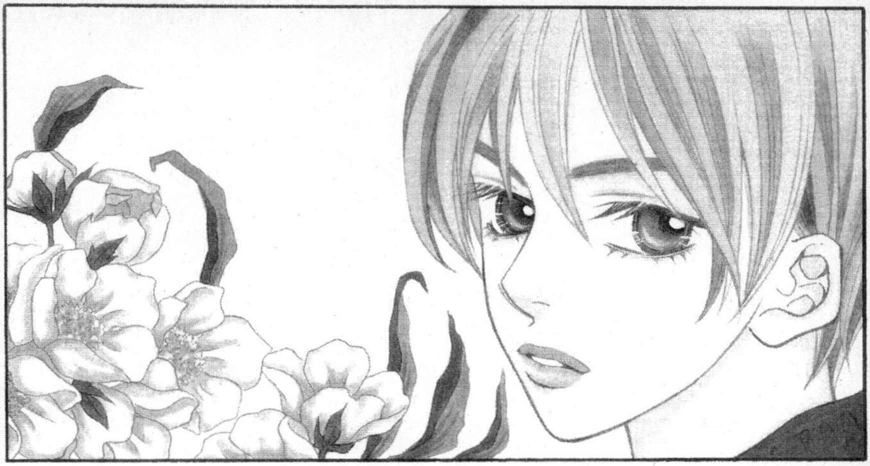
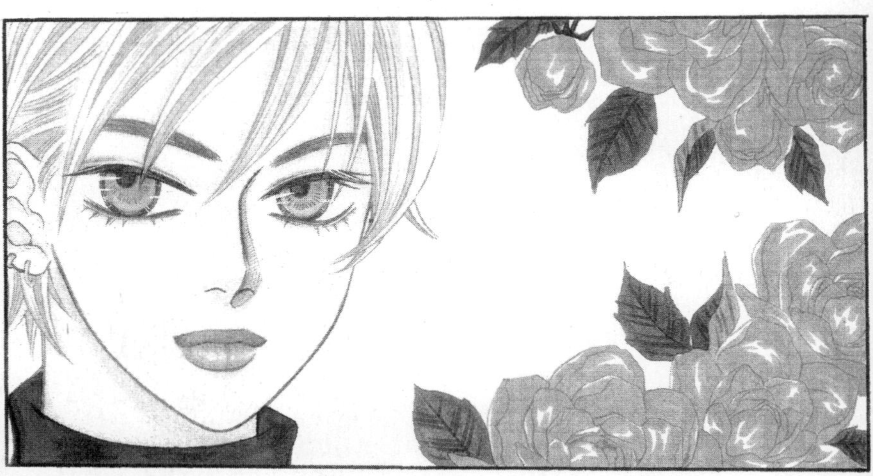

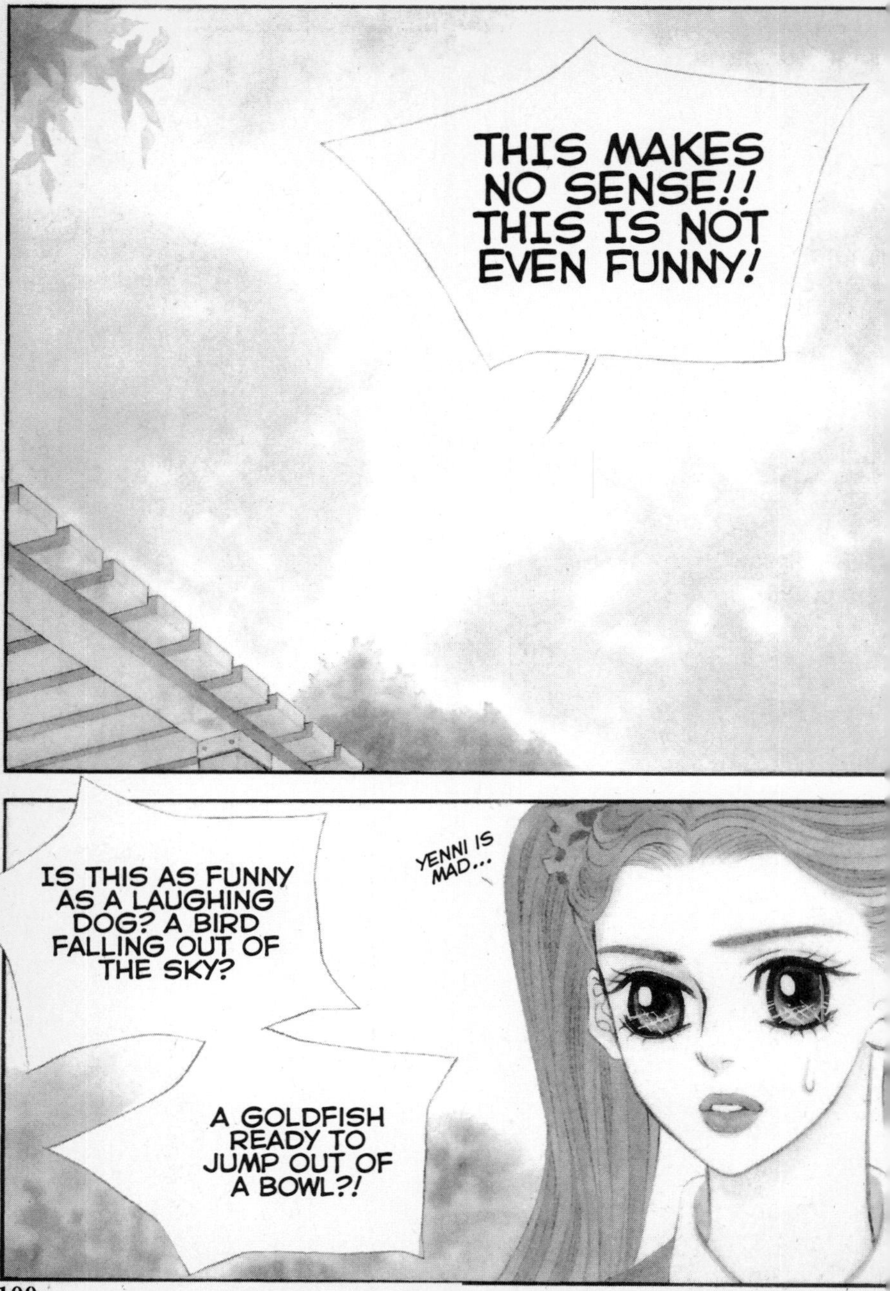
THIS MAKES NO SENSE!! THIS IS NOT EVEN FUNNY!
IS THIS AS FUNNY AS A LAUGHING DOG? A BIRD FALLING OUT OF THE SKY?
YENNI IS MAD...
A GOLDFISH READY TO JUMP OUT OF A BOWL?!

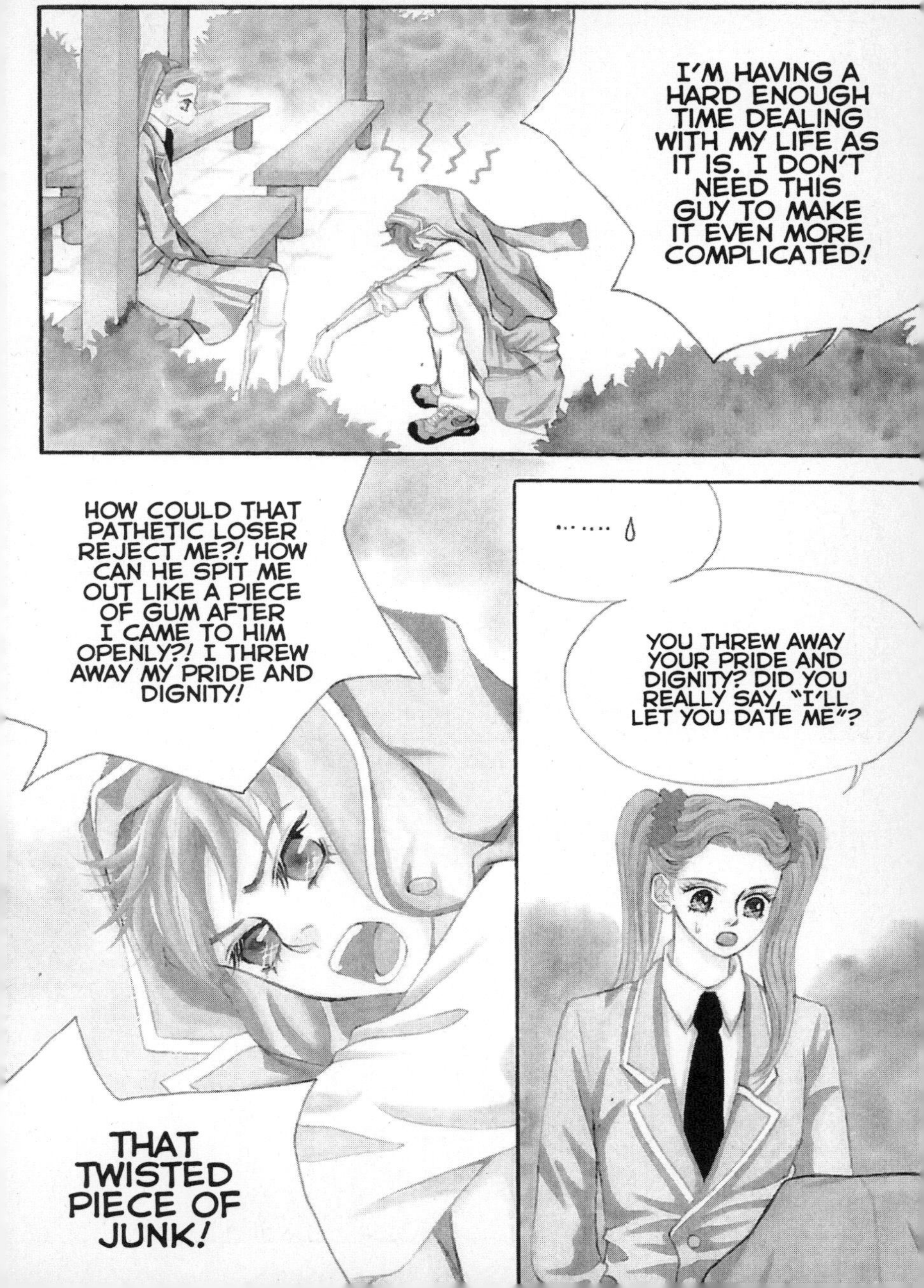
I'M HAVING A HARD ENOUGH TIME DEALING WITH MY LIFE AS IT IS. I DON'T NEED THIS GUY TO MAKE IT EVEN MORE COMPLICATED!
HOW COULD THAT PATHETIC LOSER REJECT ME?! HOW CAN HE SPIT ME OUT LIKE A PIECE OF GUM AFTER I CAME TO HIM OPENLY?! I THREW AWAY MY PRIDE AND DIGNITY!
THAT TWISTED PIECE OF JUNK!
YOU THREW AWAY YOUR PRIDE AND DIGNITY? DID YOU REALLY SAY, "I'LL LET YOU DATE ME"?

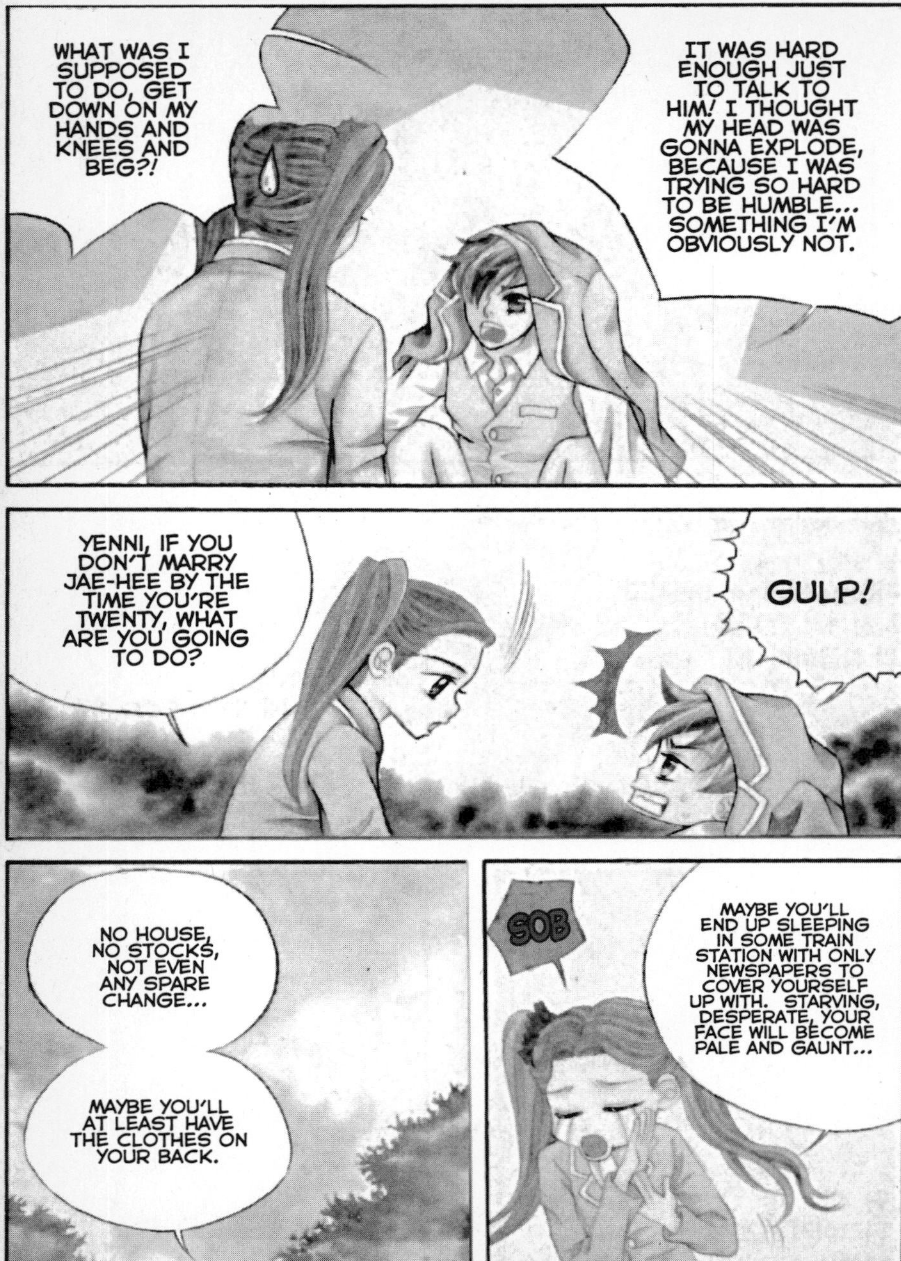
WHAT WAS I SUPPOSED TO DO, GET DOWN ON MY HANDS AND KNEES AND BEG?!
IT WAS HARD ENOUGH JUST TO TALK TO HIM! I THOUGHT MY HEAD WAS GONNA EXPLODE, BECAUSE I WAS TRYING SO HARD TO BE HUMBLE... SOMETHING I'M OBVIOUSLY NOT.
YENNI, IF YOU DON'T MARRY JAE-HEE BY THE TIME YOU'RE TWENTY, WHAT ARE YOU GOING TO DO?
GULP!
NO HOUSE, NO STOCKS, NOT EVEN ANY SPARE CHANGE...
MAYBE YOU'LL AT LEAST HAVE THE CLOTHES ON YOUR BACK.
SOB
MAYBE YOU'LL END UP SLEEPING IN SOME TRAIN STATION WITH ONLY NEWSPAPERS TO COVER YOURSELF UP WITH. STARVING, DESPERATE, YOUR FACE WILL BECOME PALE AND GAUNT...

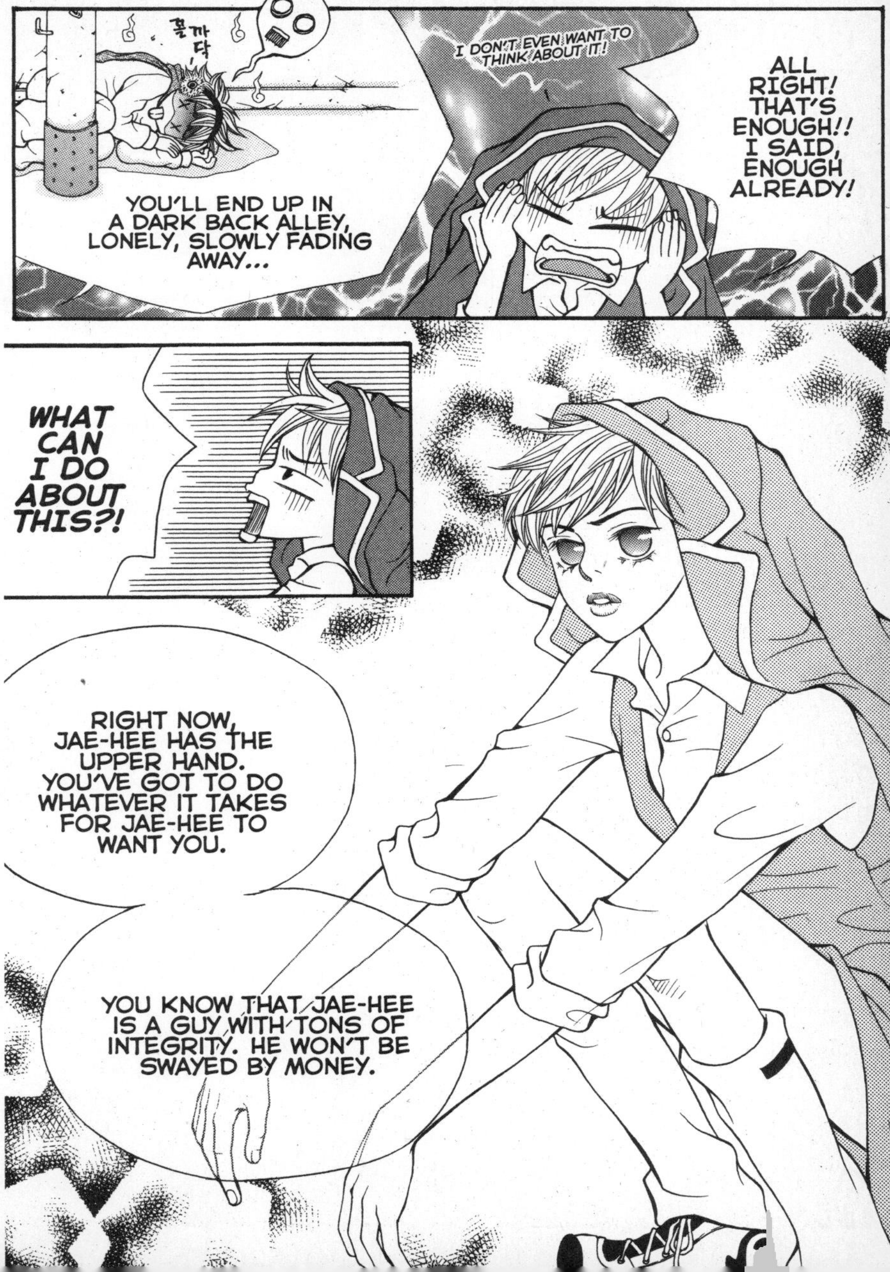
꼴까닥
YOU'LL END UP IN A DARK BACK ALLEY, LONELY, SLOWLY FADING AWAY...
I DON'T EVEN WANT TO THINK ABOUT IT!
ALL RIGHT! THAT'S ENOUGH!! I SAID, ENOUGH ALREADY!
WHAT CAN I DO ABOUT THIS?!
RIGHT NOW, JAE-HEE HAS THE UPPER HAND. YOU'VE GOT TO DO WHATEVER IT TAKES FOR JAE-HEE TO WANT YOU.
YOU KNOW THAT JAE-HEE IS A GUY WITH TONS OF INTEGRITY. HE WON'T BE SWAYED BY MONEY.

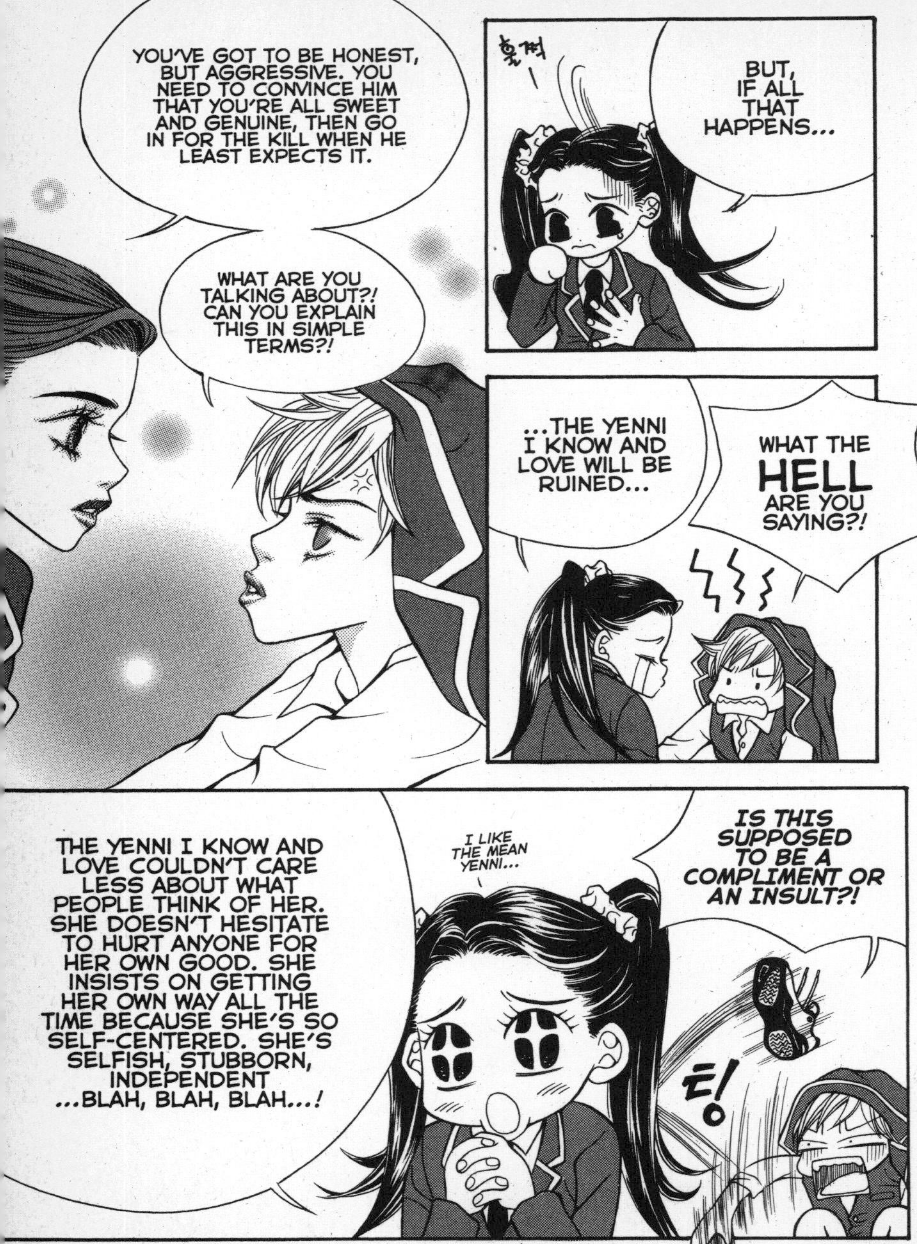
YOU'VE GOT TO BE HONEST, BUT AGGRESSIVE. YOU NEED TO CONVINCE HIM THAT YOU'RE ALL SWEET AND GENUINE, THEN GO IN FOR THE KILL WHEN HE LEAST EXPECTS IT.
WHAT ARE YOU TALKING ABOUT?! CAN YOU EXPLAIN THIS IN SIMPLE TERMS?!
BUT, IF ALL THAT HAPPENS...
...THE YENNI I KNOW AND LOVE WILL BE RUINED...
WHAT THE HELL ARE YOU SAYING?!
THE YENNI I KNOW AND LOVE COULDN'T CARE LESS ABOUT WHAT PEOPLE THINK OF HER. SHE DOESN'T HESITATE TO HURT ANYONE FOR HER OWN GOOD. SHE INSISTS ON GETTING HER OWN WAY ALL THE TIME BECAUSE SHE'S SO SELF-CENTERED. SHE'S SELFISH, STUBBORN, INDEPENDENT ...BLAH, BLAH, BLAH...!
I LIKE THE MEAN YENNI...
IS THIS SUPPOSED TO BE A COMPLIMENT OR AN INSULT?!

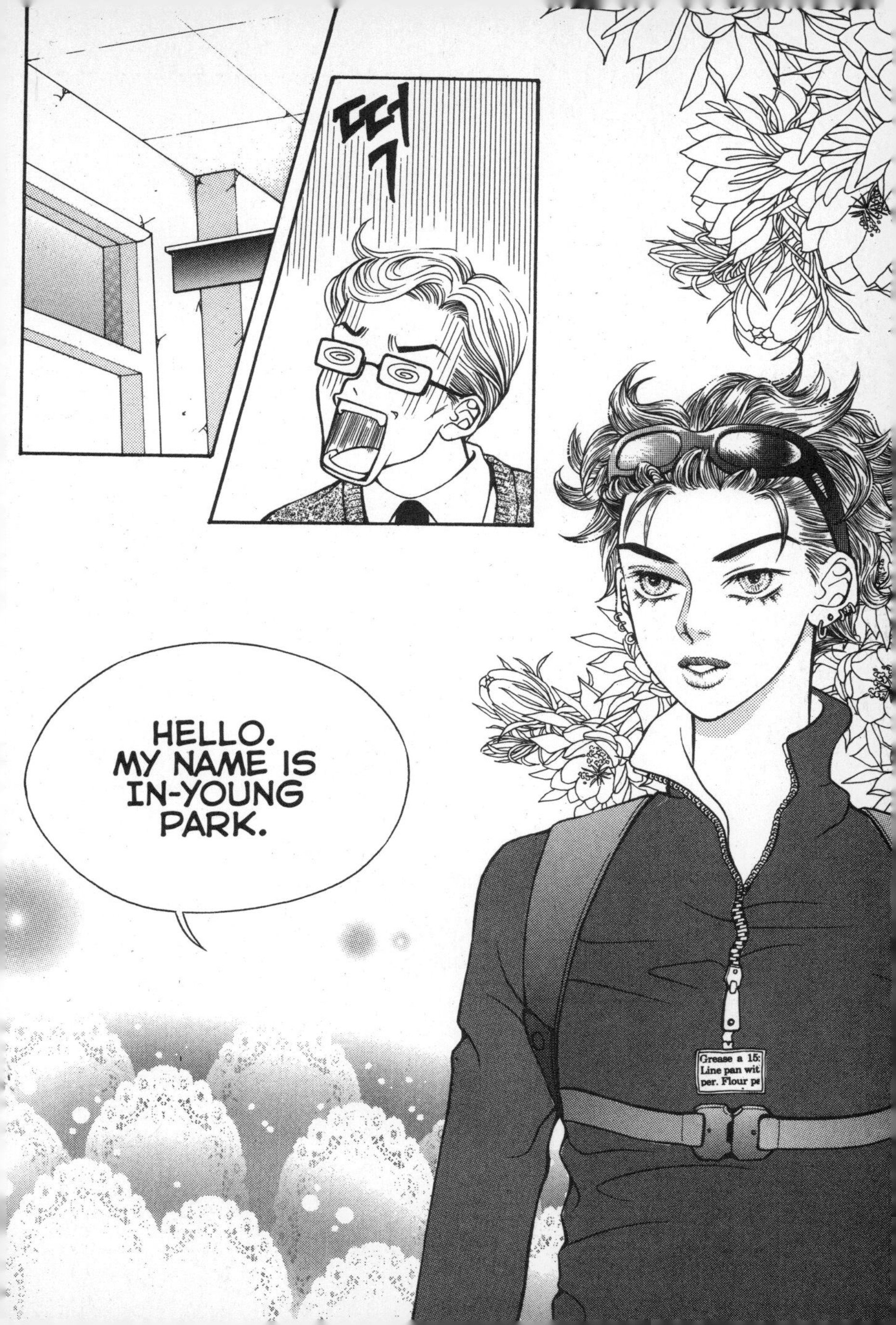
떡
HELLO. MY NAME IS IN-YOUNG PARK.
Grease a 15: Line pan wit per. Flour pe

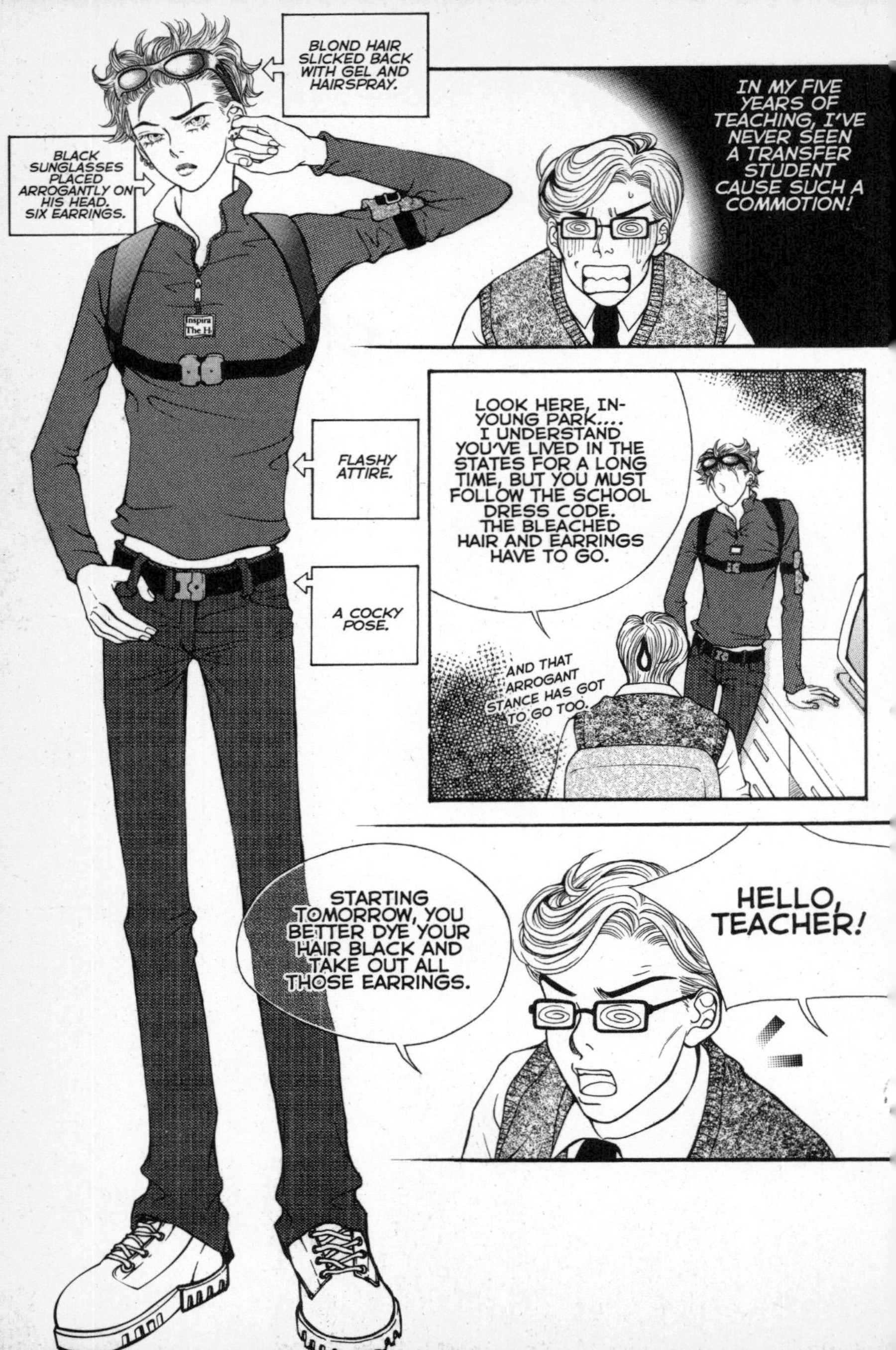
BLOND HAIR SLICKED BACK WITH GEL AND HAIRSPRAY.
BLACK SUNGLASSES PLACED ARROGANTLY ON HIS HEAD. SIX EARRINGS.
FLASHY ATTIRE.
A COCKY POSE.
IN MY FIVE YEARS OF TEACHING, I'VE NEVER SEEN A TRANSFER STUDENT CAUSE SUCH A COMMOTION!
LOOK HERE, IN-YOUNG PARK.... I UNDERSTAND YOU'VE LIVED IN THE STATES FOR A LONG TIME, BUT YOU MUST FOLLOW THE SCHOOL DRESS CODE. THE BLEACHED HAIR AND EARRINGS HAVE TO GO.
AND THAT ARROGANT STANCE HAS GOT TO GO TOO.
STARTING TOMORROW, YOU BETTER DYE YOUR HAIR BLACK AND TAKE OUT ALL THOSE EARRINGS.
HELLO, TEACHER!

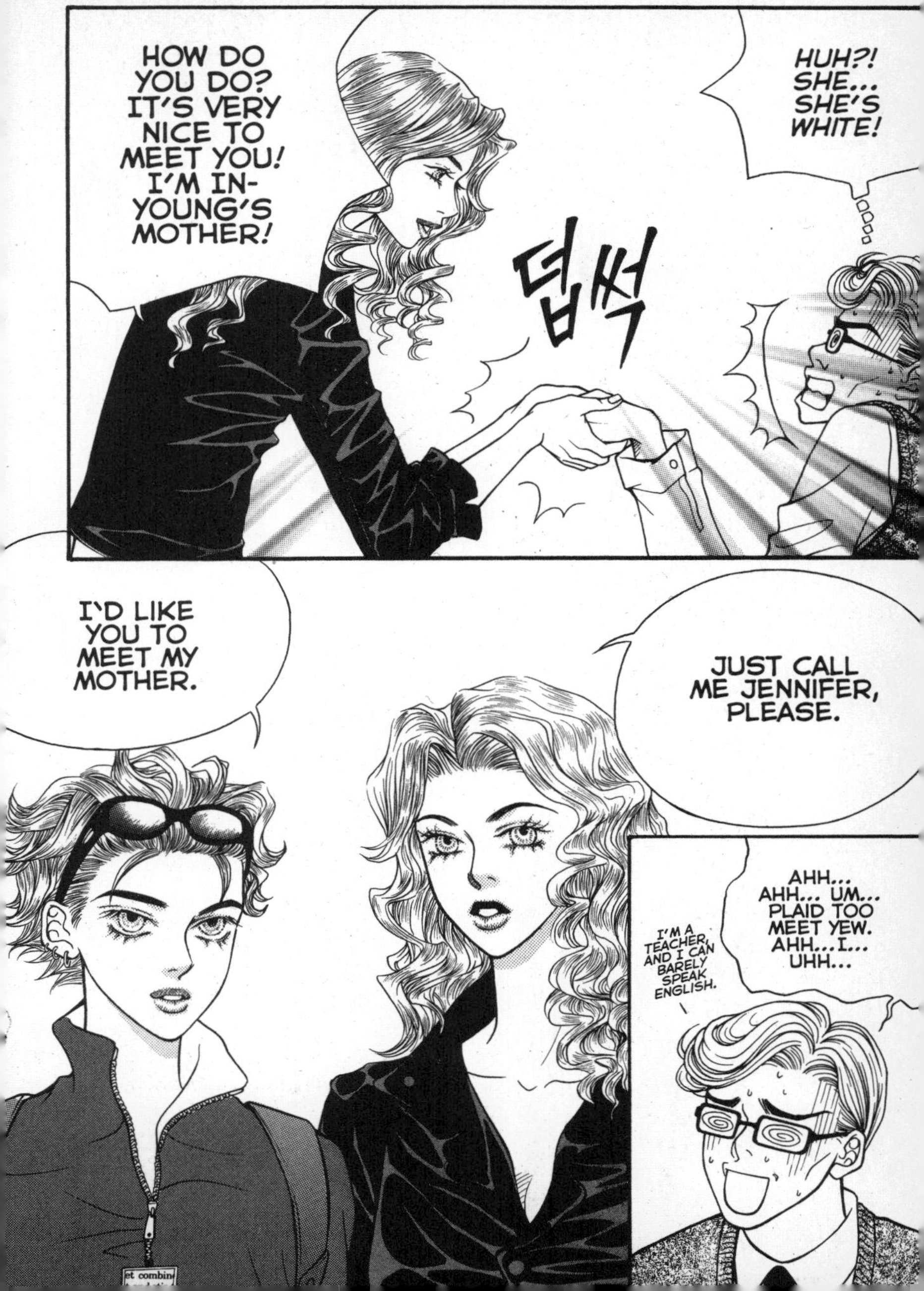
HOW DO YOU DO? IT'S VERY NICE TO MEET YOU! I'M IN-YOUNG'S MOTHER!
덥석
HUH?! SHE... SHE'S WHITE!
I'D LIKE YOU TO MEET MY MOTHER.
JUST CALL ME JENNIFER, PLEASE.
AHH... AHH... UM... PLAID TOO MEET YEW. AHH...I... UHH...
I'M A TEACHER, AND I CAN BARELY SPEAK ENGLISH.

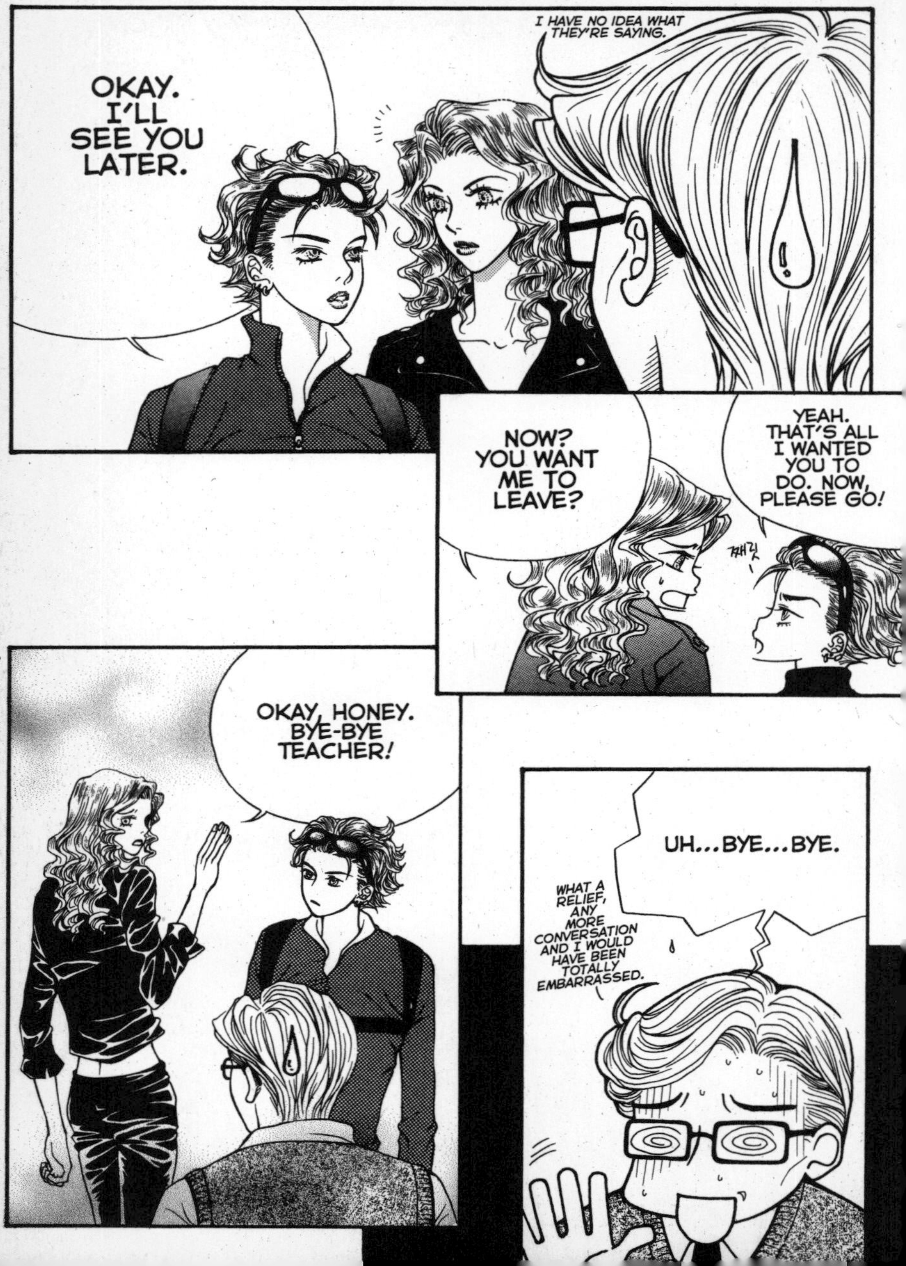

OKAY. I'LL SEE YOU LATER.
I HAVE NO IDEA WHAT THEY'RE SAYING.
NOW? YOU WANT ME TO LEAVE?
YEAH. THAT'S ALL I WANTED YOU TO DO. NOW, PLEASE GO!
째릿
OKAY, HONEY. BYE-BYE TEACHER!
UH...BYE...BYE.
WHAT A RELIEF, ANY MORE CONVERSATION AND I WOULD HAVE BEEN TOTALLY EMBARRASSED.

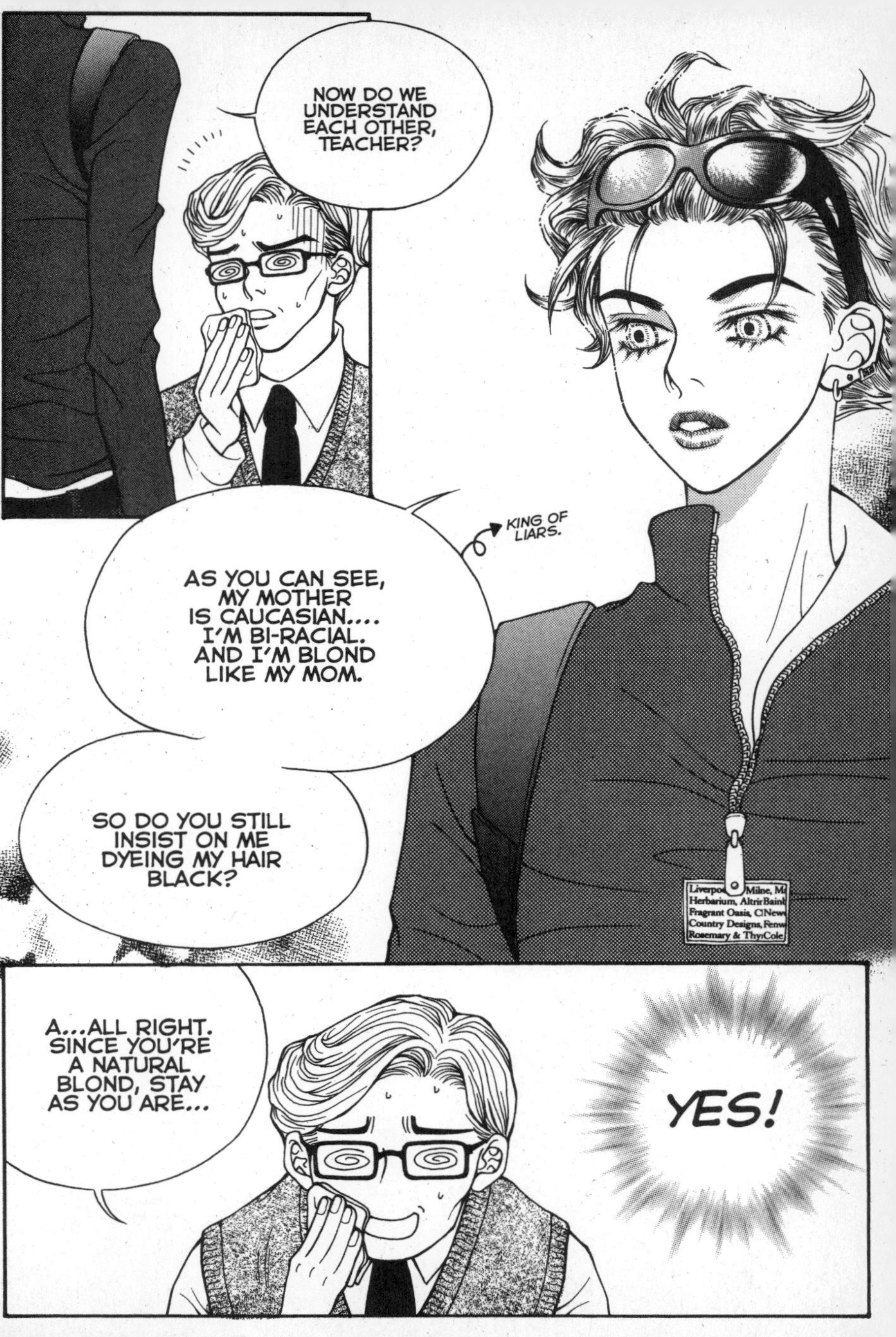
NOW DO WE UNDERSTAND EACH OTHER, TEACHER?
AS YOU CAN SEE, MY MOTHER IS CAUCASIAN.... I'M BI-RACIAL. AND I'M BLOND LIKE MY MOM.
KING OF LIARS.
SO DO YOU STILL INSIST ON ME DYEING MY HAIR BLACK?
A...ALL RIGHT. SINCE YOU'RE A NATURAL BLOND, STAY AS YOU ARE...
YES!

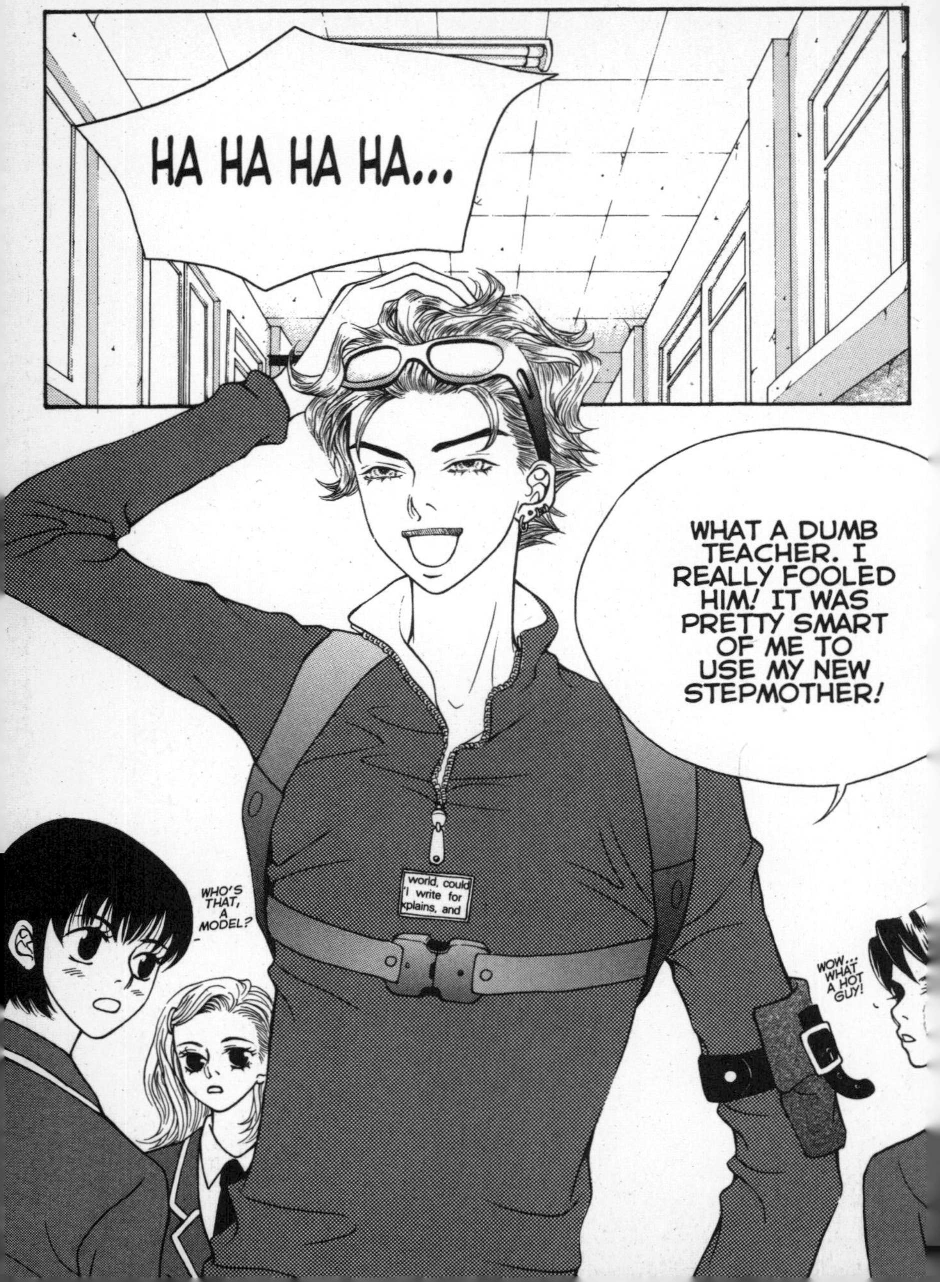
HA HA HA HA...
WHAT A DUMB TEACHER. I REALLY FOOLED HIM! IT WAS PRETTY SMART OF ME TO USE MY NEW STEPMOTHER!
WHO'S THAT, A MODEL?
world, could 'I write for kplains, and
WOW... WHAT A HOT GUY!

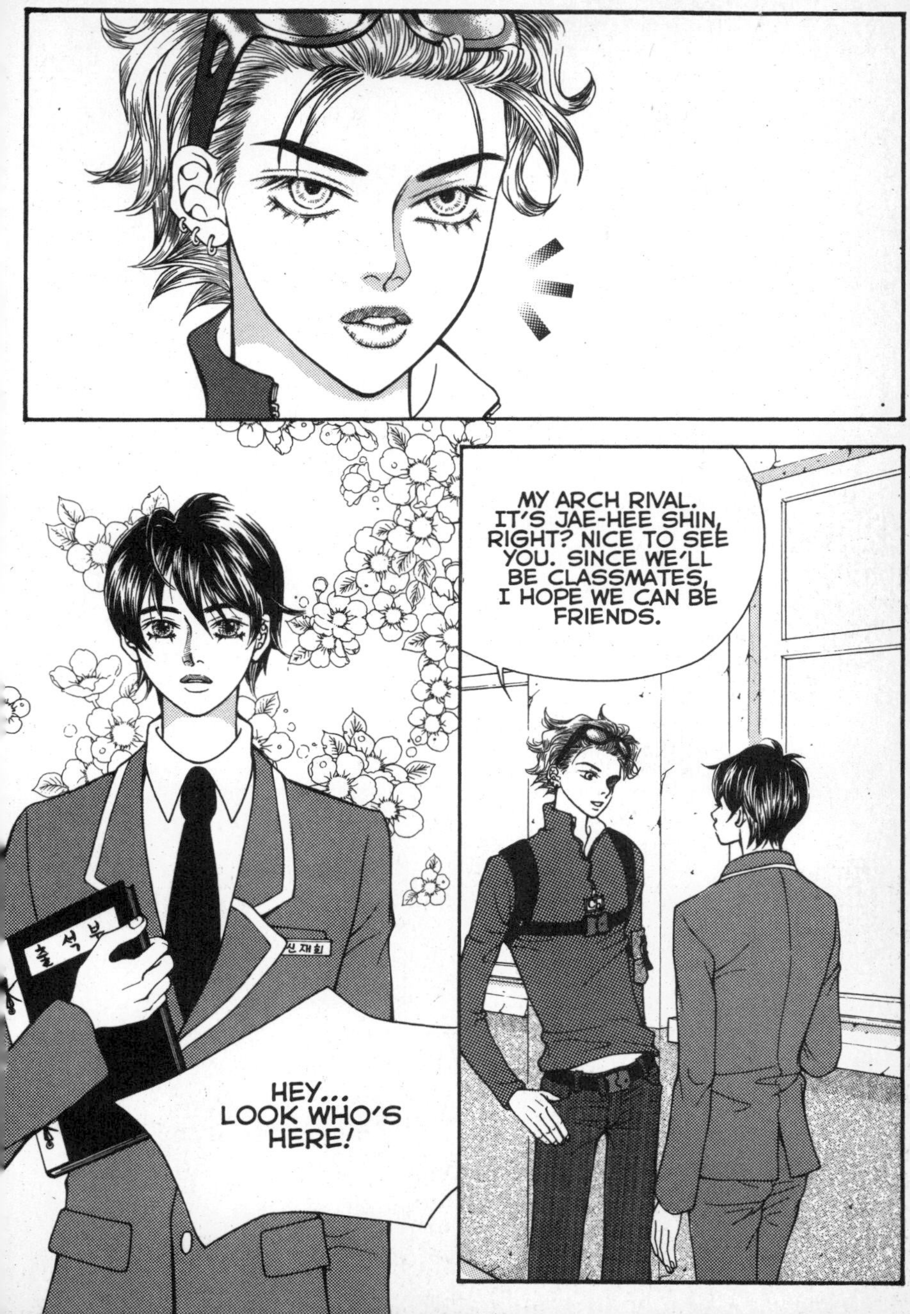

출석부
신재희
HEY... LOOK WHO'S HERE!
MY ARCH RIVAL. IT'S JAE-HEE SHIN, RIGHT? NICE TO SEE YOU. SINCE WE'LL BE CLASSMATES, I HOPE WE CAN BE FRIENDS.

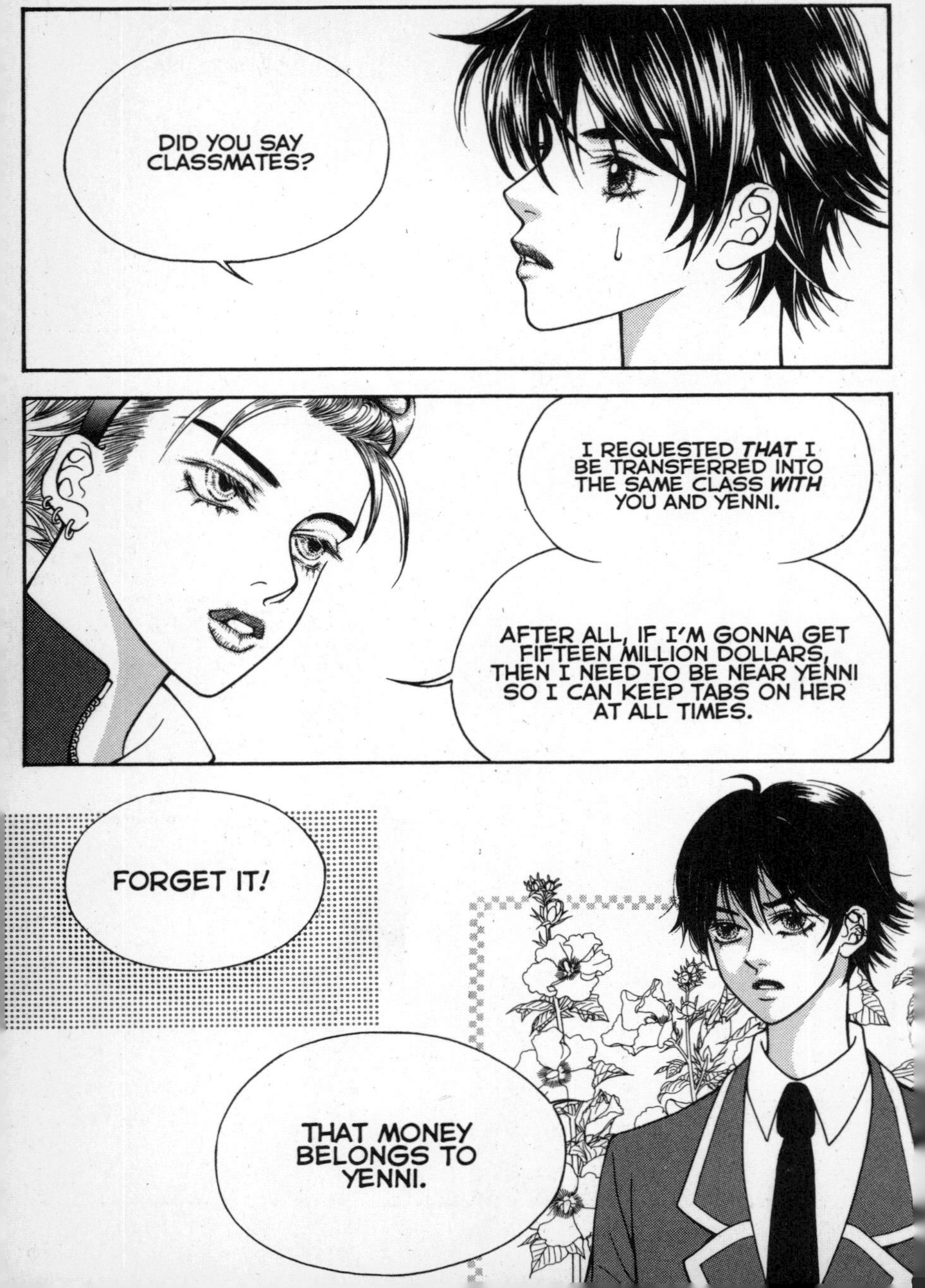
DID YOU SAY CLASSMATES?
I REQUESTED *THAT* I BE TRANSFERRED INTO THE SAME CLASS *WITH* YOU AND YENNI.
AFTER ALL, IF I'M GONNA GET FIFTEEN MILLION DOLLARS, THEN I NEED TO BE NEAR YENNI SO I CAN KEEP TABS ON HER AT ALL TIMES.
FORGET IT!
THAT MONEY BELONGS TO YENNI.

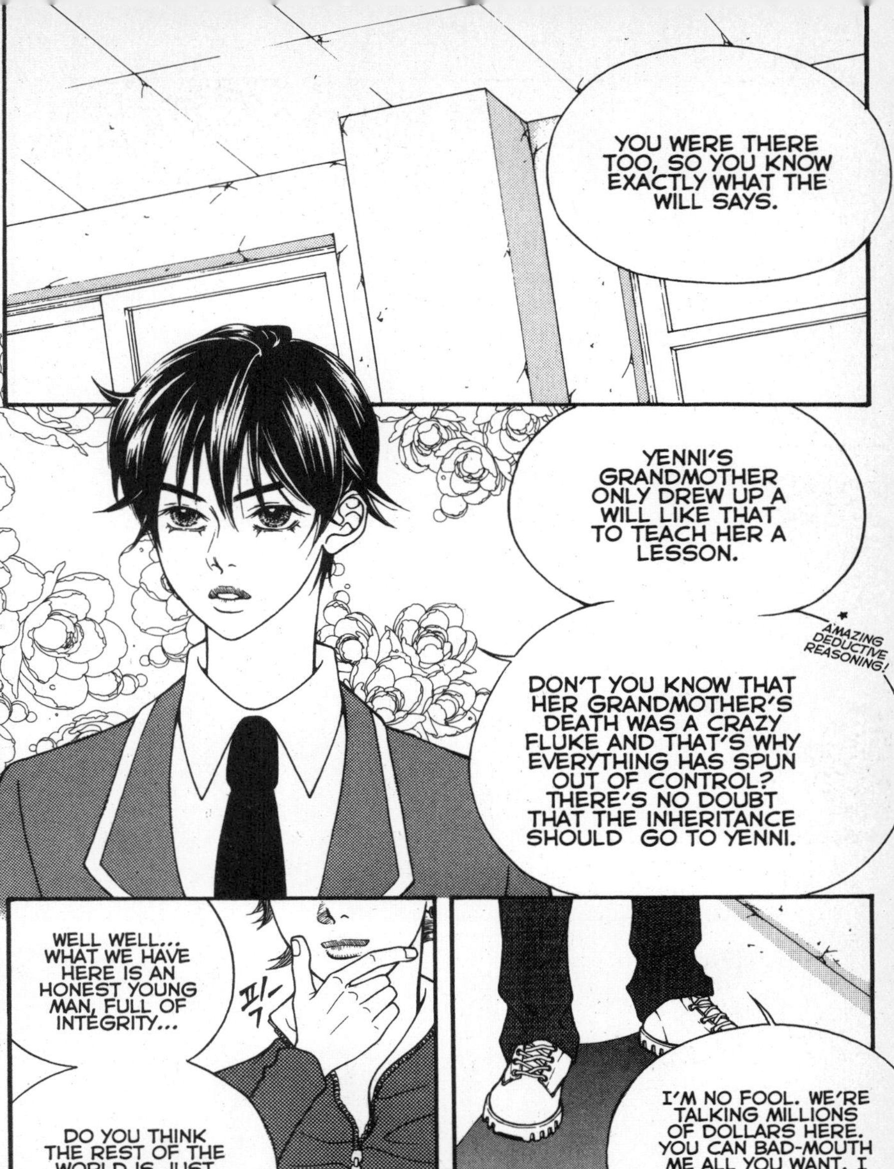
YOU WERE THERE TOO, SO YOU KNOW EXACTLY WHAT THE WILL SAYS.
YENNI'S GRANDMOTHER ONLY DREW UP A WILL LIKE THAT TO TEACH HER A LESSON.
AMAZING DEDUCTIVE REASONING!
DON'T YOU KNOW THAT HER GRANDMOTHER'S DEATH WAS A CRAZY FLUKE AND THAT'S WHY EVERYTHING HAS SPUN OUT OF CONTROL? THERE'S NO DOUBT THAT THE INHERITANCE SHOULD GO TO YENNI.
WELL WELL... WHAT WE HAVE HERE IS AN HONEST YOUNG MAN, FULL OF INTEGRITY...
DO YOU THINK THE REST OF THE WORLD IS JUST AS NAÏVE AND INNOCENT?
I'M NO FOOL. WE'RE TALKING MILLIONS OF DOLLARS HERE. YOU CAN BAD-MOUTH ME ALL YOU WANT. I DON'T CARE AS LONG AS I GET THE MONEY.

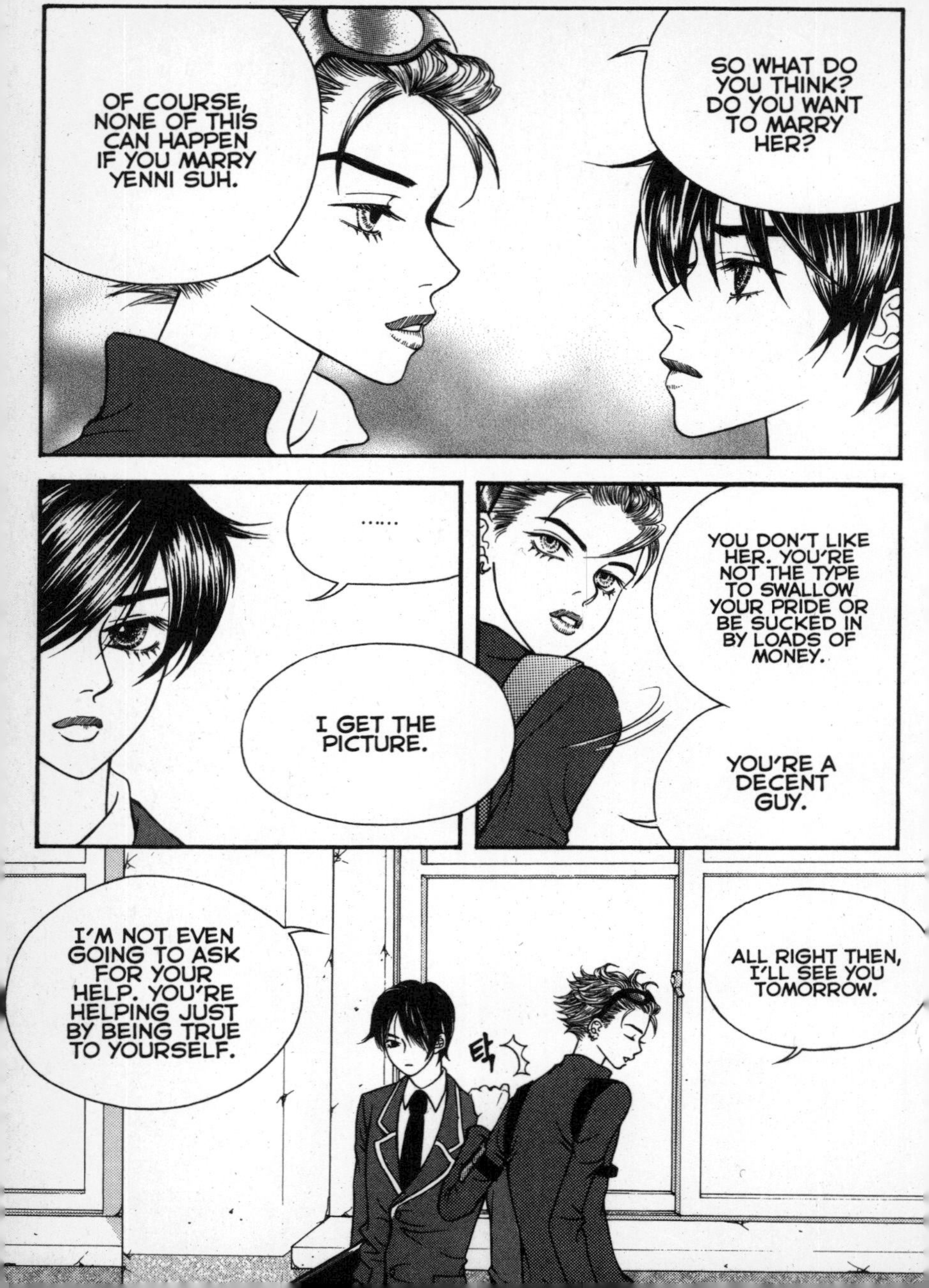
OF COURSE, NONE OF THIS CAN HAPPEN IF YOU MARRY YENNI SUH.
SO WHAT DO YOU THINK? DO YOU WANT TO MARRY HER?
......
I GET THE PICTURE.
YOU DON'T LIKE HER. YOU'RE NOT THE TYPE TO SWALLOW YOUR PRIDE OR BE SUCKED IN BY LOADS OF MONEY.
YOU'RE A DECENT GUY.
I'M NOT EVEN GOING TO ASK FOR YOUR HELP. YOU'RE HELPING JUST BY BEING TRUE TO YOURSELF.
탁
ALL RIGHT THEN, I'LL SEE YOU TOMORROW.

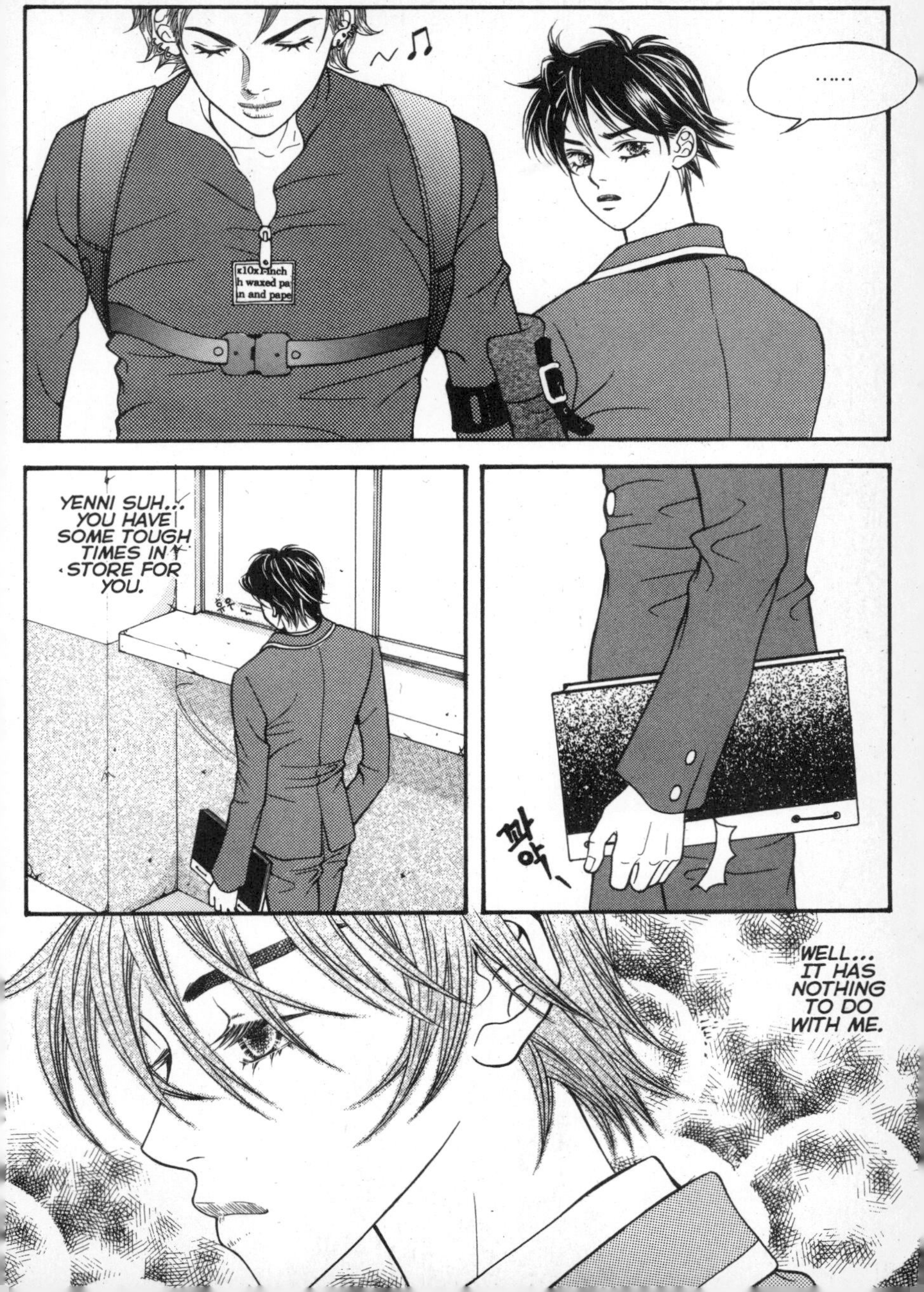
~♪
......
x10x1-inch
h waxed pa
in and pape
YENNI SUH... YOU HAVE SOME TOUGH TIMES IN STORE FOR YOU.
파악、
WELL... IT HAS NOTHING TO DO WITH ME.

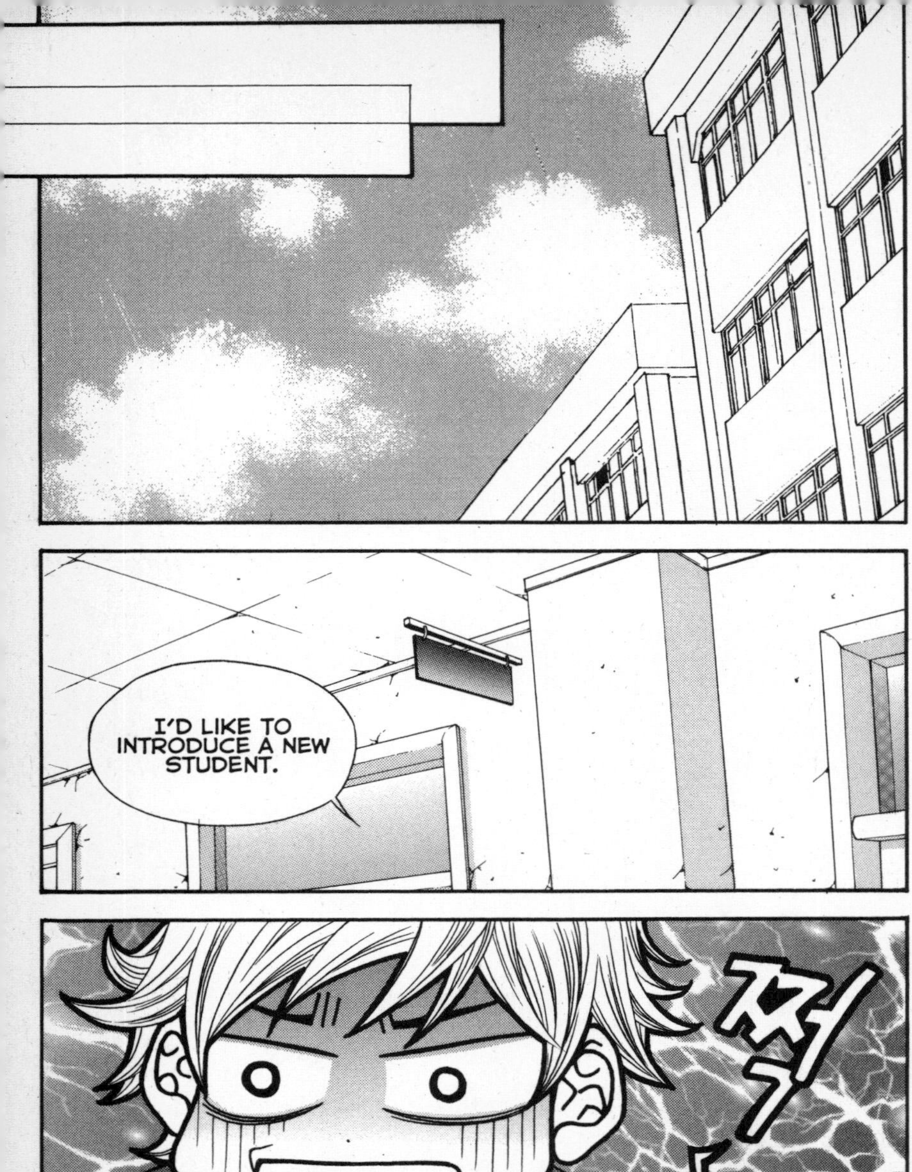
I'D LIKE TO INTRODUCE A NEW STUDENT.

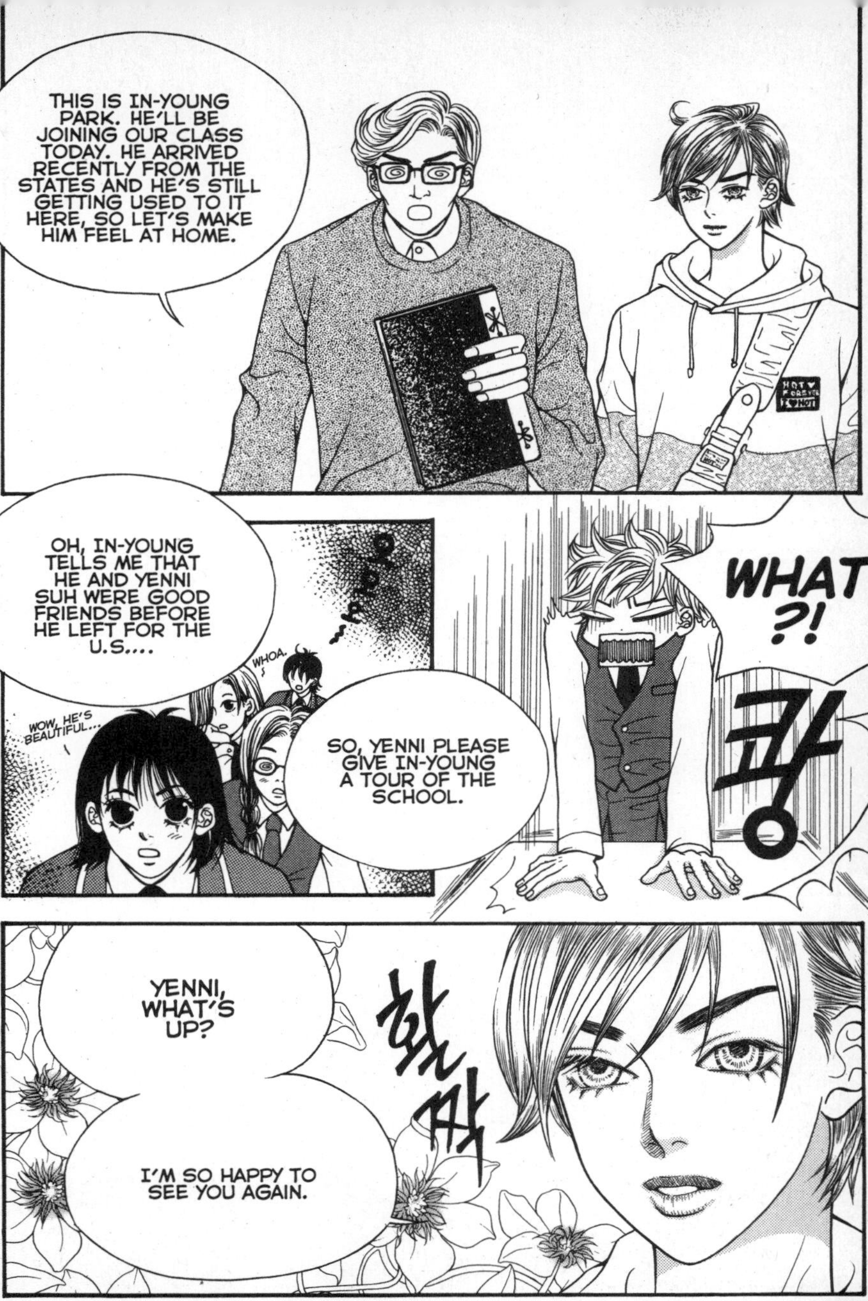
THIS IS IN-YOUNG PARK. HE'LL BE JOINING OUR CLASS TODAY. HE ARRIVED RECENTLY FROM THE STATES AND HE'S STILL GETTING USED TO IT HERE, SO LET'S MAKE HIM FEEL AT HOME.
OH, IN-YOUNG TELLS ME THAT HE AND YENNI SUH WERE GOOD FRIENDS BEFORE HE LEFT FOR THE U.S....
WHOA.
WOW, HE'S BEAUTIFUL...
SO, YENNI PLEASE GIVE IN-YOUNG A TOUR OF THE SCHOOL.
WHAT ?!
쾅
YENNI, WHAT'S UP?
I'M SO HAPPY TO SEE YOU AGAIN.
활짝

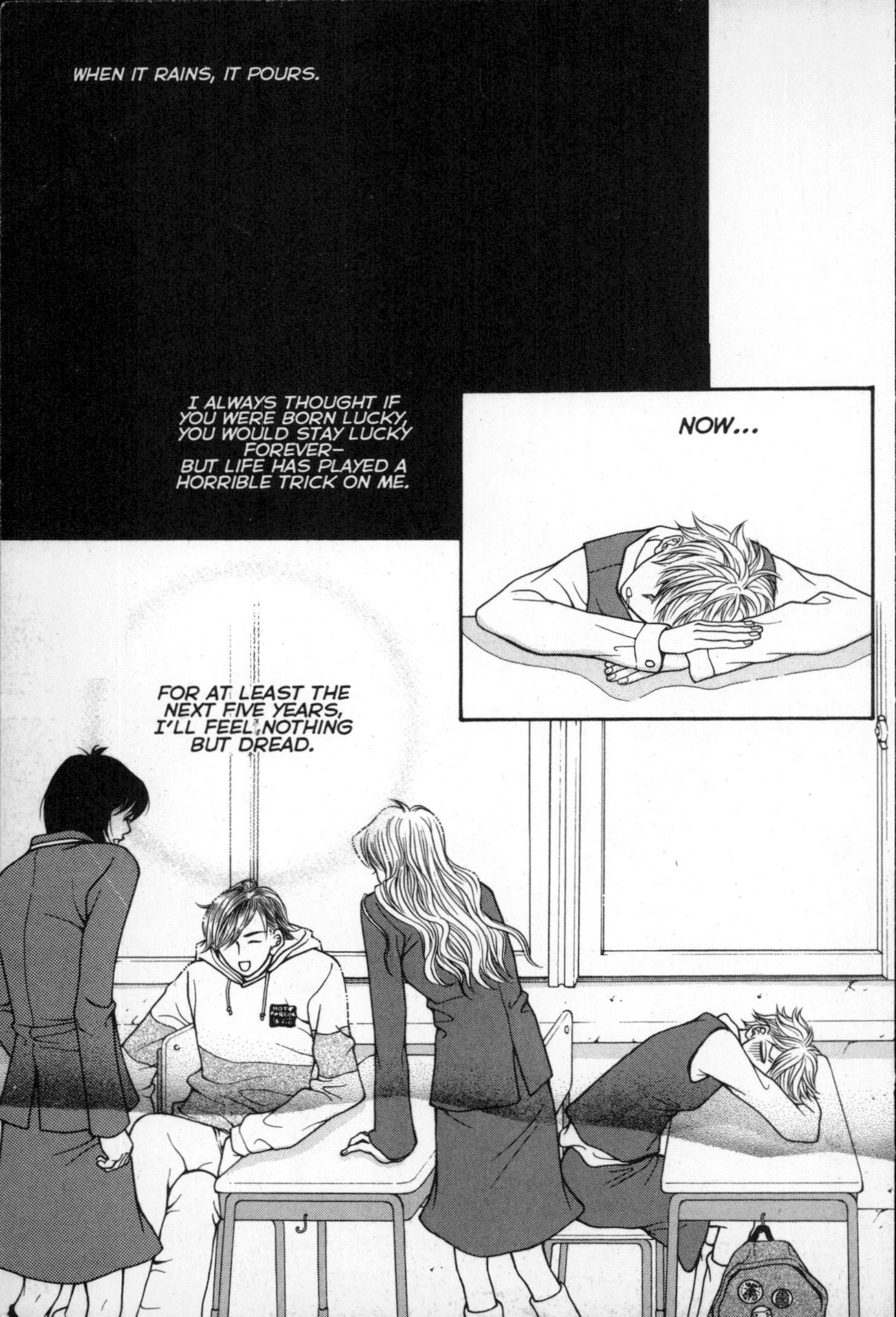
WHEN IT RAINS, IT POURS.
I ALWAYS THOUGHT IF YOU WERE BORN LUCKY, YOU WOULD STAY LUCKY FOREVER– BUT LIFE HAS PLAYED A HORRIBLE TRICK ON ME.
NOW...
FOR AT LEAST THE NEXT FIVE YEARS, I'LL FEEL NOTHING BUT DREAD.

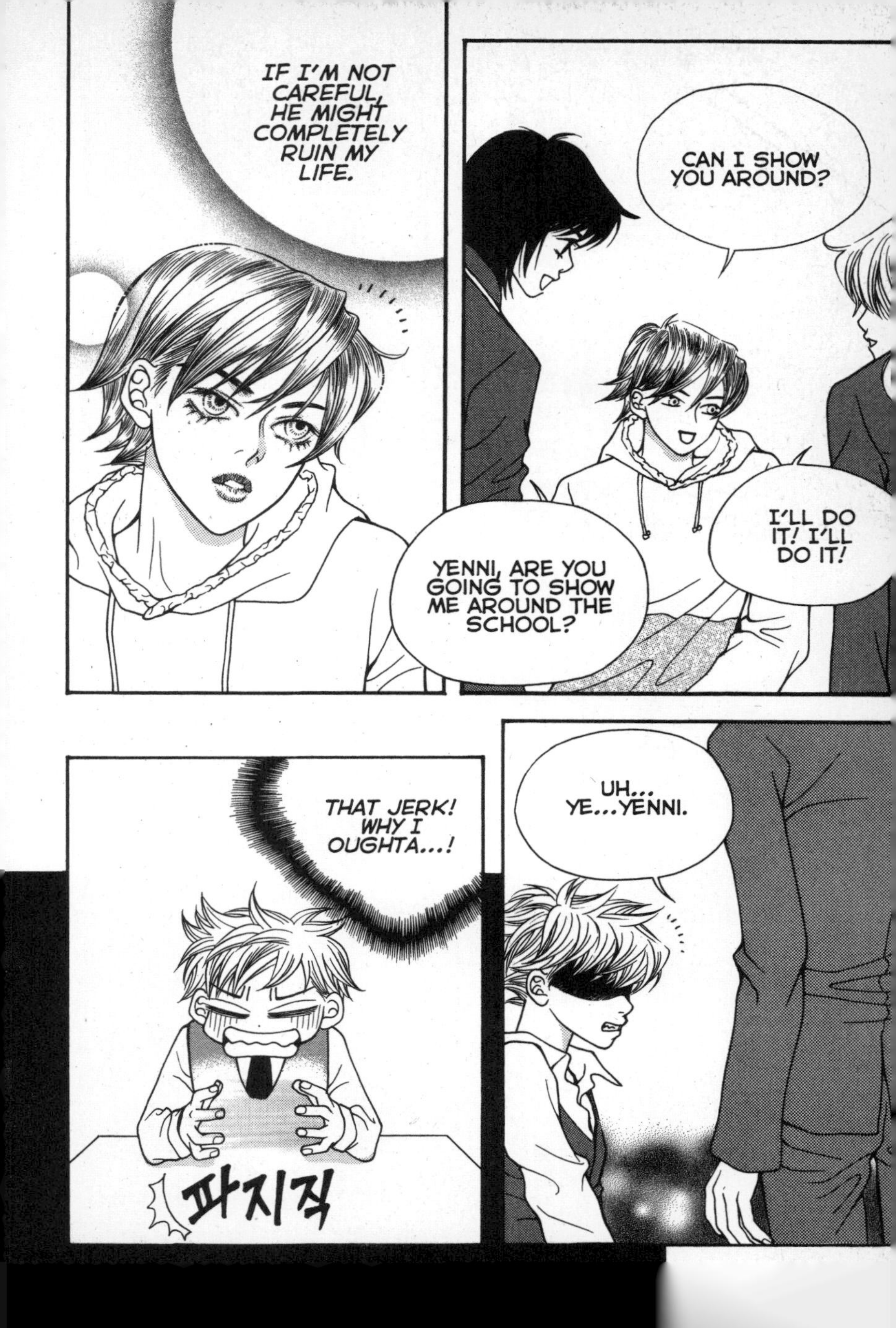
IF I'M NOT CAREFUL, HE MIGHT COMPLETELY RUIN MY LIFE.
CAN I SHOW YOU AROUND?
YENNI, ARE YOU GOING TO SHOW ME AROUND THE SCHOOL?
I'LL DO IT! I'LL DO IT!
THAT JERK! WHY I OUGHTA...!
파지직
UH... YE...YENNI.

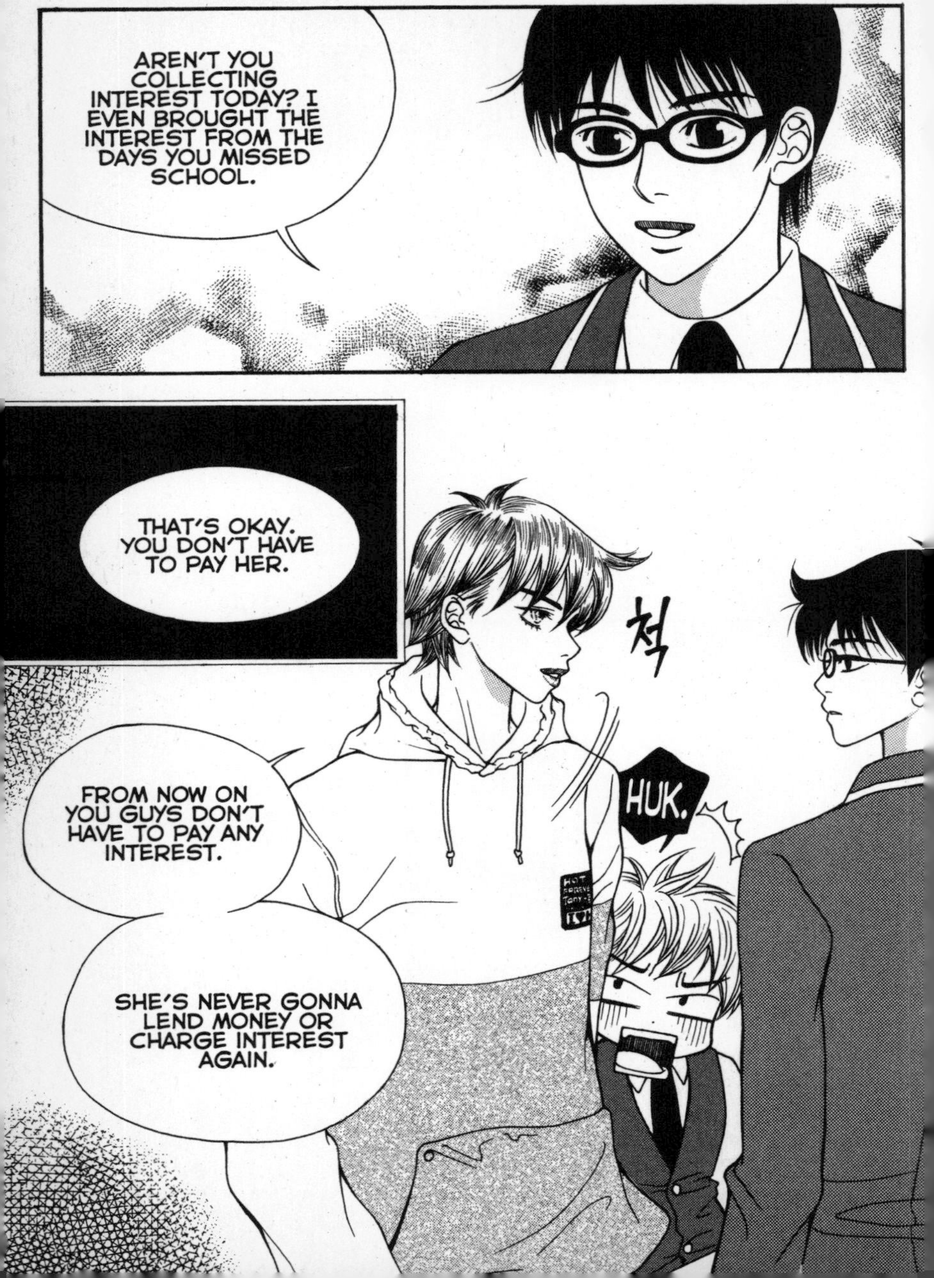
AREN'T YOU COLLECTING INTEREST TODAY? I EVEN BROUGHT THE INTEREST FROM THE DAYS YOU MISSED SCHOOL.
THAT'S OKAY. YOU DON'T HAVE TO PAY HER.
척
HUK.
FROM NOW ON YOU GUYS DON'T HAVE TO PAY ANY INTEREST.
SHE'S NEVER GONNA LEND MONEY OR CHARGE INTEREST AGAIN.

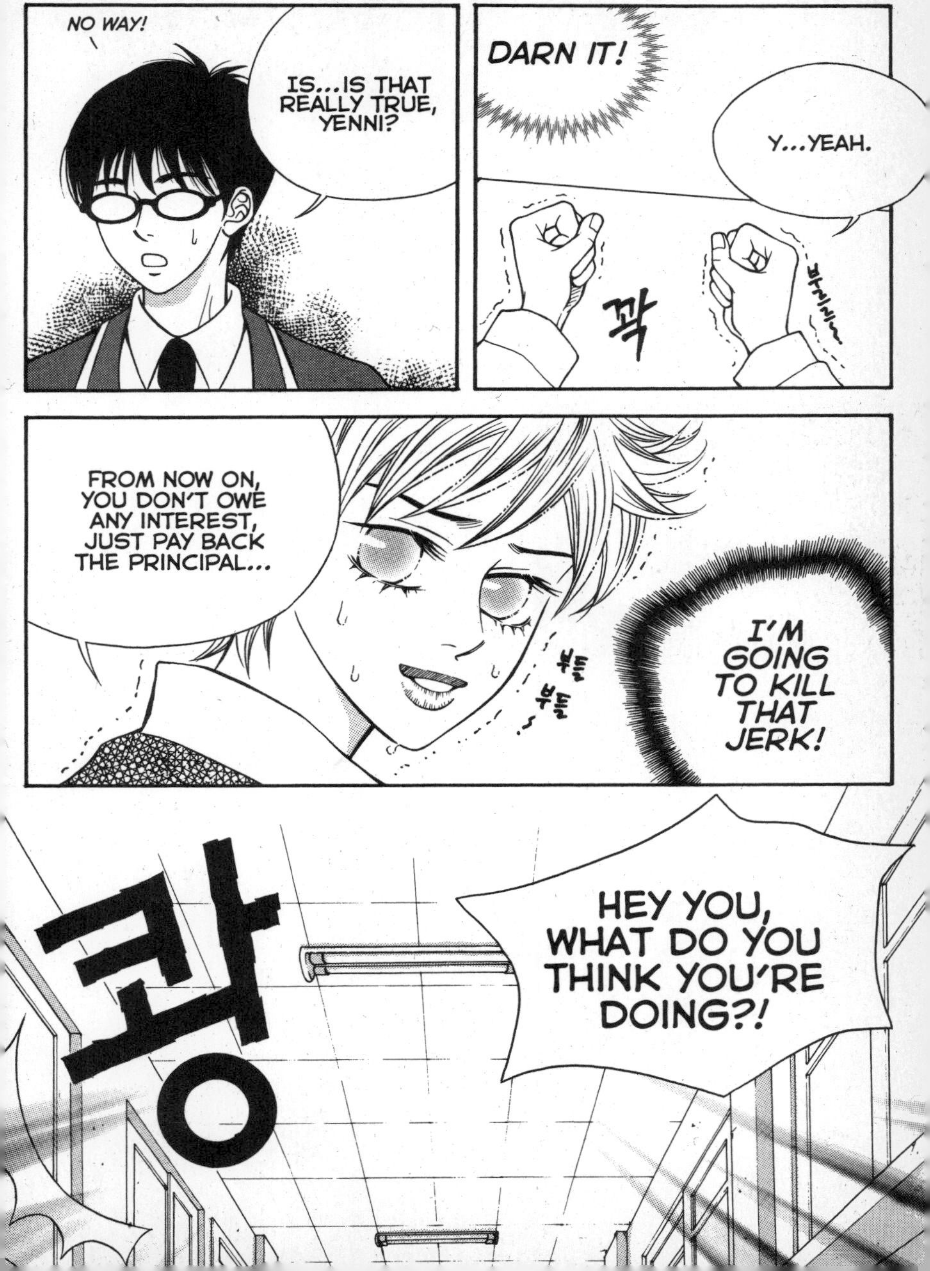
NO WAY!
IS...IS THAT REALLY TRUE, YENNI?
DARN IT!
Y...YEAH.
꽉
부르르~
FROM NOW ON, YOU DON'T OWE ANY INTEREST, JUST PAY BACK THE PRINCIPAL...
부들부들~
I'M GOING TO KILL THAT JERK!
쾅
HEY YOU, WHAT DO YOU THINK YOU'RE DOING?!

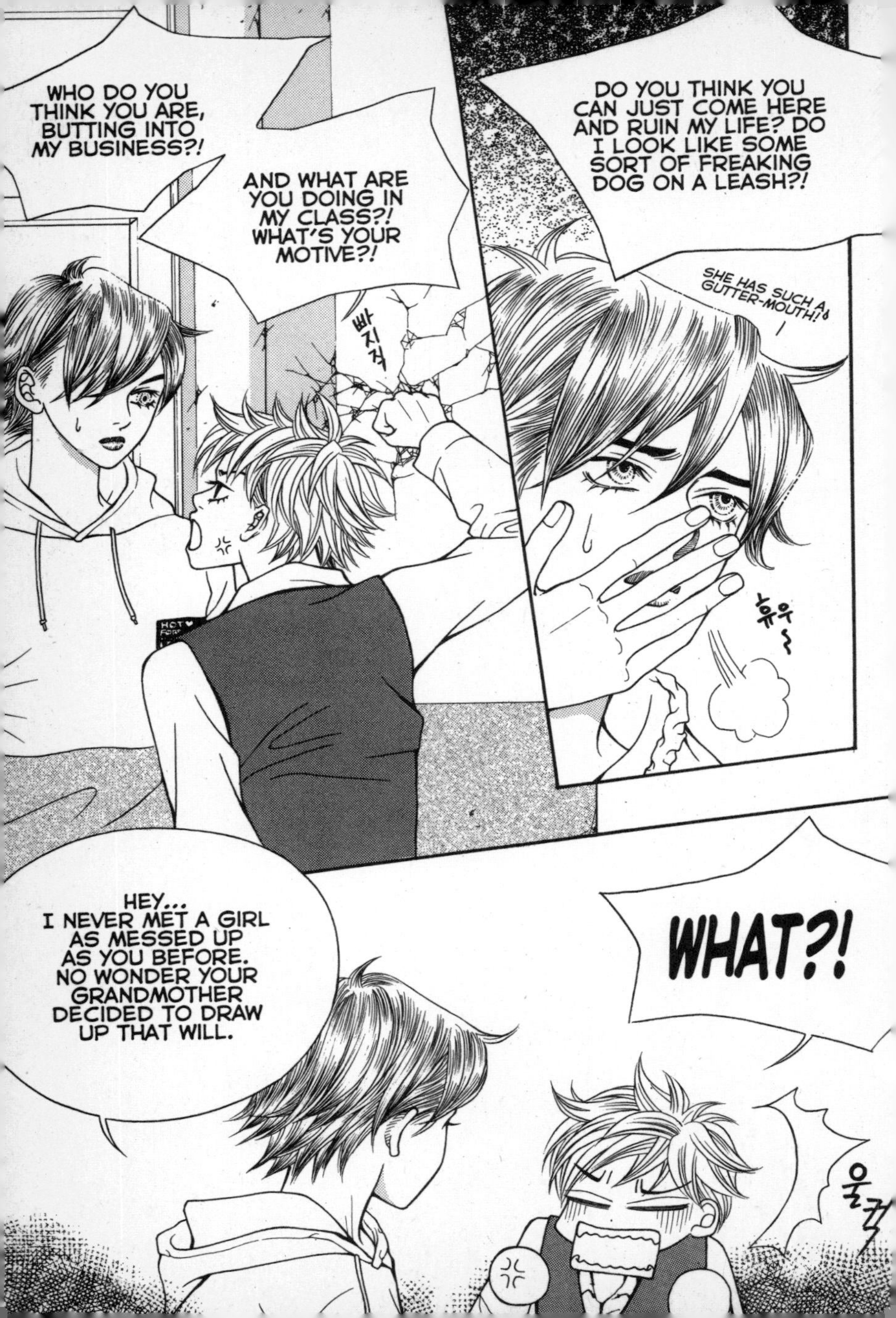
WHO DO YOU THINK YOU ARE, BUTTING INTO MY BUSINESS?!
AND WHAT ARE YOU DOING IN MY CLASS?! WHAT'S YOUR MOTIVE?!
빠지직
DO YOU THINK YOU CAN JUST COME HERE AND RUIN MY LIFE? DO I LOOK LIKE SOME SORT OF FREAKING DOG ON A LEASH?!
SHE HAS SUCH A GUTTER-MOUTH!
후우~
HEY... I NEVER MET A GIRL AS MESSED UP AS YOU BEFORE. NO WONDER YOUR GRANDMOTHER DECIDED TO DRAW UP THAT WILL.
WHAT?!
울컥

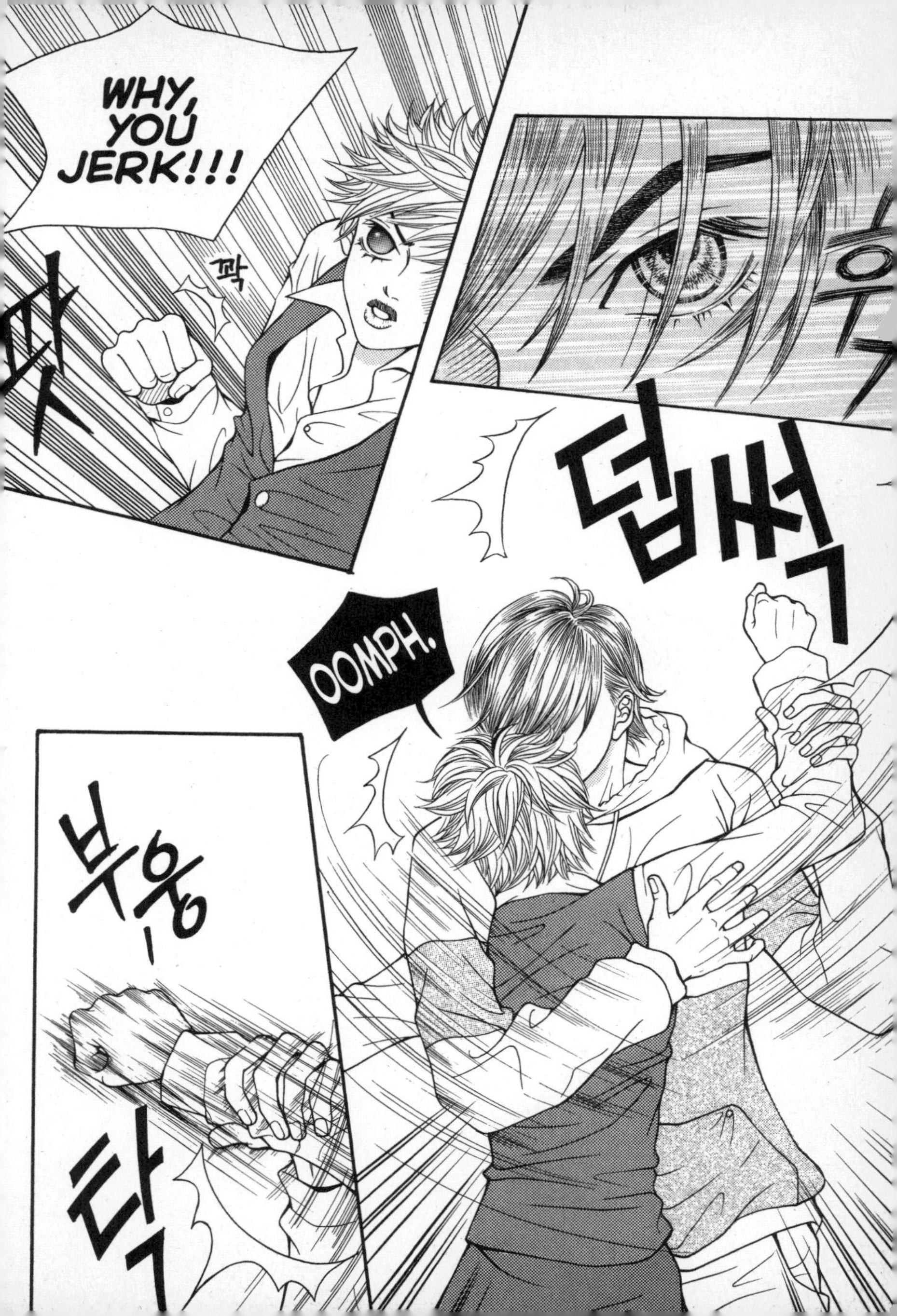
WHY, YOU JERK!!!
꽉
팍
덥썩
OOMPH.
부웅
탁

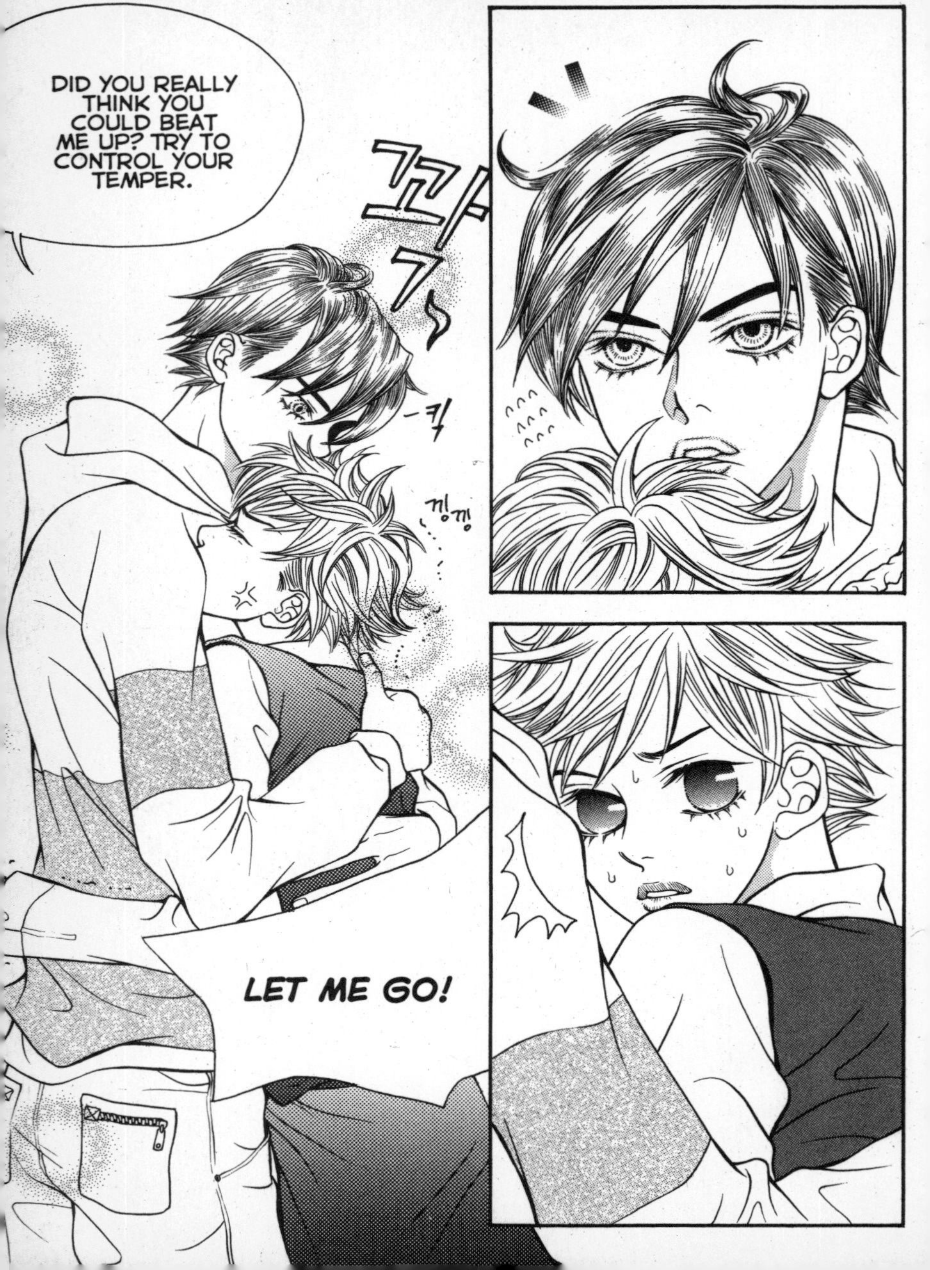
DID YOU REALLY THINK YOU COULD BEAT ME UP? TRY TO CONTROL YOUR TEMPER.
낑낑
LET ME GO!

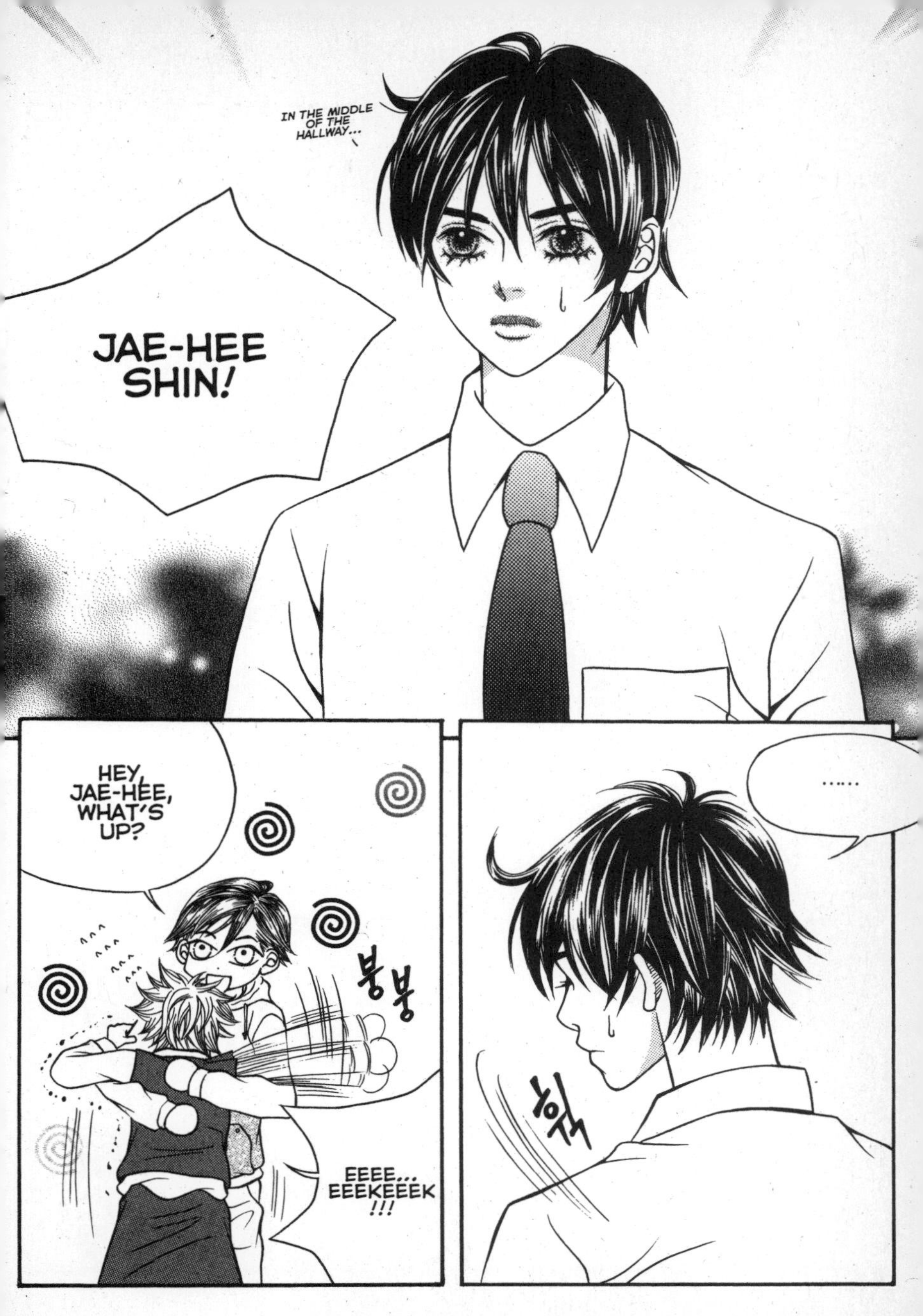
IN THE MIDDLE OF THE HALLWAY...
JAE-HEE SHIN!
HEY, JAE-HEE, WHAT'S UP?
붕붕
EEEE... EEEKEEEK !!!
......
휙

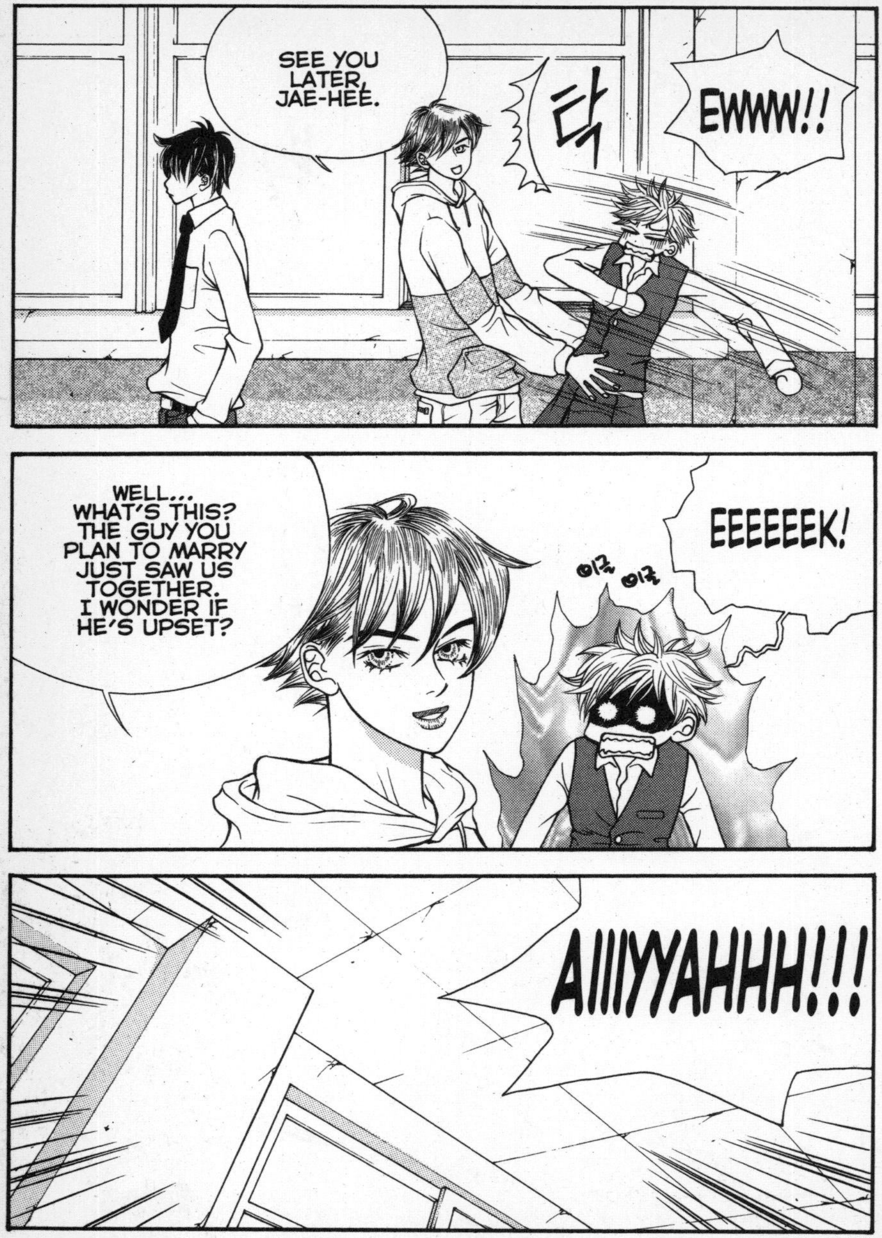
SEE YOU LATER, JAE-HEE.
탁
EWWW!!
WELL... WHAT'S THIS? THE GUY YOU PLAN TO MARRY JUST SAW US TOGETHER. I WONDER IF HE'S UPSET?
EEEEEEK!
이글 이글
AIIIYYAHHH!!!

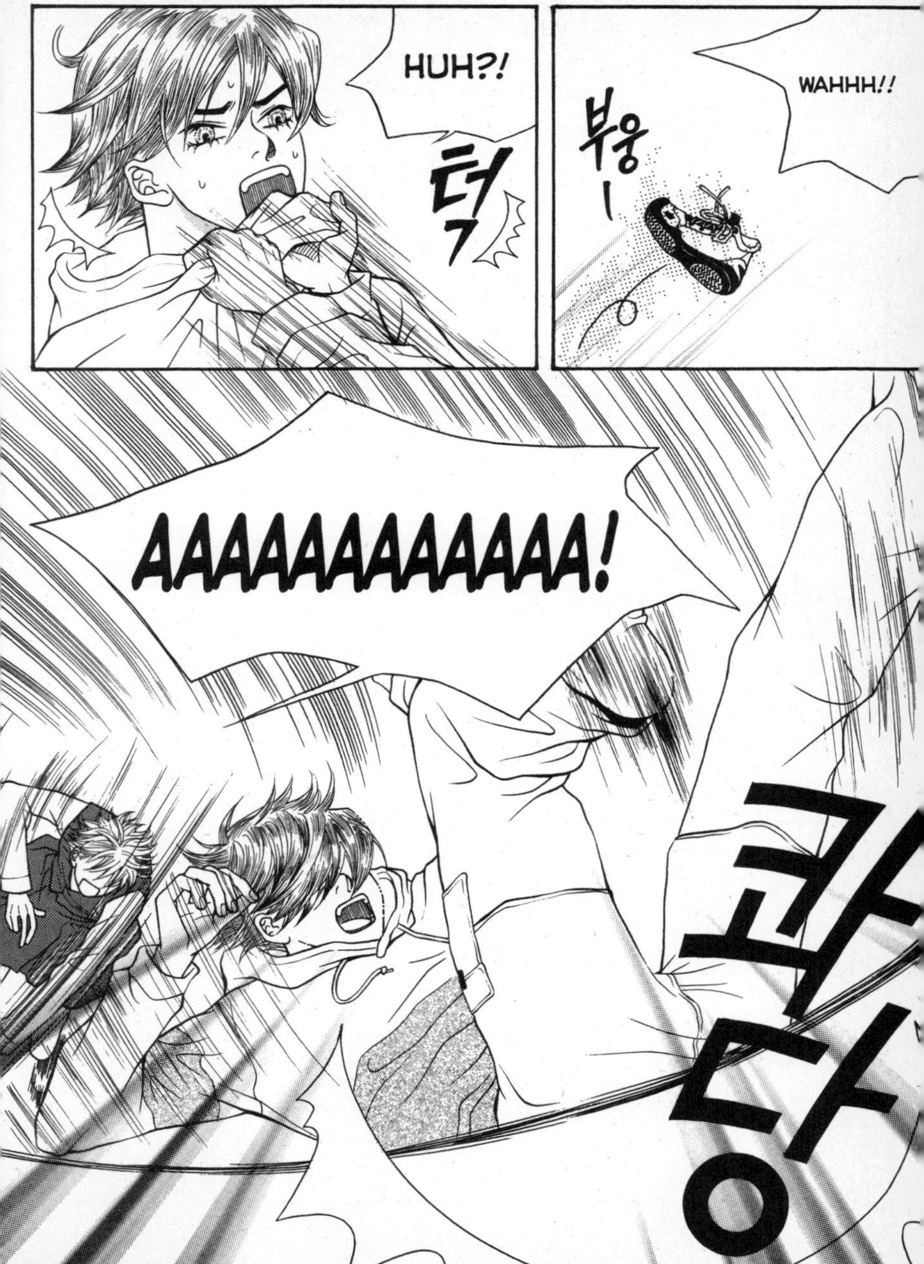
HUH?!
헉
부웅-
WAHHH!!
AAAAAAAAAAAAA!
콰당

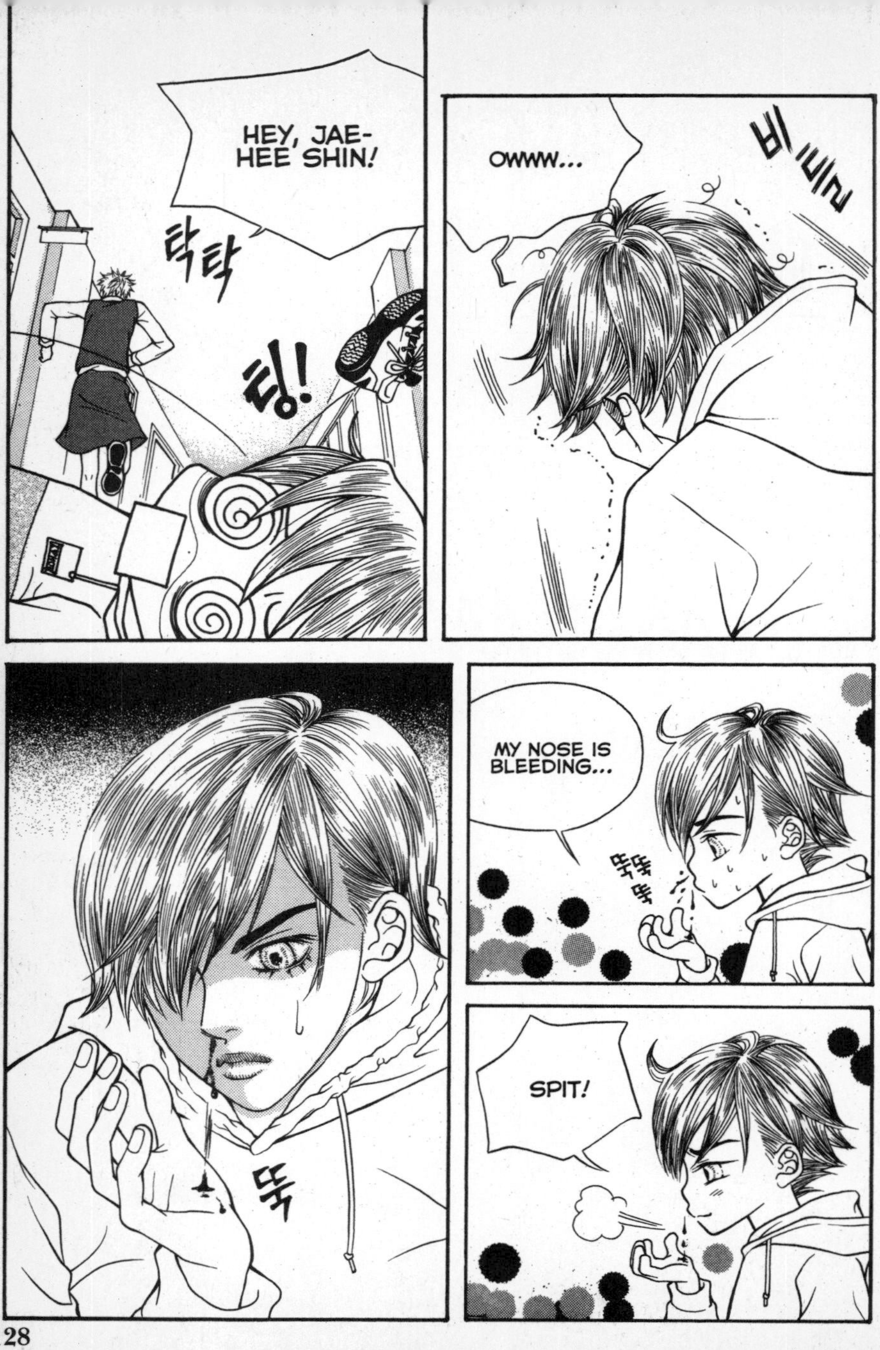
HEY, JAE-HEE SHIN!
탁탁
탕!
OWWW...
비틀
뚝
MY NOSE IS BLEEDING...
뚝뚝 뚝
SPIT!

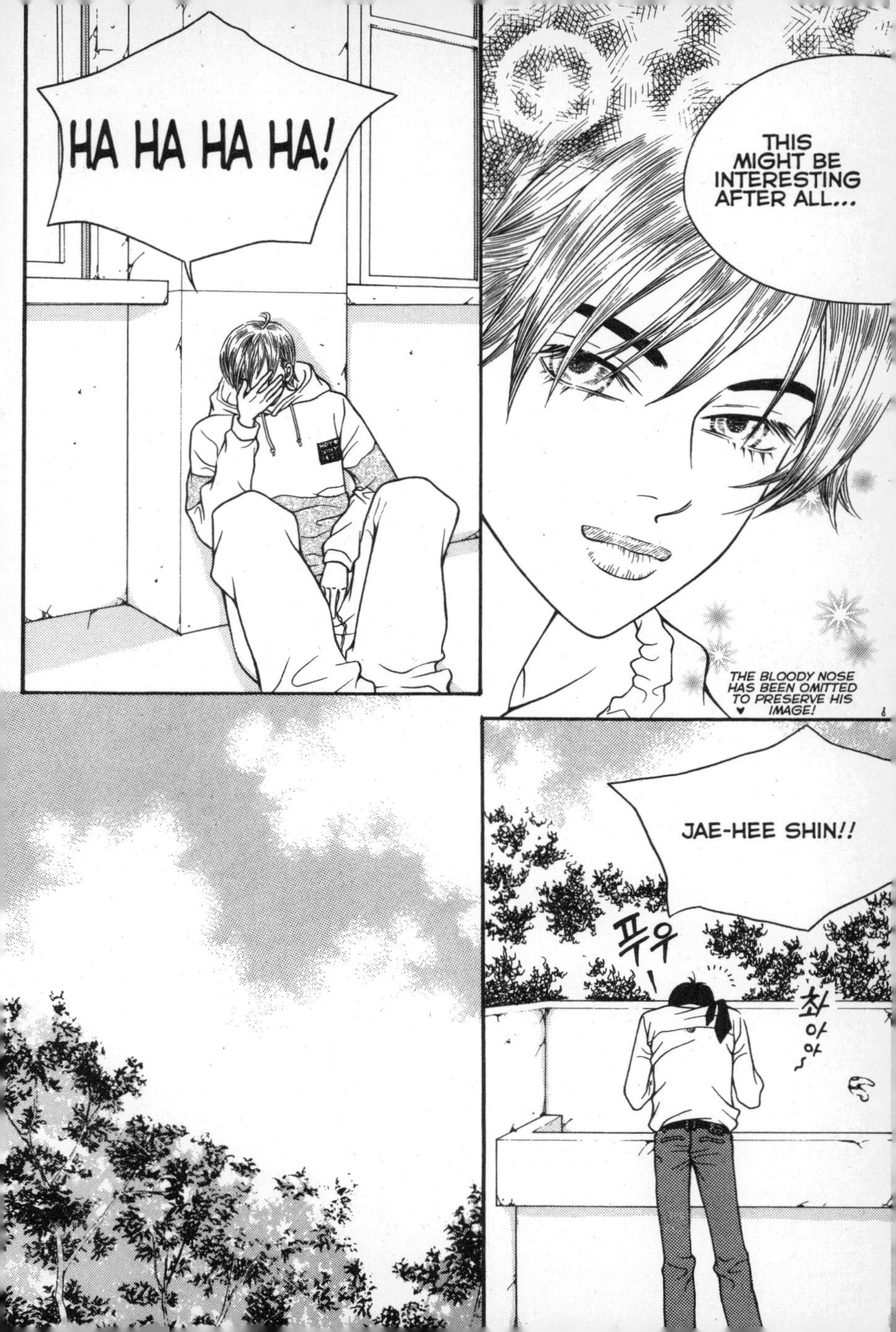
HA HA HA HA HA!
THIS MIGHT BE INTERESTING AFTER ALL...
THE BLOODY NOSE HAS BEEN OMITTED TO PRESERVE HIS IMAGE! ♥
JAE-HEE SHIN!!
푸우
촤아아~

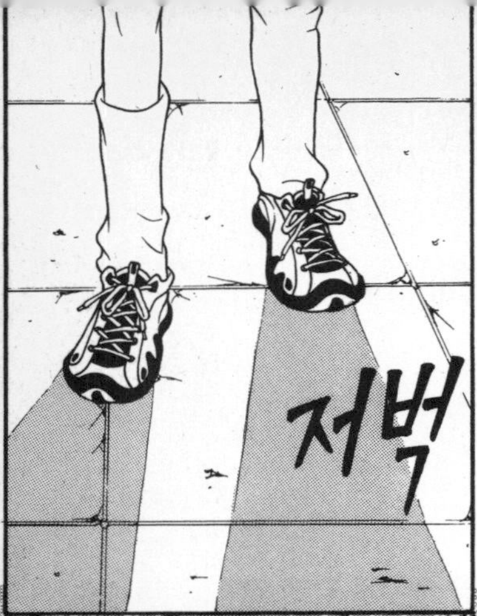
저벅
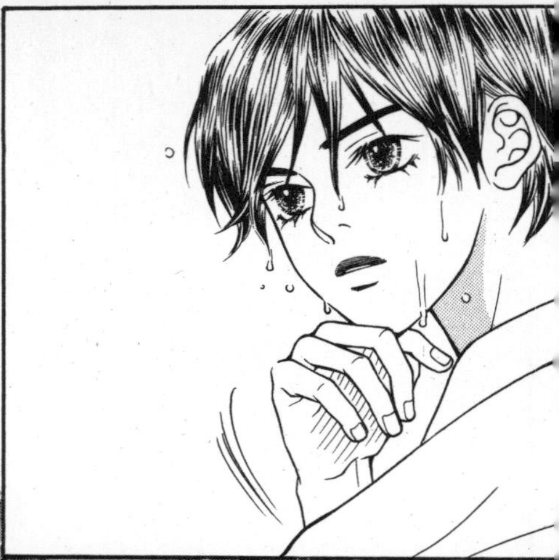
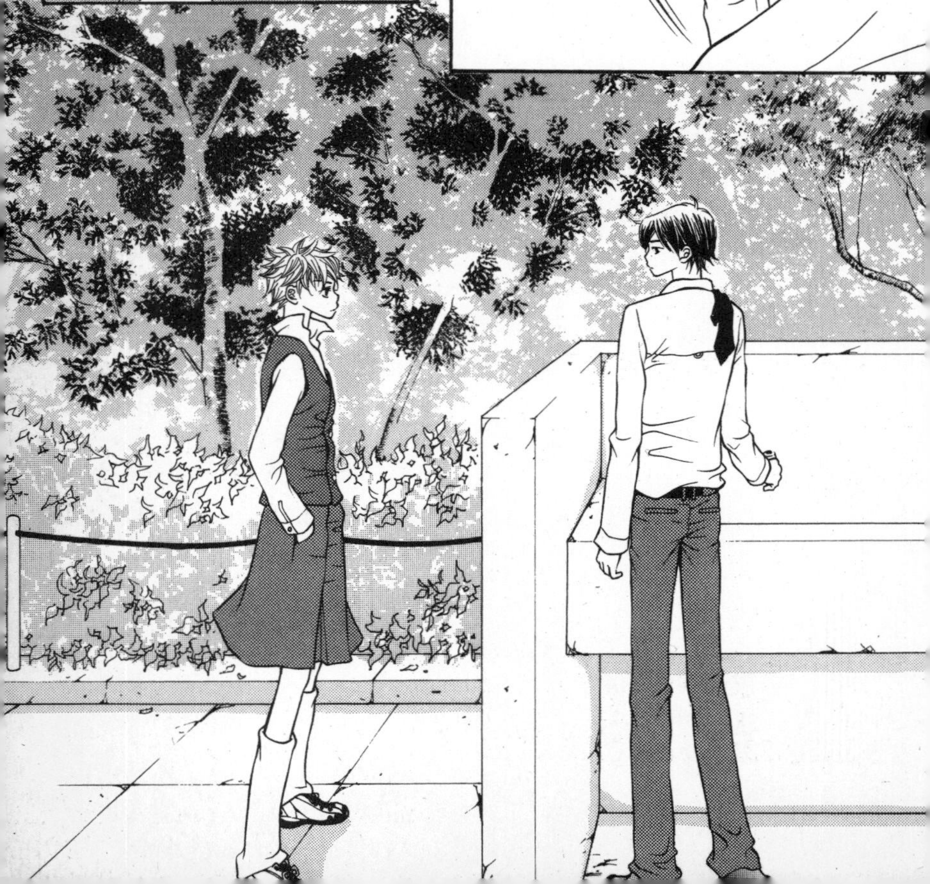

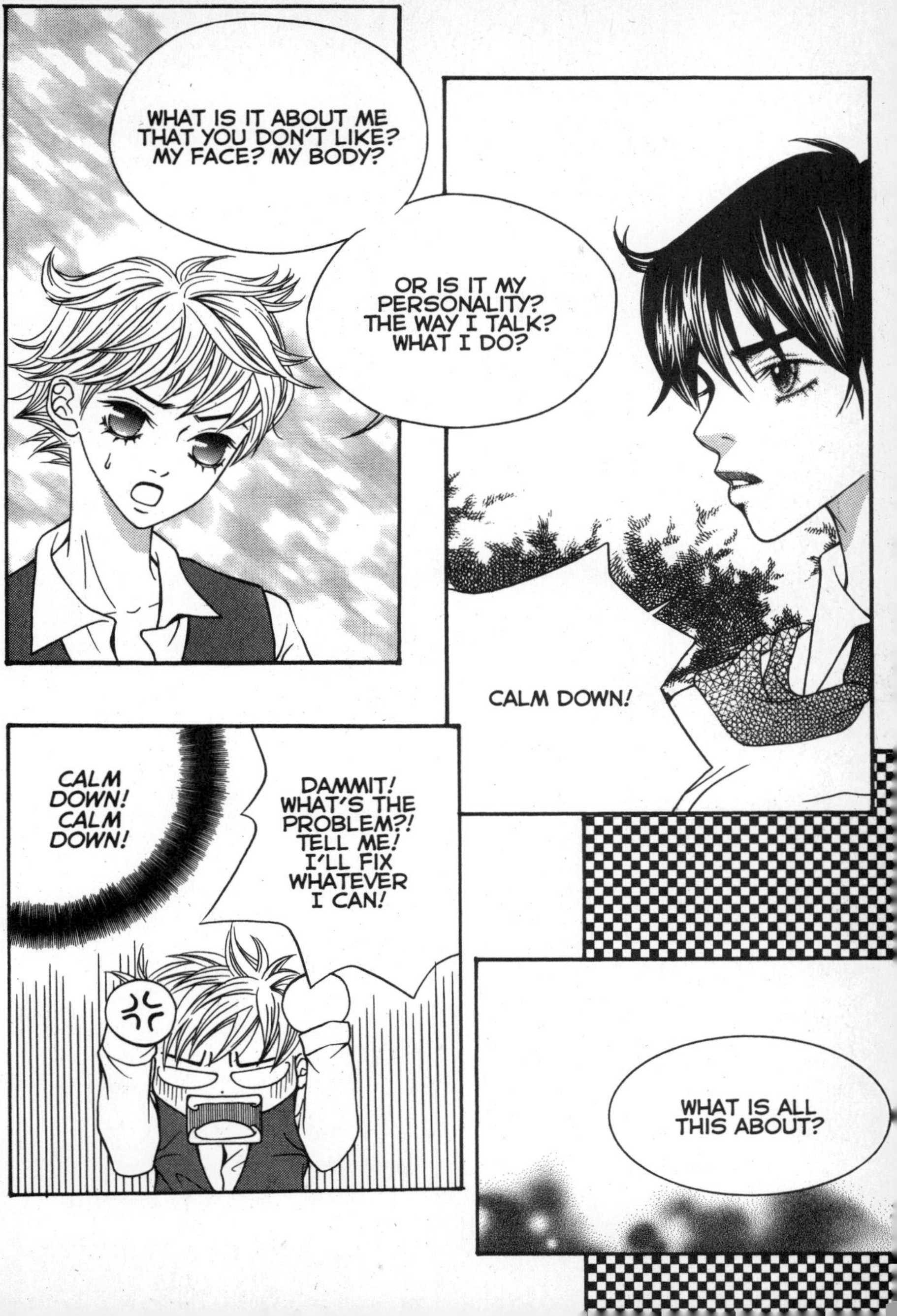
WHAT IS IT ABOUT ME THAT YOU DON'T LIKE? MY FACE? MY BODY?
OR IS IT MY PERSONALITY? THE WAY I TALK? WHAT I DO?
CALM DOWN!
CALM DOWN! CALM DOWN!
DAMMIT! WHAT'S THE PROBLEM?! TELL ME! I'LL FIX WHATEVER I CAN!
WHAT IS ALL THIS ABOUT?

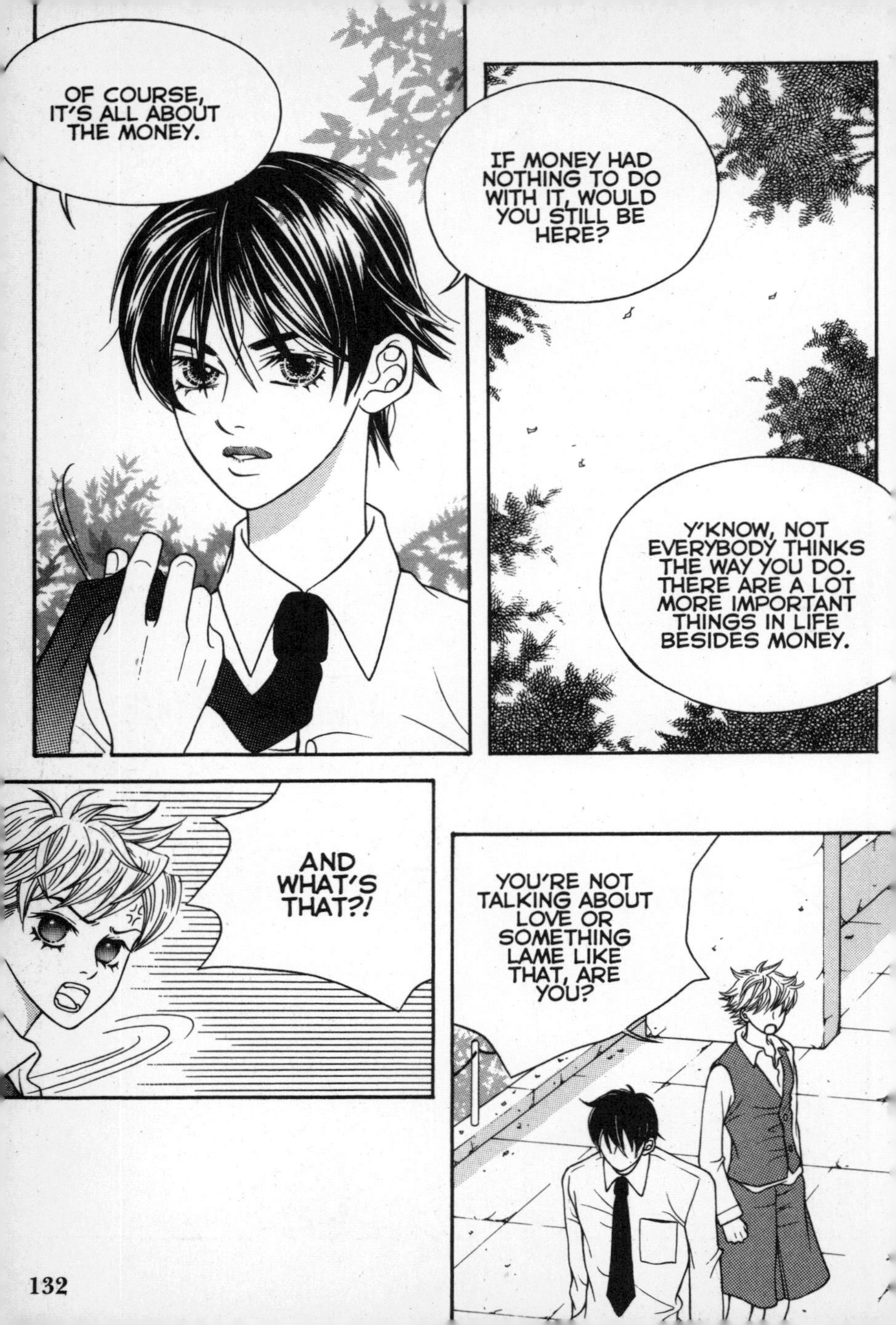
OF COURSE, IT'S ALL ABOUT THE MONEY.
IF MONEY HAD NOTHING TO DO WITH IT, WOULD YOU STILL BE HERE?
Y'KNOW, NOT EVERYBODY THINKS THE WAY YOU DO. THERE ARE A LOT MORE IMPORTANT THINGS IN LIFE BESIDES MONEY.
AND WHAT'S THAT?!
YOU'RE NOT TALKING ABOUT LOVE OR SOMETHING LAME LIKE THAT, ARE YOU?

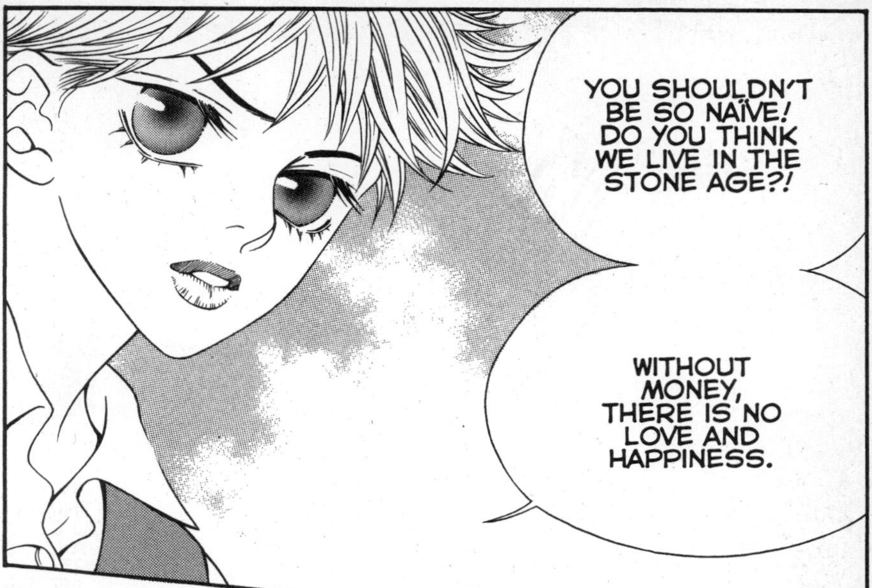
YOU SHOULDN'T BE SO NAÏVE! DO YOU THINK WE LIVE IN THE STONE AGE?!
WITHOUT MONEY, THERE IS NO LOVE AND HAPPINESS.

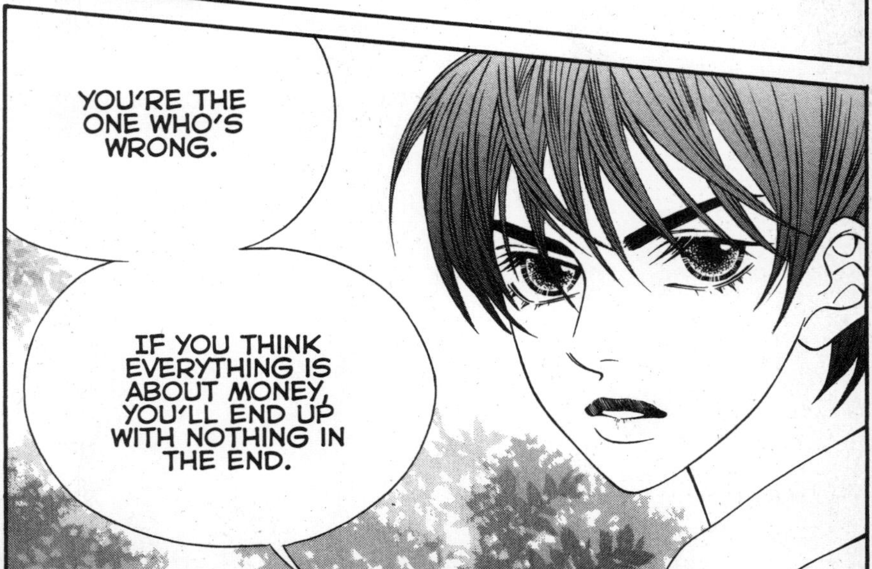
YOU'RE THE ONE WHO'S WRONG.
IF YOU THINK EVERYTHING IS ABOUT MONEY, YOU'LL END UP WITH NOTHING IN THE END.

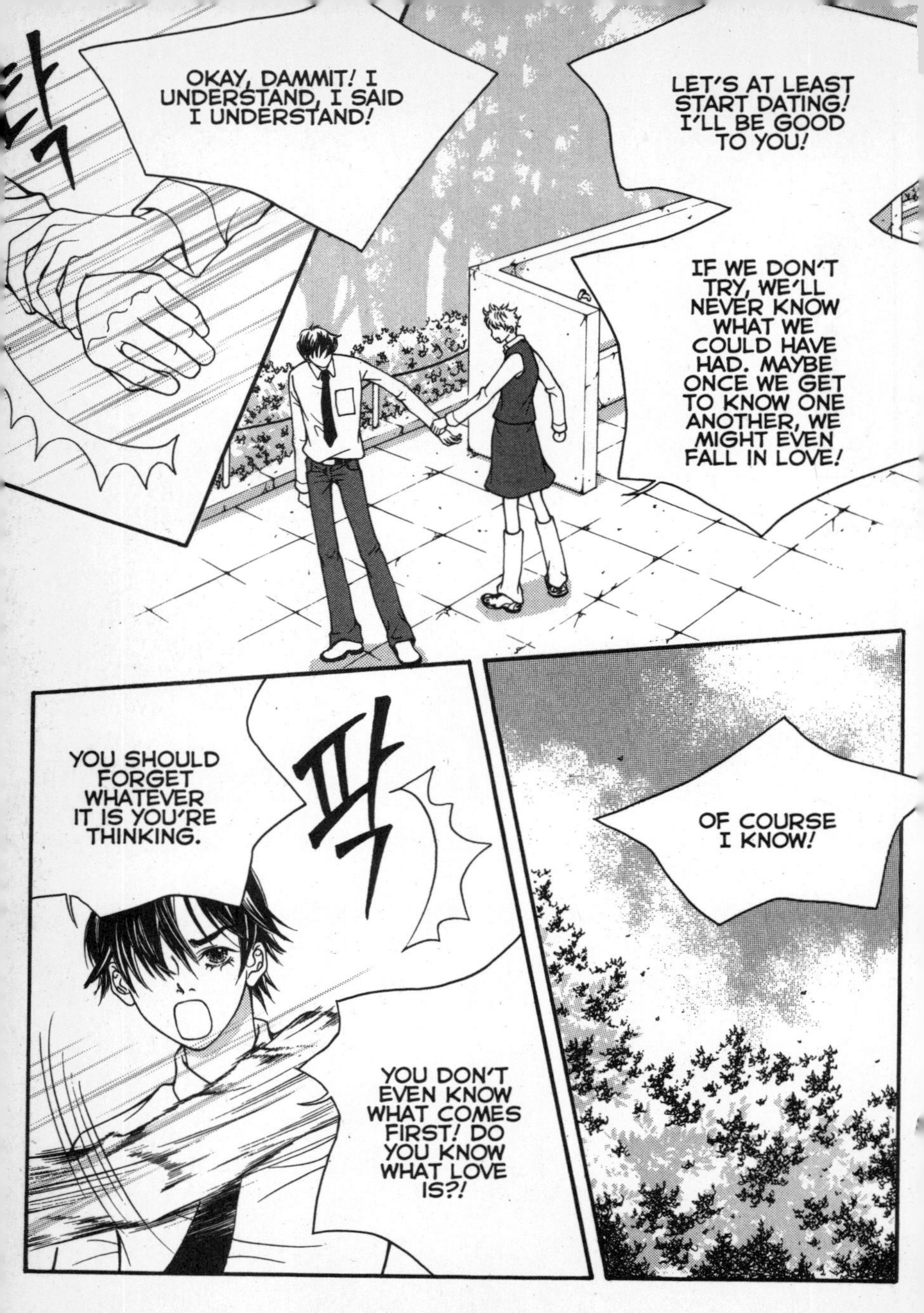
OKAY, DAMMIT! I UNDERSTAND, I SAID I UNDERSTAND!
LET'S AT LEAST START DATING! I'LL BE GOOD TO YOU!
IF WE DON'T TRY, WE'LL NEVER KNOW WHAT WE COULD HAVE HAD. MAYBE ONCE WE GET TO KNOW ONE ANOTHER, WE MIGHT EVEN FALL IN LOVE!
YOU SHOULD FORGET WHATEVER IT IS YOU'RE THINKING.
YOU DON'T EVEN KNOW WHAT COMES FIRST! DO YOU KNOW WHAT LOVE IS?!
OF COURSE I KNOW!

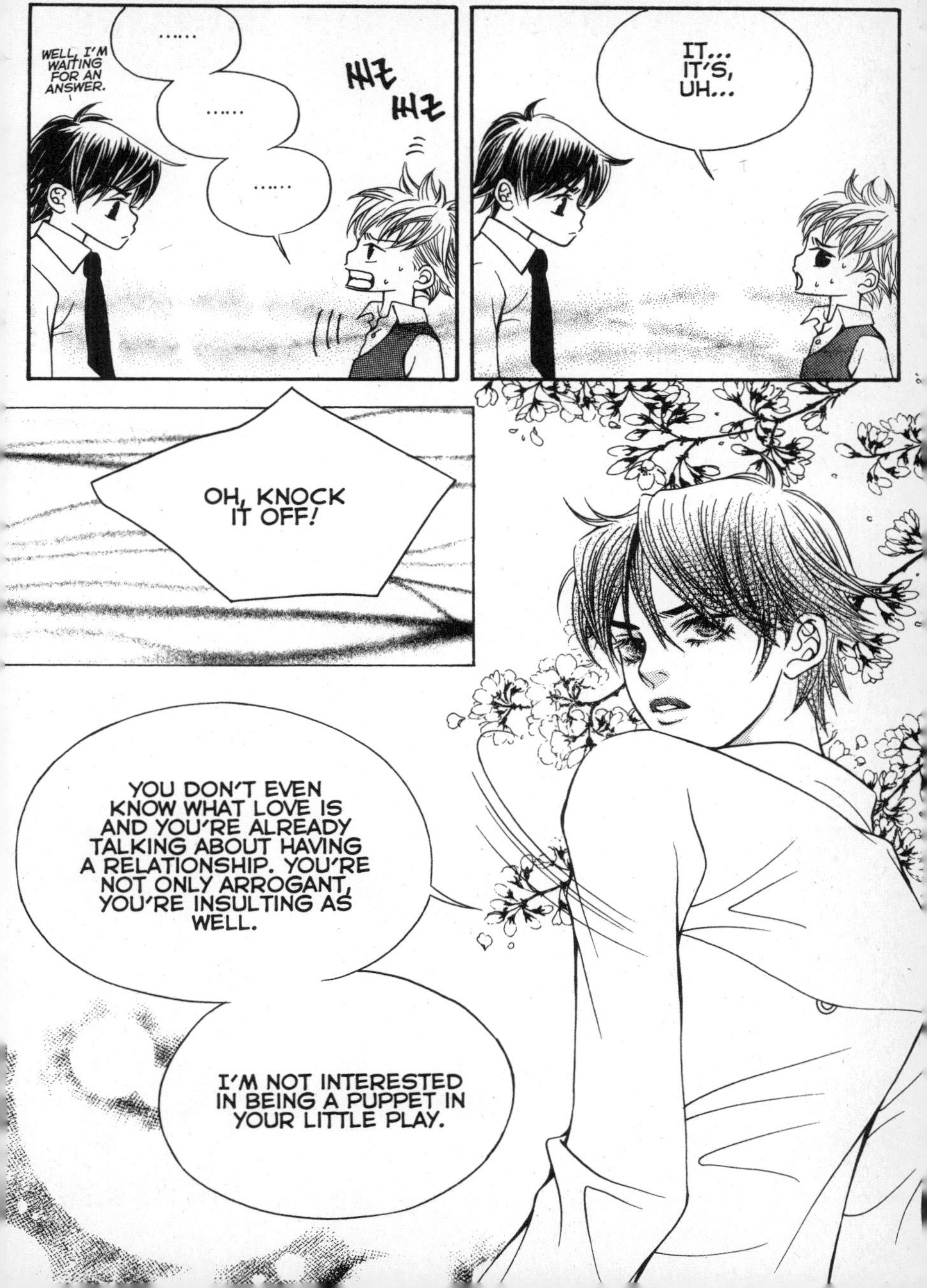

WELL, I'M WAITING FOR AN ANSWER.
……
……
……
IT... IT'S, UH...
OH, KNOCK IT OFF!
YOU DON'T EVEN KNOW WHAT LOVE IS AND YOU'RE ALREADY TALKING ABOUT HAVING A RELATIONSHIP. YOU'RE NOT ONLY ARROGANT, YOU'RE INSULTING AS WELL.
I'M NOT INTERESTED IN BEING A PUPPET IN YOUR LITTLE PLAY.

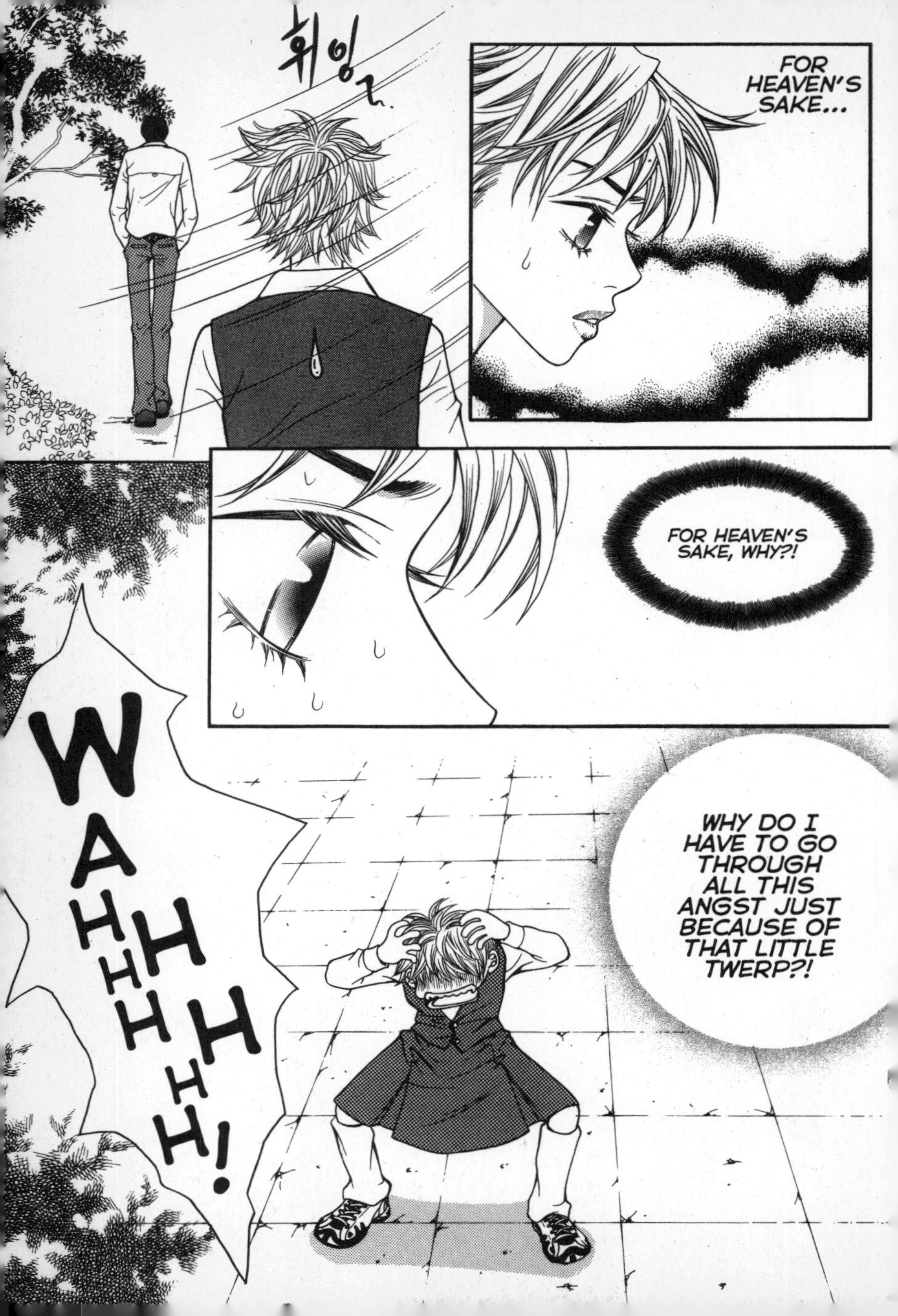
휘잉~
FOR HEAVEN'S SAKE...
FOR HEAVEN'S SAKE, WHY?!
WAHHHHHHH!
WHY DO I HAVE TO GO THROUGH ALL THIS ANGST JUST BECAUSE OF THAT LITTLE TWERP?!

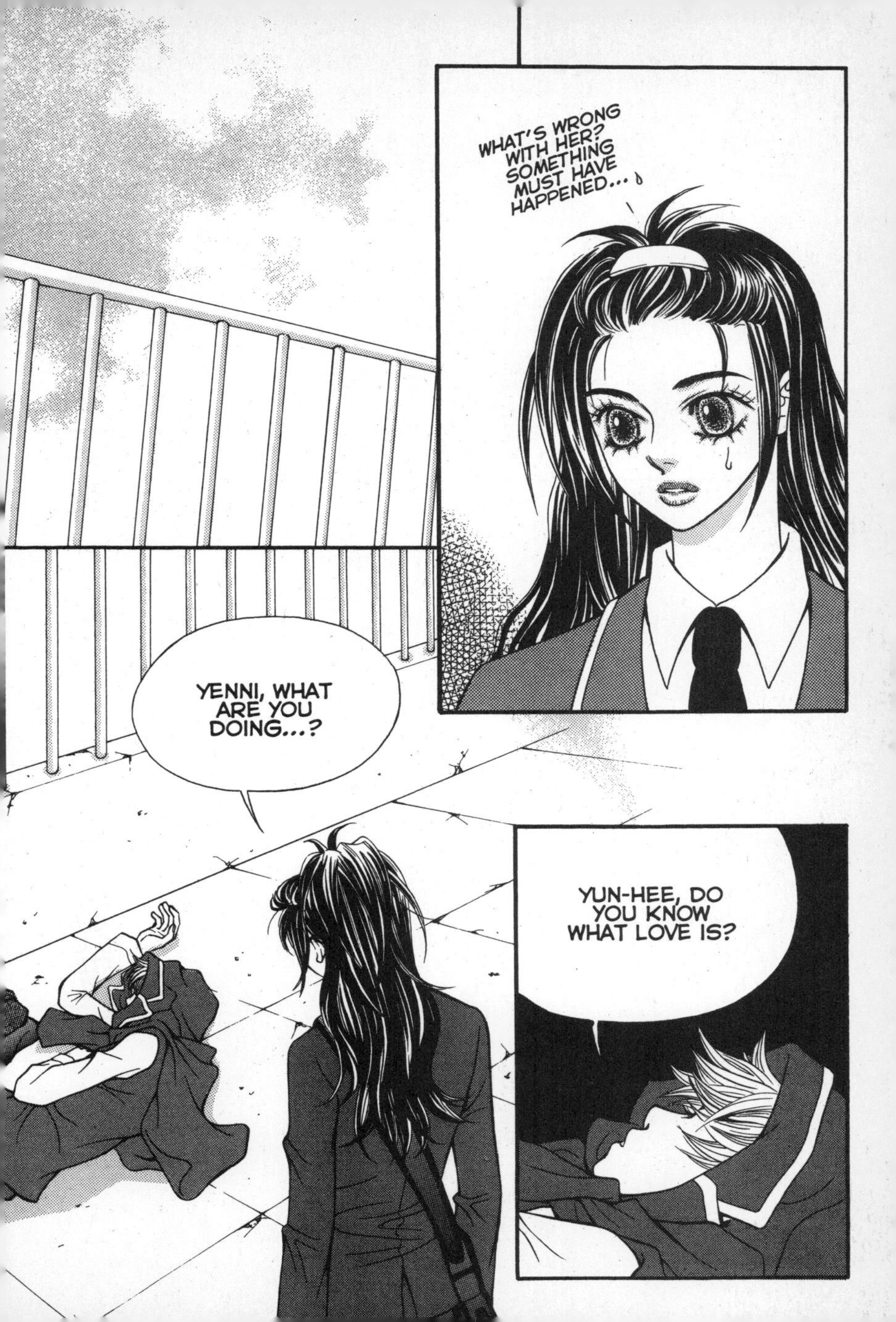
YENNI, WHAT ARE YOU DOING...?
WHAT'S WRONG WITH HER? SOMETHING MUST HAVE HAPPENED...
YUN-HEE, DO YOU KNOW WHAT LOVE IS?

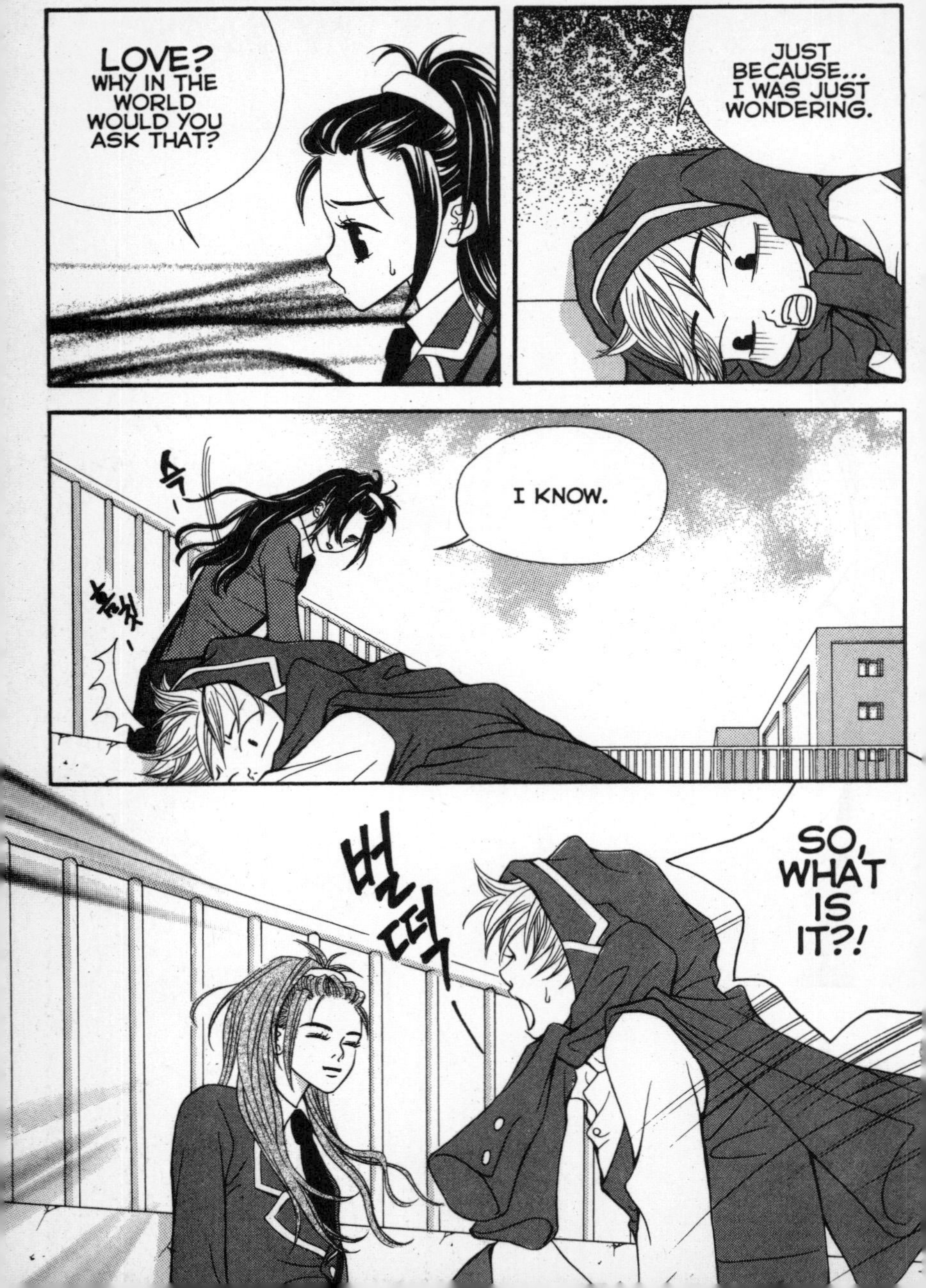
LOVE? WHY IN THE WORLD WOULD YOU ASK THAT?
JUST BECAUSE... I WAS JUST WONDERING.
슥
I KNOW.
벌떡
SO, WHAT IS IT?!

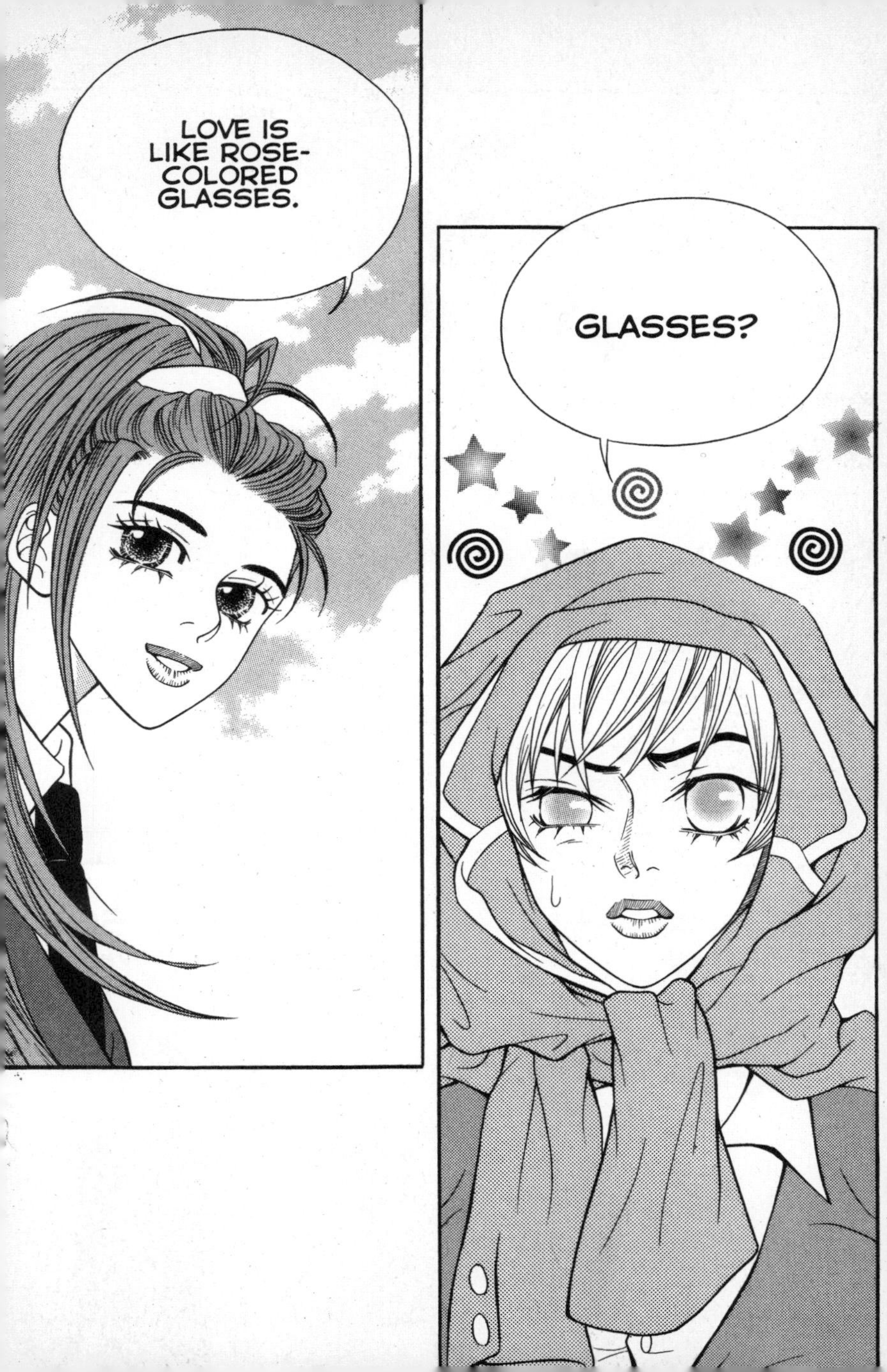
LOVE IS LIKE ROSE-COLORED GLASSES.
GLASSES?

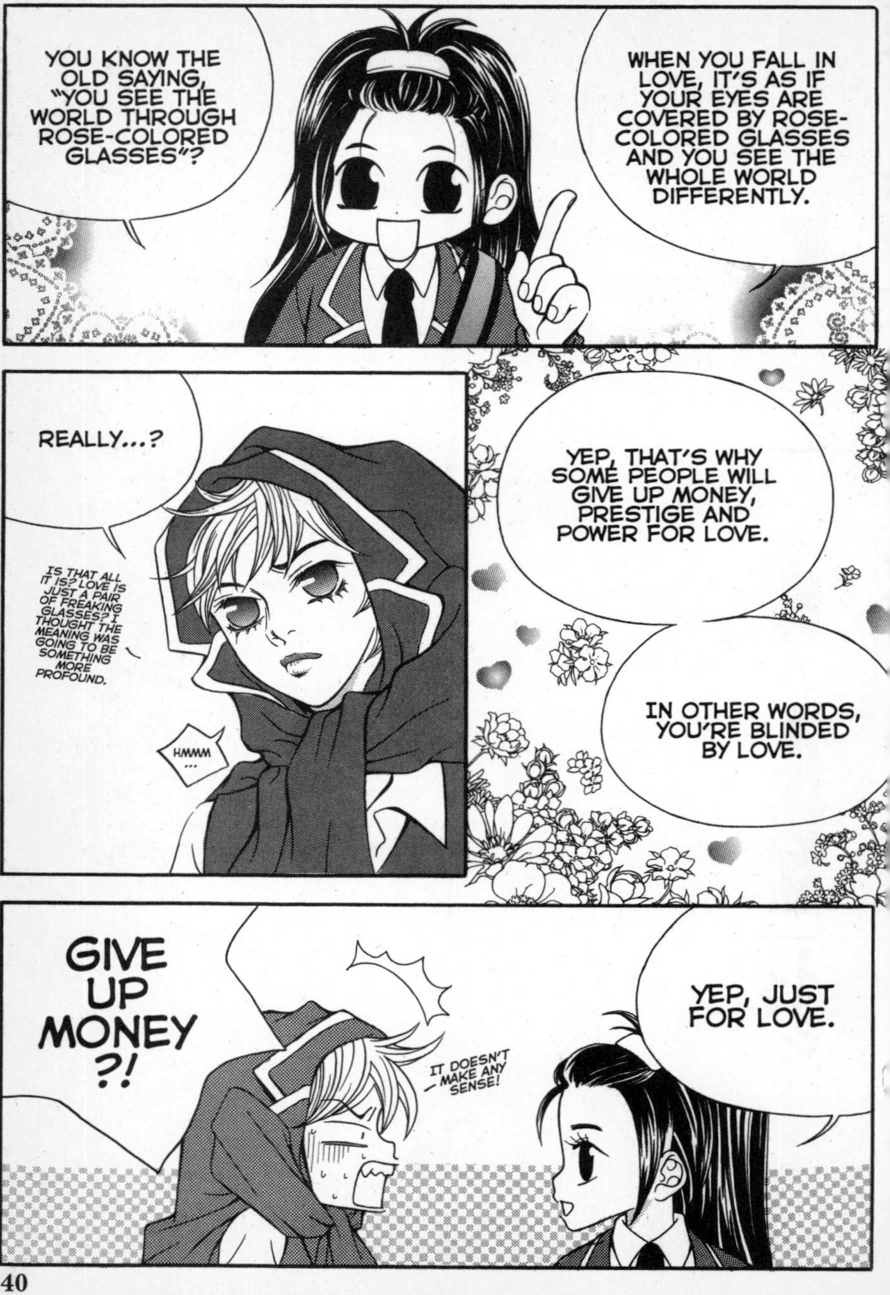
YOU KNOW THE OLD SAYING, "YOU SEE THE WORLD THROUGH ROSE-COLORED GLASSES"?
WHEN YOU FALL IN LOVE, IT'S AS IF YOUR EYES ARE COVERED BY ROSE-COLORED GLASSES AND YOU SEE THE WHOLE WORLD DIFFERENTLY.
REALLY...?
IS THAT ALL IT IS? LOVE IS JUST A PAIR OF FREAKING GLASSES? I THOUGHT THE MEANING WAS GOING TO BE SOMETHING MORE PROFOUND.
HMMM ...
YEP, THAT'S WHY SOME PEOPLE WILL GIVE UP MONEY, PRESTIGE AND POWER FOR LOVE.
IN OTHER WORDS, YOU'RE BLINDED BY LOVE.
GIVE UP MONEY ?!
IT DOESN'T MAKE ANY SENSE!
YEP, JUST FOR LOVE.

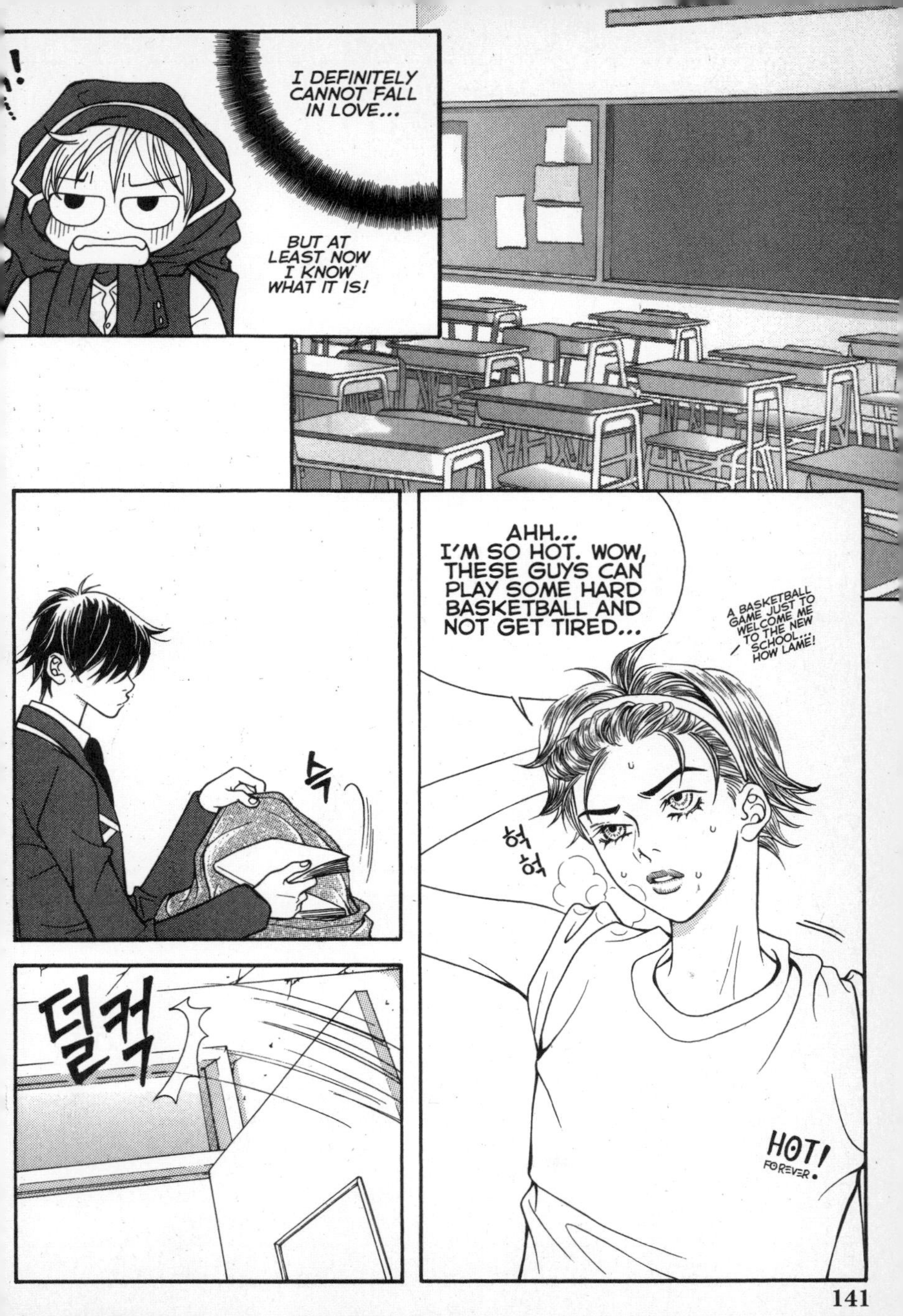

!
I DEFINITELY CANNOT FALL IN LOVE...
BUT AT LEAST NOW I KNOW WHAT IT IS!
슥
덜컥
AHH... I'M SO HOT. WOW, THESE GUYS CAN PLAY SOME HARD BASKETBALL AND NOT GET TIRED...
A BASKETBALL GAME JUST TO WELCOME ME TO THE NEW SCHOOL... HOW LAME!
헉 헉
HOT! FOREVER.

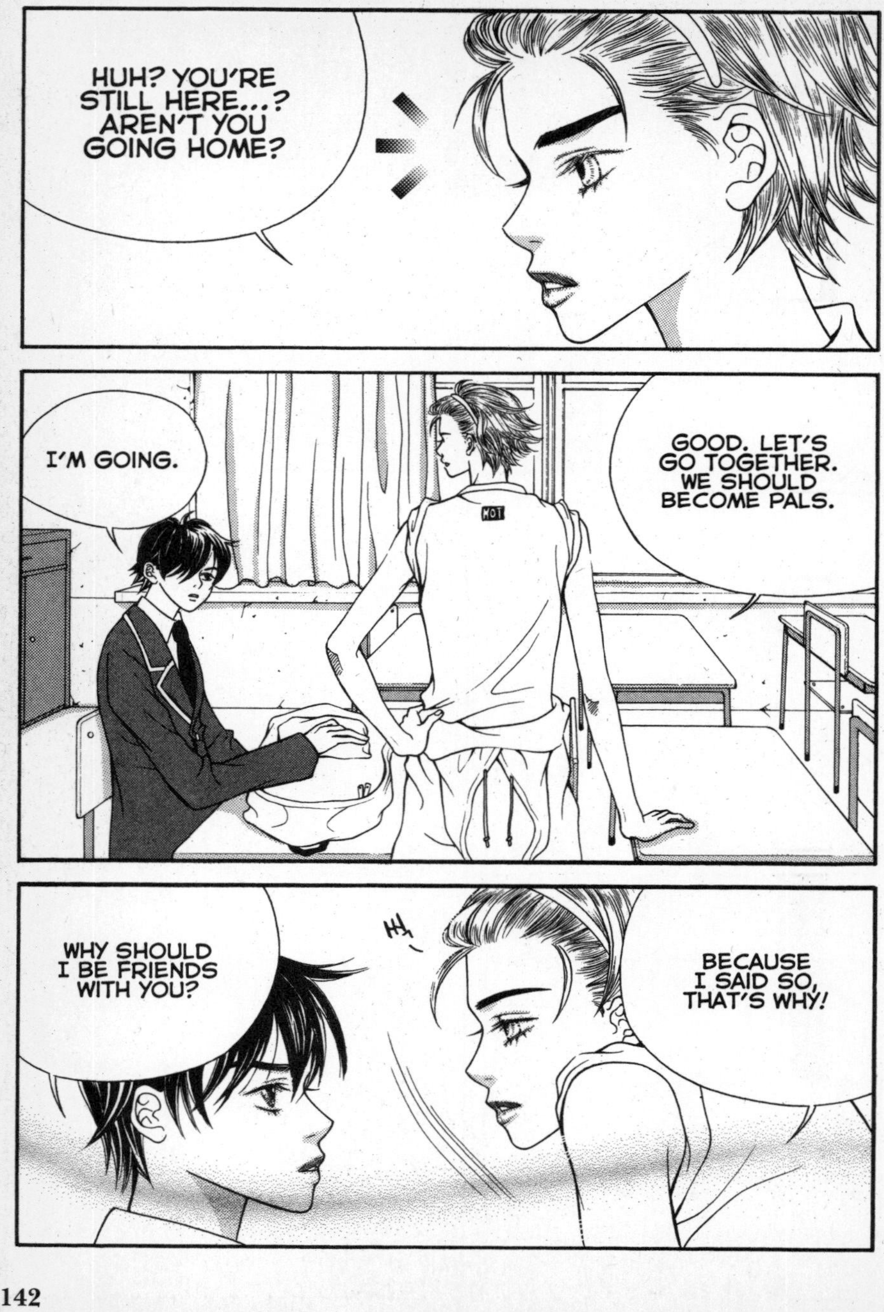
HUH? YOU'RE STILL HERE...? AREN'T YOU GOING HOME?
I'M GOING.
GOOD. LET'S GO TOGETHER. WE SHOULD BECOME PALS.
WHY SHOULD I BE FRIENDS WITH YOU?
BECAUSE I SAID SO, THAT'S WHY!

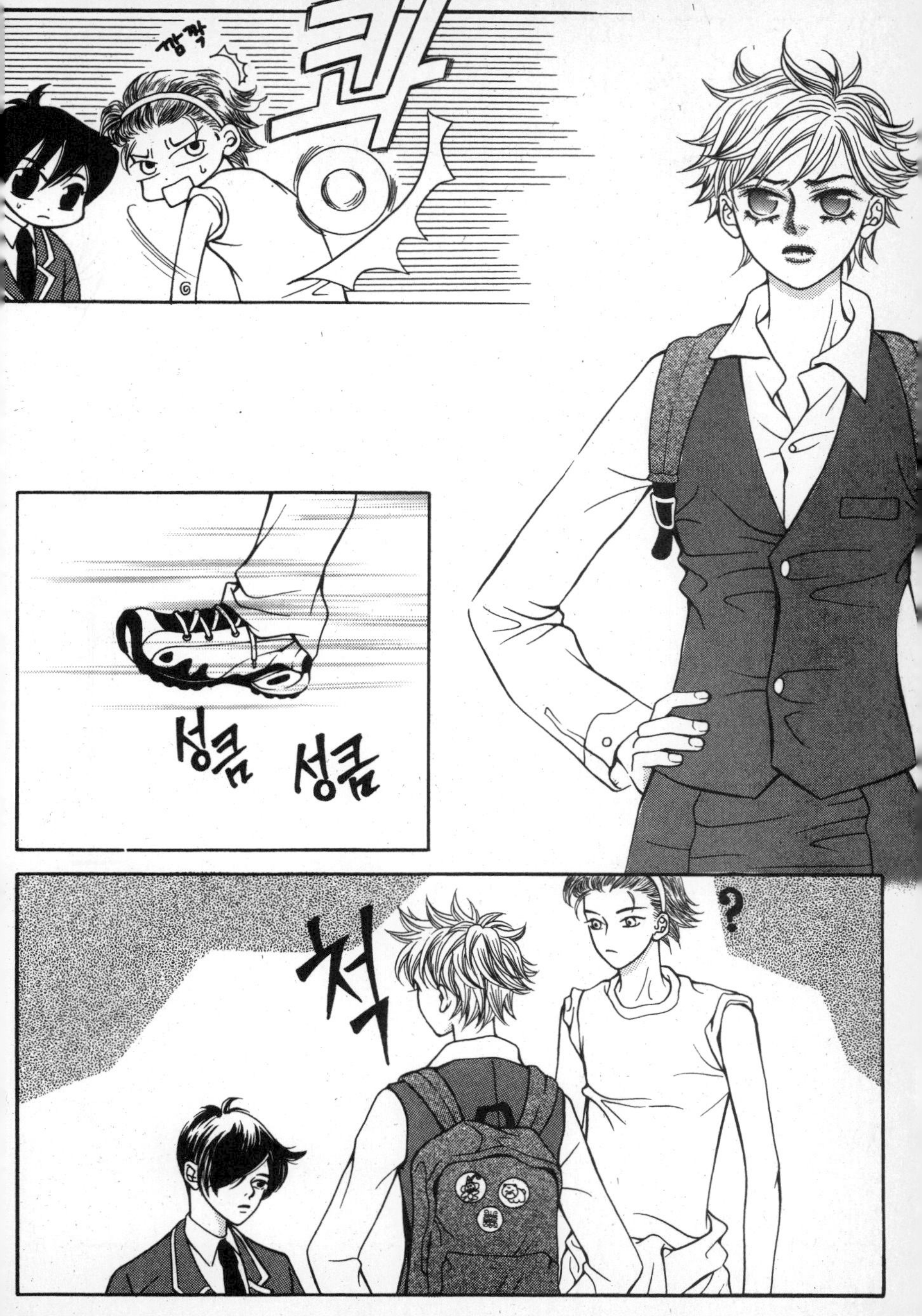
깜짝
콰
성큼 성큼
척
?

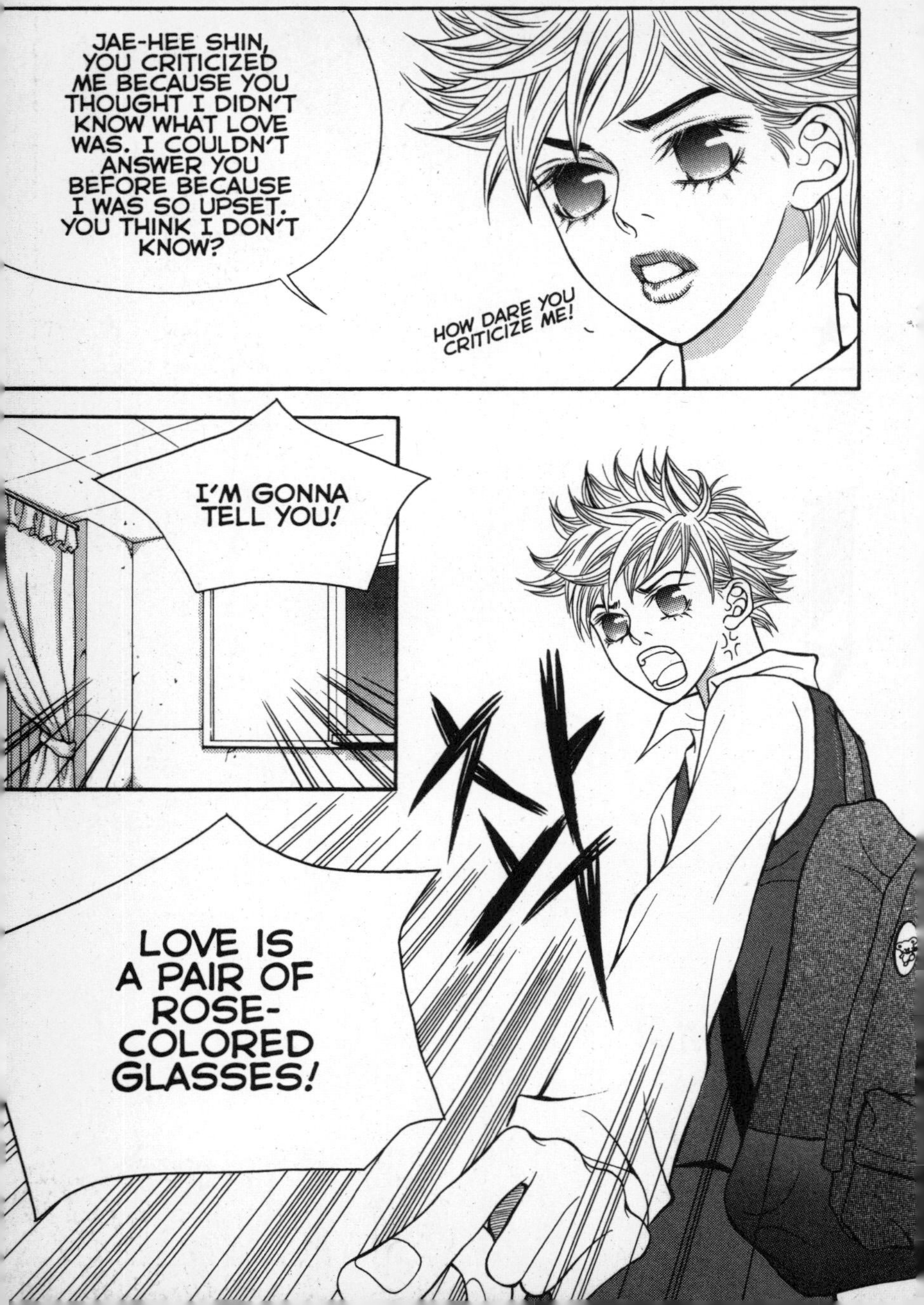
JAE-HEE SHIN, YOU CRITICIZED ME BECAUSE YOU THOUGHT I DIDN'T KNOW WHAT LOVE WAS. I COULDN'T ANSWER YOU BEFORE BECAUSE I WAS SO UPSET. YOU THINK I DON'T KNOW?
HOW DARE YOU CRITICIZE ME!
I'M GONNA TELL YOU!
LOVE IS A PAIR OF ROSE-COLORED GLASSES!

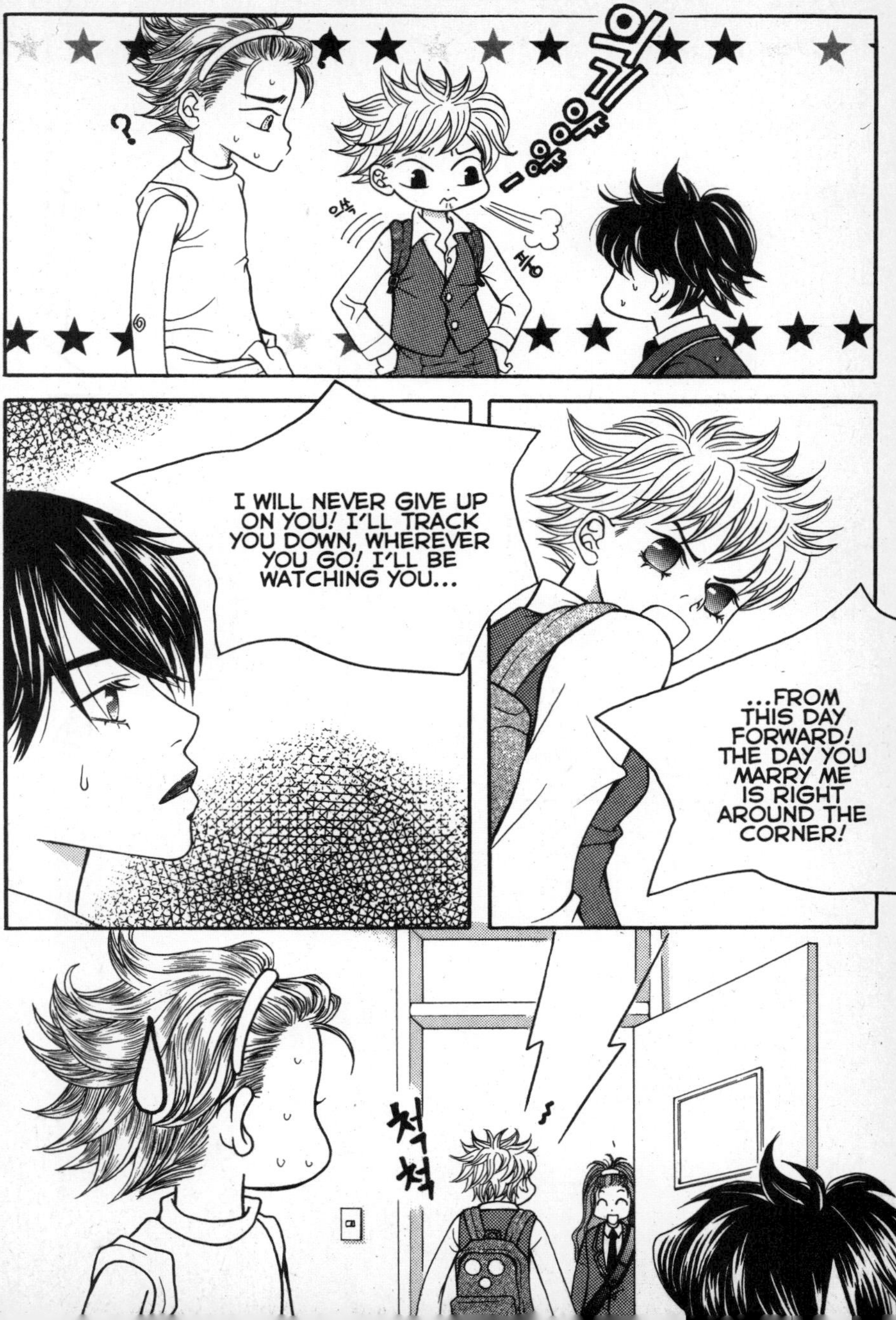

으쓱
흥
I WILL NEVER GIVE UP ON YOU! I'LL TRACK YOU DOWN, WHEREVER YOU GO! I'LL BE WATCHING YOU...
...FROM THIS DAY FORWARD! THE DAY YOU MARRY ME IS RIGHT AROUND THE CORNER!
척척

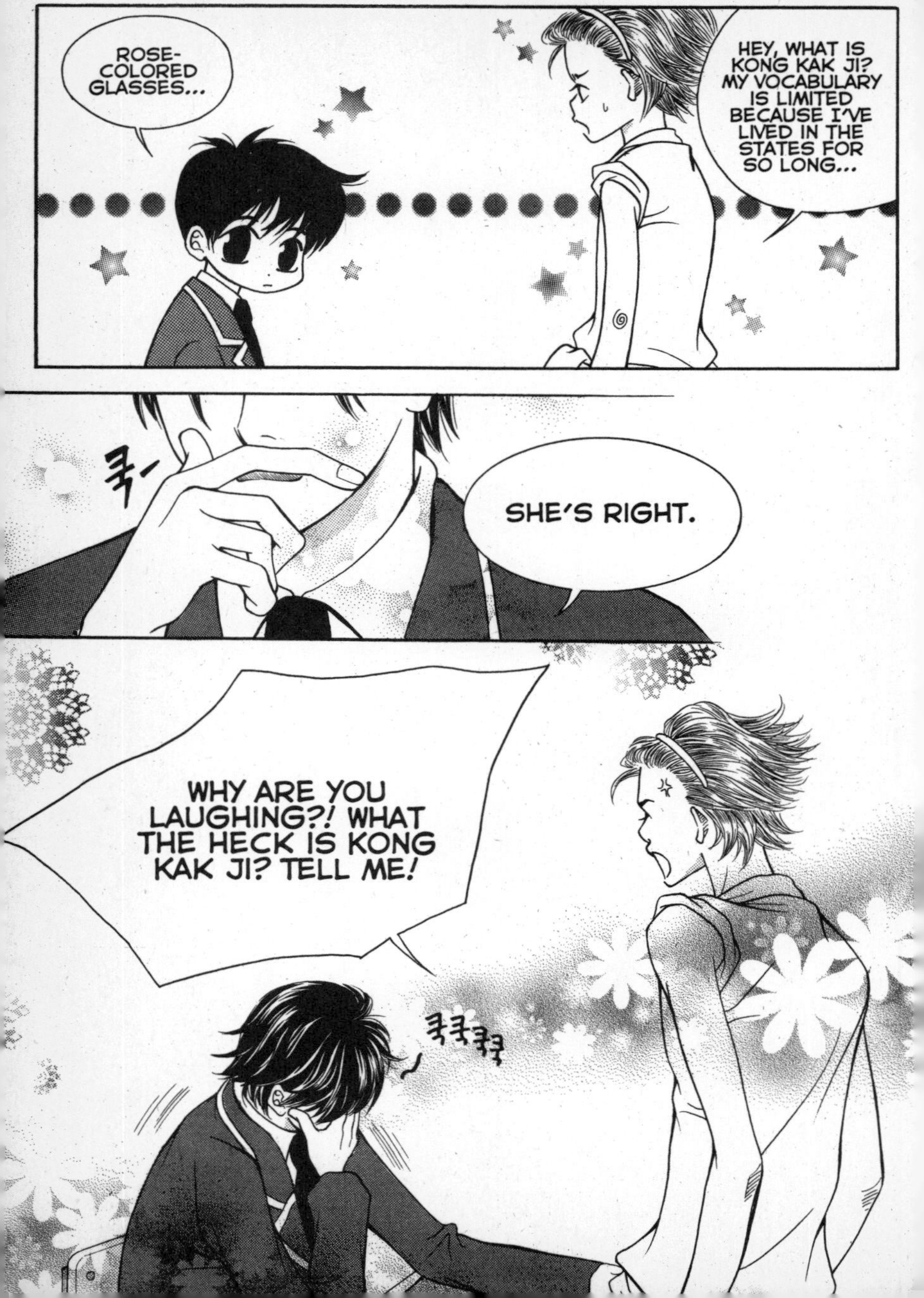
ROSE-COLORED GLASSES...
HEY, WHAT IS KONG KAK JI? MY VOCABULARY IS LIMITED BECAUSE I'VE LIVED IN THE STATES FOR SO LONG...
ㅋ~
SHE'S RIGHT.
WHY ARE YOU LAUGHING?! WHAT THE HECK IS KONG KAK JI? TELL ME!
ㅋㅋㅋㅋ~

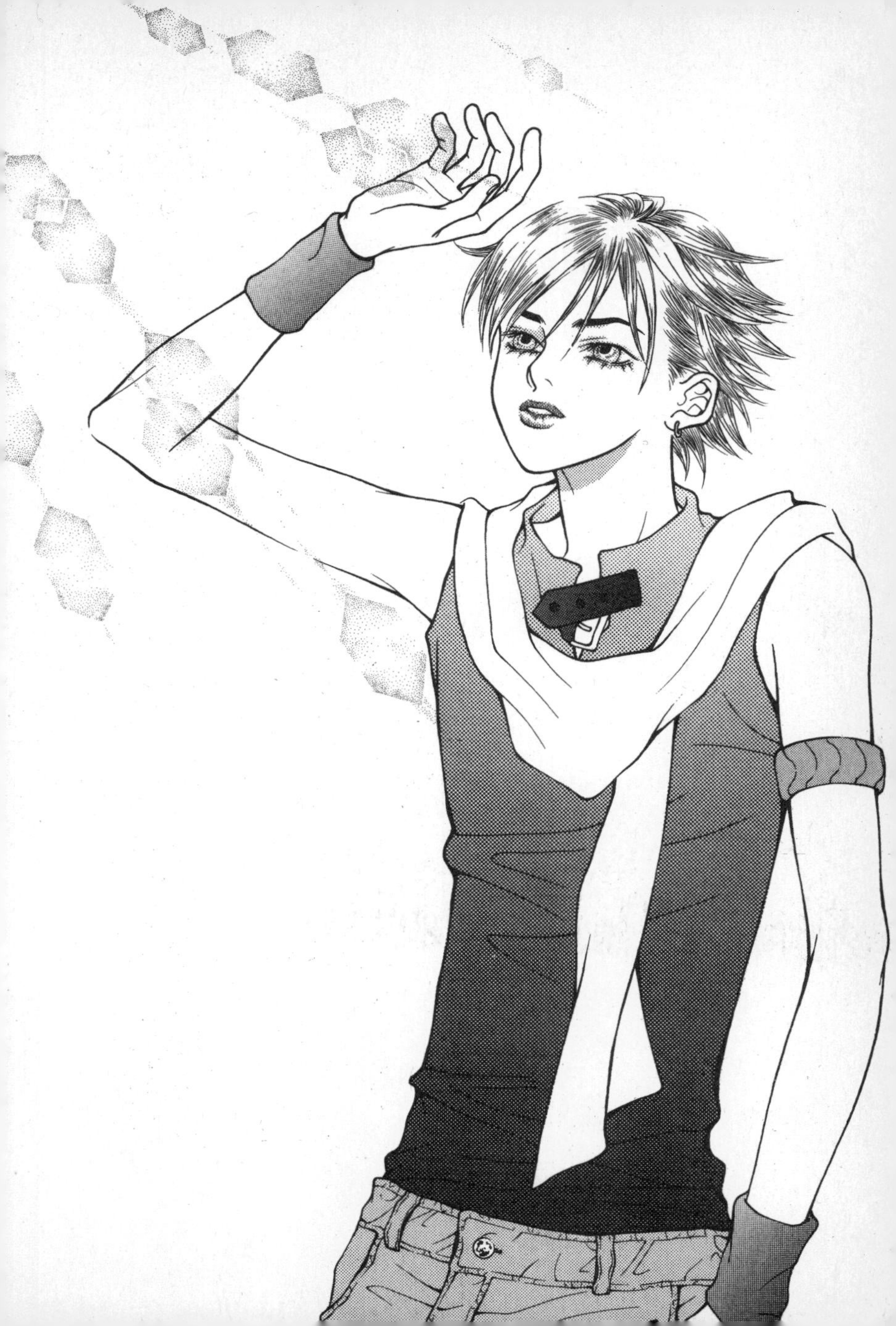

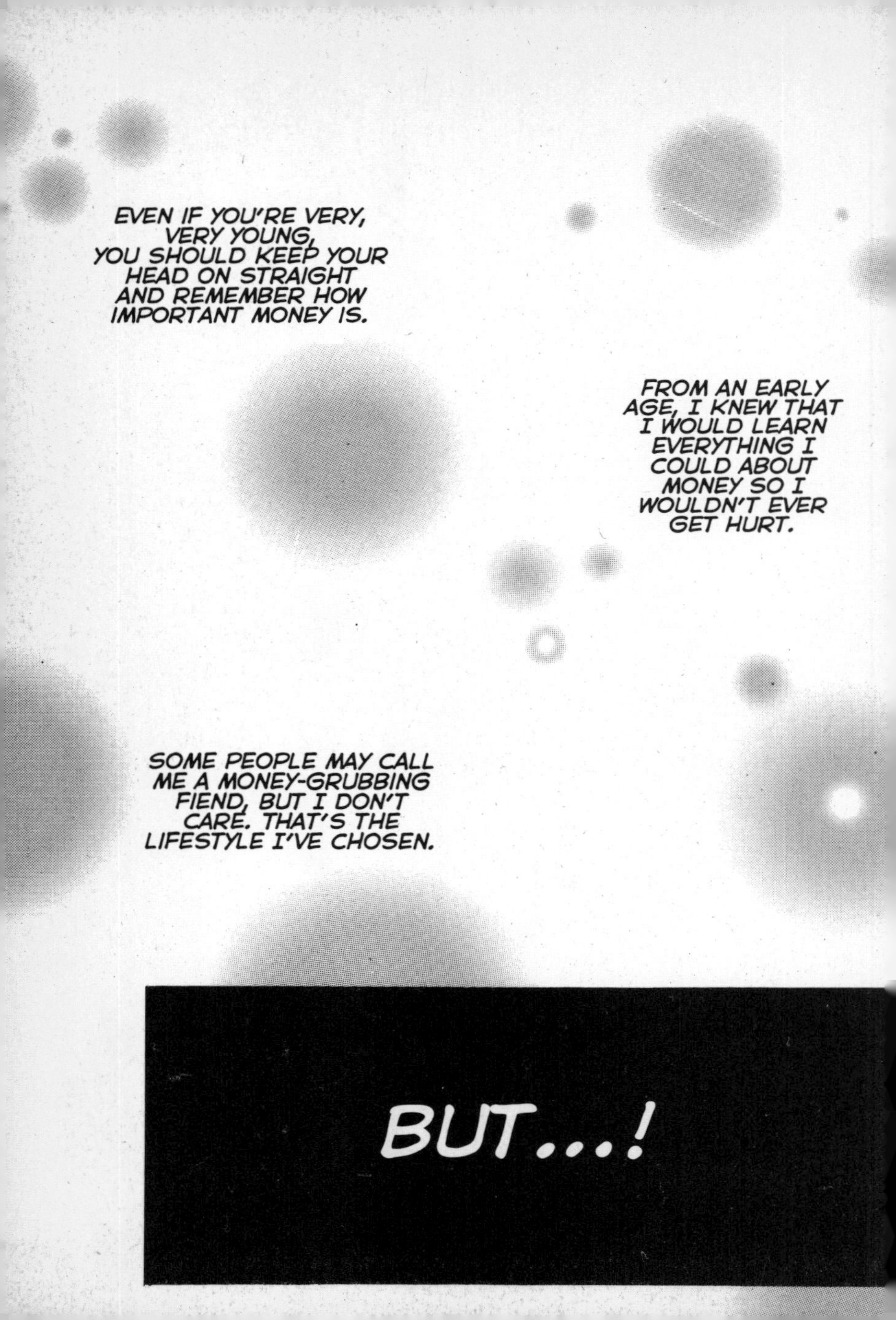
EVEN IF YOU'RE VERY, VERY YOUNG, YOU SHOULD KEEP YOUR HEAD ON STRAIGHT AND REMEMBER HOW IMPORTANT MONEY IS.
FROM AN EARLY AGE, I KNEW THAT I WOULD LEARN EVERYTHING I COULD ABOUT MONEY SO I WOULDN'T EVER GET HURT.
SOME PEOPLE MAY CALL ME A MONEY-GRUBBING FIEND, BUT I DON'T CARE. THAT'S THE LIFESTYLE I'VE CHOSEN.
BUT...!

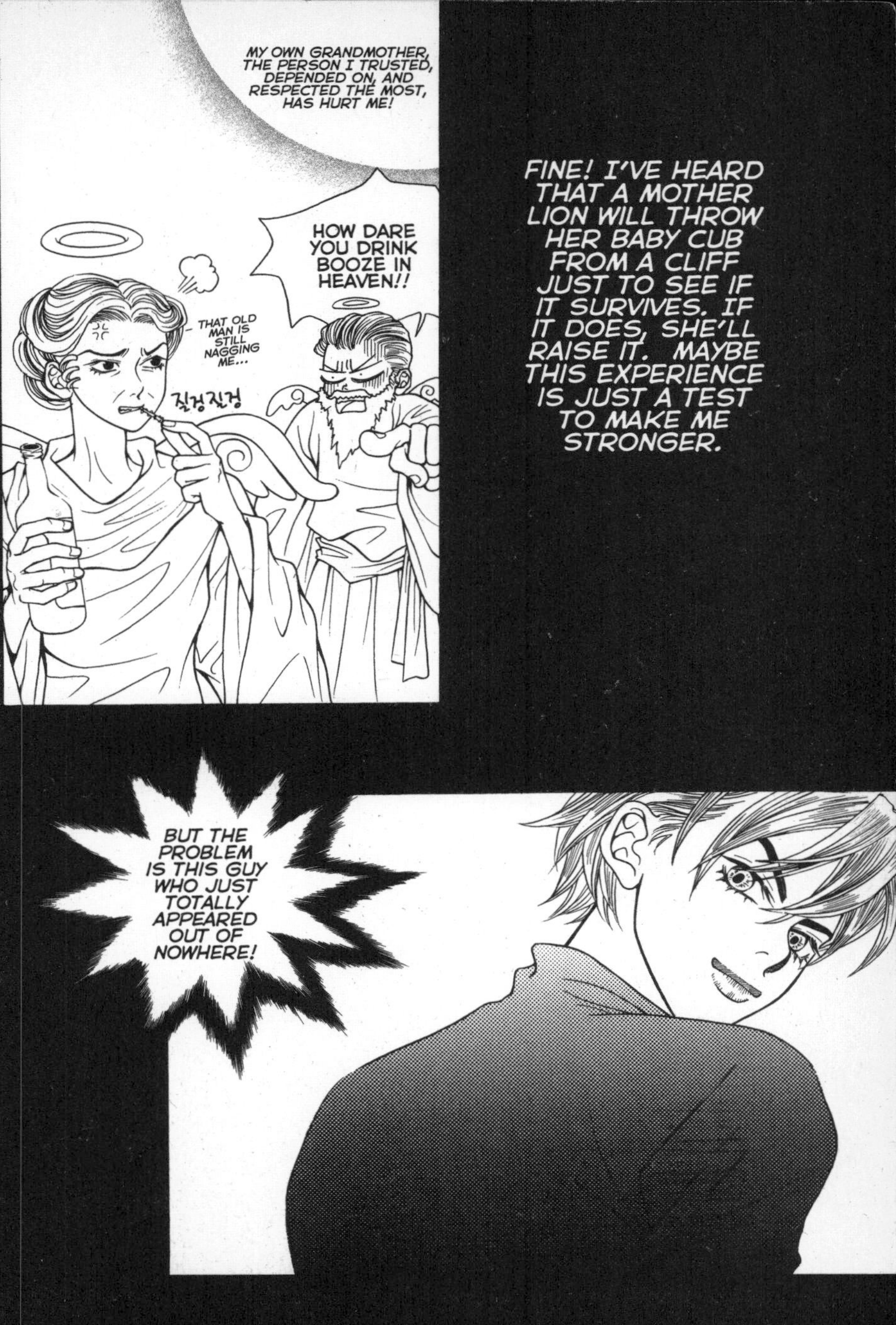
MY OWN GRANDMOTHER, THE PERSON I TRUSTED, DEPENDED ON, AND RESPECTED THE MOST, HAS HURT ME!
HOW DARE YOU DRINK BOOZE IN HEAVEN!!
THAT OLD MAN IS STILL NAGGING ME...
질겅질겅
FINE! I'VE HEARD THAT A MOTHER LION WILL THROW HER BABY CUB FROM A CLIFF JUST TO SEE IF IT SURVIVES. IF IT DOES, SHE'LL RAISE IT. MAYBE THIS EXPERIENCE IS JUST A TEST TO MAKE ME STRONGER.
BUT THE PROBLEM IS THIS GUY WHO JUST TOTALLY APPEARED OUT OF NOWHERE!

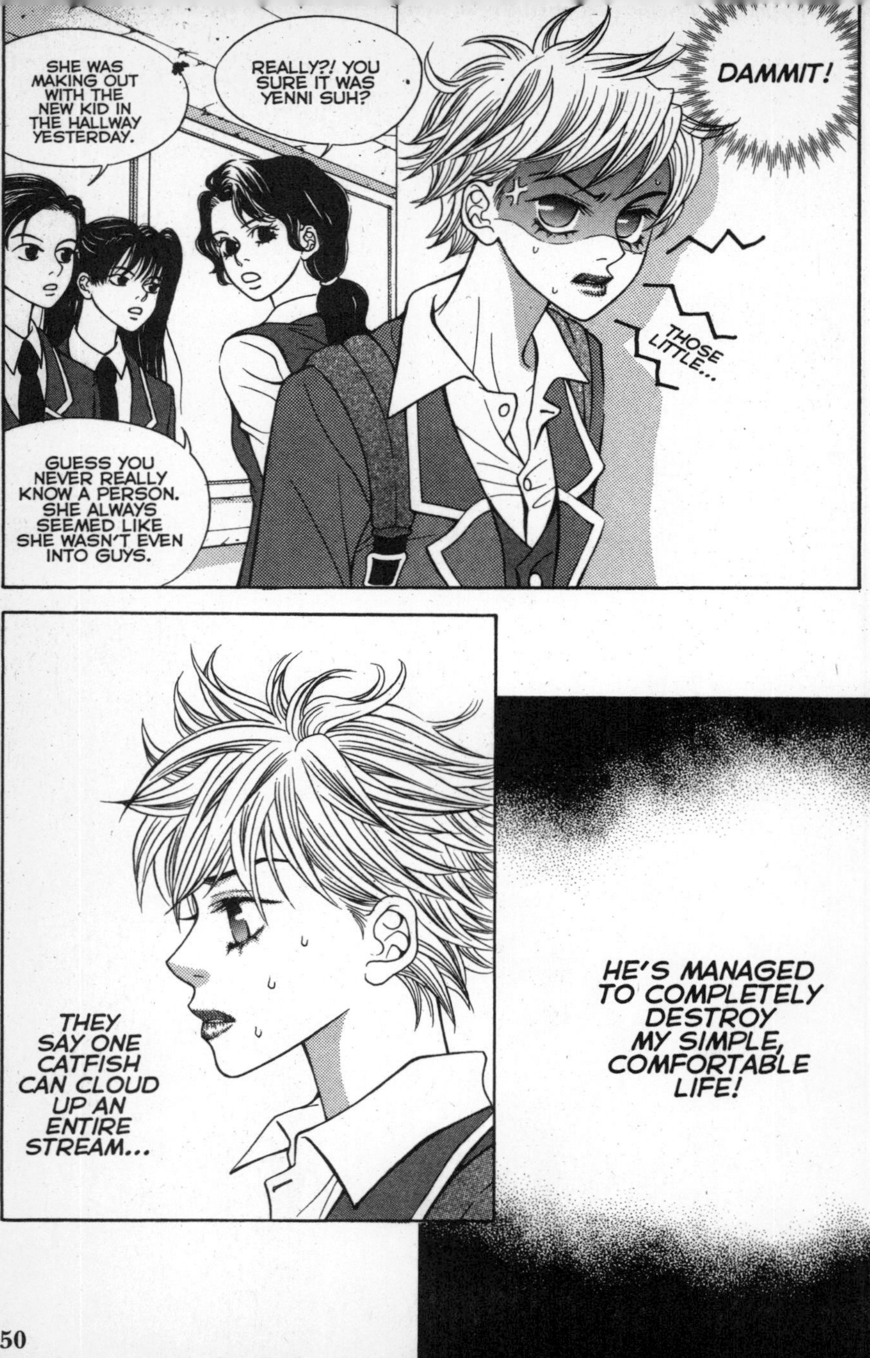
SHE WAS MAKING OUT WITH THE NEW KID IN THE HALLWAY YESTERDAY.
REALLY?! YOU SURE IT WAS YENNI SUH?
DAMMIT!
THOSE LITTLE...
GUESS YOU NEVER REALLY KNOW A PERSON. SHE ALWAYS SEEMED LIKE SHE WASN'T EVEN INTO GUYS.
THEY SAY ONE CATFISH CAN CLOUD UP AN ENTIRE STREAM...
HE'S MANAGED TO COMPLETELY DESTROY MY SIMPLE, COMFORTABLE LIFE!

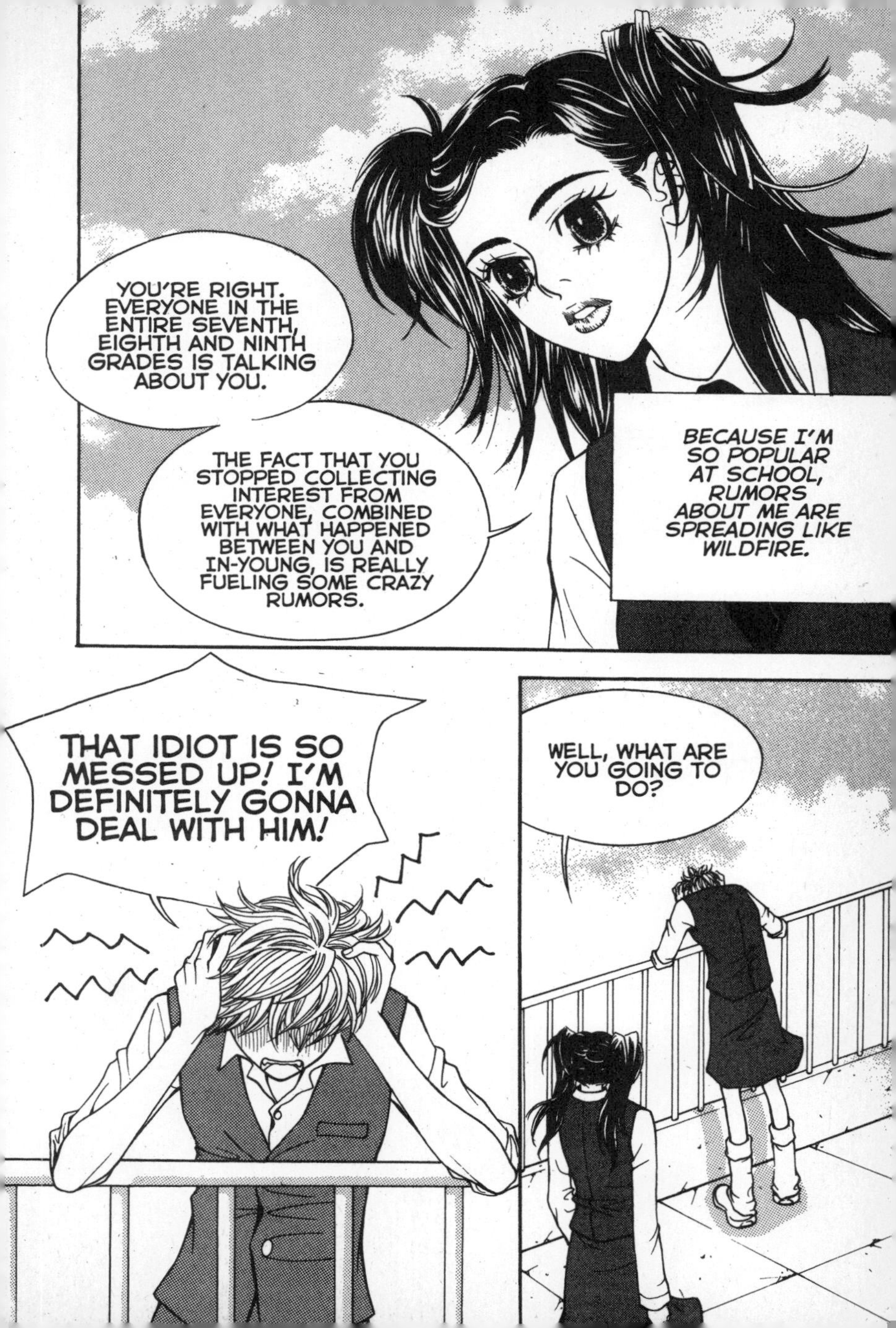
BECAUSE I'M SO POPULAR AT SCHOOL, RUMORS ABOUT ME ARE SPREADING LIKE WILDFIRE.
YOU'RE RIGHT. EVERYONE IN THE ENTIRE SEVENTH, EIGHTH AND NINTH GRADES IS TALKING ABOUT YOU.
THE FACT THAT YOU STOPPED COLLECTING INTEREST FROM EVERYONE, COMBINED WITH WHAT HAPPENED BETWEEN YOU AND IN-YOUNG, IS REALLY FUELING SOME CRAZY RUMORS.
WELL, WHAT ARE YOU GOING TO DO?
THAT IDIOT IS SO MESSED UP! I'M DEFINITELY GONNA DEAL WITH HIM!

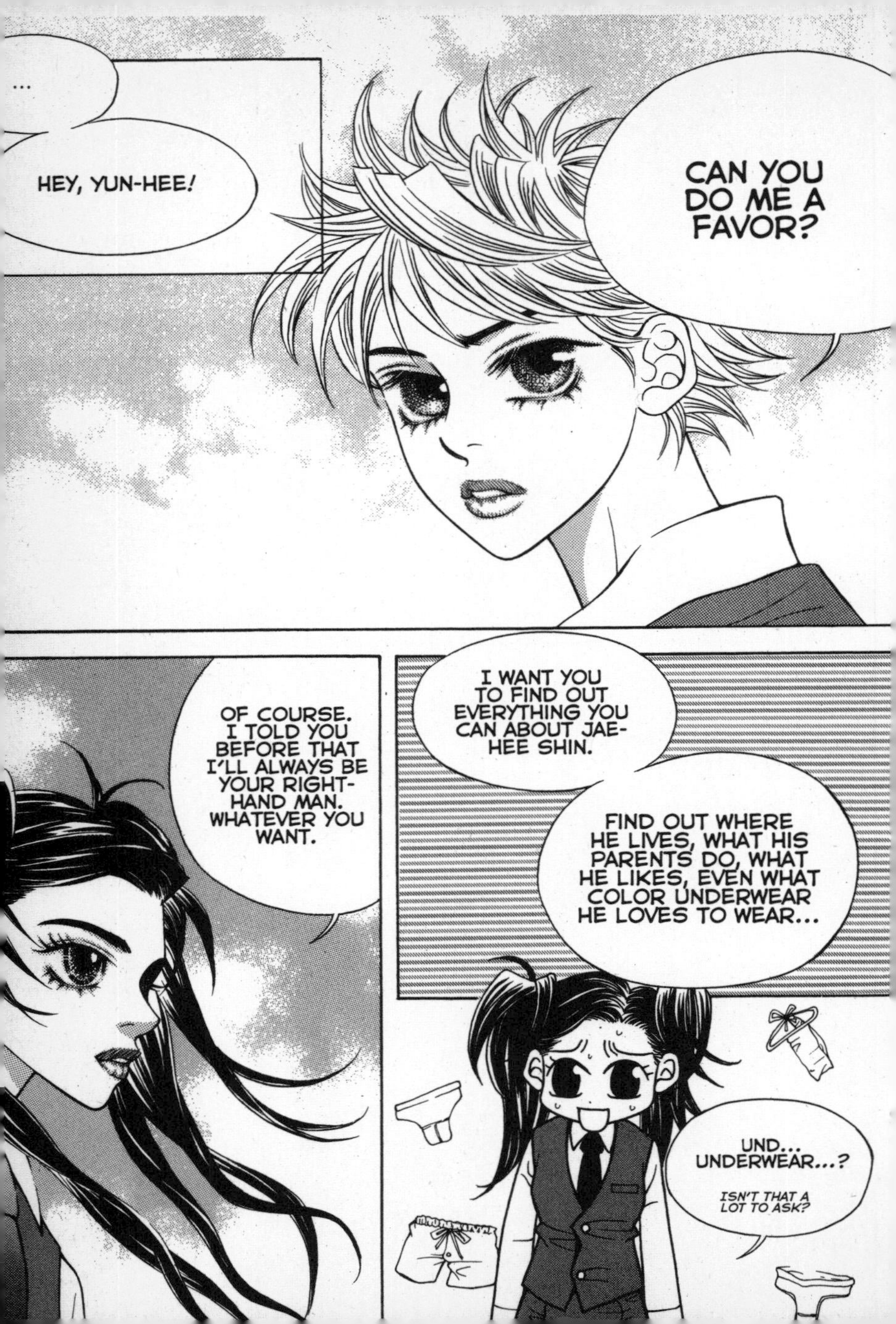
...
HEY, YUN-HEE!
CAN YOU DO ME A FAVOR?
OF COURSE. I TOLD YOU BEFORE THAT I'LL ALWAYS BE YOUR RIGHT-HAND MAN. WHATEVER YOU WANT.
I WANT YOU TO FIND OUT EVERYTHING YOU CAN ABOUT JAE-HEE SHIN.
FIND OUT WHERE HE LIVES, WHAT HIS PARENTS DO, WHAT HE LIKES, EVEN WHAT COLOR UNDERWEAR HE LOVES TO WEAR...
UND... UNDERWEAR...?
ISN'T THAT A LOT TO ASK?

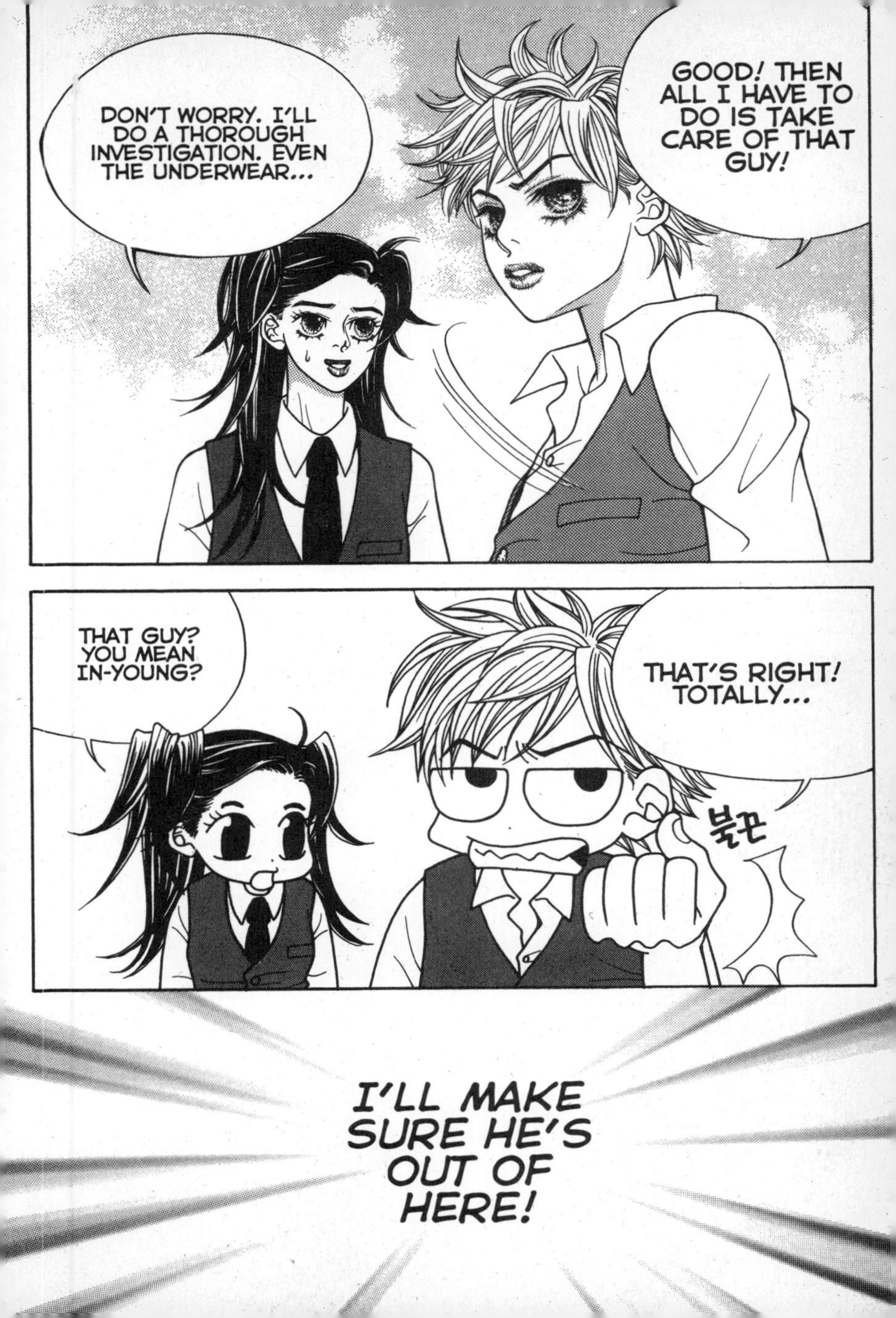
DON'T WORRY. I'LL DO A THOROUGH INVESTIGATION. EVEN THE UNDERWEAR...
GOOD! THEN ALL I HAVE TO DO IS TAKE CARE OF THAT GUY!
THAT GUY? YOU MEAN IN-YOUNG?
THAT'S RIGHT! TOTALLY...
불끈
I'LL MAKE SURE HE'S OUT OF HERE!

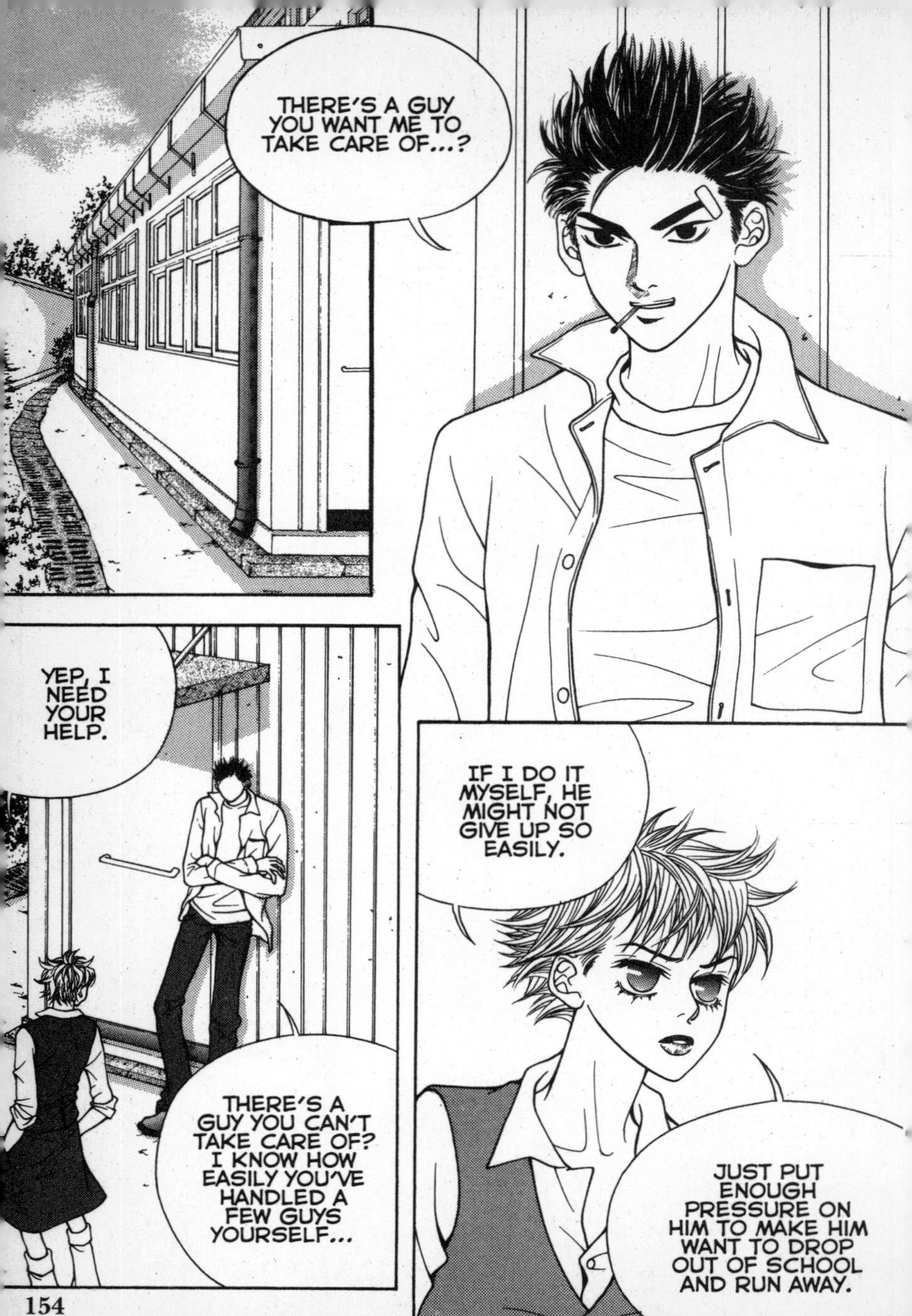
THERE'S A GUY YOU WANT ME TO TAKE CARE OF...?
YEP, I NEED YOUR HELP.
THERE'S A GUY YOU CAN'T TAKE CARE OF? I KNOW HOW EASILY YOU'VE HANDLED A FEW GUYS YOURSELF...
IF I DO IT MYSELF, HE MIGHT NOT GIVE UP SO EASILY.
JUST PUT ENOUGH PRESSURE ON HIM TO MAKE HIM WANT TO DROP OUT OF SCHOOL AND RUN AWAY.

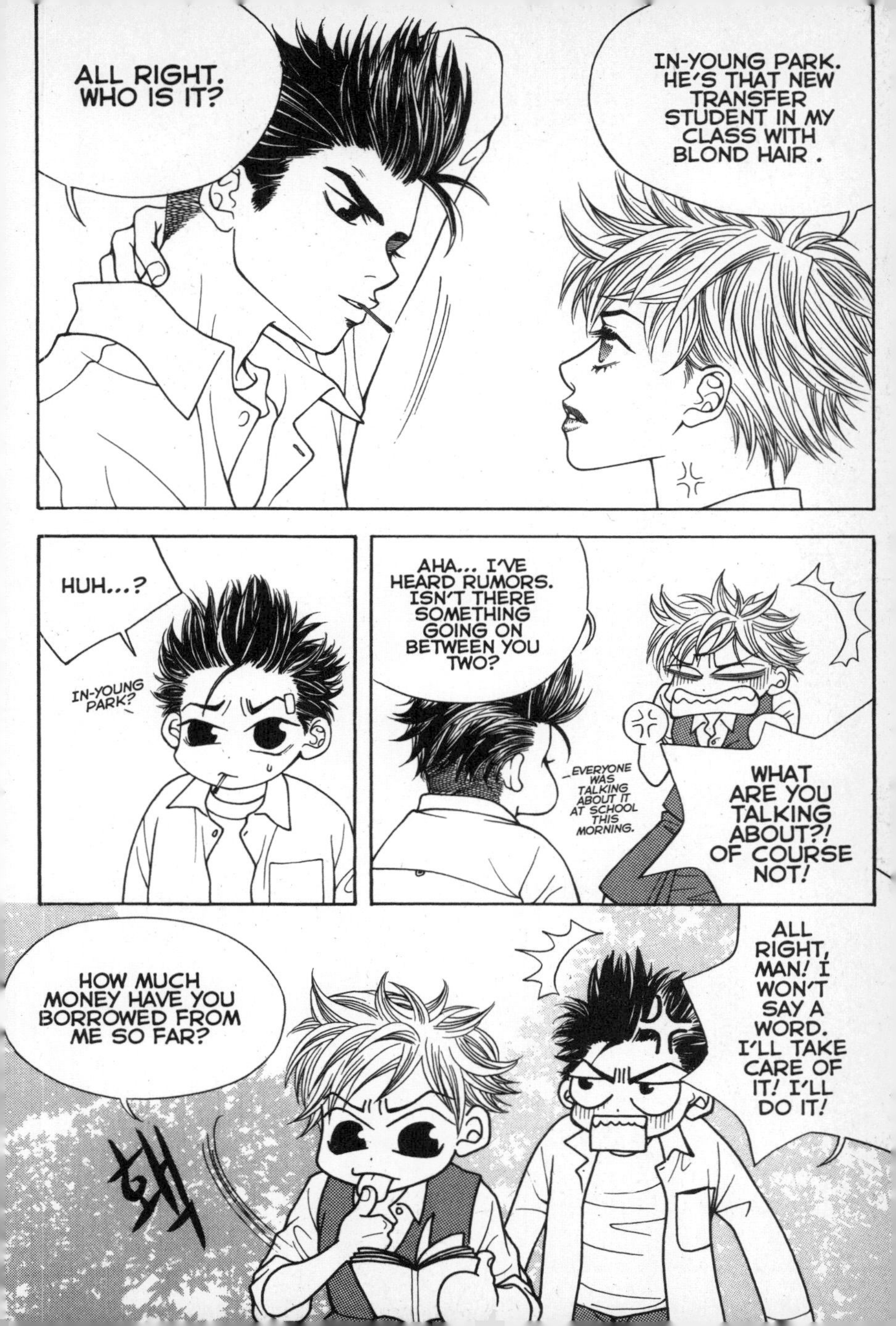
ALL RIGHT. WHO IS IT?
IN-YOUNG PARK. HE'S THAT NEW TRANSFER STUDENT IN MY CLASS WITH BLOND HAIR .
HUH...?
IN-YOUNG PARK?
AHA... I'VE HEARD RUMORS. ISN'T THERE SOMETHING GOING ON BETWEEN YOU TWO?
EVERYONE WAS TALKING ABOUT IT AT SCHOOL THIS MORNING.
WHAT ARE YOU TALKING ABOUT?! OF COURSE NOT!
HOW MUCH MONEY HAVE YOU BORROWED FROM ME SO FAR?
ALL RIGHT, MAN! I WON'T SAY A WORD. I'LL TAKE CARE OF IT! I'LL DO IT!

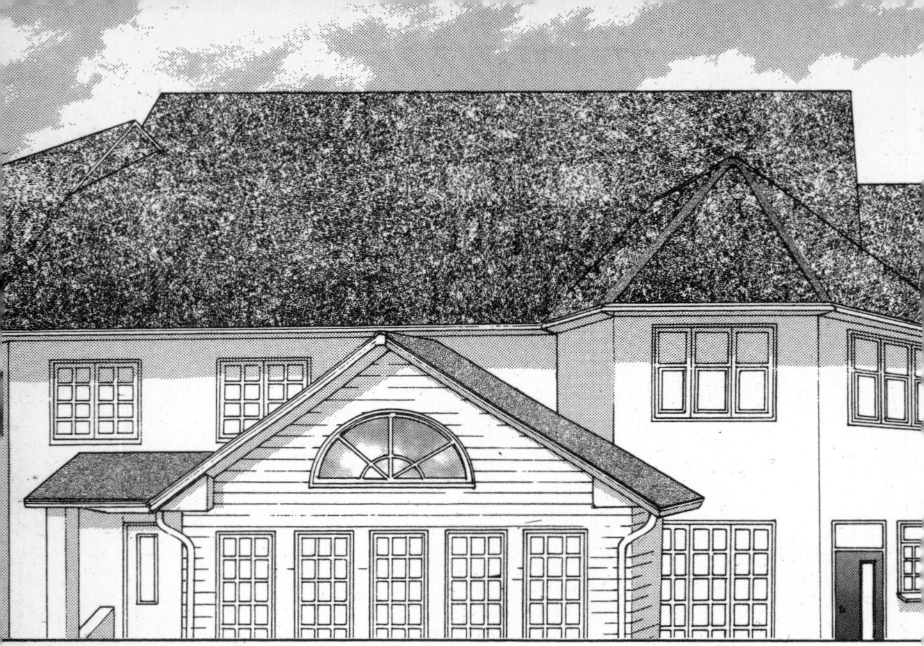

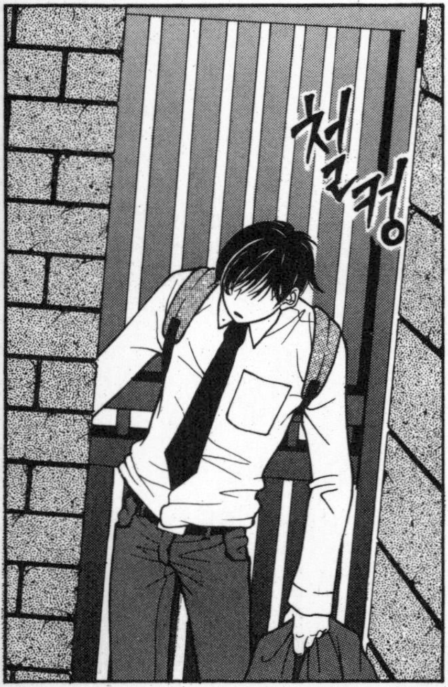
철컹

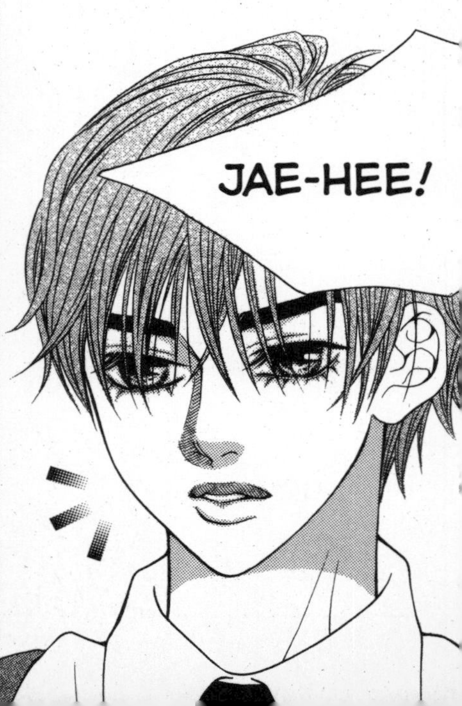
JAE-HEE!

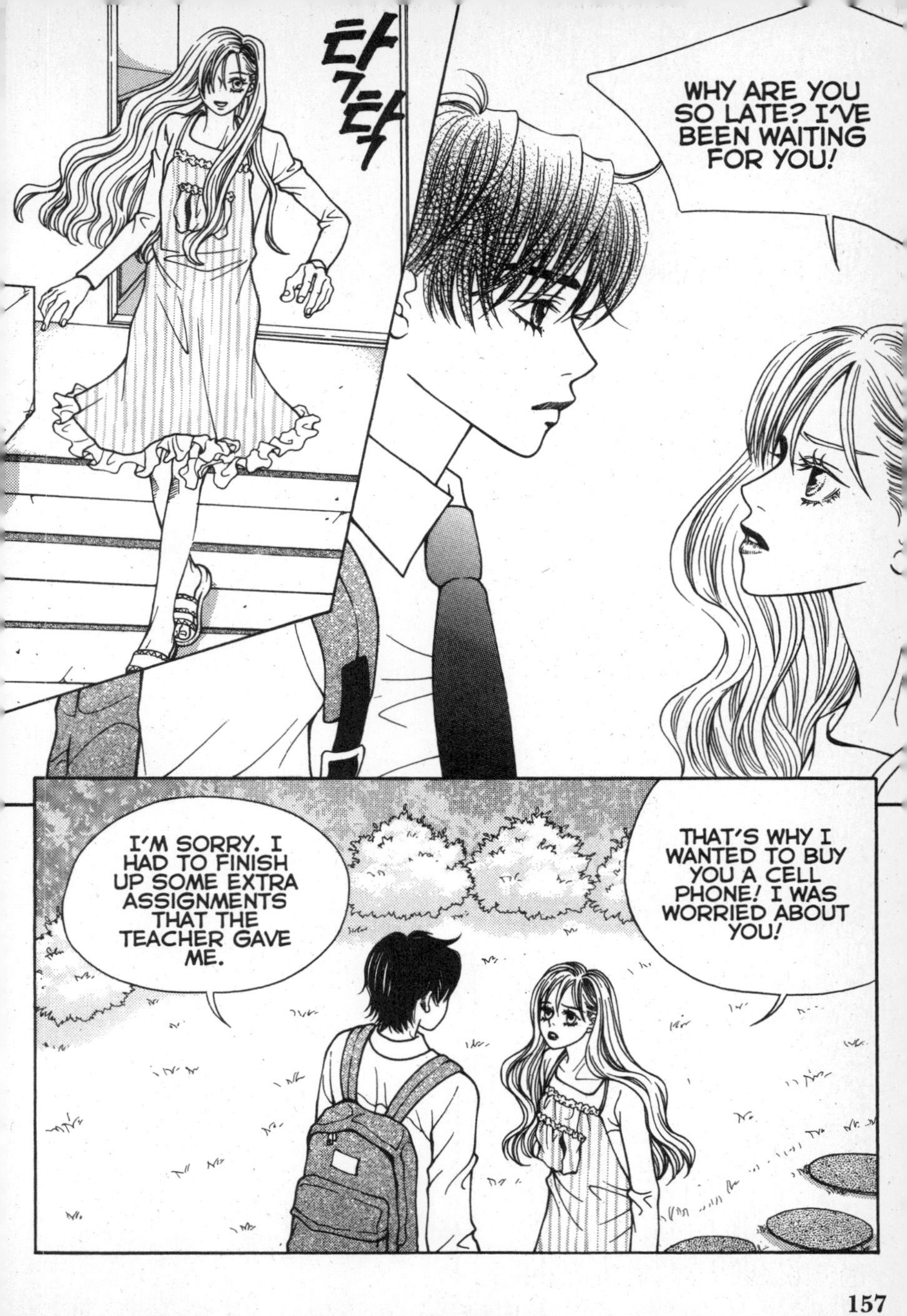
WHY ARE YOU SO LATE? I'VE BEEN WAITING FOR YOU!
I'M SORRY. I HAD TO FINISH UP SOME EXTRA ASSIGNMENTS THAT THE TEACHER GAVE ME.
THAT'S WHY I WANTED TO BUY YOU A CELL PHONE! I WAS WORRIED ABOUT YOU!

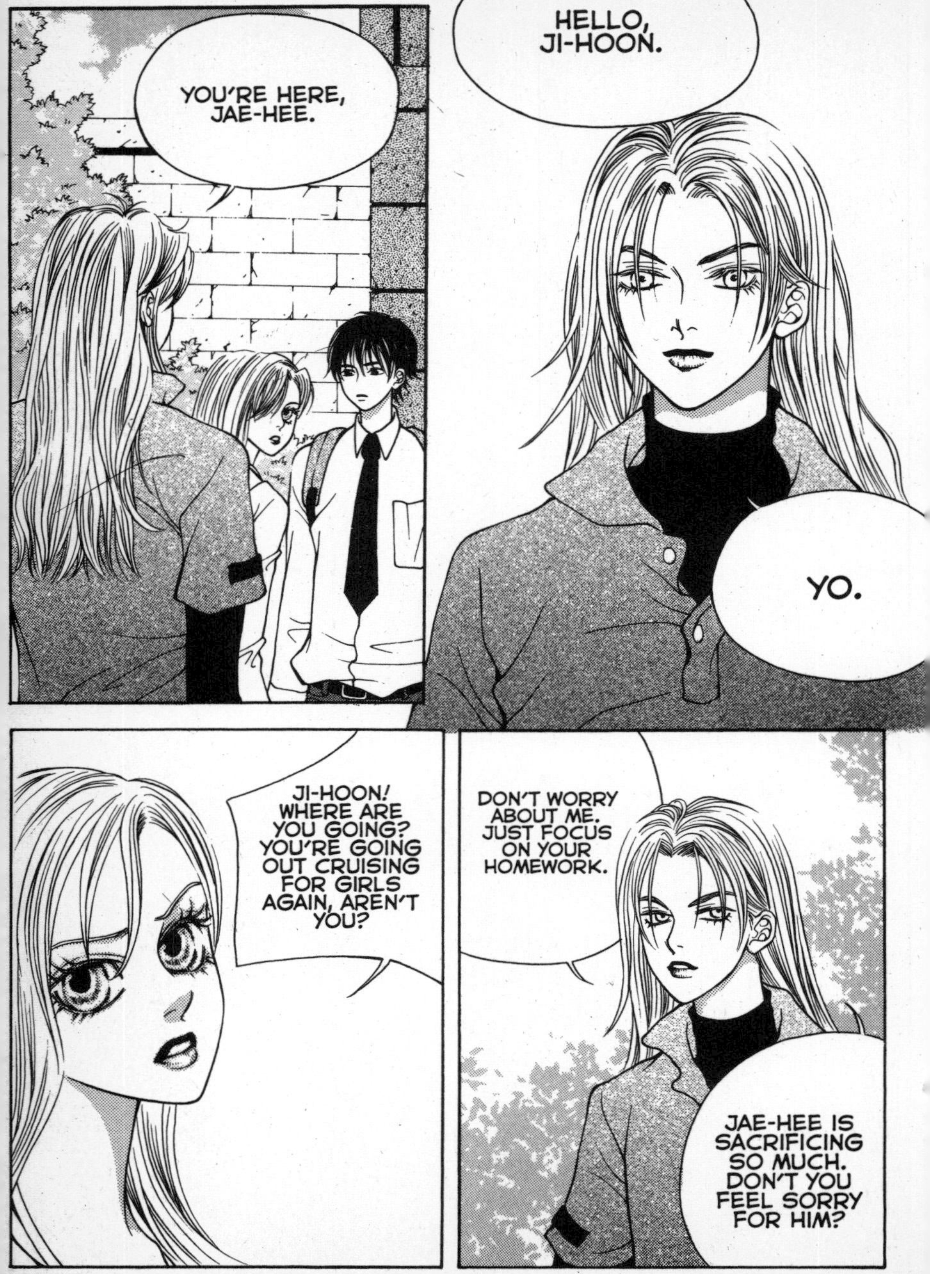
YOU'RE HERE, JAE-HEE.
HELLO, JI-HOON.
YO.
JI-HOON! WHERE ARE YOU GOING? YOU'RE GOING OUT CRUISING FOR GIRLS AGAIN, AREN'T YOU?
DON'T WORRY ABOUT ME. JUST FOCUS ON YOUR HOMEWORK.
JAE-HEE IS SACRIFICING SO MUCH. DON'T YOU FEEL SORRY FOR HIM?

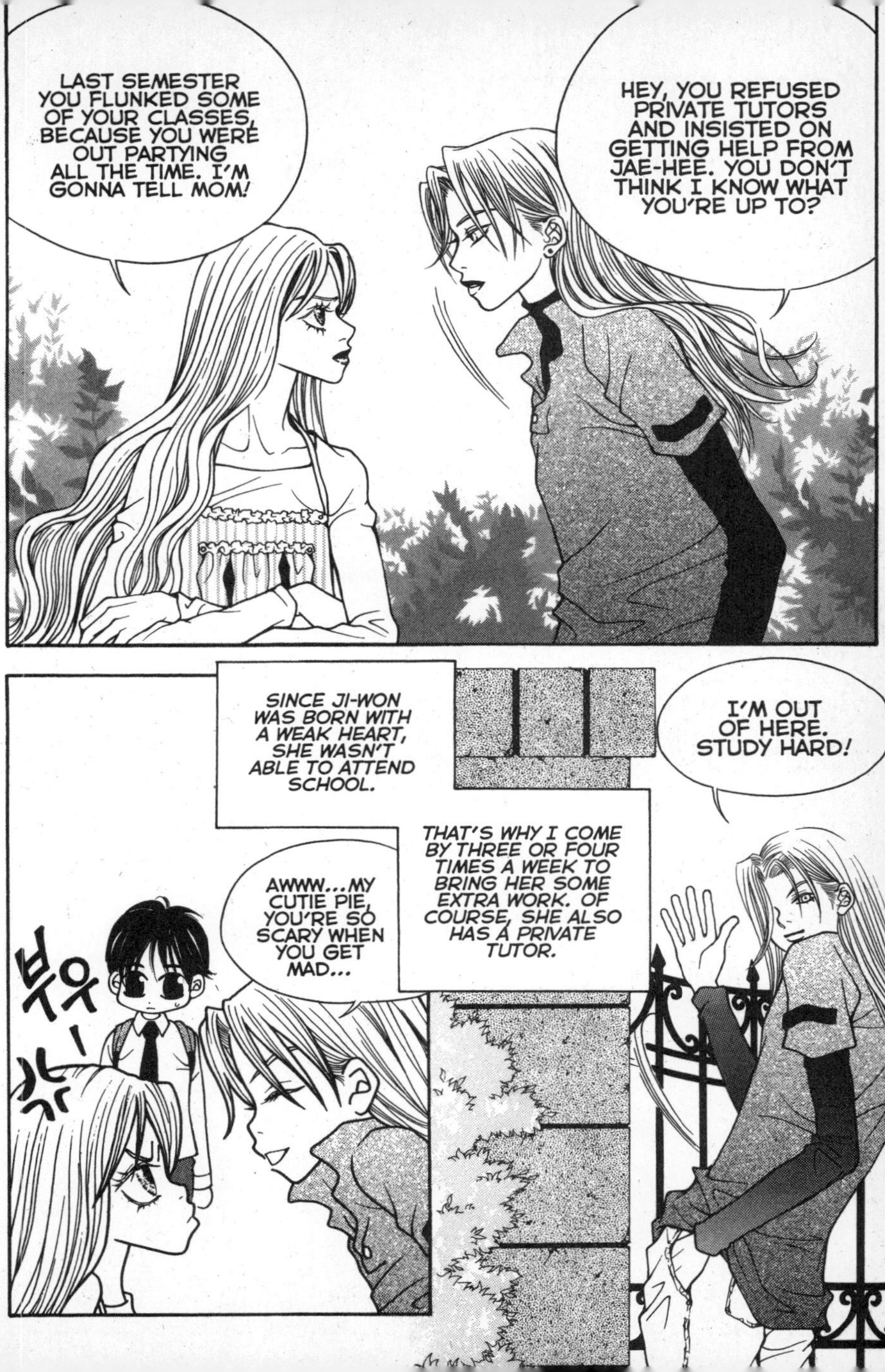
LAST SEMESTER YOU FLUNKED SOME OF YOUR CLASSES, BECAUSE YOU WERE OUT PARTYING ALL THE TIME. I'M GONNA TELL MOM!
HEY, YOU REFUSED PRIVATE TUTORS AND INSISTED ON GETTING HELP FROM JAE-HEE. YOU DON'T THINK I KNOW WHAT YOU'RE UP TO?
SINCE JI-WON WAS BORN WITH A WEAK HEART, SHE WASN'T ABLE TO ATTEND SCHOOL.
I'M OUT OF HERE. STUDY HARD!
THAT'S WHY I COME BY THREE OR FOUR TIMES A WEEK TO BRING HER SOME EXTRA WORK. OF COURSE, SHE ALSO HAS A PRIVATE TUTOR.
AWWW...MY CUTIE PIE, YOU'RE SO SCARY WHEN YOU GET MAD...

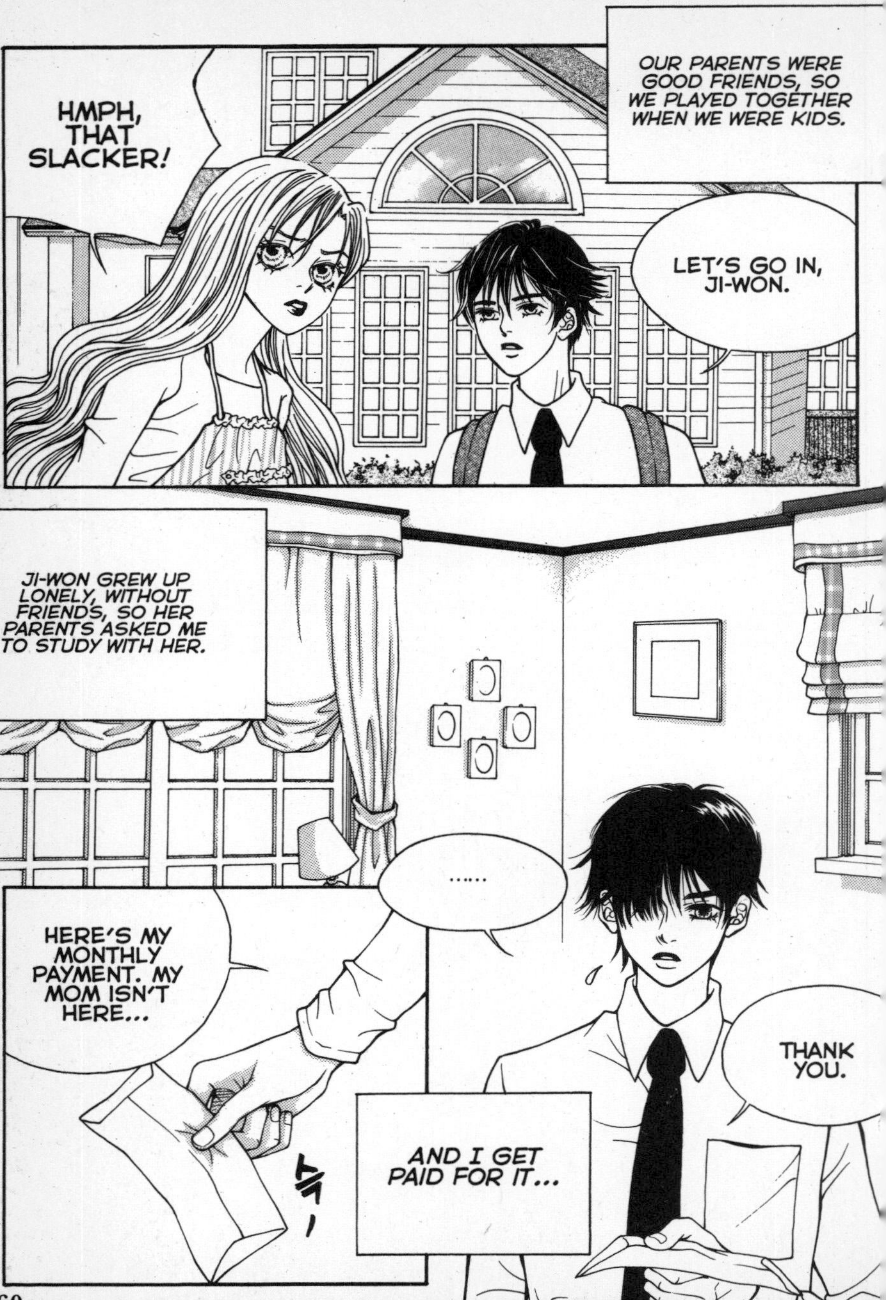
HMPH, THAT SLACKER!
OUR PARENTS WERE GOOD FRIENDS, SO WE PLAYED TOGETHER WHEN WE WERE KIDS.
LET'S GO IN, JI-WON.
JI-WON GREW UP LONELY, WITHOUT FRIENDS, SO HER PARENTS ASKED ME TO STUDY WITH HER.
......
HERE'S MY MONTHLY PAYMENT. MY MOM ISN'T HERE...
THANK YOU.
AND I GET PAID FOR IT...

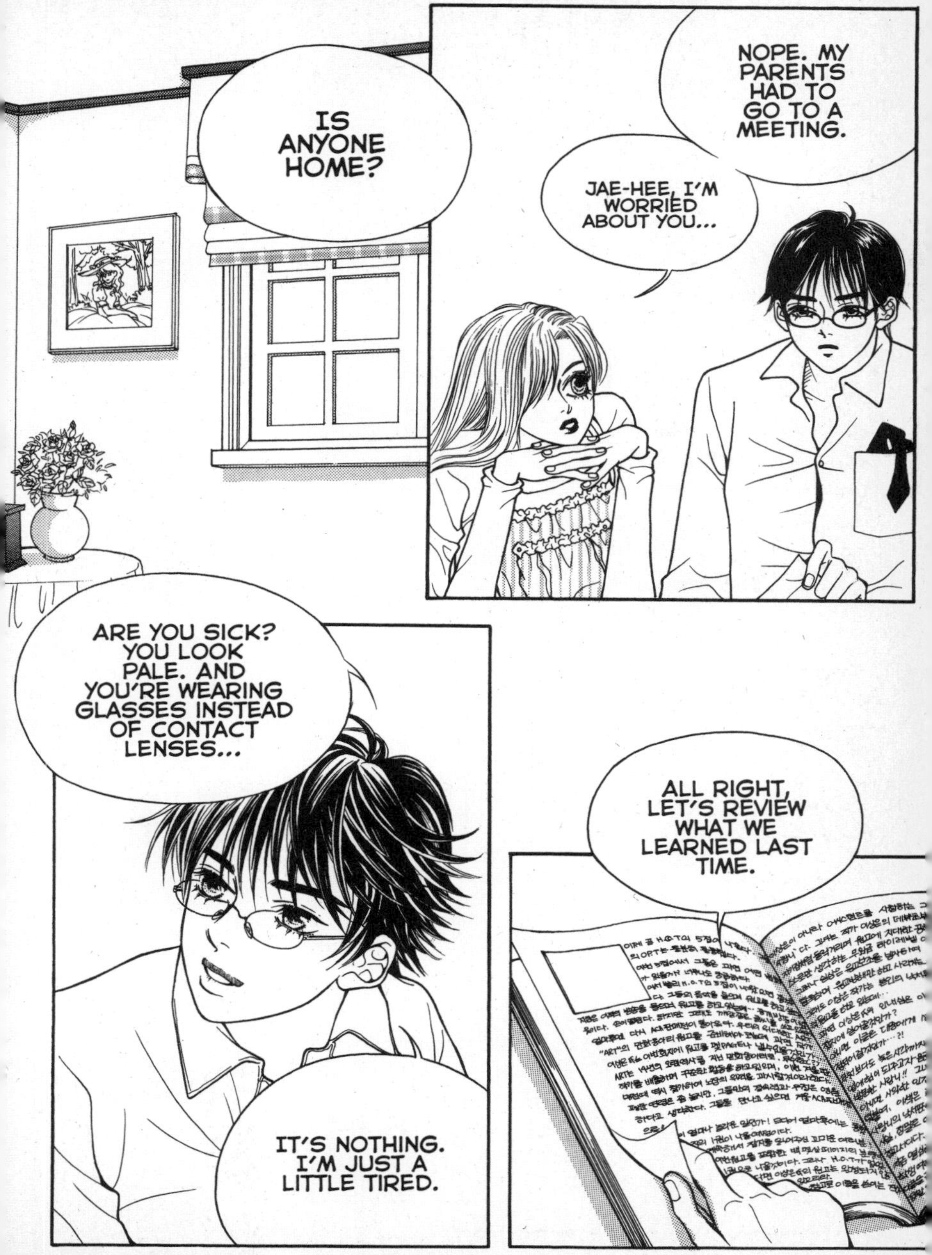
IS ANYONE HOME?
NOPE. MY PARENTS HAD TO GO TO A MEETING.
JAE-HEE, I'M WORRIED ABOUT YOU...
ARE YOU SICK? YOU LOOK PALE. AND YOU'RE WEARING GLASSES INSTEAD OF CONTACT LENSES...
IT'S NOTHING. I'M JUST A LITTLE TIRED.
ALL RIGHT, LET'S REVIEW WHAT WE LEARNED LAST TIME.

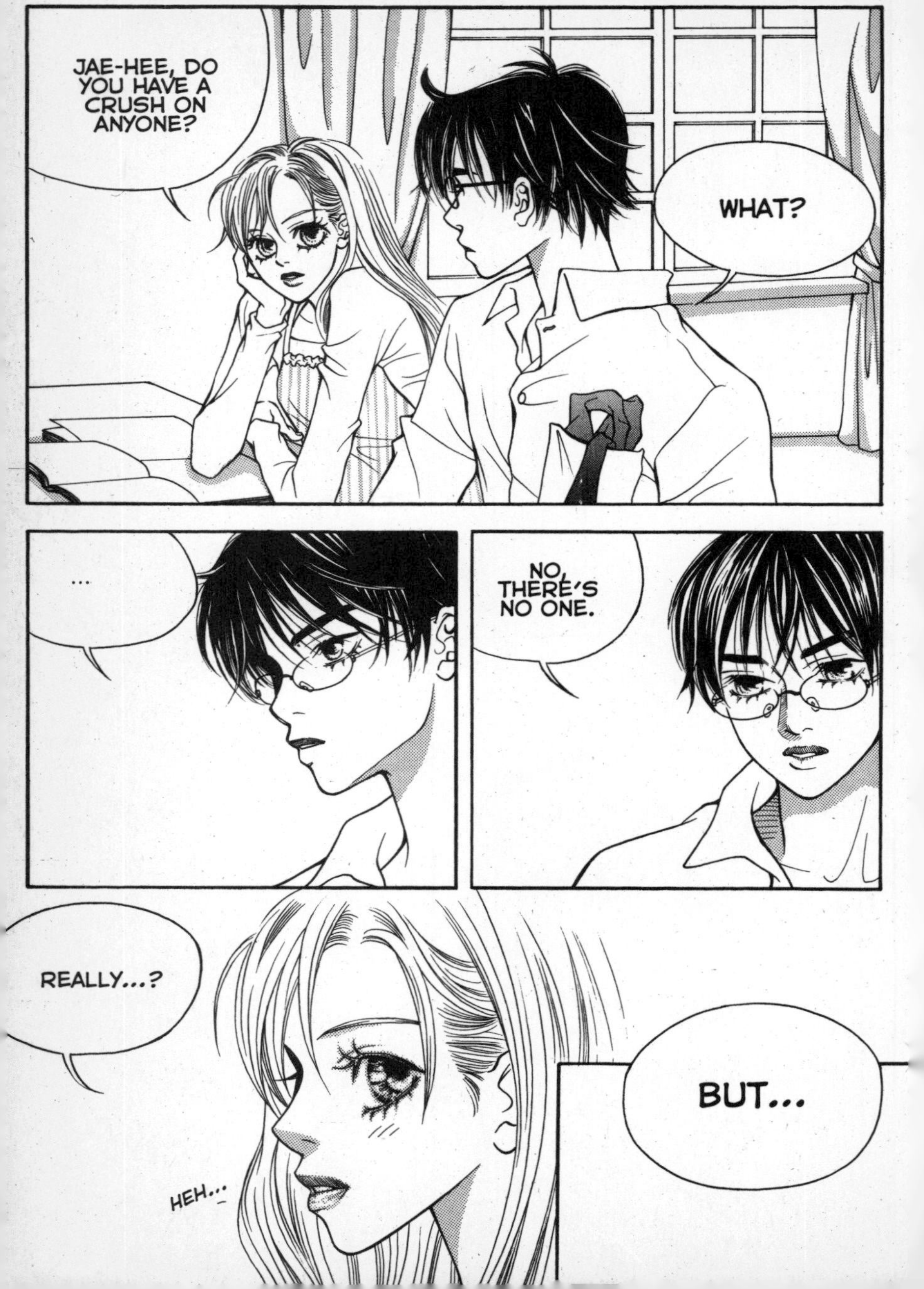
JAE-HEE, DO YOU HAVE A CRUSH ON ANYONE?
WHAT?
...
NO, THERE'S NO ONE.
REALLY...?
HEH...
BUT...

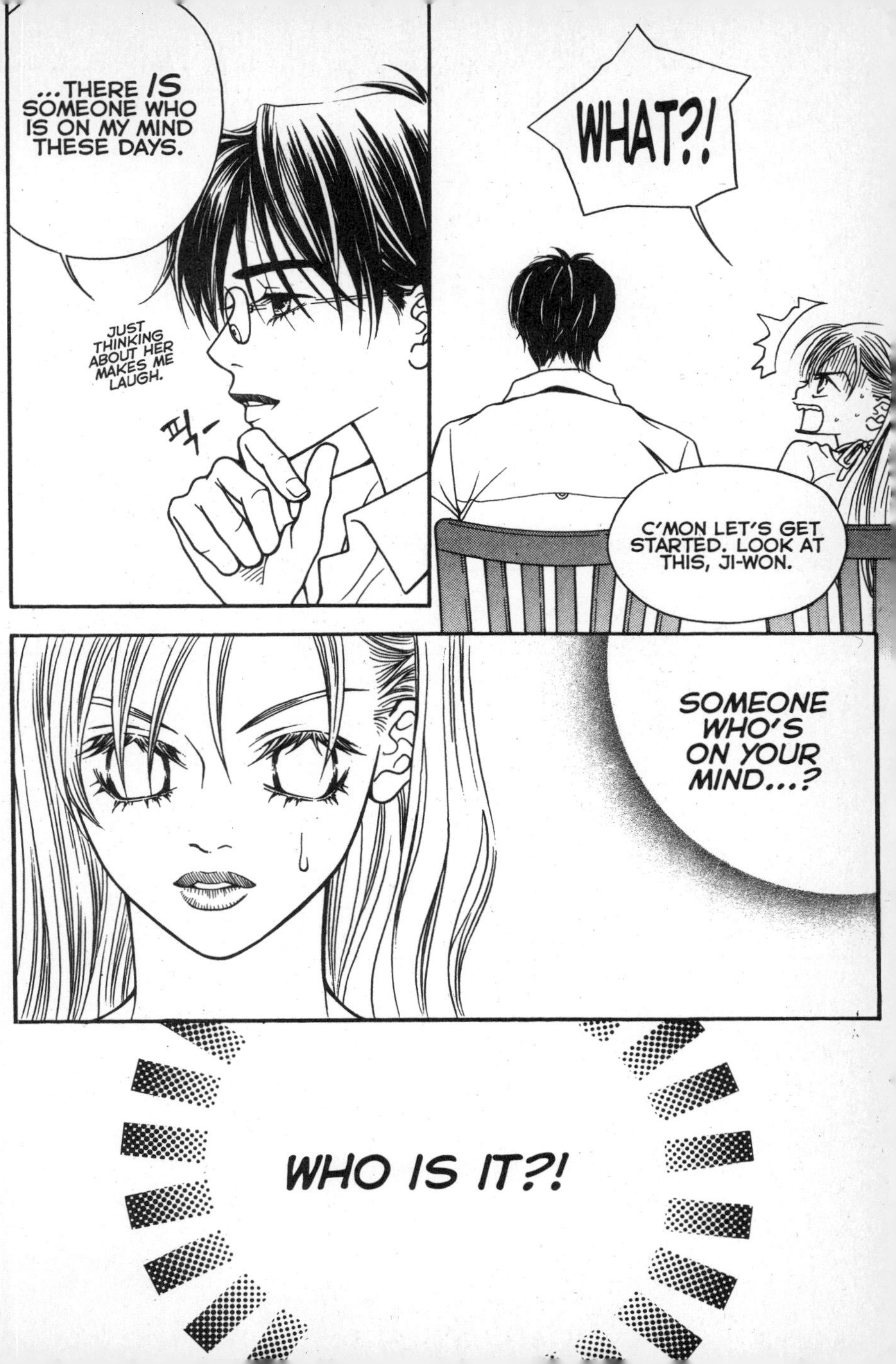
...THERE IS SOMEONE WHO IS ON MY MIND THESE DAYS.
JUST THINKING ABOUT HER MAKES ME LAUGH.
WHAT?!
C'MON LET'S GET STARTED. LOOK AT THIS, JI-WON.
SOMEONE WHO'S ON YOUR MIND...?
WHO IS IT?!

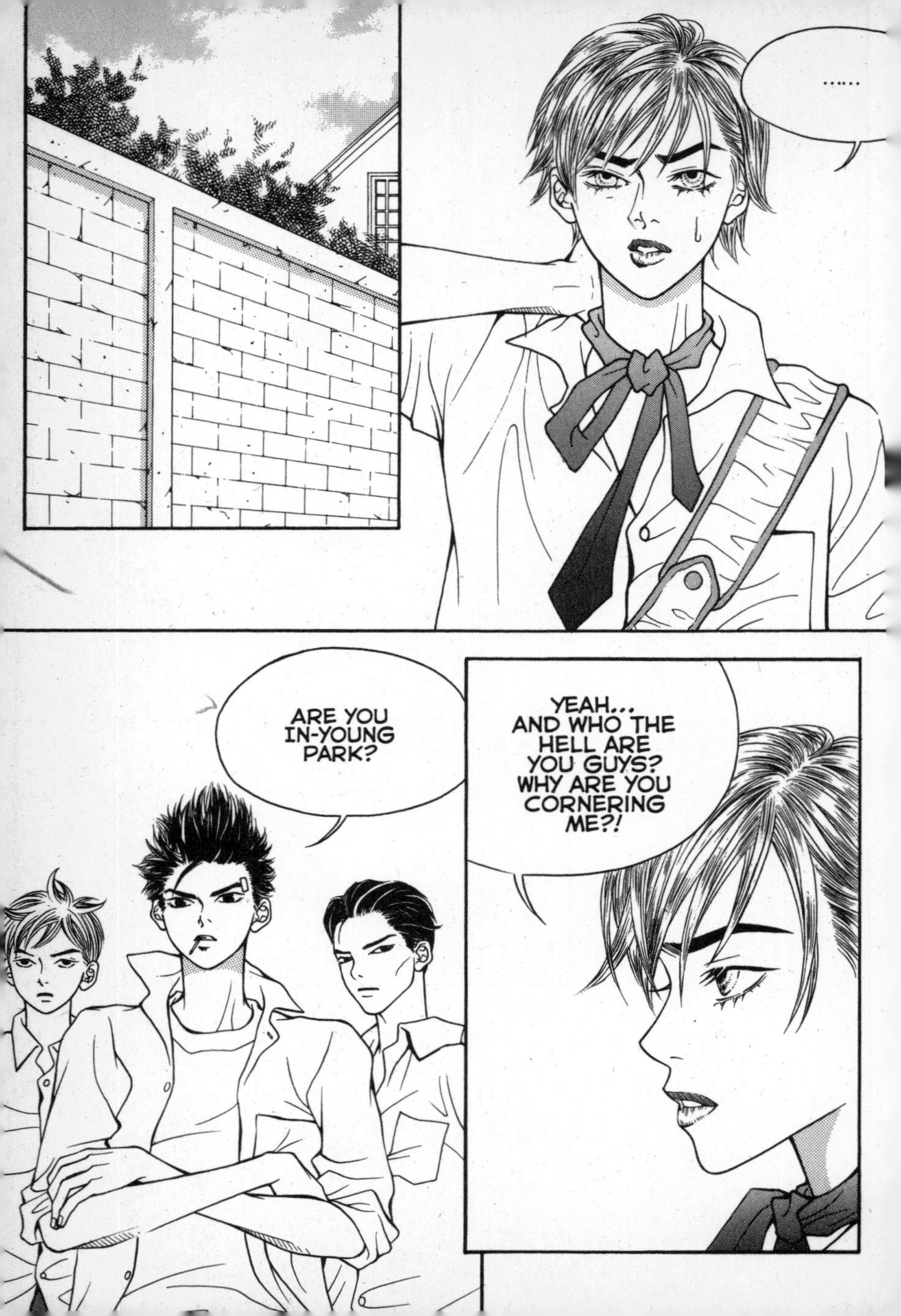
......
ARE YOU IN-YOUNG PARK?
YEAH... AND WHO THE HELL ARE YOU GUYS? WHY ARE YOU CORNERING ME?!

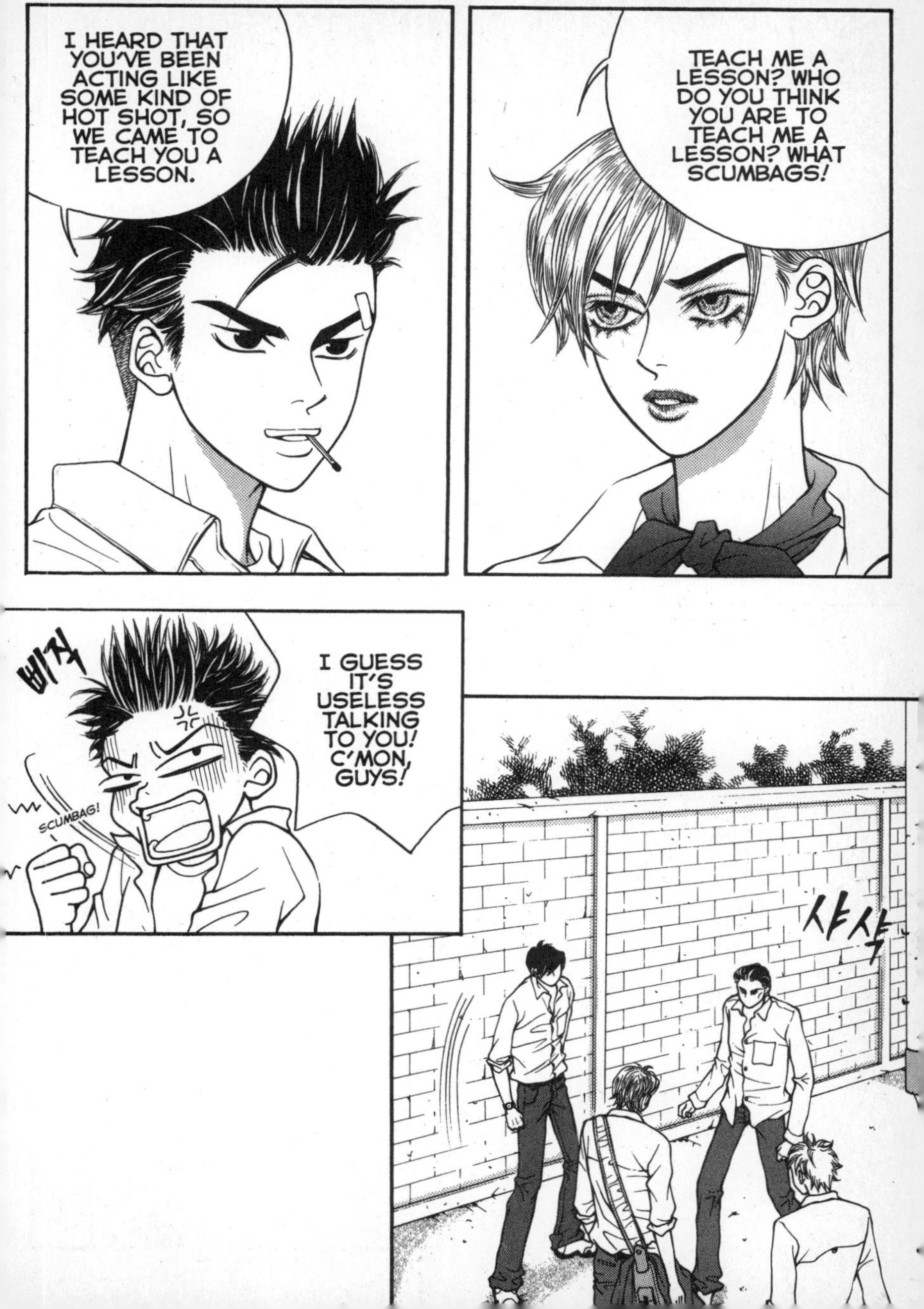
I HEARD THAT YOU'VE BEEN ACTING LIKE SOME KIND OF HOT SHOT, SO WE CAME TO TEACH YOU A LESSON.
TEACH ME A LESSON? WHO DO YOU THINK YOU ARE TO TEACH ME A LESSON? WHAT SCUMBAGS!
빠직
I GUESS IT'S USELESS TALKING TO YOU! C'MON, GUYS!
SCUMBAG!
샤샥

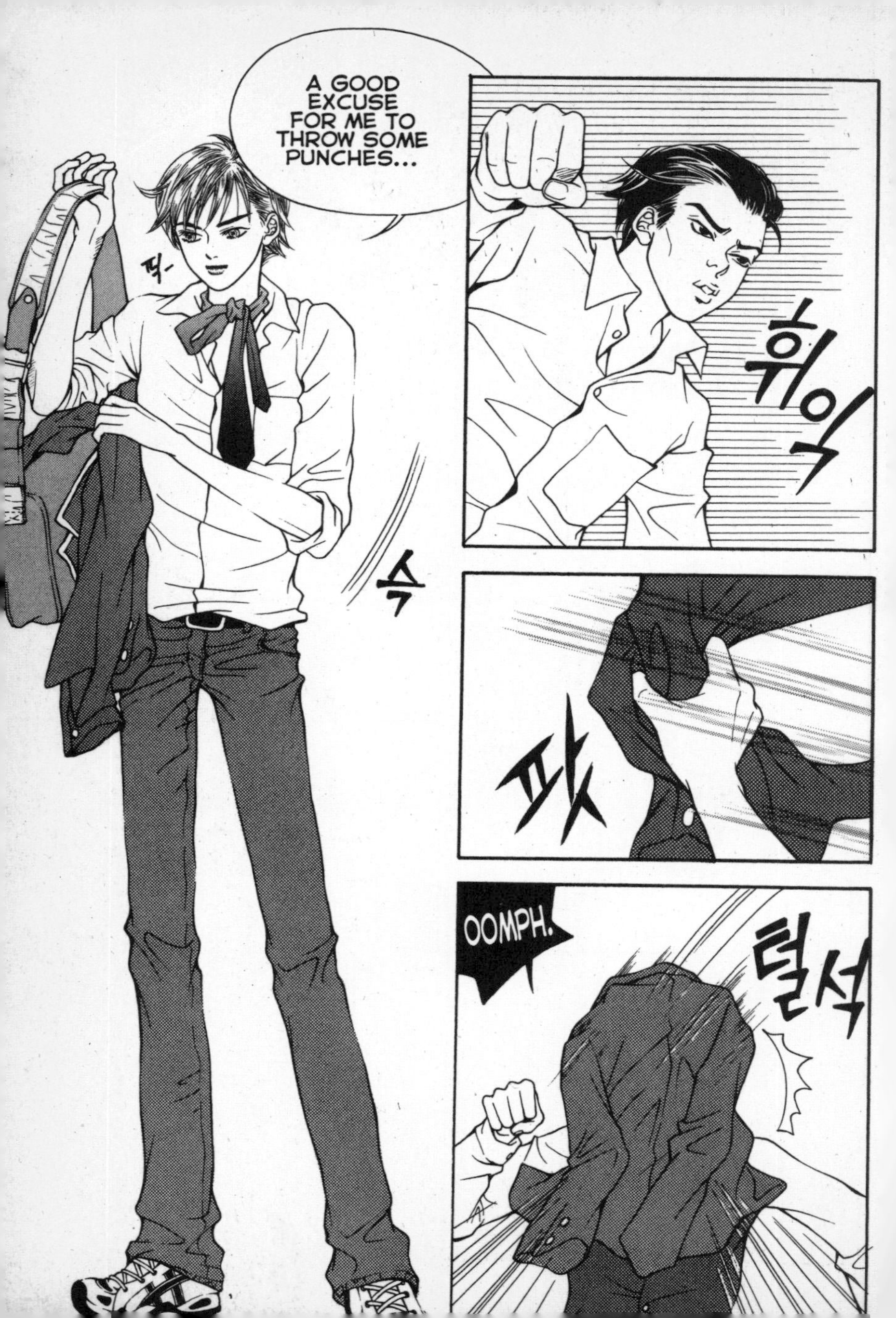
A GOOD EXCUSE FOR ME TO THROW SOME PUNCHES...
슥
휘익
팍
OOMPH.
털석

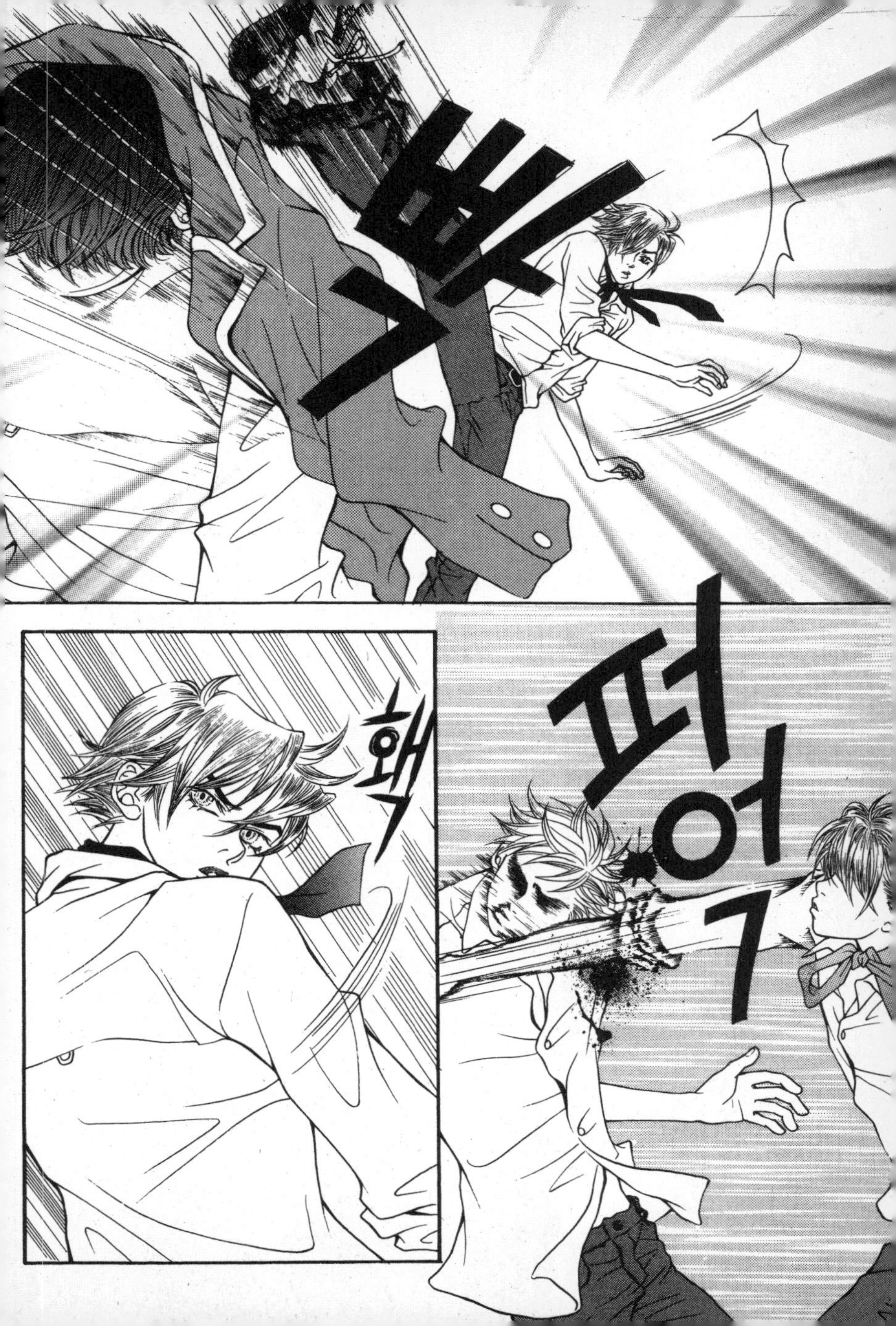
빡
홱
퍼억

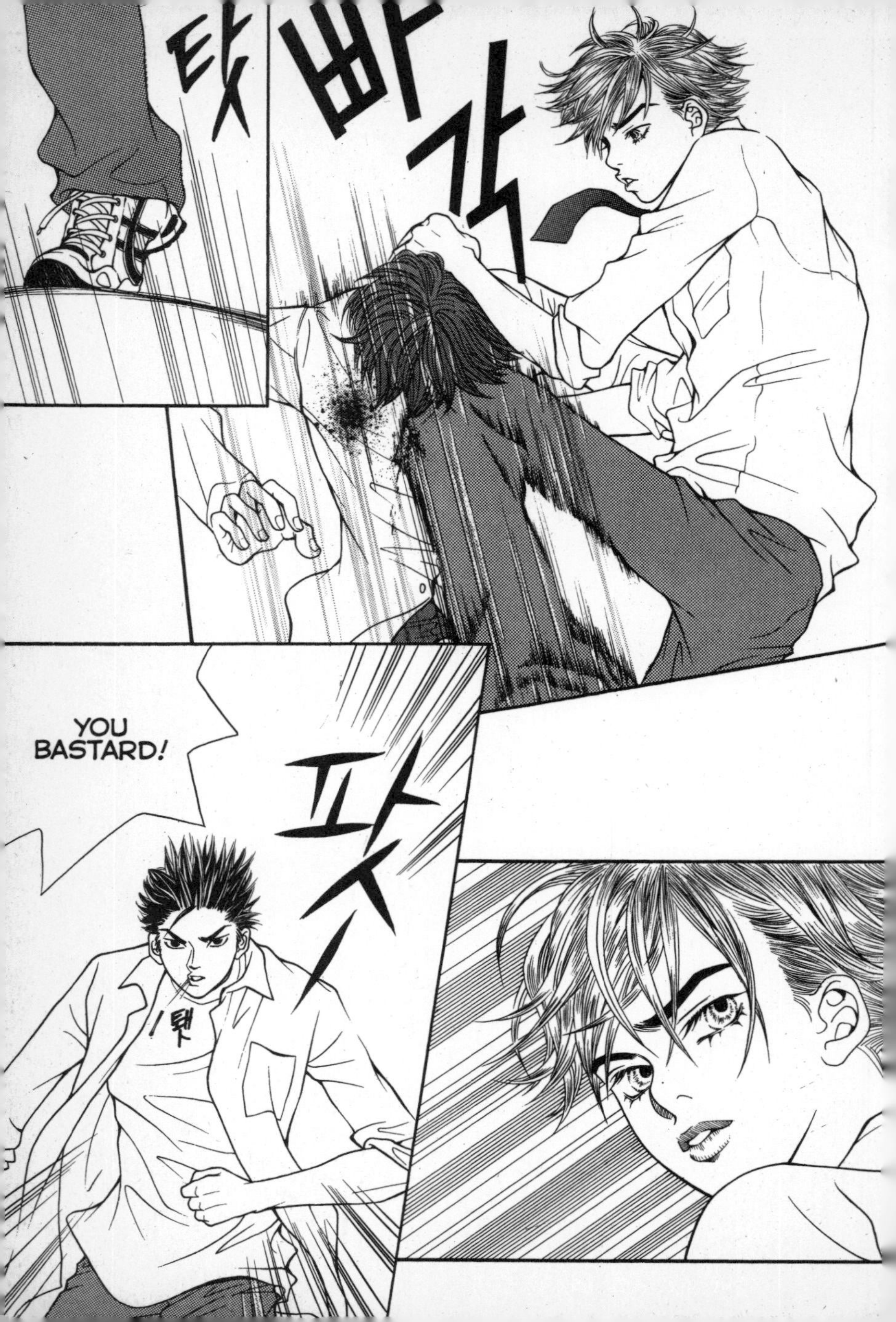
탁
빠각
YOU BASTARD!
팟
퉤!

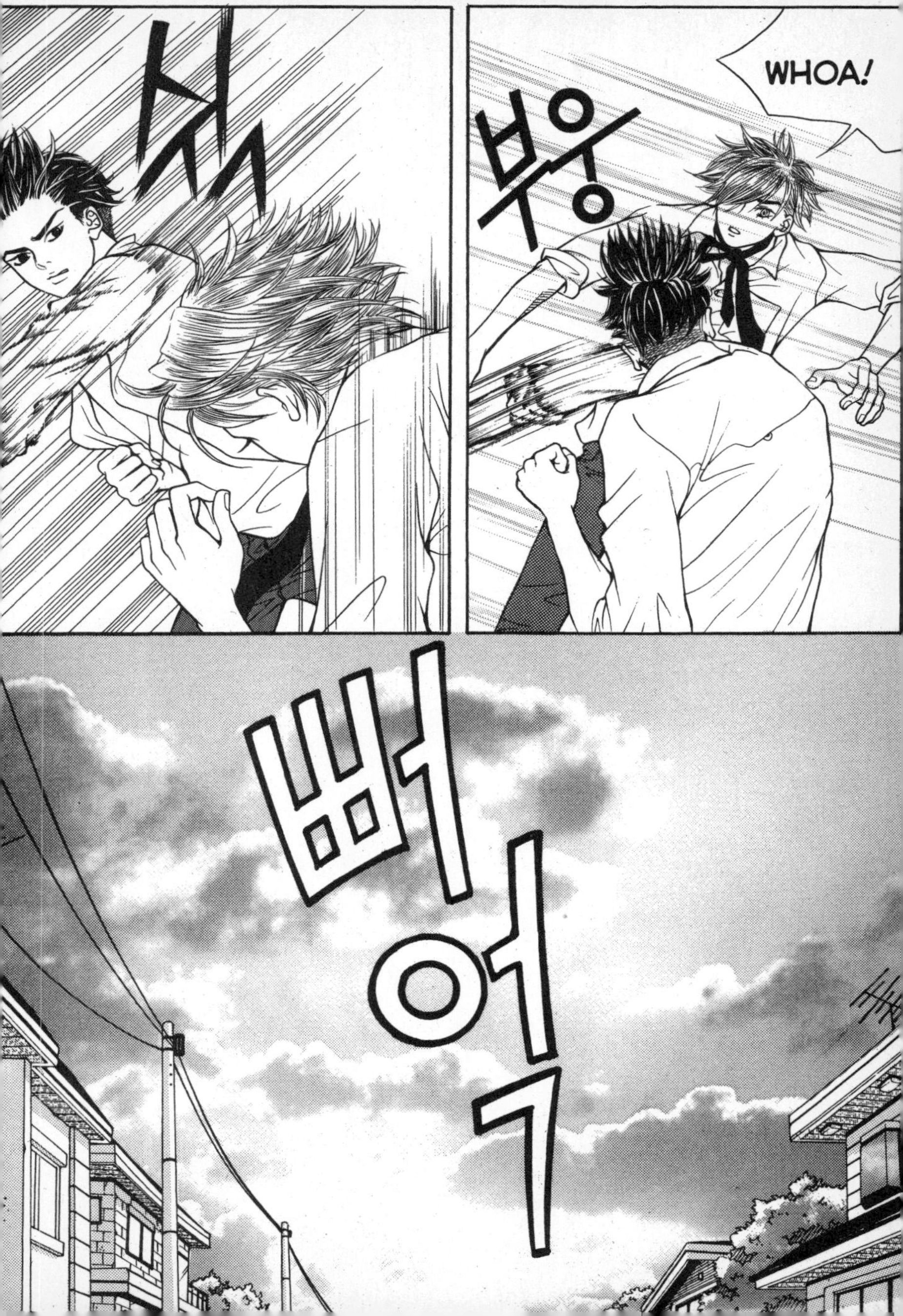
WHOA!

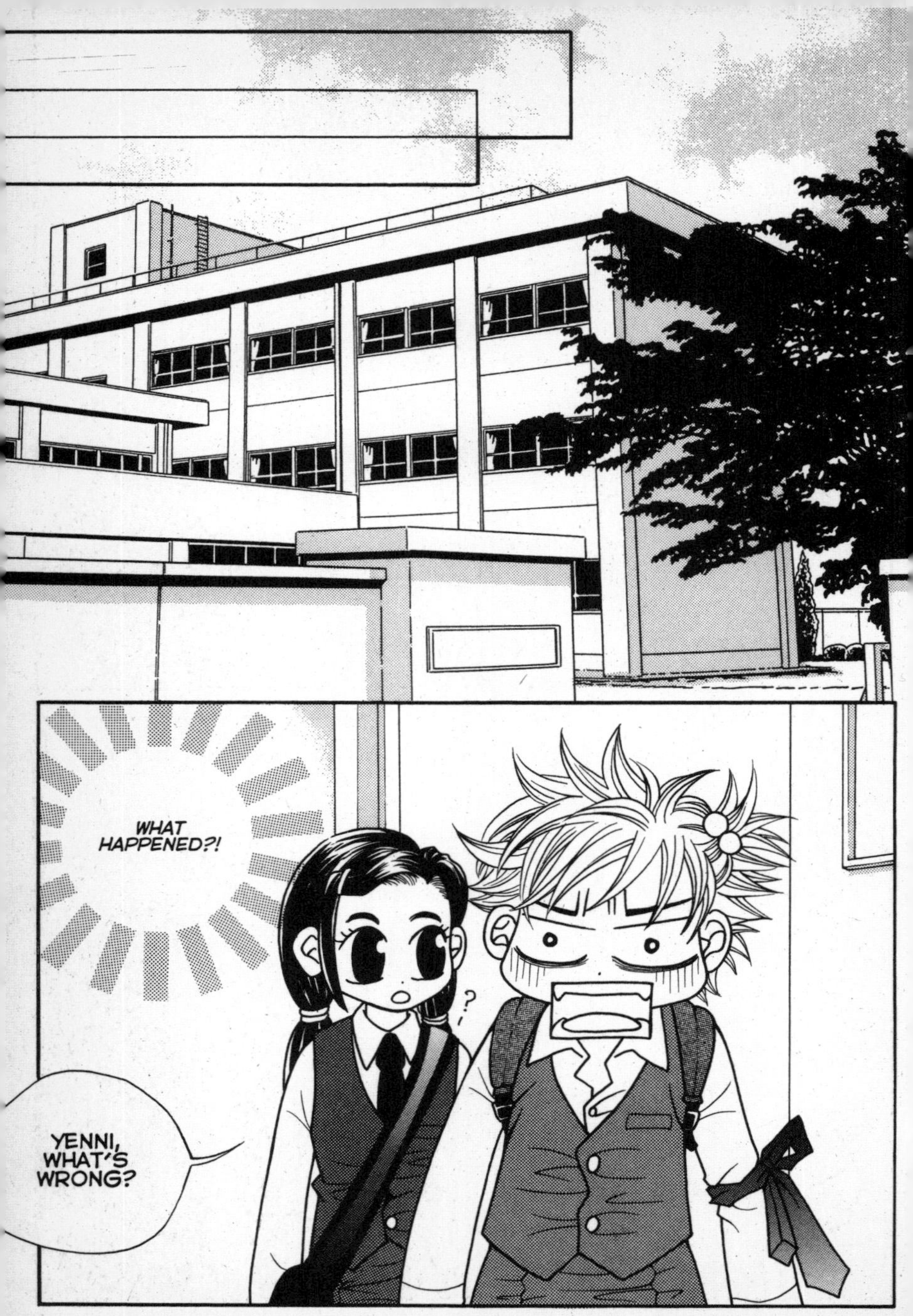
WHAT HAPPENED?!
YENNI, WHAT'S WRONG?

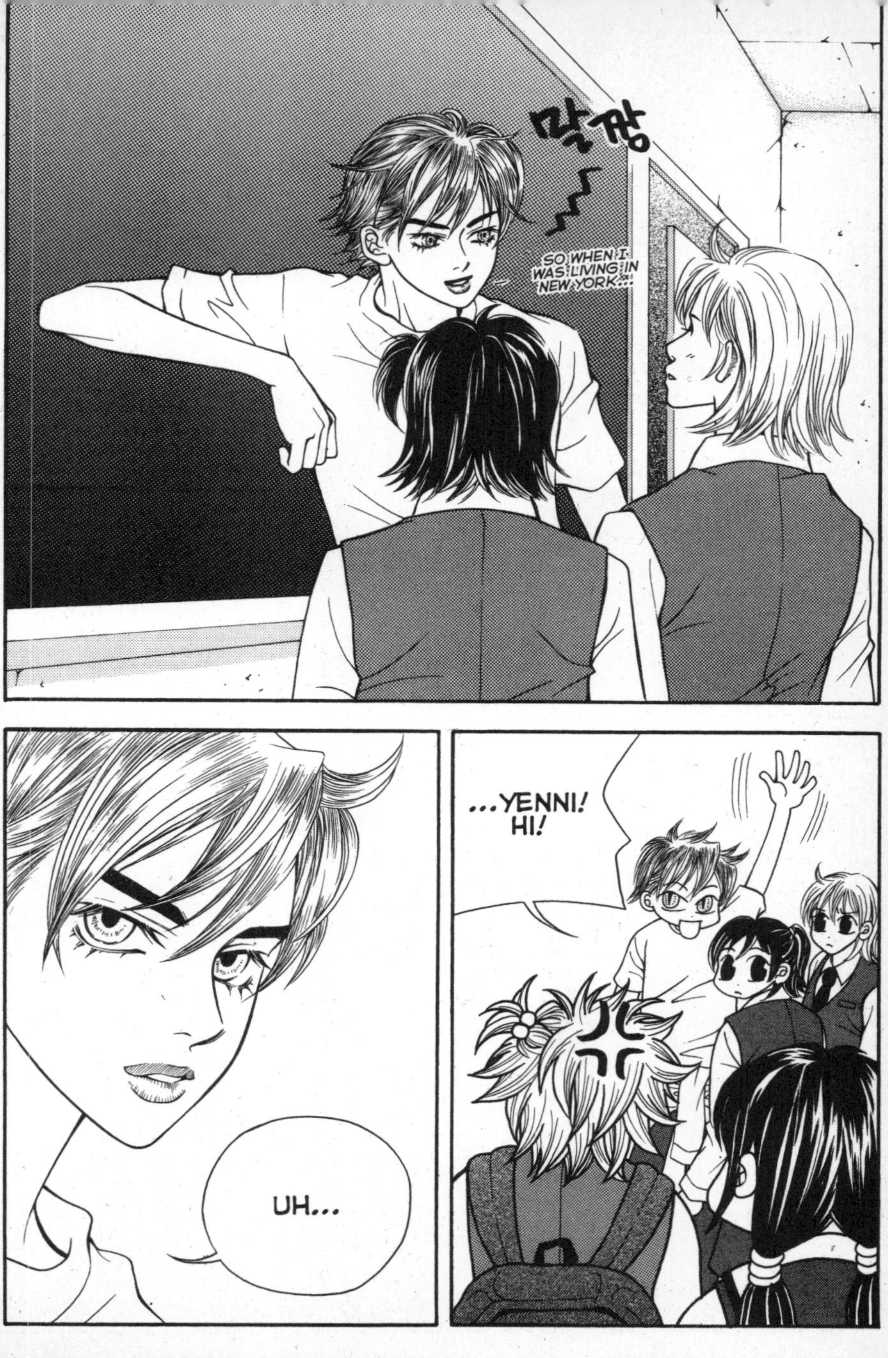
깔깡
SO WHEN I WAS LIVING IN NEW YORK...
UH...
...YENNI! HI!

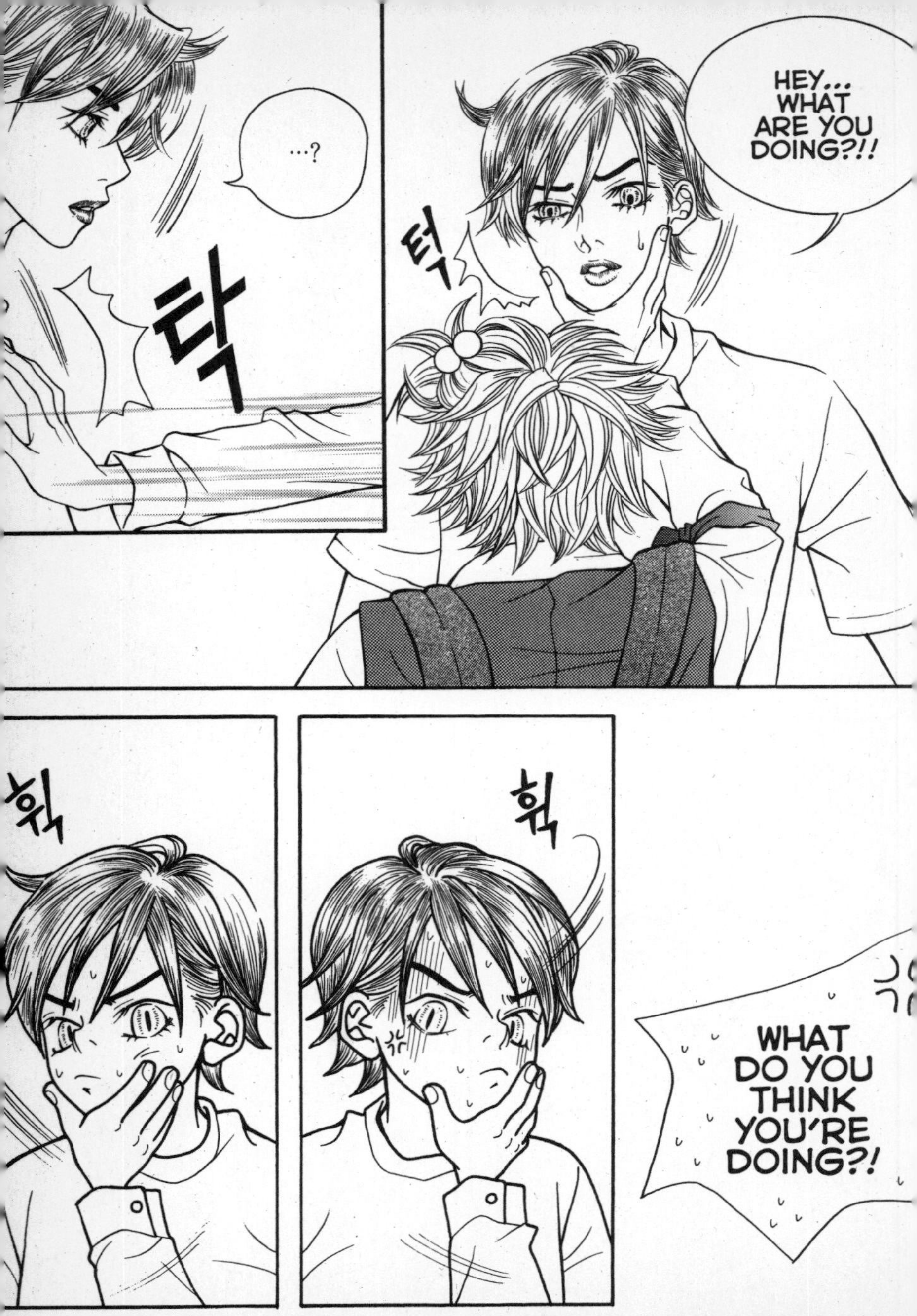
...?
탁
턱
HEY... WHAT ARE YOU DOING?!!
휙
휙
WHAT DO YOU THINK YOU'RE DOING?!

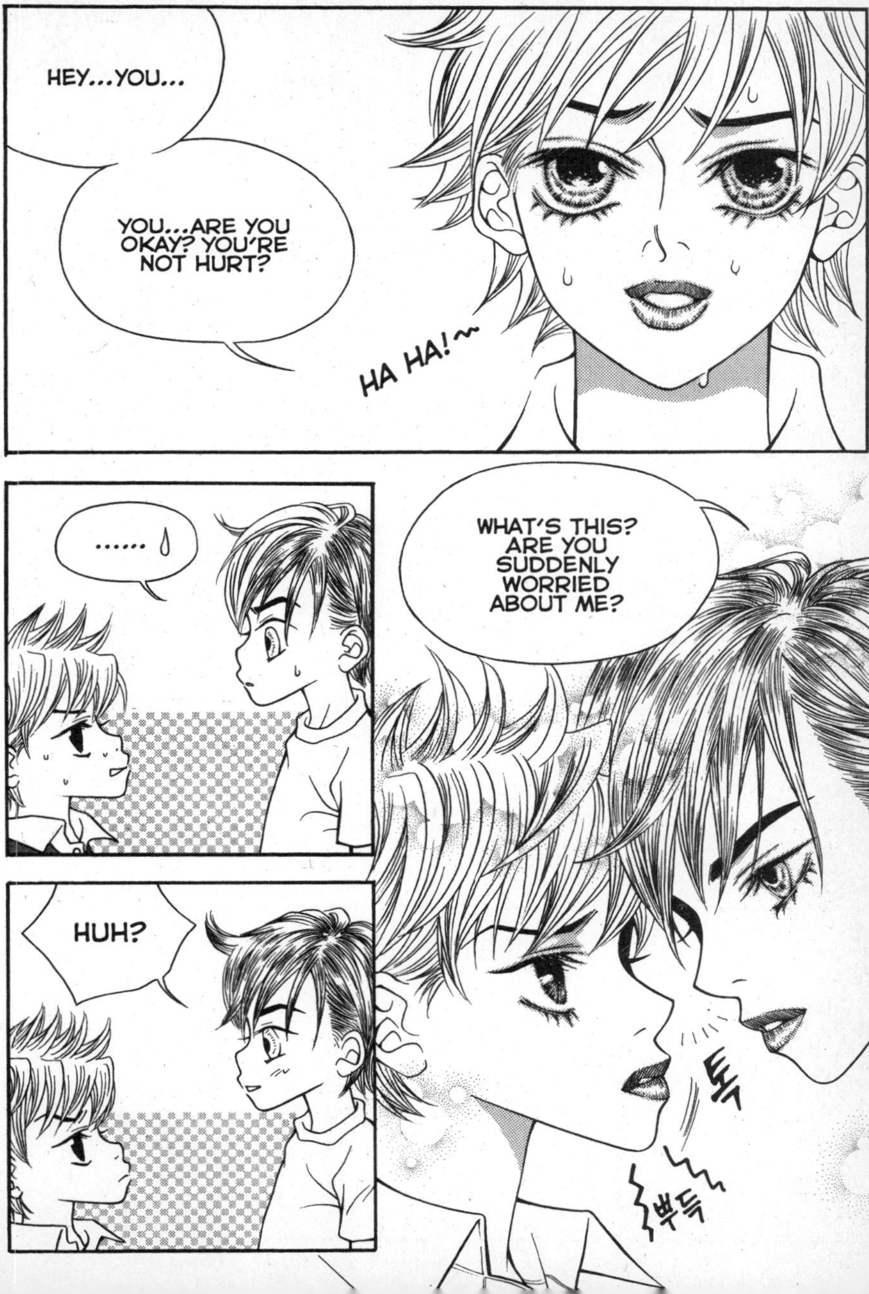
HEY...YOU...
YOU...ARE YOU OKAY? YOU'RE NOT HURT?
HA HA!~
......
HUH?
WHAT'S THIS? ARE YOU SUDDENLY WORRIED ABOUT ME?
톡
부득

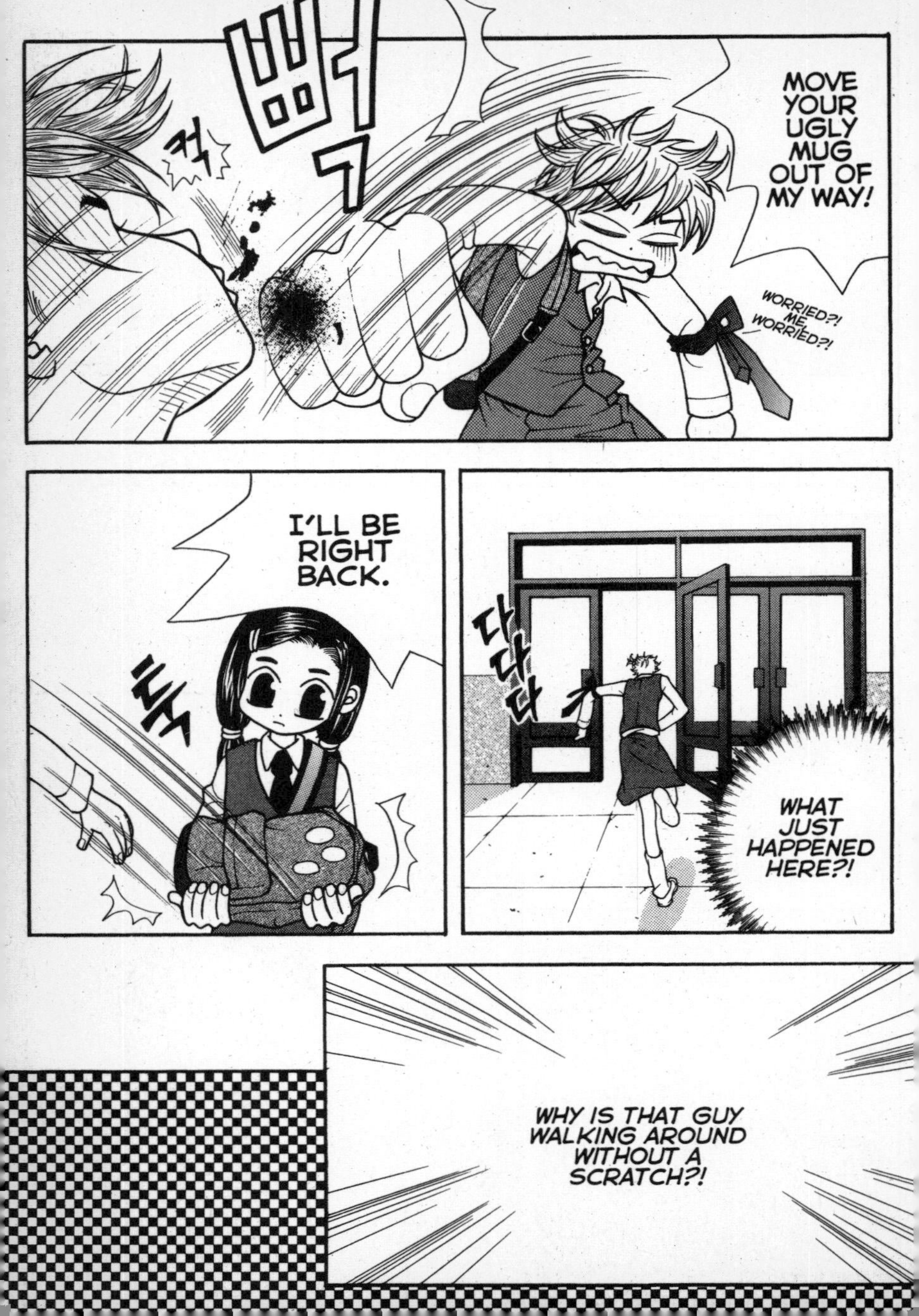
뻑
컥
MOVE YOUR UGLY MUG OUT OF MY WAY!
WORRIED?! ME WORRIED?!
I'LL BE RIGHT BACK.
다다다
WHAT JUST HAPPENED HERE?!
WHY IS THAT GUY WALKING AROUND WITHOUT A SCRATCH?!

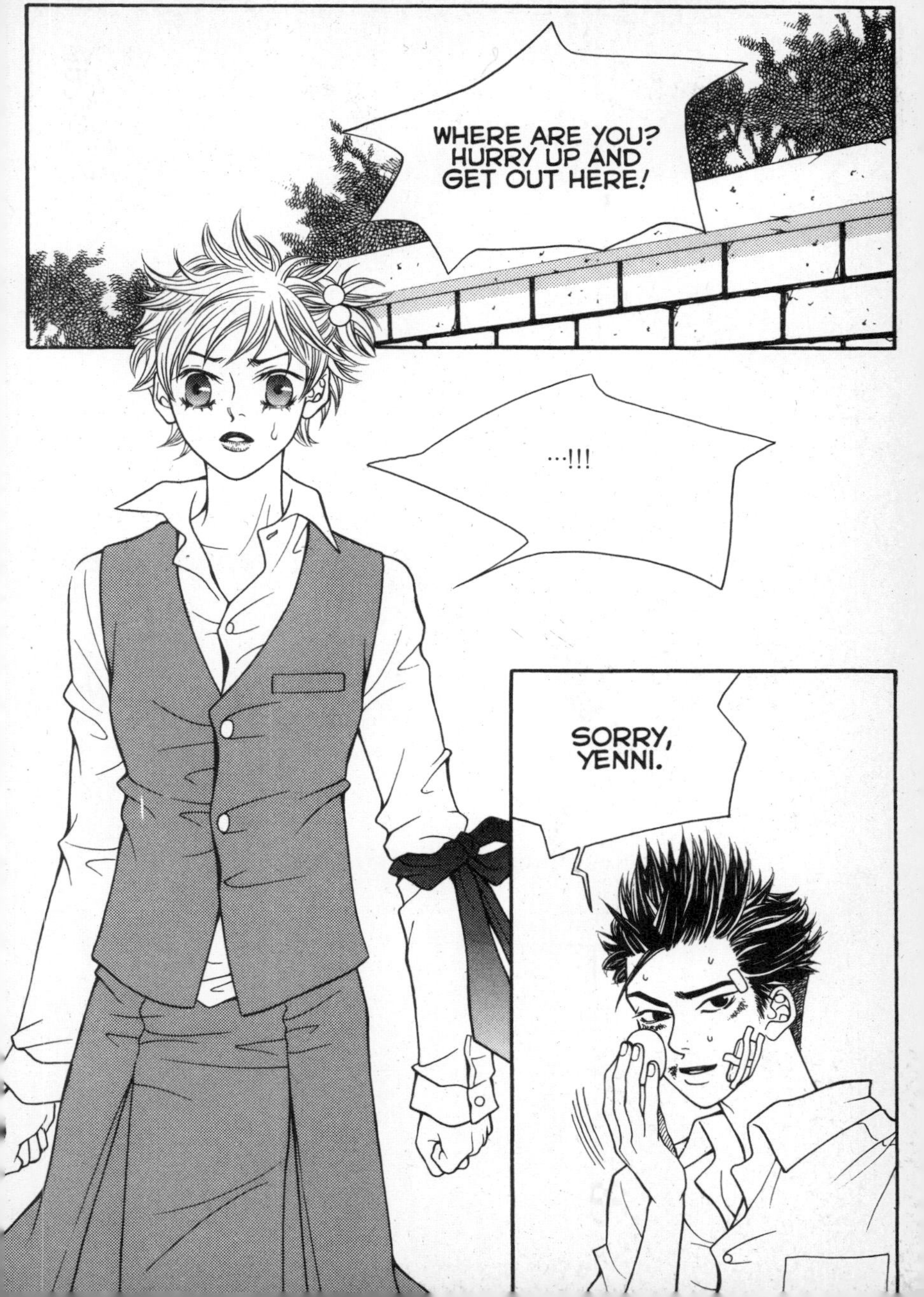
WHERE ARE YOU? HURRY UP AND GET OUT HERE!
...!!!
SORRY, YENNI.

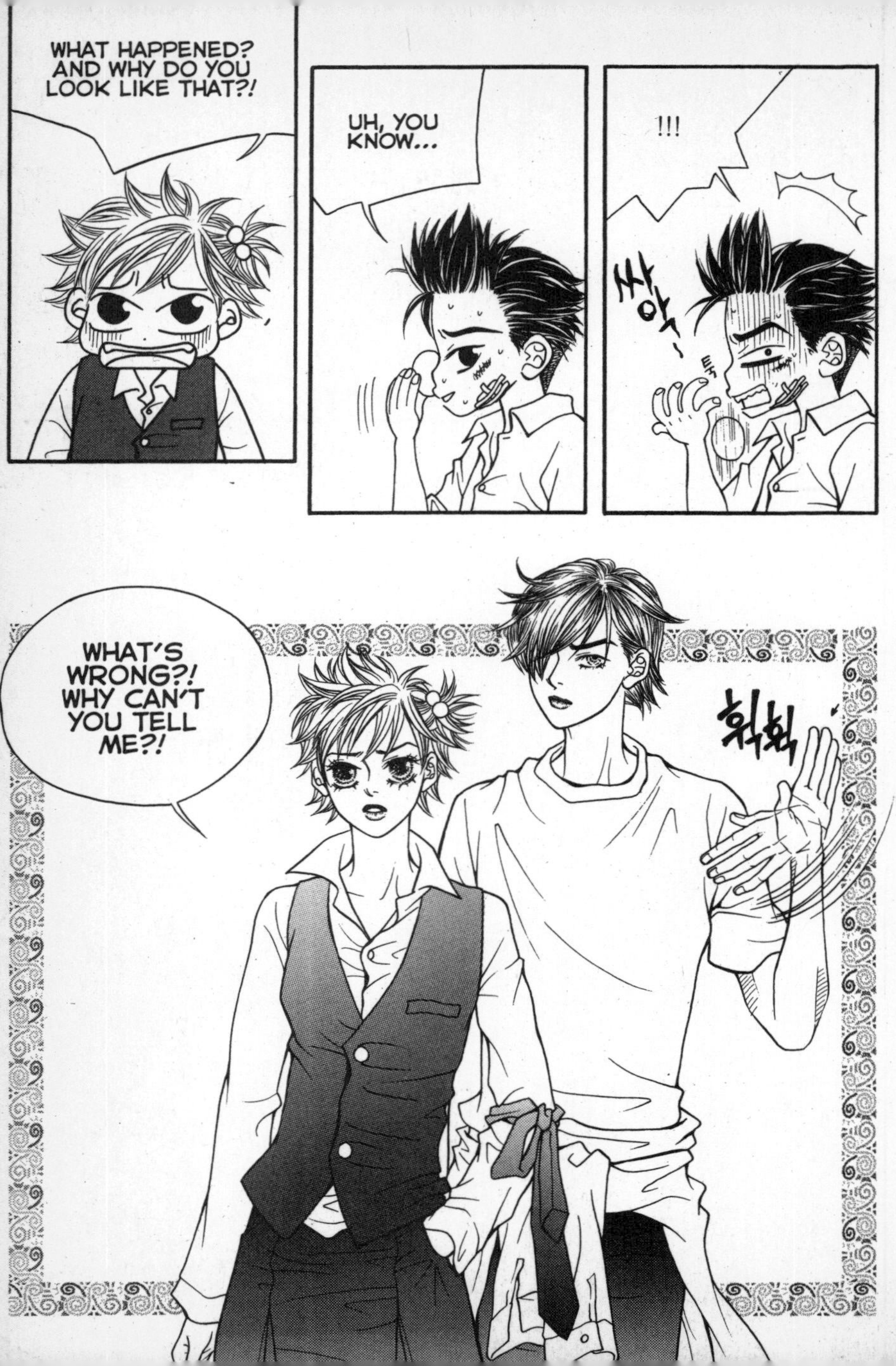
WHAT HAPPENED? AND WHY DO YOU LOOK LIKE THAT?!
UH, YOU KNOW...
!!!
싸악~
툭
WHAT'S WRONG?! WHY CAN'T YOU TELL ME?!
휙휙

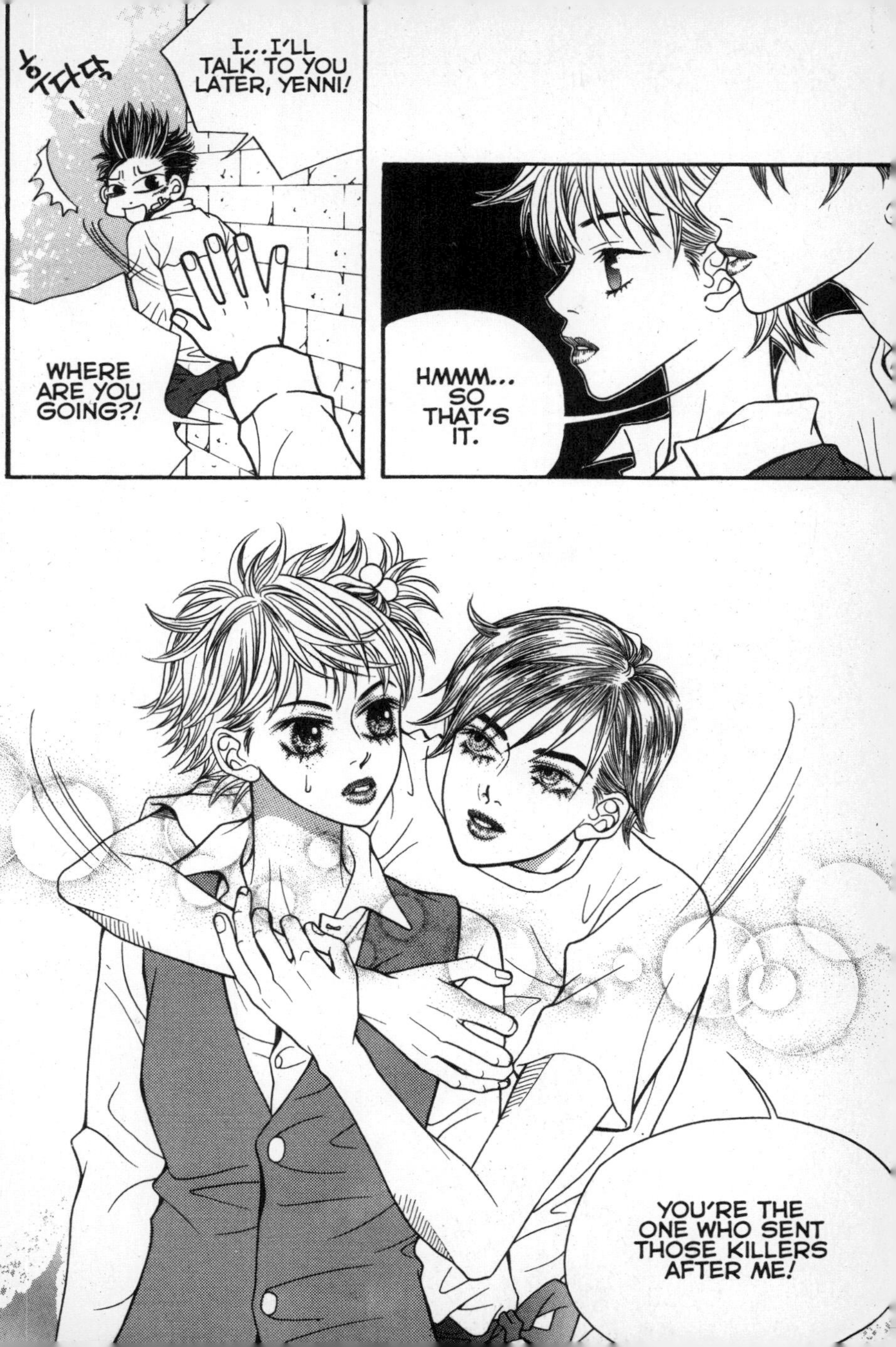
I...I'LL TALK TO YOU LATER, YENNI!
WHERE ARE YOU GOING?!
HMMM... SO THAT'S IT.
YOU'RE THE ONE WHO SENT THOSE KILLERS AFTER ME!

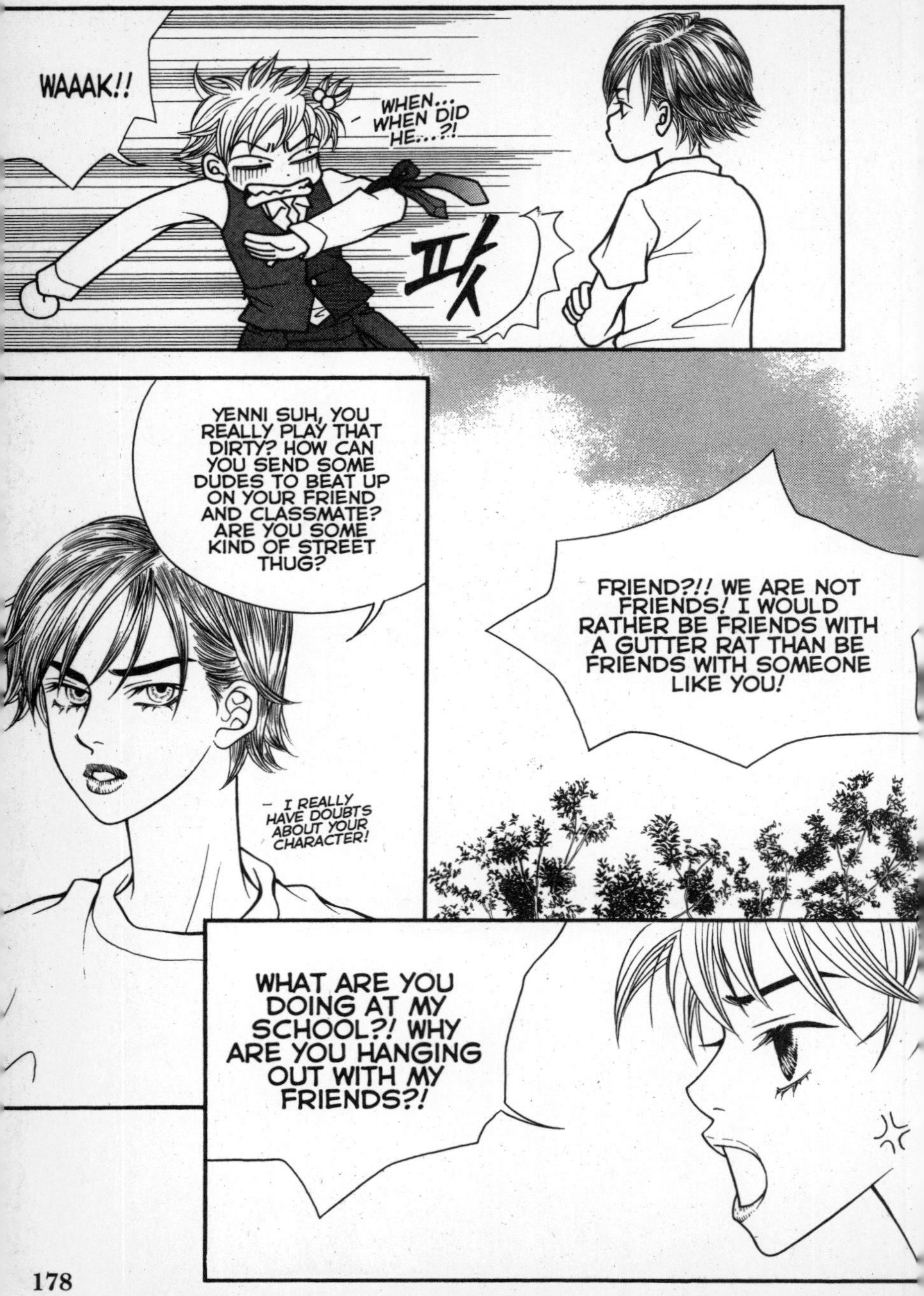
WAAAK!!
WHEN... WHEN DID HE...?!
YENNI SUH, YOU REALLY PLAY THAT DIRTY? HOW CAN YOU SEND SOME DUDES TO BEAT UP ON YOUR FRIEND AND CLASSMATE? ARE YOU SOME KIND OF STREET THUG?
- I REALLY HAVE DOUBTS ABOUT YOUR CHARACTER!
FRIEND?!! WE ARE NOT FRIENDS! I WOULD RATHER BE FRIENDS WITH A GUTTER RAT THAN BE FRIENDS WITH SOMEONE LIKE YOU!
WHAT ARE YOU DOING AT MY SCHOOL?! WHY ARE YOU HANGING OUT WITH MY FRIENDS?!

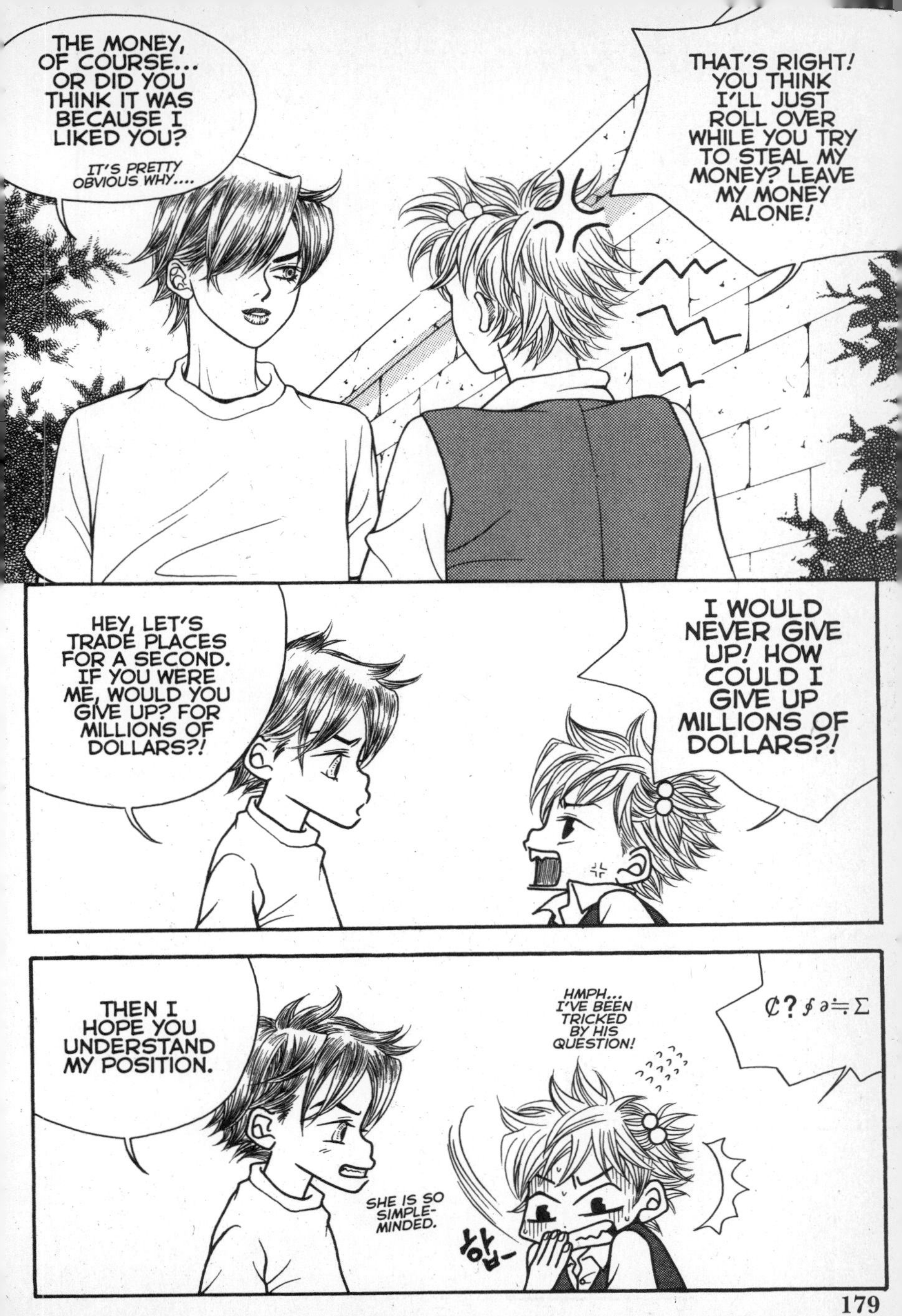
THE MONEY, OF COURSE... OR DID YOU THINK IT WAS BECAUSE I LIKED YOU?
IT'S PRETTY OBVIOUS WHY....
THAT'S RIGHT! YOU THINK I'LL JUST ROLL OVER WHILE YOU TRY TO STEAL MY MONEY? LEAVE MY MONEY ALONE!
HEY, LET'S TRADE PLACES FOR A SECOND. IF YOU WERE ME, WOULD YOU GIVE UP? FOR MILLIONS OF DOLLARS?!
I WOULD NEVER GIVE UP! HOW COULD I GIVE UP MILLIONS OF DOLLARS?!
THEN I HOPE YOU UNDERSTAND MY POSITION.
HMPH... I'VE BEEN TRICKED BY HIS QUESTION!
¢?∮∂≒Σ
SHE IS SO SIMPLE-MINDED.
합-

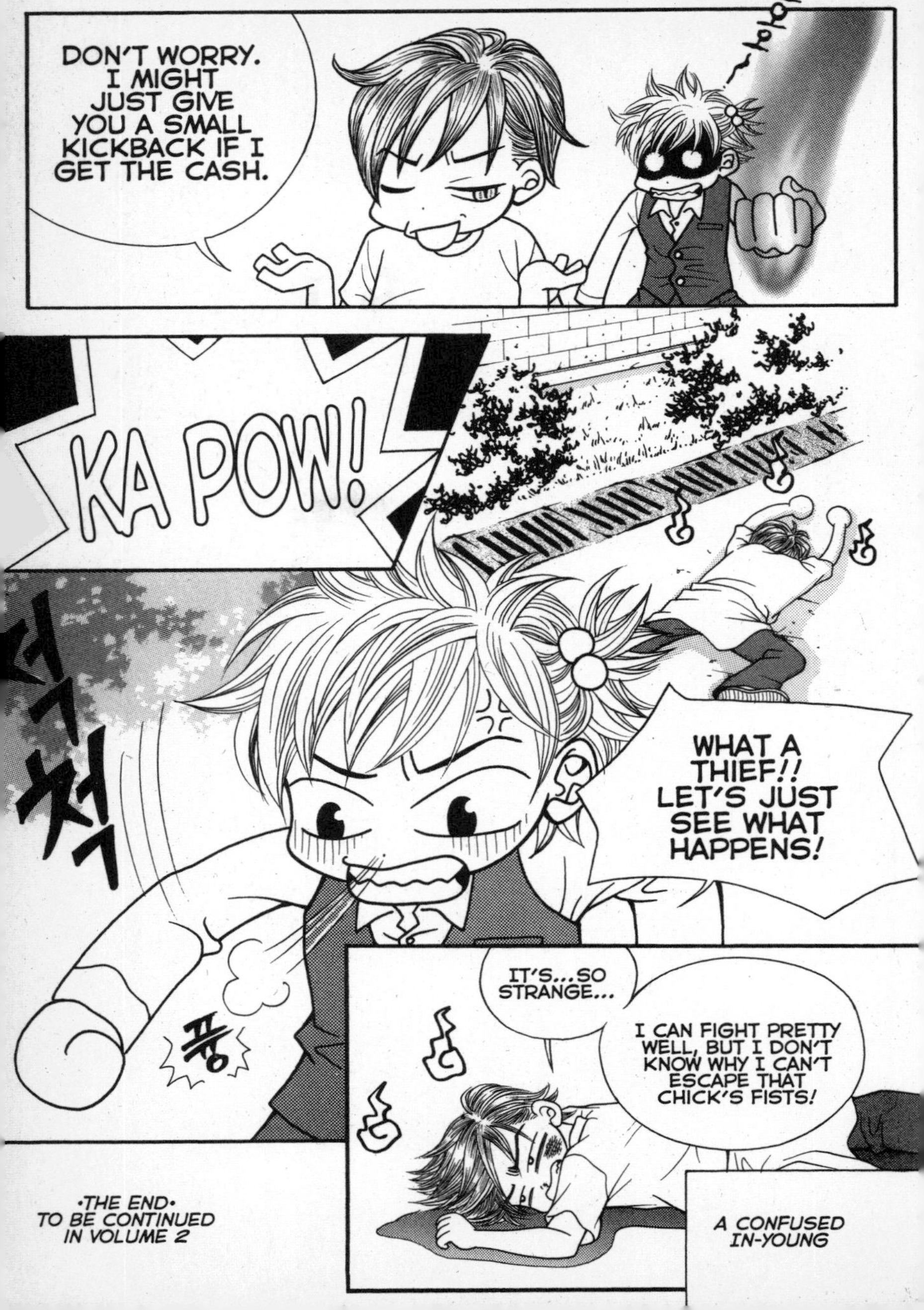
DON'T WORRY. I MIGHT JUST GIVE YOU A SMALL KICKBACK IF I GET THE CASH.
KA POW!
WHAT A THIEF!! LET'S JUST SEE WHAT HAPPENS!
IT'S...SO STRANGE...
I CAN FIGHT PRETTY WELL, BUT I DON'T KNOW WHY I CAN'T ESCAPE THAT CHICK'S FISTS!
•THE END• TO BE CONTINUED IN VOLUME 2
A CONFUSED IN-YOUNG

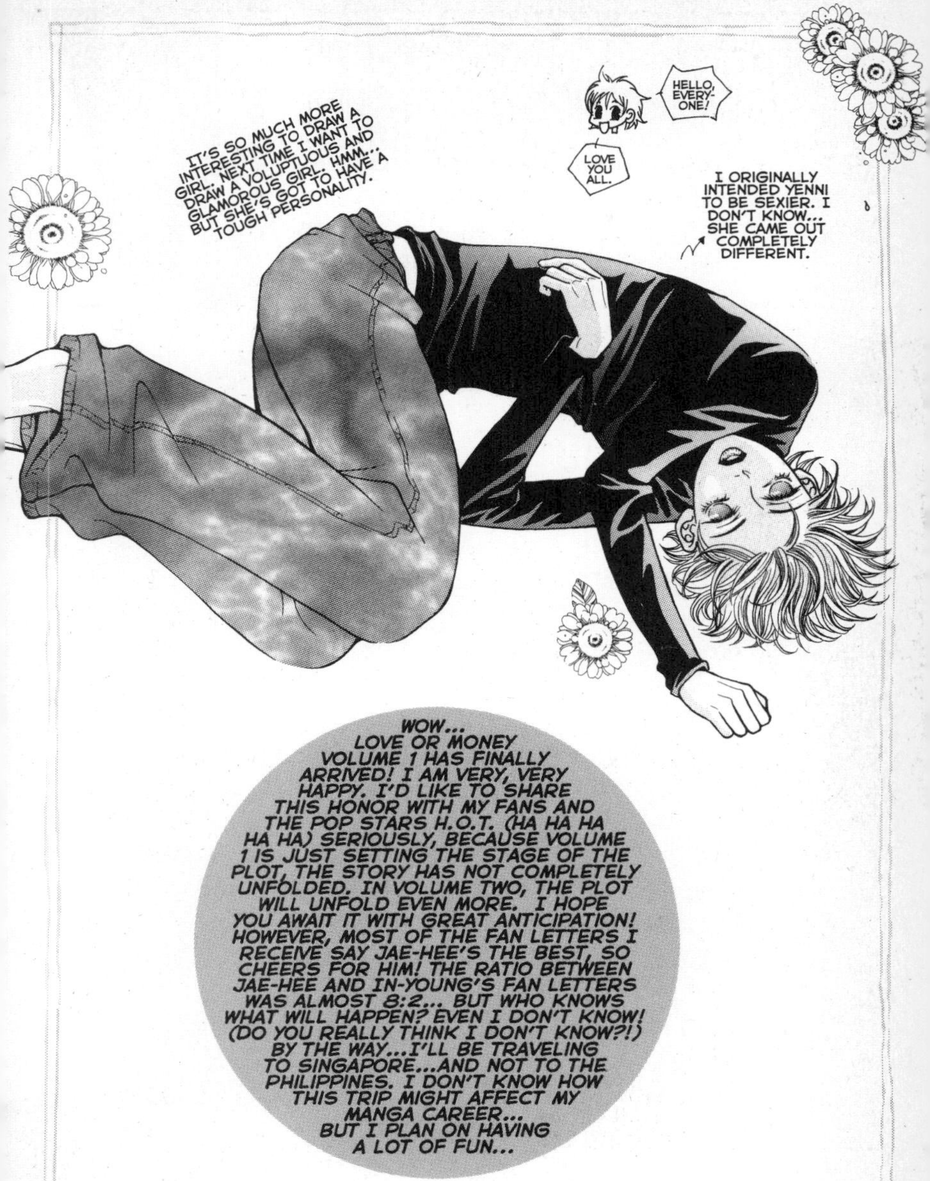
HELLO, EVERY-ONE!
LOVE YOU ALL.
IT'S SO MUCH MORE INTERESTING TO DRAW A GIRL. NEXT TIME I WANT TO DRAW A VOLUPTUOUS AND GLAMOROUS GIRL. HMM... BUT SHE'S GOT TO HAVE A TOUGH PERSONALITY.
I ORIGINALLY INTENDED YENNI TO BE SEXIER. I DON'T KNOW... SHE CAME OUT COMPLETELY DIFFERENT.

WOW... LOVE OR MONEY VOLUME 1 HAS FINALLY ARRIVED! I AM VERY, VERY HAPPY. I'D LIKE TO SHARE THIS HONOR WITH MY FANS AND THE POP STARS H.O.T. (HA HA HA HA HA) SERIOUSLY, BECAUSE VOLUME 1 IS JUST SETTING THE STAGE OF THE PLOT, THE STORY HAS NOT COMPLETELY UNFOLDED. IN VOLUME TWO, THE PLOT WILL UNFOLD EVEN MORE. I HOPE YOU AWAIT IT WITH GREAT ANTICIPATION! HOWEVER, MOST OF THE FAN LETTERS I RECEIVE SAY JAE-HEE'S THE BEST, SO CHEERS FOR HIM! THE RATIO BETWEEN JAE-HEE AND IN-YOUNG'S FAN LETTERS WAS ALMOST 8:2... BUT WHO KNOWS WHAT WILL HAPPEN? EVEN I DON'T KNOW! (DO YOU REALLY THINK I DON'T KNOW?!) BY THE WAY...I'LL BE TRAVELING TO SINGAPORE...AND NOT TO THE PHILIPPINES. I DON'T KNOW HOW THIS TRIP MIGHT AFFECT MY MANGA CAREER... BUT I PLAN ON HAVING A LOT OF FUN...

IN THE NEXT

LOVE OR MONEY

VOLUME 2

YENNI'S PLAN IS WORKING OUT
PERFECTLY! SHE MANAGES TO
CONVINCE JAY AND HIS FAMILY TO
MOVE IN. WHAT SHE DIDN'T EXPECT
WAS FOR IN-YOUNG TO SHOW UP
AND "SQUAT" ON HER PLANS.
IN-YOUNG'S INTENTIONS ARE TO
INTERFERE WITH YENNI'S PLAN...
BUT HAS HE SUDDENLY FALLEN
HEAD OVER HEELS FOR HER? ON
THE OTHER HAND, JAY HAS HAD
FEELINGS FOR YENNI SINCE THEIR
CHILDHOOD DAYS. UNFORTUNATELY,
YENNI DOESN'T REMEMBER
ANYTHING ABOUT JAY FROM HER
CHILDHOOD! JAY MUST STEP
UP OR FACE BEING FORGOTTEN
COMPLETELY.

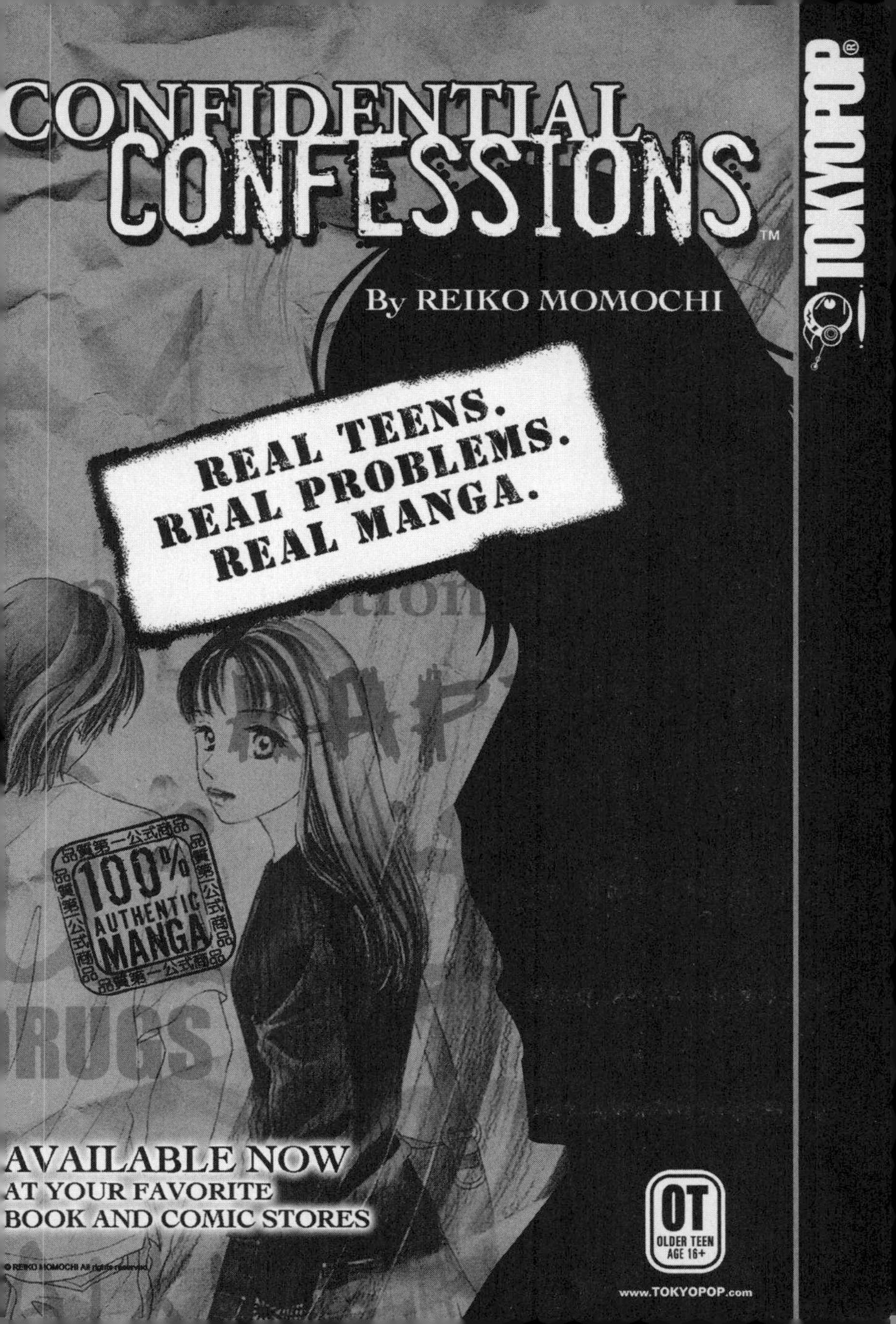
CONFIDENTIAL CONFESSIONS™
By REIKO MOMOCHI
REAL TEENS.
REAL PROBLEMS.
REAL MANGA.
100% AUTHENTIC MANGA
AVAILABLE NOW
AT YOUR FAVORITE
BOOK AND COMIC STORES
OT OLDER TEEN AGE 16+
© REIKO MOMOCHI All rights reserved.
www.TOKYOPOP.com
TOKYOPOP®

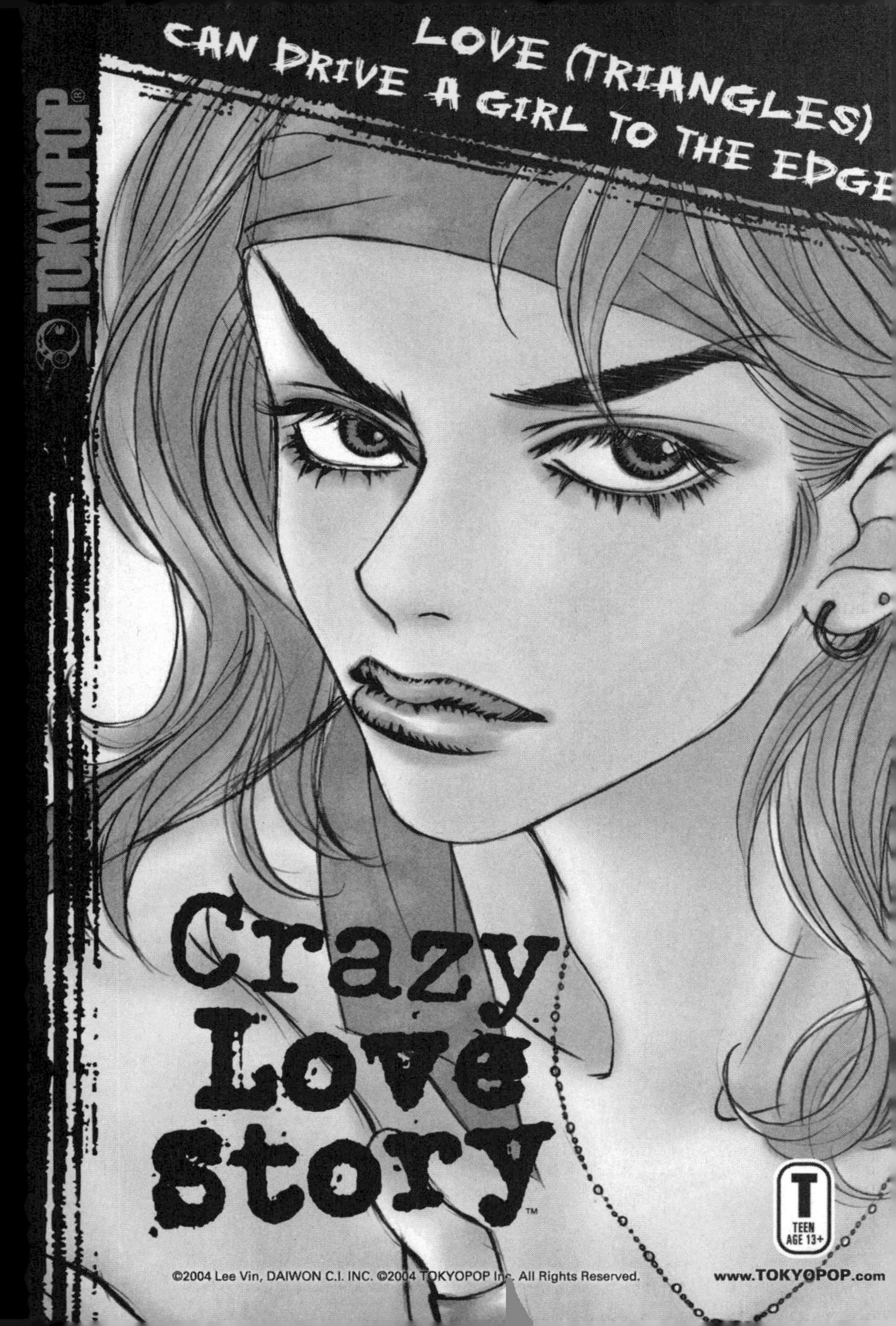
LOVE (TRIANGLES)
CAN DRIVE A GIRL TO THE EDGE
TOKYOPOP®
Crazy Love Story™
T TEEN AGE 13+
©2004 Lee Vin, DAIWON C.I. INC. ©2004 TOKYOPOP Inc. All Rights Reserved.
www.TOKYOPOP.com

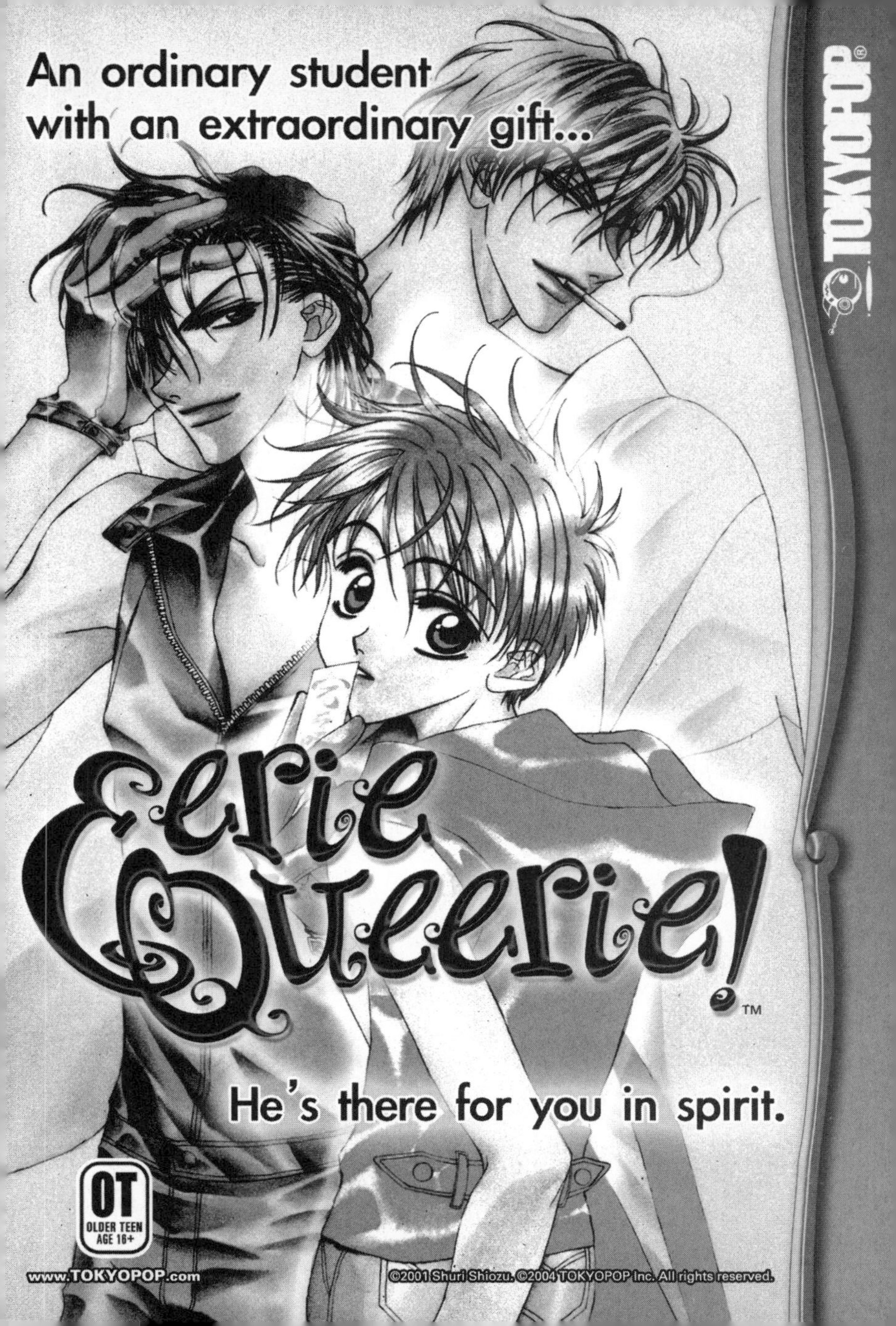
An ordinary student
with an extraordinary gift...
TOKYOPOP®
Eerie Queerie!™
He's there for you in spirit.
OT
OLDER TEEN
AGE 16+
www.TOKYOPOP.com
©2001 Shuri Shiozu. ©2004 TOKYOPOP Inc. All rights reserved.

ALSO AVAILABLE FROM 🎬 TOKYOPOP®

MANGA

.HACK//LEGEND OF THE TWILIGHT
@LARGE
ABENOBASHI: MAGICAL SHOPPING ARCADE
A.I. LOVE YOU
AI YORI AOSHI
ALICHINO
ANGELIC LAYER
ARM OF KANNON
BABY BIRTH
BATTLE ROYALE
BATTLE VIXENS
BOYS BE...
BRAIN POWERED
BRIGADOON
B'TX
CANDIDATE FOR GODDESS, THE
CARDCAPTOR SAKURA
CARDCAPTOR SAKURA - MASTER OF THE CLOW
CHOBITS
CHRONICLES OF THE CURSED SWORD
CLAMP SCHOOL DETECTIVES
CLOVER
COMIC PARTY
CONFIDENTIAL CONFESSIONS
CORRECTOR YUI
COWBOY BEBOP
COWBOY BEBOP: SHOOTING STAR
CRAZY LOVE STORY
CRESCENT MOON
CROSS
CULDCEPT
CYBORG 009
D•N•ANGEL
DEARS
DEMON DIARY
DEMON ORORON, THE
DEUS VITAE
DIGIMON
DIGIMON TAMERS
DIGIMON ZERO TWO
DOLL
DRAGON HUNTER
DRAGON KNIGHTS
DRAGON VOICE
DREAM SAGA
DUKLYON: CLAMP SCHOOL DEFENDERS
EERIE QUEERIE!
ERICA SAKURAZAWA: COLLECTED WORKS
ET CETERA
ETERNITY
EVIL'S RETURN
FAERIES' LANDING
FAKE
FLCL
FLOWER OF THE DEEP SLEEP, THE
FORBIDDEN DANCE
FRUITS BASKET

G GUNDAM
GATEKEEPERS
GETBACKERS
GIRL GOT GAME
GRAVITATION
GTO
GUNDAM SEED ASTRAY
GUNDAM WING
GUNDAM WING: BATTLEFIELD OF PACIFISTS
GUNDAM WING: ENDLESS WALTZ
GUNDAM WING: THE LAST OUTPOST (G-UNIT)
HANDS OFF!
HAPPY MANIA
HARLEM BEAT
HYPER RUNE
I.N.V.U.
IMMORTAL RAIN
INITIAL D
INSTANT TEEN: JUST ADD NUTS
ISLAND
JING: KING OF BANDITS
JING: KING OF BANDITS - TWILIGHT TALES
JULINE
KARE KANO
KILL ME, KISS ME
KINDAICHI CASE FILES, THE
KING OF HELL
KODOCHA: SANA'S STAGE
LAMENT OF THE LAMB
LEGAL DRUG
LEGEND OF CHUN HYANG, THE
LES BIJOUX
LOVE HINA
LOVE OR MONEY
LUPIN III
LUPIN III: WORLD'S MOST WANTED
MAGIC KNIGHT RAYEARTH I
MAGIC KNIGHT RAYEARTH II
MAHOROMATIC: AUTOMATIC MAIDEN
MAN OF MANY FACES
MARMALADE BOY
MARS
MARS: HORSE WITH NO NAME
MINK
MIRACLE GIRLS
MIYUKI-CHAN IN WONDERLAND
MODEL
MOURYOU KIDEN: LEGEND OF THE NYMPHS
NECK AND NECK
ONE
ONE I LOVE, THE
PARADISE KISS
PARASYTE
PASSION FRUIT
PEACH GIRL
PEACH GIRL: CHANGE OF HEART
PET SHOP OF HORRORS
PITA-TEN
PLANET LADDER

08.20.04T

ALSO AVAILABLE FROM  TOKYOPOP®

PLANETES
PRESIDENT DAD
PRIEST
PRINCESS AI
PSYCHIC ACADEMY
QUEEN'S KNIGHT, THE
RAGNAROK
RAVE MASTER
REALITY CHECK
REBIRTH
REBOUND
REMOTE
RISING STARS OF MANGA
SABER MARIONETTE J
SAILOR MOON
SAINT TAIL
SAIYUKI
SAMURAI DEEPER KYO
SAMURAI GIRL REAL BOUT HIGH SCHOOL
SCRYED
SEIKAI TRILOGY, THE
SGT. FROG
SHAOLIN SISTERS
SHIRAHIME-SYO: SNOW GODDESS TALES
SHUTTERBOX
SKULL MAN, THE
SNOW DROP
SORCERER HUNTERS
STONE
SUIKODEN III
SUKI
TAROT CAFÉ, THE
THREADS OF TIME
TOKYO BABYLON
TOKYO MEW MEW
TOKYO TRIBES
TRAMPS LIKE US
UNDER THE GLASS MOON
VAMPIRE GAME
VISION OF ESCAFLOWNE, THE
WARCRAFT
WARRIORS OF TAO
WILD ACT
WISH
WORLD OF HARTZ
X-DAY
ZODIAC P.I.

NOVELS

CLAMP SCHOOL PARANORMAL INVESTIGATORS
SAILOR MOON

ART BOOKS

ART OF CARDCAPTOR SAKURA
ART OF MAGIC KNIGHT RAYEARTH, THE
PEACH: MIWA UEDA ILLUSTRATIONS
CLAMP NORTHSIDE
CLAMP SOUTHSIDE

ANIME GUIDES

COWBOY BEBOP
GUNDAM TECHNICAL MANUALS
SAILOR MOON SCOUT GUIDES

TOKYOPOP KIDS

STRAY SHEEP

CINE-MANGA™

ALADDIN
CARDCAPTORS
DUEL MASTERS
FAIRLY ODDPARENTS, THE
FAMILY GUY
FINDING NEMO
G.I. JOE SPY TROOPS
GREATEST STARS OF THE NBA: SHAQUILLE O'NEAL
GREATEST STARS OF THE NBA: TIM DUNCAN
JACKIE CHAN ADVENTURES
JIMMY NEUTRON: BOY GENIUS, THE ADVENTURES OF
KIM POSSIBLE
LILO & STITCH: THE SERIES
LIZZIE MCGUIRE
LIZZIE MCGUIRE MOVIE, THE
MALCOLM IN THE MIDDLE
POWER RANGERS: DINO THUNDER
POWER RANGERS: NINJA STORM
PRINCESS DIARIES 2
RAVE MASTER
SHREK 2
SIMPLE LIFE, THE
SPONGEBOB SQUAREPANTS
SPY KIDS 2
SPY KIDS 3-D: GAME OVER
TEENAGE MUTANT NINJA TURTLES
THAT'S SO RAVEN
TOTALLY SPIES
TRANSFORMERS: ARMADA
TRANSFORMERS: ENERGON

You want it? We got it!
A full range of TOKYOPOP
products are available now at:
www.TOKYOPOP.com/shop

08.20.04T

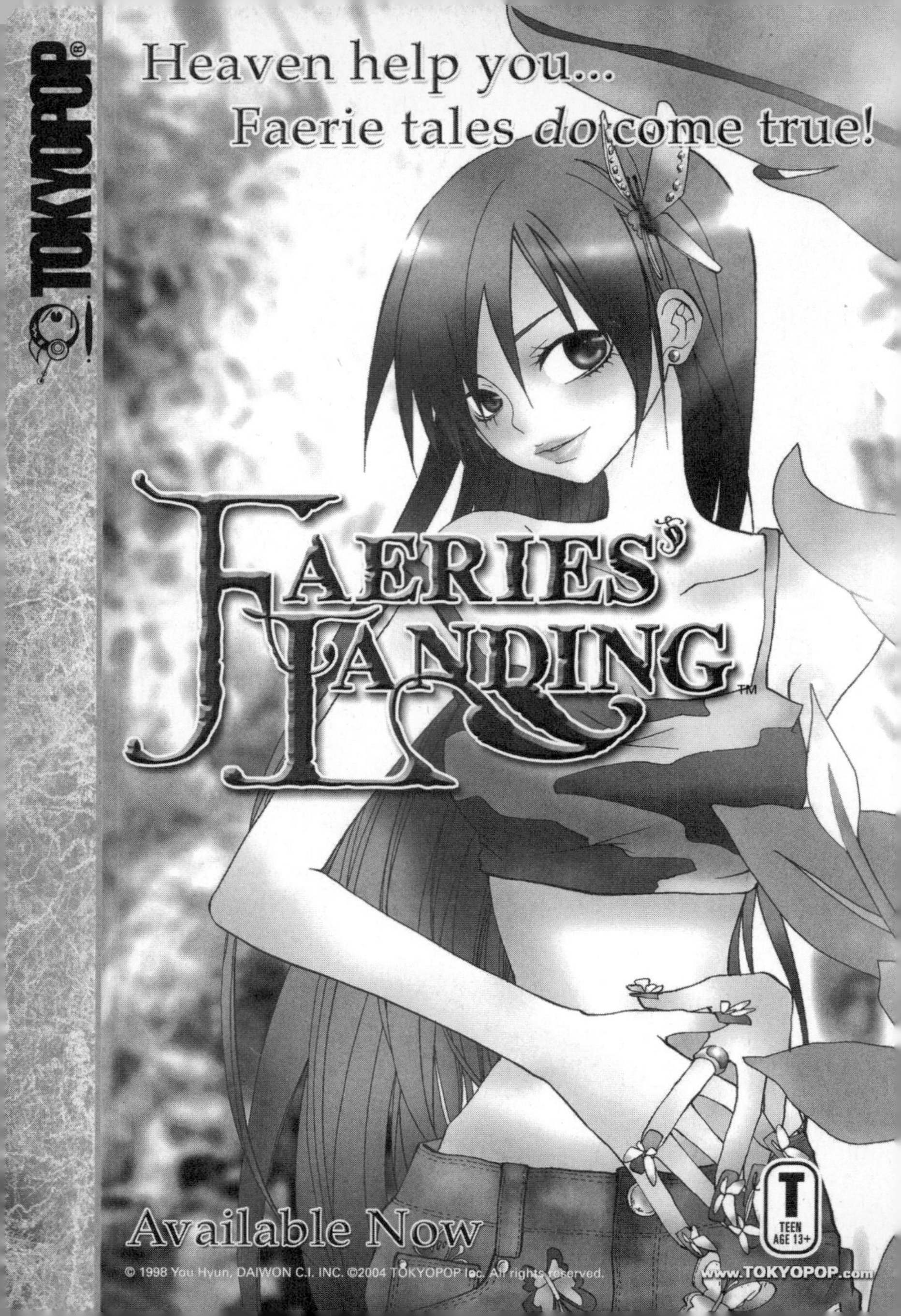
TOKYOPOP®
Heaven help you...
Faerie tales *do* come true!
FAERIES' LANDING™
T TEEN AGE 13+
Available Now
© 1998 You Hyun, DAIWON C.I. INC. ©2004 TOKYOPOP Inc. All rights reserved.
www.TOKYOPOP.com

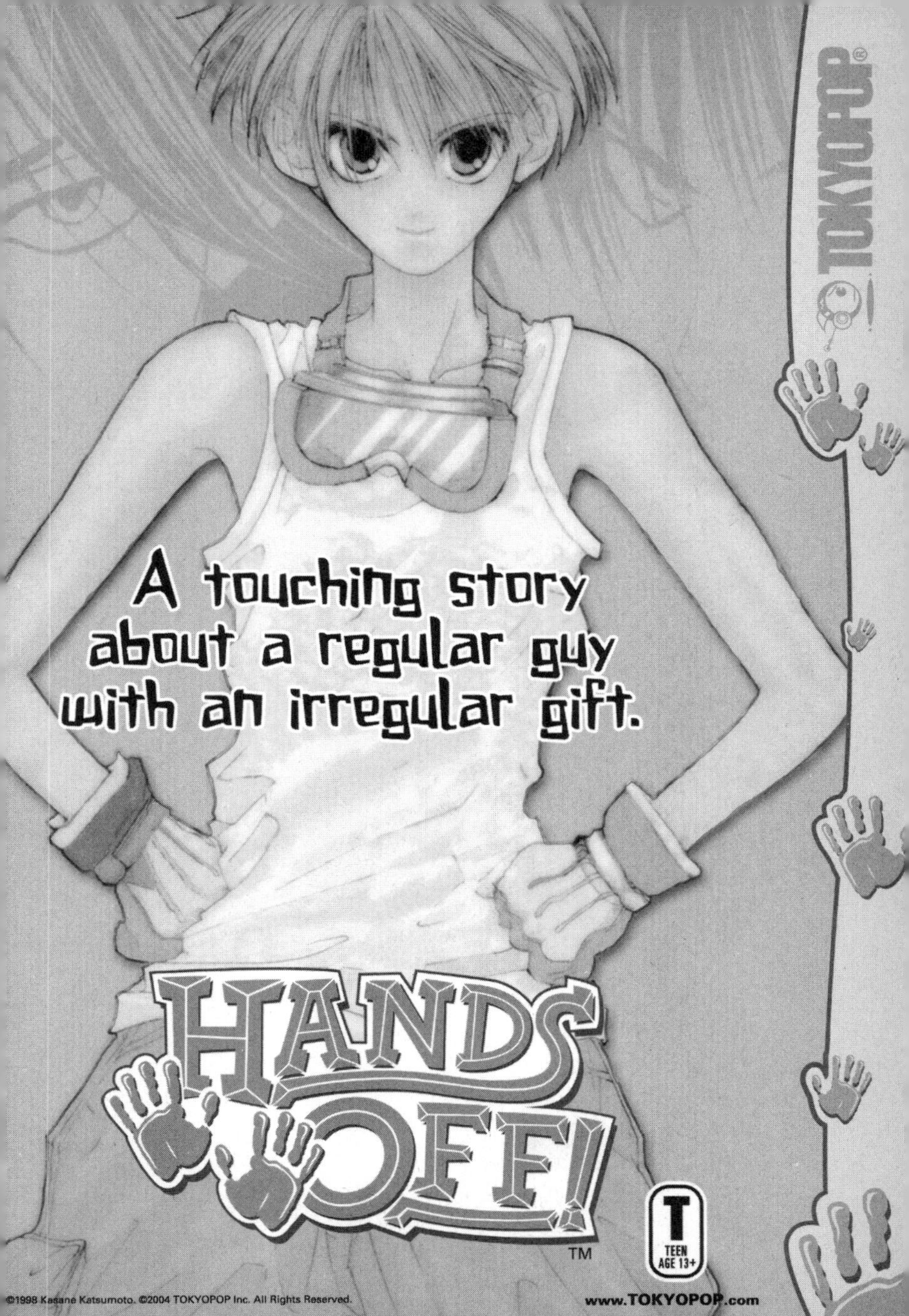
A touching story
about a regular guy
with an irregular gift.
TOKYOPOP
HANDS OFF!
TM
T
TEEN
AGE 13+

Snow Drop

Like a fragile flower,
   love often blooms in unlikely places.

www.TOKYOPOP.com

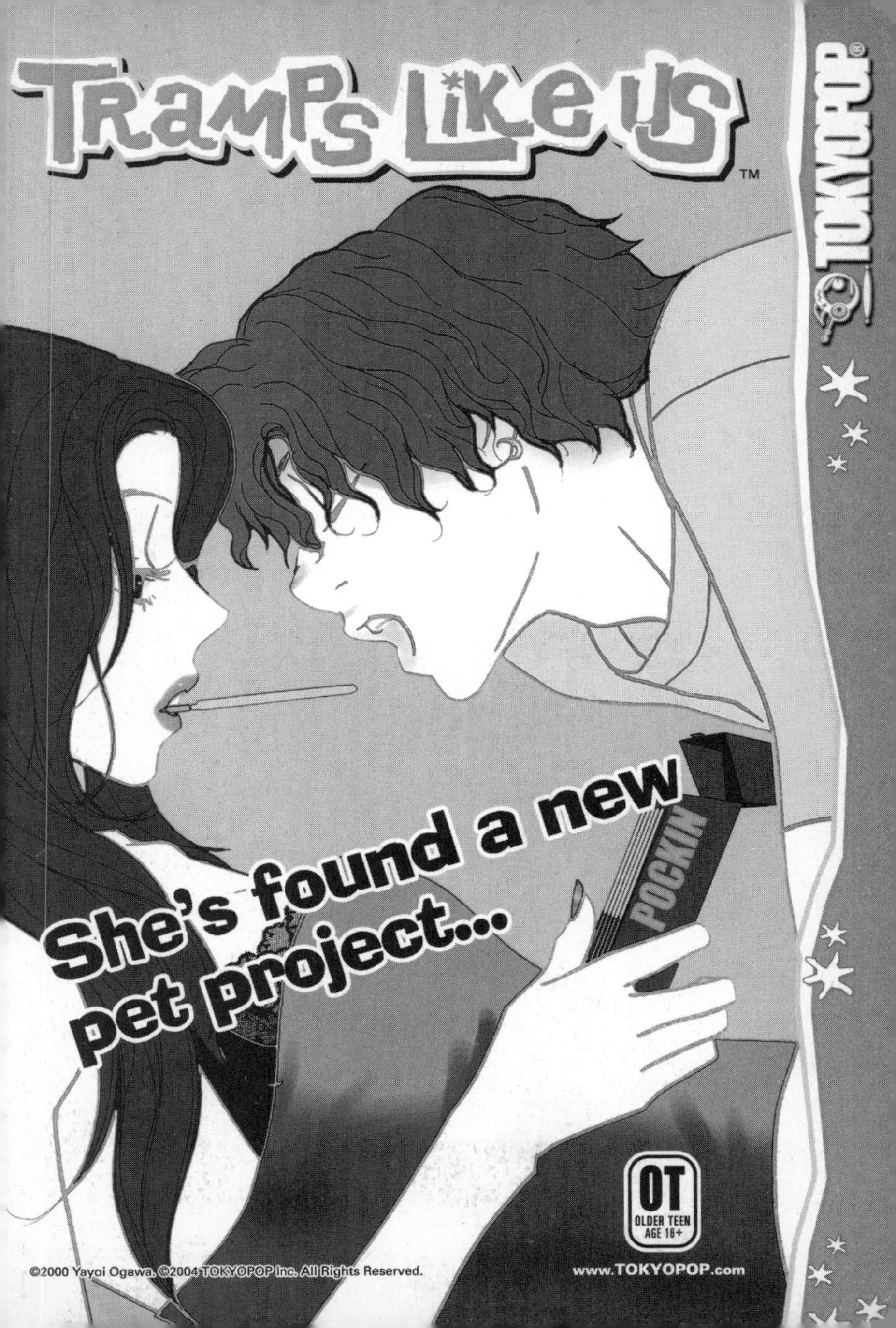
TRAMPS LIKE US™
TOKYOPOP
POCKIN
She's found a new pet project...
OT
OLDER TEEN AGE 16+
©2000 Yayoi Ogawa. ©2004 TOKYOPOP Inc. All Rights Reserved.
www.TOKYOPOP.com

Princess Ai™

A Diva torn
from Chaos...

A Savior doomed
to Love

Created by
Courtney Love
and D.J. Milky

3 1901 04538 0112

TEEN
AGE 13+

©2003 TOKYOPOP Inc. and Kitty Radio, Inc. All Rights Reserved.

www.TOKYOPOP.com